EXPLAINING PO

This unique text offers a comprehensive overview of who participates in politics and why, how social and political institutions shape that involvement, and, ultimately, what form citizen political participation takes. Drawing on a multitude of factors to explain politics and political behavior, Woshinsky shows that political outcomes depend on a complex interplay between individuals and their environment. Psychology, personality, and ideology, together with culture, institutions, and social context shape political behavior. *Explaining Politics* offers a wealth of comparative examples and practical applications through a lively and engaging narrative.

Oliver H. Woshinsky is Professor Emeritus at the University of Southern Maine and author of several previous books. He has taught undergraduates for over three decades and has lived and taught in France, Russia, and the UK.

EXPLAINING POLITICS

Culture, institutions, and political behavior

Oliver H. Woshinsky

Routledge
Taylor & Francis Group

NEW YORK AND LONDON

First published 2008
by Routledge
270 Madison Ave, New York, NY 10016

Simultaneously published in the UK
by Routledge
2 Park Square, Milton Park, Abingdon, Oxon OX14 4RN

Routledge is an imprint of the Taylor & Francis Group, an informa business

© 2008 Taylor & Francis

Typeset in Bembo by
RefineCatch Limited, Bungay, Suffolk
Printed and bound in the United States of America on acid-free paper by
Sheridan Books, Inc

Library of Congress Cataloging in Publication Data
Woshinsky, Oliver H.
Explaining politics : culture, institutions, and political behavior /
Oliver H. Woshinsky
p. cm.
Includes index
ISBN–13: 978–0–415–96078–6 (pbk.: alk. paper)
ISBN–10: 0–415–96078–9 (pbk.: alk. paper)

ISBN–13: 978–0–203–93318–3 (ebook)
ISBN–10: 0–203–93318–4 (ebook)
1. Political culture.   2. Political participation.   I. Title.
JA75.7.W67   2008
320—dc22
2007038212

To my son, David,
to my long-time friends and colleagues, Richard Maiman and
William Coogan,
and to the students of the University of Southern Maine

CONTENTS

CONTENTS

CONTENTS

CONTENTS

PREFACE

In March, 1952, Harry Truman had been President of the USA for nearly 7 years. His Democratic Party had won five straight presidential elections. Democrats had controlled the White House for two decades and dominated both houses of Congress for nearly all of the past 22 years. But Truman and the Democrats were in trouble. They were seen as "soft" on domestic communists, weak in pursuing the Korean War, and tainted with scandals.

Deeply unpopular himself, Truman faced the daunting prospect of a re-election run that fall against the nation's beloved Second World War leader, General Dwight David Eisenhower. In the end, he bowed to the inevitable. On March 29, the nation learned that Truman would not be a candidate to succeed himself in the Oval Office.[1]

Democratic Party prospects for the presidency at that point were bleak. In July, the party faithful met in Chicago to choose someone as their sacrificial lamb in the fall campaign. They turned to Adlai Stevenson, the eloquent and intellectual Governor of Illinois, who took on the thankless task with grace and humor. He ran such a creditable race that he was re-nominated for the job in 1956. Still, few people ever believed that Stevenson could beat the man known affectionately to a grateful nation as Ike. He was, in fact, soundly defeated in both his efforts. After 20 years of Democratic presidents, the nation was ready for a change, and a national hero like Eisenhower was probably unbeatable under any conditions.

At a low moment towards the end of his second campaign, an adoring woman rushed up to shake Stevenson's hand after one of his whistle-stop speeches. "Oh, Governor Stevenson," she gushed, "that was such a thoughtful presentation—and so persuasive. I'm sure that every thinking American will be voting for you on election day!"

"That's not enough," quipped the disheartened candidate. "I need a majority!"[2]

Like Adlai Stevenson, a distant relative of mine, I too worry that American politics suffers from a shortage of thinking citizens. Yet also like Stevenson, I remain eternally hopeful. Stevenson stayed active in American politics right up to the day of his death in 1965—of a heart attack on a street in London, while serving as American Ambassador to the United Nations. My own career has been entirely academic, but I feel a certain kinship with Stevenson's mission: to make democratic politics understandable to a broad range of interested citizens.

For over three decades I touted, to often skeptical students, the benefits of the democratic process. Still concerned that too few people think about politics rationally, I continue trying to explain, to as broad an audience as possible, how political life works. I write this book in the hopes of reaching all thinking citizens who want a primer on politics.

Although designed for anyone with a political interest, the book is also clearly intended as a textbook. It is aimed at students in introductory-level courses of political science. Assuming that most readers have had little formal training in the study of politics, I provide an extensive Glossary of Terms at the end of the text. There, words found in **bold** within each chapter are given brief definitions. For aid to both teachers and students, I have provided several questions at the end of each chapter. They are aimed at provoking thought and debate—and possibly to suggest research topics for course papers.

No work is the product of a single mind. We are all shaped by countless teachers, mentors, and friends. In an earlier book, I provided a short history of my life, acknowledging the many who influenced my intellectual development.[3] To avoid repetition, I shall thank here only the specific people who have helped on this particular project.

My University of Southern Maine colleagues, Richard Maiman and William Coogan, read parts of the manuscript and provided insightful comments. Three other USM colleagues, Lynn Kuzma, Ron Schmidt, and Robert Klotz, offered helpful suggestions at crucial moments. I received valuable research assistance and advice from librarians Virginia Hopcroft of Bowdoin College and Zip Kellogg of the University of Southern Maine. Amelia Golden, administrative assistant at the USM Political Science Department, provided useful technical help whenever I asked. Amy Fleig, a USM political science major and now a graduate student at the University of Massachusetts, reviewed the entire manuscript, provided helpful commentary, and made many excellent suggestions.

I owe a special debt of gratitude to the hundreds of undergraduates at the University of Southern Maine who have been subjected to the words that follow. For several years, I used introductory students as unwitting subjects of an experiment, one designed to test the ideas and the mode of presentation within these pages. My students' feedback helped enormously as I refined the chapters and moved the draft into final form.

I have been especially lucky in my collaboration with Routledge. Robert Tempio encouraged me to undertake the project, and Michael Kerns took it over and became a supportive editor. I've had admirable editorial assistance from Angela Chnapko and Elizabeth Renner, along with good project support from Felisa Salvago-Keyes. I am especially grateful to the four anonymous reviewers that Routledge provided. Their extensive comments were both encouraging and helpful. I wish I could sit down with each of them for an extended conversation on the many points I could not integrate into the manuscript, try as I might.

My wife, Pat Garrett, read and commented on most of the book. More important, she provided the loving encouragement and moral support that helped me stay with the project. We all need an enthusiastic backer, and I have the very best!

Portland, Maine
June 20, 2007

INTRODUCTION

Personality and environment

Electioneering strategy: it's not the same old battlefield

Why do people act as they do? It's an age-old question. Political scientists narrow the focus to ask why people behave as they do in *politics*. Let's begin by examining the behavior of some successful (and not so successful) presidential candidates.

Imagine a George W. Bush in sixteenth-century England. He is an ambitious man, who has long dreamed of ruling his country. For years, he has planned and schemed to attain the throne. Now in his early 50s, he is ready to move toward his heart's desire.

Here's how he does it. He walks from door to door in every town in the land asking people to support him. At each door, he denounces "the incompetence and immorality of that out-of-touch old scoundrel, Henry VIII." He gives speeches in market squares railing against Henry's ruinous war policies, his heavy taxes, and his oppression of minorities (the nation's Catholics). He demands an end to "the elitist privileges of an arrogant aristocracy." He advocates a reduction in taxes for all English citizens. Most dramatically, Bush calls on "the ordinary people of this great land of ours" to "rise up and place *me* on the throne of England." "Oust that illegitimate Henry VIII and his brutal gang of greedy free-loaders," Bush cries.

How would Bush's bid for power work in these circumstances?

Obviously, these tactics—which sound plausible, even necessary, when Bush used them as an opposition leader in late twentieth-century America —would be disastrous if used in sixteenth-century England. At the first sign that one of his subjects was trying to replace him, the real Henry VIII would have had the man arrested, tortured, tried for treason, and hanged. A George W. Bush of that time, hoping to replace Henry on the throne of England, would have had to behave in a quite different fashion.

Let's go back to the 1530s. A rival for Henry's position would, for starters, have to become a threatening military leader. He would have to develop fierce loyalties among some of the leading noblemen of the day, become a beloved figure among the nation's peasants, and get an archbishop or two to

1

swear that the "real" line of succession to the throne ran through the ancient House of Bush. Even after those moves, any pretender to the throne would have to raise an army, challenge Henry's military forces on the battlefield, and win decisive victories over him in armed combat.

A battlefield strategy of this sort in contemporary America would prove as absurd as an electioneering strategy in sixteenth-century England.

The modern race to power: different tactics for different times

As we know, George W. Bush was successful in adjusting his ambition to his time and place. Rather than raise a rebel army, he raised money for television ads. Rather than perfect his military skills, he perfected his public-relations skills. Rather than aim his efforts at an elite, he focused on persuading the great mass of citizens. He became President of the USA because he understood what's required to win power in a modern democracy. You must persuade large numbers of people to vote for you. Bush honed his skills toward that end rather than toward winning power in a dictatorship.

Of course, not all who want to become president succeed, even if they understand the requirements. Let's look at four people who in recent times might have become president—but didn't. Let's start with Mario Cuomo and Colin Powell. Both men, one a Democrat, one a Republican, were once national figures with excellent chances for the presidency. Cuomo, a popular Governor of New York, was considered a front-runner for the Democratic nomination in 1988. General Powell, a respected military man and former Chairman of the Joint Chiefs of Staff, was deemed to have a good shot at the Republican nomination in 2000. Yet neither man made it to the White House. Indeed, both men declined even to run for their party's nomination.

Two other men were once deemed strong candidates for the White House: Gary Hart and George Romney. Hart had been a respected Senator from Colorado and a serious challenger to Walter Mondale in the 1984 race for the Democratic nomination. After Mondale's defeat at the hands of incumbent president Ronald Reagan, Hart was seen as front-runner for the Democratic nomination in 1988.

Romney had been a successful businessman and popular Governor of Michigan. He looked like a serious contender for the Republican nomination in 1968. Unlike the wavering Cuomo and Powell, both of these men *did* begin campaign activity that they hoped would take them to the White House.

Neither made it far. Both dropped out of the race early, after taking actions that produced devastating political consequences. Hart, a married man with a wandering eye, was caught having an affair with a young unmarried model. Romney prominently changed his position on the war in Vietnam. He had been a supporter of the war until he started running for

2

president at a time when the national mood was shifting against it. Declaring that he now opposed the war, Romney claimed that his former position had occurred after he had been "brainwashed" by military leaders during his inspection tour of American efforts in that country.

Romney's statement made him look like a weak flip-flopper. Hart simply looked like a lecherous philanderer. After these incidents, both men were ridiculed mercilessly in the media, and both became the targets of popular jokes. Inevitably, both ended their campaigns soon after these disclosures.

What do these histories suggest about the likelihood of successful political action? Why did Bush and the others behave as they did?

Here we see the importance of the **environmental setting** for determining one's actions. Bush became President because he understood that in a mass democracy, persuasion of the many is key to victory. He also understood that in American democracy, in particular, it is vital to build an image of friendliness, accessibility, and sympathetic caring for average people.

In trying to project those traits, Bush worked to embody key norms in American democratic culture. But that's not all he needed. He benefited enormously from several other situational factors. First, he was campaigning after 8 years of a troubled Democratic presidency. Many Americans were "ready for a change." Second, a downturn in the economy had begun. As a result, many voters had become jittery about keeping the incumbent party in office. Third, his opponent, Al Gore, seemed to lack both charisma and that affable "common touch" essential to successful campaigners in the USA. Beyond all this, Bush benefited from the third-party candidacy of Ralph Nader, who took crucial votes from Gore, particularly in the key state of Florida.[1]

A final environmental factor that gave Bush the presidency was the Electoral College. We shall discuss this unique institution in Chapter 10.[2] Here we need only point out that Bush ultimately became president because he won a majority of Electors. In a country without this institution, he would have lost his race to Al Gore, who, despite everything, finished half a million votes ahead of Bush in the popular count.

Presidential behavior

Bush took advantage of the situation in which he operated. But it was not *just* the situation that allowed him to become President. Central to the achievement was his combination of personal skills and attitudes. He was a dynamic, likeable, empathetic man with relatively Centrist political views—at least that's how he projected himself and was seen at the time. The American public likes friendly leaders, and it prefers Centrist policies to those of the Right or Left. Bush's personality and political preferences made him a strong candidate at the particular moment that he chose to run for office.

George W. Bush, in other words, became president not just because of who he was and not just because of the circumstances in which he chose to run, but because of those two factors combined. Their complex interplay made him president. The odds favored a talented challenger, and Bush had the personality traits that made him that talented challenger.

Managing behavior and environment

In like manner, we can explain the behavior of the four *unsuccessful* candidates. They failed not just because of personality problems and not just because of environmental factors, but through a combination of the two. Take Cuomo and Powell. For years, both men had been widely seen as excellent potential candidates. Many thought they would take the presidency and even go down in history as great leaders. Yet both took themselves out of the race months before it even began. They never sought the job for which they were supposedly destined. What happened?

We can start to explain these events by focusing on personality. Simplifying, we might say that neither man had that "fire in the belly" needed to run a serious campaign. Both looked down the road and saw they would have to commit years to an energy-sapping, mind-numbing grind of hand-shaking, fund-raising, and travel. In addition, that draining activity would be accompanied by vicious attacks on their ideas and their character by a throng of dedicated enemies. Neither could stomach this daunting prospect.

At first glance, personality seems the only factor influencing Cuomo and Powell—their inability to stand the heat of the campaign kitchen. The same could be said for the unsuccessful runs of Hart and Romney. Both men made personal decisions that led to failure. Hart pursued a woman he wasn't married to, and Romney released a statement that made him look weak and indecisive.

Yet in all four cases, failure to achieve the presidency reflected much more than personal weakness. The situation, or political environment, played a major role. Cuomo and Powell backed out of a presidential campaign under the conditions of late-twentieth-century American politics. In that historical era (that is, our era), no one can become president without running for the job for years, personally raising millions of dollars, and suffering vitriolic criticism each step of the way. Politics doesn't have to be like that. Indeed, it wasn't like that even within the USA just a few decades before.

Running for president had been a modest affair well into the twentieth century. In many circumstances, political leaders and men of national stature like Cuomo or Powell were simply handed their party's nomination at a national convention. They did not necessarily work hard to get it. For one thing, there were no primaries to suffer. For another, politicians didn't barnstorm around the country, even after getting the nomination. Until the twentieth century, it was considered "unseemly" for presidential candidates to "beg" for votes. Party activists did the campaign work, persuading and rounding up voters. Men with the temperament of a Cuomo or a Powell, happy to lead but unwilling to campaign, could plausibly become president in nineteenth-century America.[3]

In the same vein, both Hart and Romney would have had better shots at the presidency in a different environment. In many a culture, personal habits (like drinking or philandering) are deemed irrelevant to leadership skills and would be ignored as a factor in choosing a president. In many cultures in the past, the media was not particularly intrusive in political life (and that is still true in many places today). One misspoken phrase or action (Howard Dean's "scream," Romney's "brainwashed" comment) would not have been viewed and discussed a thousand times a day across the land until the unfortunate actor was embarrassed into ignominious retreat from public life.

In many times or places, people like Cuomo, Powell, Hart, and Romney might well have succeeded in their desire to attain national leadership. Likewise, in another time and place (e.g., Russia in 1900) someone like George W. Bush would have had no chance at his society's top job. Political behavior results not just from what a person is like and not just from the situation a person faces, but from a complex interplay between these two factors.

Political behavior as a product of personality and environment

These insights lead us to a famous principle in social science. At any given time, behavior results from an interaction between the individual (with his or her particular set of personality traits) and the external, situational forces that shape and narrow the range of that individual's possible choices. *Behavior occurs when a given individual facing a specific environment makes a decision about how to act in that environment.*

This perspective can be condensed, for ease of understanding, into a simple equation. It is usually written,

$$B = f[OE]$$

where:

B stands for **behavior**
f [ ] stands for "a **function of**"
O stands for the **organism**
E stands for the **environment**.

The equation can be read this way: "Behavior is a function of the interaction between the organism and its environment."[4]

In plain English, this means that to understand people's behavior in any situation, you must understand their attitudes, values, personality traits—and

5

the circumstances they are confronting. You cannot ignore either the psychological aspects of behavior (what's in the mind of the "organism"—that is, the individual) or the social-economic-political circumstances (the environment) within which the individual must act.

These points can be illustrated by a simple diagram (Figure I.1).

Keep this model firmly in mind. To explain political behavior, we shall examine both environmental influences and personality tendencies. Each factor is crucial for understanding human actions. Sometimes it is the environment that is dominant. People behave as they do because they find themselves in a particular set of circumstances. Whatever your personality, if you live in an oppressive dictatorship and you are told to vote on election day . . ., then you vote on election day. Likewise, no matter who you are, if you live in a democracy, you do *not* run for office on the platform that opposition party leaders should be shot.

But individual differences also matter. If we hold environment constant and just look at people in the same time and place, we find wide variation, not uniformity. In 1950 in the USA, for example, active politicians from similar states included the liberal Adlai Stevenson from Illinois and the conservative Joseph McCarthy next door in Wisconsin.[5] In 1900 in Russia one could find the absolute monarch Nicholas II and the revolutionary communist, Vladimir Ilyich Lenin. And of course in America today in any community one finds ardent conservatives and zealous liberals who share, in all other respects, apparently identical features (ethnicity, social status, gender, etc.).

Environment alone does not determine behavior. Neither does personality. Sometimes one of those factors is determinative, sometimes the other. Most often, it is a combination of the two.

My friend, James Payne, used to tell an amusing story to illustrate this point. In 1961, he spent his junior year of college in Lima, Peru. When he went to movie theatres there, he noticed that everyone was smoking, despite an abundant number of highly visible No Smoking signs. He chalked this behavior up to "the wild, undisciplined nature of the Spanish temperament" and lit his own cigarettes with impunity.

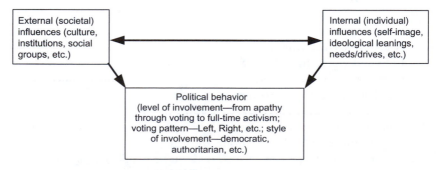

Figure I.1 Explaining behavior: The model.

Then during a vacation week he traveled to a distant town to see more of the country. Having enjoyed all the local tourist sites, he dropped in one evening at the nearest cinema to take in a film. Settling comfortably into his seat, he promptly started puffing on a cigarette, ignoring as usual all the signs forbidding that habit. The young man to his right quickly leaned Payne's way and whispered, "There's no smoking in this theatre!" Startled, my friend replied that everyone smoked at the theatres in Lima. "Yes," came the response, "but here they give fines!"

Behavior in this case is influenced partly by the specific traits of the individual (one's a smoker or not, one's "undisciplined" or not) and partly by the individual's environment (fines or not).

Conclusion

Behavior occurs when a particular person (an organism) faces a particular situation (the environment). Only through the interplay of individual and institution can we explain political outcomes. People act in politics to satisfy personal motives, beliefs, and ambitions. But they also act as they do because their culture compels them or because institutions demand it. Politics, like life, is complex, and there are no simple explanations. Only by examining the relationship between internal and external forces can we start to understand political realities.

Questions for discussion

1   Bush campaigned for president in 2000, while calling himself "a compassionate conservative." Does this phrase resonate with the norms and values of the American people? Did it help or hurt him in his efforts towards winning the White House?

2   In a celebrated incident, Howard Dean, a leading Democratic candidate for the presidency in 2004, was filmed yelling like a wild man in front of cheering supporters after a disappointing third-place finish in the Iowa caucuses. Why did that video, known as "the scream" and re-played repeatedly on television and the Internet, hurt Dean's chances of becoming president?

3   A series of commercials known as "the Swift Boat ads" downplayed John Kerry's military achievements in the Vietnam War. Kerry, running for president against George W. Bush in 2004, had made much of his military service. To what extent did these ads, widely believed to have cost Kerry the election, reflect environmental or personal factors?

Part I

CULTURE AND POLITICS

1

THE IMPACT OF CULTURE

Geography and cultural difference

People behave, from one place to another, in remarkably dissimilar ways. Brazilians bear hug when they meet friends. The French shake hands formally, and the Japanese bow. Transferring the pattern of one culture to another can produce dramatic misunderstandings. Bear hugging a Japanese businessman would hardly improve your chances for a contract. Fail to shake hands with a Frenchwoman each time you meet, and she will see you as a boor and a cad.[1]

Anecdotal accounts of human diversity can be fascinating, and they can also make a serious point. It pays to understand the variety of human mores, because every social pattern impinges in some way on politics. Candidates for office in Japan or France do not throw their arms around constituents while campaigning; in Brazil they do. Try it in Japan, or fail to do it in Brazil, and you will get nowhere in your bid for office.

In the same manner, what you eat (far-fetched though it may seem) will influence your political fortune. Imagine a politician in Israel known to dine on roast pig. Or an American politician who admits to loathing hot dogs and apple pie, or a Hindu politician in India caught eating a steak. All three would soon be ex-politicians, having horrified most other members of their culture.

P.J. O'Rourke, the flamboyant American journalist, once described some harrowing (though hilarious) adventures in Lebanon for his bestseller, *Holidays in Hell*. One day he and his guide roamed the countryside looking for a farmer he was supposed to interview.

> "It's hard to know what your driver is doing when he talks to natives. He'll pull up somewhere and make a preliminary oration, which draws five or six people to the car window. Then each of them speaks in turn. There will be a period of gesturing, some laughter, much arm clasping and handshaking, and a long speech by the eldest or most prominent bystander.

Then your driver will deliver an impassioned soliloquy. This will be answered at length by each member of the audience and by anyone else who happens by. Another flurry of arm grabbing, shoulder slapping and handshakes follows, then a series of protracted and emotional good-byes.

'What did you ask them?' you'll say to your driver.

'Do they know of your friend.'

'What did they tell you?'

'No.' "[2]

Cultures vary. People differ radically from each other, depending on where they live and how they have been raised. Despite the old cliché, people are emphatically *not* "just the same the world over."

As human behavior varies from place to place, so too does political behavior. The direct American manner of asking questions would get nowhere in a Lebanese village. In like vein, a "straight-talking," "no-nonsense" American-style politician would fail miserably there in a bid for office. That behavior would be seen as coarse and rude. By the same token, the circuitous and loquacious style of Lebanese interaction would spell career disaster for any American politician dim enough to adopt it.

Political behavior and culture

No human activity occurs in a vacuum. Everything we do takes place within a system of norms and expectations that shape our behavior. Whether we are going to a wedding, shopping, running for office, or yes, eating, we will act in ways dictated by our culture. *To understand behavior anywhere, then, we must understand the culture in which that behavior occurs. Likewise, to understand politics anywhere, we must understand the culture within which political acts are embedded.*

Let's return to the George W. Bush we've already met in that "alternate universe." Say that our ambitious friend settles on another tactic for gaining power. He invites his chief political rival and his rival's leading followers to a magnificent feast. After the meal, supporters of Bush build a huge fire in the back yard. There he proceeds to toss onto the blaze several valuable paintings by Picasso that had been hanging on the walls of his estate. Not to be outdone, Bush's rival sends his backers out to the driveway, where they unload from his van a large number of expensive Monet paintings. (He "just happens" to have brought these along.) The man and his cronies proceed calmly to toss these works of art onto the same bonfire that had destroyed the Picassos.

Unfazed, Bush simply orders more valuable paintings to be torn from his walls and burned, while his rival urges his supporters to bring in more art from the van for the same purpose. After some hours of this mutual destruction, Bush's rival runs out of paintings, to the raucous jeers of Bush and his people. The defeated guests slink away, shamefaced, and all the people of the land acknowledge the greatness of their new leader, George W. Bush.

Naturally, seeking public support in this way would appear insane to contemporary Americans. Yet it was standard fare in the rivalries for status and power of traditional *Kwakiutl* society. The Kwakiutl, a tribe of Native Americans who have lived for centuries in the Pacific Northwest, established hierarchical dominance by public displays of wealth. For them, nothing indicated wealth better than the easy ability to destroy objects of value.

What was the rationale here? Conspicuous destruction implies enormous wealth. A leader thereby shows that the destroyed objects, valuable as they may appear to outsiders, mean little to him because he has so many of them. "I can destroy all these goods," he is saying, "because I have so many more that even this level of destruction means nothing to me. But if you run out of goods to destroy, then that means that you had much less than I did to begin with. Thus, you rank much lower in status than I do, and your public humiliation testifies to my greatness and superiority."[3]

This contest of powerful leaders was known as a "potlatch," and these ritual ceremonies of material destruction were quite common in Kwakiutl culture. Of course, they didn't destroy paintings, but they did ruin equivalent works of art. They burnt beautiful blankets, for instance, and broke artistically etched copper engravings.[4]

Naturally, this type of power-seeking behavior, while rational among the Kwakiutl, would bring a political claimant nothing but derision in contemporary Washington. It might lead to an appointment with a psychiatrist, but never to power. Thus, a George Bush of our time and place—that is to say, any American politician in the early twenty-first century—would never behave in this manner.

Socioeconomics and political action

Culture provides the setting within which politics occurs.[5] And cultures vary enormously from place to place, from era to era. Imagine the following scene. Your neighbors, a poor but hardworking couple with several young children, tell you that they see no sense in keeping their twelve-year-old son in school. Instead, they have pulled him out of classes and sent him to work in the local coal mine. After working 12 hours a day for 6 days a week, the boy brings home enough money to save the family from destitution. These neighbors express nothing but pleasure at this improvement in their fortunes.

Outraged, you report your neighbor to local government officials, only to be told that they can do nothing about the situation. Indeed, they inform you that you are a nosy busybody and should start minding your own affairs.

Individuals, they say, are free to sell their labor, or the labor of their dependents, as they see fit. Interfering with "the sanctity of contracts" is neither the business of government officials nor of prying neighbors. Stunned, you slink out of City Hall and ask yourself: "What kind of society am I living in anyway?"

As it turns out, you are not living in contemporary Bangladesh. Nor are you living in Thailand, Nigeria, or Guatemala, all countries where the scenario just sketched might be plausible. You are indeed living in the United States, but through a time-warp accident, it's not the United States of today—but of 1900. Economic and social conditions were rather different then, and they shaped the politics of that time in ways different from those we recognize today.

In 1900, no society was wealthy enough to fund government for a role that today we take for granted: provider of a social safety net. In our time if a family cannot make ends meet, it can receive a range of government assistance. The USA provides less of a safety net than many modern nations do, but we still have food stamps, Medicaid, Medicare, social security, unemployment compensation, and various other programs to help the unfortunate. The nation has become much wealthier since 1900; it is also become more willing to use public funds to aid the less fortunate.

Indeed, governments everywhere have enacted laws to help families make ends meet. Foremost among such measures in the USA are those insuring a minimum level of pay (minimum-wage bills) and reduced rates of taxation for lower-income groups (e.g., the earned-income tax credit). Governments in other industrialized nations use other methods, but they achieve the same results. As a consequence of twentieth-century economic policy-making, few families in wealthy countries today find themselves in such dire straits that they would need to send young children into dangerous and grueling jobs for 50 or more hours a week.

Even very poor families that might want to send their children to work are legally prohibited from doing so. Indeed, they are *required* to take advantage of one of the major government-benefit programs in modern societies: free education for all. In most developed nations, children are legally obliged to attend school until they are essentially adults (15 or older, depending on the country). Anyone who takes a 12-year-old out of school could be in serious trouble. This was true almost nowhere in 1900.[6]

The troubles of anyone trying to follow the 1900 scenario today do not stop with school authorities. Sending children to work in a coal mine could land parents in jail for child abuse. They might have children taken from them by angry state officials. Anyone who cooperated with the parents and actually put this child to work could be hauled into court for violating child-labor laws.

Furthermore, any attempt to put children into a standard workplace would meet stiff resistance from employed adult workers. They would see this action as a threat to their own livelihoods. Various forms of protest, from lawsuits to full-blown strikes, would promptly ensue. Most significant of all, a cascade of politicians, media figures, and community leaders, once the story became known, would rise up to denounce "this travesty of parental responsibility."

Living as we do in one of the world's wealthy, modern societies, we know that forcing children to do dangerous work for long hours during regular school time is unthinkable. Yet, just a few decades ago in all the world's "wealthy, modern societies," it was just as unthinkable to do otherwise. Few politicians, government officials, or public figures worried much about this widespread practice.

From these examples, we can conclude that *what is legally, morally, and politically unthinkable in one era can be standard and normal in another.* Thus, to understand political action (or any human behavior, for that matter), we must place it in its proper historical and cultural context.

Changing class structure/changing perspectives on class

The reason for these different perspectives on child labor is simple. Over the past century, personal wealth in advanced industrial nations has shot up dramatically. Whereas societies in 1900 were too poor to provide assistance to the large number of people who lived in poverty, over 100 years later, many nations are wealthy enough to provide generous assistance to the (now) relatively small number of impoverished citizens.

In addition, attitudes towards the poor have changed. Along with their increasing wealth, citizens in modern societies have come to believe that it is right and proper to help the needy. Indeed, ignoring their plight would be considered shocking. To illustrate, the Pew Research Center found in March, 2007, that 69 percent of Americans believed that "it is the responsibility of government to take care of people who can't take care of themselves." These attitudes are consistent and long term. They reflect similar findings from similar polls by the same organization over the previous two decades. More striking, over half of respondents agreed that "government should help the needy even if it means greater debt."[7]

Given the different political climate, politicians who might have been silent in 1900 would today react with outrage at the discovery of a factory operating under nineteenth-century working conditions. Politicians, like the rest of us, pay attention to social expectations. Like the rest of us, they do not wish to commit professional suicide. They pass the laws expected of them in their time, and they avoid passing the laws that are seen by contemporaries as outrageous.

Changing times . . . changing popular political ideas

This discussion leads to another important conclusion: *Political ideas reflect the conditions of the age.* No one was touting the virtues of democracy in Henry VIII's time. No one today hails the benefits of an absolute monarch. Political ideas go hand in hand with the social and economic conditions of the time.

In an age when poverty was near-universal, society—acting collectively through government—could do little to alleviate that condition. Thus, no one advocated government safety-net programs. Instead, citizens and politicians alike developed ideas to justify and rationalize the then current (and seemingly inevitable) government policy of non-intervention in citizens' lives. Societies in the past just were not rich enough to help the huge number of people living in poverty. In 1900, for instance, wealth *per capita* in the USA (technically, GDP *per capita* in constant 2000 dollars) came to US$4,943. In 2000, that figure was US$34,788, a seven-fold increase in wealth.[8] It is clearly easier to consider helping others when you are seven times richer than you once were.

Political philosophies of an earlier day helped better-off citizens justify a harsh reality: no one, including government, could provide a decent life for most people. A popular belief known as **Social Darwinism** held sway for decades, starting in the late nineteenth century. It stressed "survival of the fittest," suggesting that those who do well in any society earn their position through superior talent and effort. These people *should* reap great benefits, the argument went. To discourage these achievers and encourage non-productive "slackers" would be to elevate the weak and incompetent to positions of power and status at the expense of the robust and effective. That would undermine national vitality and lead to "social decadence." Naturally, such beliefs helped those who already enjoyed money and power justify their situation. It further allowed them to rationalize government policies that kept the poor in their place "for the good of society."

Not everyone accepted that conclusion. A few in any age fail to reflect society's mainstream ideas. But would-be leaders in 1900 who argued for government assistance to the poor got nowhere. They were called socialists (at best), and few were elected to high office anywhere before the twentieth century. In fact, in most places people who advocated these policies were variously harassed, persecuted, arrested, beaten, and even put to death by governments of the day.

Times change, ideas change. Today, people who espouse the policies of governmental *non*-intervention that held sway in 1900 are called libertarians, and most of them are just as unelectable as socialists were a few decades back.[9] Many societies have become wealthy enough to provide modest (even generous) social safety nets, and most citizens accept that providing various forms of social aid is one of government's major functions. The term **welfare state** is commonly used to describe governments in modern nations.

In this transformation, we see again that the dominant ideas of an age reflect, in significant ways, the socioeconomic conditions of the time. No Duke called for a welfare state during the poverty-stricken Middle Ages. No senator in industrially-advanced countries today calls for the re-introduction of serfdom. *Like all of us, politicians reflect their time.*

The context of politics

This notion of politics as embedded within a cultural, social, and historical context helps enormously to explain why people behave as they do. Let us look at a few examples that would perplex a visiting Martian—that is, someone with no context for understanding human action.

In 1942, all American politicians were denouncing "the Japs" as hated enemies. In 2006, no American politician would call anyone "a Jap," and most American leaders would refer to citizens of Japan as "our good friends and close allies, the Japanese." "What's going on here?" the Martian might wonder. Of course, *we* know that 60 years of history have changed the relationship between the Americans and Japanese. The countries became closer as the Japanese adopted democracy, renounced militarism, and joined the USA during its long Cold War against communism. As a result, these nations are no longer deadly enemies, but allies and friends.

When an American male politician meets a European male politician, both men wear suits. When an Arab leader meets the Pope, both men wear robes. Why, the Martian might wonder, can't the Pope wear a business suit while meeting with a robe-wearing American president? *We* know, of course, that such action is impossible. The clothes-wearing habits of our leaders, and the rest of us, are determined by social and cultural expectations. Violating those expectations just isn't done; violations bring heavy penalties. Ridicule, loss of the public's confidence, and ousting from office are some of the results likely to occur when politicians violate strong social norms.

Our Martian friend might wonder why women comprise more than 40 percent of leadership positions in Sweden, but exactly 0 percent in Saudi Arabia. To explain this *political* fact, we would need an extended description of the different *cultures* of these two nations. It is impossible to understand the political role women play anywhere without examining the culture in which they must operate. You will not find strong female leaders in countries with profoundly traditionalistic norms about woman's "rightful" place at home with children. Even in modern nations like the USA, many social conservatives believe women should be home-makers, not career-makers.

Conclusion

People are deeply influenced by their culture and their historical era. The **norms** of their time and place dictate how they will behave: how they will dress, how they will work, how they will play . . . and how they will act in politics. In short, environment plays a major role in shaping political action. Beyond that, environments (especially cultures) shape the character of entire political systems. It is time to take a close look at that key phenomenon.

Questions for discussion

1   Do politicians really "reflect their time and place," as the author argues? Can you think of any successful politicians who seem exceptions to that rule?
2   If politics does reflect culture and society, why are so few upper-level politicians women or minorities, in an era when those groups are supposedly accorded full social and legal rights?
3   Has the "survival of the fittest" philosophy really disappeared in our culture?

2

CULTURES AND CONFLICT

Some years ago, I heard an odd story from my colleague at the University of Southern Maine, Leonard Shedletsky. He had been visiting Glasgow, Scotland, a city divided by class and religious tensions. The Protestant majority and the Catholic minority lived in separate neighborhoods, belonged to separate clubs, drank in separate pubs, and viewed each other with hostility. The antagonism between these two groups reflected a spill-over effect from the violent Catholic–Protestant clashes taking place at that time in neighboring Northern Ireland. Their division was symbolized by separate colors representing each group (Green for Catholics; Orange for Protestants).

My friend was taking a bus across town one day, when he noticed a 10-year-old boy eyeing him suspiciously.

"How are you?" my friend asked expansively. "I've come all the way from America to visit your country."

"Are you Orange or Green?" the boy asked, curtly.

Taken aback, my friend replied that he was neither, he was just a visiting tourist from the United States. Not to be put off, the boy pressed his point: "But are you Orange or Green?"

Despite my friend's effort to change the topic, the boy kept putting his question: "Are you Orange or Green?" In desperation, my friend came up with a way to end the questioning: "I can't be Orange, and I can't be Green," he said. "I'm Jewish."

The boy thought this over for a minute, then turned back to my friend and said, "O.K., but are you Jewish Orange or Jewish Green?"

Conflict, cooperation, and indifference: three major social forces

As this story illustrates, **conflict** and **cooperation** both lie at the heart of the human condition. It is crucial for this boy to know whether the stranger is an enemy or a friend. Where he lives, only one option is possible. He is ready to fear the newcomer or share confidences, depending on the answer to one all-important question: the stranger's identity. A third possibility, neutrality and indifference, does not occur to him.

Each culture provides a lens through which inhabitants see the world. That lens can allow hostility, friendship, or indifference to filter in—or some combination of the three. A hostile attitude toward others leads to conflict, a central feature of life. People do compete for everything: land, jobs, money, love, respect.

But conflict alone does not explain all social behavior. People also cooperate with each other. They mingle in friendly groups. They eat, drink, and play together. They work together for common goals. Collaboration is another key aspect of social behavior.

Finally, people often have little to do with each other. They simply go about their own business, holding neither a positive nor a negative attitude toward the others, if they think of them at all. The mix of conflict, indifference, and cooperation in a given society determines what its social process will look like. Variations in that mix lead to diverse political patterns.

Politics in some places is quiet, almost boring. Go to Switzerland, Norway, New Zealand, and small towns in New England, Iowa, or Oregon. In places like these, political activity frequently reflects the cooperative side of human nature. One hears practical debate about the wisdom of building a new sports arena versus renovating the old one. Moderate voices urge a new sewer system, constructive critics examine current school programs, productive suggestions are made for improving neighborhood parks. Eventually votes are taken. Some policies muster majority support and are implemented, while others lose and are put aside. Citizens move on to other issues. Tempers do occasionally flare, but the process generally proceeds in an orderly, business-like, and often courteous manner.

On the other side of the conflict-cooperation continuum—in Northern Ireland, Rwanda, Colombia, Bosnia, Afghanistan, and many other places—politics gets intense, confrontational. Conflict dominates; violence is common. People shout, point accusing fingers, pound tables, and it does not stop there. Kidnappings, assassinations, guerrilla warfare, and other forms of brutality occur with regularity. Conflict moves beyond words into armed battles between rival individuals and groups.

Towards the middle of the conflict-cooperation spectrum lies indifference. This attitude characterized citizens of the various American states for much of the country's history. Before the age of modern communications (e.g., in 1900), residents of Vermont and Kansas were not particularly friendly towards each other, nor were they especially hostile. They lived far apart, and little that happened in one state affected people in the other. These citizens could live their entire lives and rarely think about each other. This kind of neutrality is most likely when people have little interaction with each other. People form emotional attitudes, whether positive or negative, toward others that they know well.[1]

The precise mix of conflict, indifference, and cooperation varies from place to place. Even in the same setting, it can vary over time. Politics in the USA has been relatively calm through much of its history, but violence rose to dramatically high levels in the 1860s during a bloody civil war. Human societies oscillate between extreme levels of conflict (war, civil war, anarchy) and extreme levels of cooperation (building projects, government reforms, economic advances).[2]

Conflict produces politics

Although people can be both cooperative and confrontational, political scientists stress conflict. We study politics, after all, and we would have no politics to study without conflict. If all citizens agreed on everything, they would not need separate parties to advance different perspectives. They would not need public debate to determine which policy options to adopt. They would not need courts to resolve disputes (there would be no disputes). It is because conflict produces politics that political scientists focus on it: on disagreement and competition. Without social struggles, we would be out of work.

This emphasis on conflict can lead political scientists to see conflict-producing elements even in forms of cooperation. We point out, for instance, that groups of people working together can paradoxically intensify conflict. A group of friendly, cooperating people, like the "Orange" in Northern Ireland or Glasgow, can run headlong into another group (the "Green") who are also cooperating, but to achieve opposing goals. Thus, some types of cooperation can produce deep and bitter conflict, as my friend learned during his trip to the British Isles.

Looking at all the conflict in the world, many well-meaning people have asked, "Can't we eliminate conflict, and thereby eliminate politics?" Many have dreamed of a golden age, when people will become uniformly coopera-tive, when no conflicts will occur, when politics becomes a thing of the past. This sounds reasonable. People as diverse as Plato and Karl Marx have imagined a world without conflict. But do not hold your breath. Conflict is central to the human condition. So too (therefore) is politics, which is *society's way of dealing with conflict.* Those who dream of eliminating either element from human affairs are doomed to disappointment.[3]

Some may find this conclusion bleak, but let us put it in perspective. For one thing, conflict is not *all* that occurs in society. Cooperation plays a major and valuable role.[4] People are much more than conflictual, competitive beings. The fact that confrontations are part of life should not blind us to the many cooperative forms of human behavior.

For another thing, both conflict and politics can have positive repercus-sions. The tensions that arise from clashing interests and perspectives fre-quently produce creative solutions to seemingly intractable problems. Social tensions force people to focus on issues they might otherwise ignore. Confrontations often lead to innovative policy proposals. For example, the groundbreaking civil rights laws of the 1960s followed marches and demonstrations led by people like Martin Luther King.

Conflict can even be psychologically productive. The feminist psychotherapist, Jean Baker Miller, has argued that "we all grow via conflict."[5] It "is not necessarily threatening or destructive,"[6] but rather a step that must be taken to produce a better world. "Conflict," she stresses, "is inevitable, the source of all growth, and an absolute necessity if one is to be alive."[7] For Miller, conflict is a tool for disadvantaged groups. It helps them force dominant groups to pay attention to their claims. If the conflict is then processed in a just manner, both groups win. The dominant group, by paying heed to the demands on it, becomes more human, while the disadvantaged group gains both rights and self-respect.

Conflict and politics do not always lead to violence and war. At its best, politics can produce creative compromises that significantly reduce social tension. But because it deals so directly with conflict, politics will rarely seem glamorous or attractive. Most of us shun conflict. We prefer to avoid situations of tension. Disliking conflict, we therefore dislike one effect of conflict—politics.

Yet, while we may detest politics, the alternative can be worse. If conflict cannot be resolved politically, it often degenerates into violence. In its ordinary, workaday mode, "*politics is damage control*,"[8] says Peter Berkowitz in one of the best aphorisms I know on the subject. Politics provides an arena where people can vent their hostilities, pursue their interests, and express their rivalries without actually killing each other. Like growing old, it may not be wonderful, but it is better than the alternative.

The forces behind conflict

The inevitability of conflict (and therefore politics) is an old theme. In 1788, James Madison wrote that "the causes of conflict are sown in the nature of man," and we have no reason to believe much has changed since Madison's day.[9] Madison argued that diverse human interests would always lead people to clash with each other, but he went further. Conflict, for him, lay beyond the mere struggle for resources. It was buried deep in the human psyche.

> So strong is this propensity of mankind to fall into mutual animosities that where no substantial occasion presents itself, the most frivolous and fanciful distinctions have been sufficient to kindle their unfriendly passions and excite their most violent conflicts.[10]

No matter how happy the circumstances, Madison is saying, conflict will abound.

Reasons for the inevitability of conflict are many. We will start with the basics.

Desire

First, *human desires are infinite*—or if not infinite, mighty close.[11] What would it take to make you truly, utterly happy? How about wealth—like, say, a million dollars? The answer for most people, after stopping to think a minute, would be: hardly! A new Lamborghini alone costs something in the neighborhood of a quarter of a million. A couple of those (one for you, one for your significant other), a decent yacht, a castle in Spain—and you'd suddenly find yourself with hardly a cent to your name.[12]

No, a million is not enough to buy happiness. A billion *might* do it—it might allow you to buy all the material possessions you could possibly imagine. Yet millions, and even billions, do not seem to satisfy many of the people who do achieve them. We can all think of extremely wealthy people who are still working themselves ragged, not lounging around beaches in Tahiti or basking in the sun by that castle in Spain.

The human desire for wealth is clearly large. Material plenty, however, is not all that people want from life. They also want respect, love, power, and affection. How many of those intangible qualities would it take to make you happy?

Take power, for example. The most powerful people who ever lived—Alexander the Great, Attila the Hun, Stalin, Hitler—were never content. No matter how much power they had, they never stopped trying to accumulate more. They restlessly sought to increase their power over others, or defend their power base, every second of their waking lives, right to the moment of death.

How about love? As a moonstruck teenager, I was sure that my life would be complete if I could just gain the love of the famous movie star, Marilyn Monroe. Yet to my amazement, several people who did gain Marilyn's love—including the famous baseball player, Joe DiMaggio, and the well-known playwright, Arthur Miller—found that achievement insufficient for their needs and before long, left her.

In fact, humans have a near-infinite capacity for dissatisfaction with their current lot, no matter how desirable that lot might appear to objective observers. "I want, I want, I want" captures a central human perspective.[13]

This never-ceasing need for "more" collides with a second fact. *The world's resources are finite.* Put bluntly, there are only so many goodies to go around. Whether "goodies" consist of land, wealth, positions of prestige, rare stamps, or gorgeous potential partners, the most desired things will always be scarce. Few of us will ever have enough of what we want. Few will ever achieve a state of perfect fulfillment.

Part of the problem is that we are a restless, questing species. No matter how much of any value we attain, we rarely remain satisfied. If not all of us, then certainly a large proportion will vie to extend our benefits, to do better, to improve our lot, no matter how well off we may already be. And the simple fact is that everything we seek to gain is scarce. The struggle to maximize benefits brings all of us up against others struggling toward the same end. Our multiple and incompatible goals create a prime recipe for conflict.

Selfishness

The problem is compounded by another fact of life. *Few people are saints.* "If men were angels," says Madison, wistfully, in one of his most famous passages, then we wouldn't need government and politics, because people would conduct their affairs with restraint, love, and altruism. Unfortunately, Madison hastens to add, people are *not* angels. Thus, we *do* in fact need politics ("damage control") to keep the inevitable conflicts over finite resources from getting out of hand.[14]

Many of the world's religions have tried to diminish this acquisitive side of human nature. Buddhism stresses the need to renounce worldly pleasure and find true spiritual happiness within ourselves. Christ said, "Don't lay up treasure for yourself on earth, but in heaven." Islam and Hinduism also stress the rewards to come in a future life, if one is good in this one, while Confucianism argues that we should moderate our desires in order to fit peacefully into our current social niche.

In more recent times, ethicists, philosophers, and environmentalists, among many others, have argued that we must all modify our wish for material possessions if we are to build a livable and peaceful world. Warning phrases like "the limits of growth" and "small is beautiful" have aimed to damp down levels of human acquisitiveness.[15] None of these perspectives has had much success in diminishing human desire. "I want" usually takes precedence over "I shall sacrifice."

One need not be a cynic to point this out. If most people were in fact selfless altruists, then we would have no need to sanctify the few human beings who do reach high levels of spirituality: Buddha, Gandhi, Jesus Christ. It is also true, fortunately, that few people are absolutely evil. On any scale of humanity, Adolf Hitler and Saddam Hussein stand out as extreme deviants—just as people like Mother Teresa and Francis of Assisi stand out at the other end of the scale. On a range from pure egoism to pure altruism, most people lie somewhere in the middle.

To make things more complex, most people vary up and down on that scale over the course of their lives. We are "better people" at some times than at others. We can all rise to the heights and sink to the depths. As the Roman poet, Terrence said in 163 BC, "I am human, and so nothing human is alien to me."[16] In most circumstances, however, most people focus first on

24

themselves. We struggle to gain as many advantages as possible, given our skills, resources, and location on the social ladder.

For most of us, fortunately, the lifelong struggle for privilege does not occur in a lawless vacuum. We are protected from ruthless behavior (our own, as well as that of others) by various social institutions, including laws, courts, and the police. We are also constrained by the values that we have internalized from our particular culture. Its moral and religious beliefs, its condemnation of self-serving action, its norms about helping the less fortunate: these and other widely-propagated values combine to curb our most selfish tendencies. But despite restraints and restrictions, most of us struggle to promote our own well-being as ardently as we can within our particular milieu.

Group affiliation and Jingoism

Conflict does not stop at the individual level. *Humans are social beings—that is, they are group-affiliating creatures.* Aristotle is often reported to have said, "Man is a political animal." What he actually said is that men (i.e., humans) are first and foremost members of a *polis* (the Greek word for community, which for Aristotle meant the traditional city-state of his time). Using the language of our own era, we can translate and update Aristotle in this way: People live in social groups, are defined by the groups they live in, and cannot survive on their own outside of a group. As members of a group-oriented social species, we must learn to get along with at least some other human beings in order to get through life.

Cooperative behavior works enormously to our advantage. The more people we learn to work with, the better our chances of getting through life successfully.[17] In groups, we can collectively pursue our goals more effectively than on our own. Cooperative activity has a side-effect. It produces ties of friendship and loyalty among group members. Thus, the natural human tendency toward social life produces cooperating, effective affiliations of people who know how jointly to pursue their common interests.

As we know, however, the cooperative behavior that takes place *within* groups can exacerbate levels of conflict *between* groups. Groups of people struggling to achieve incompatible goals collide with each other on a regular basis. These struggles can have vast ramifications, as they involve many people, not lone individuals. If the "groups" are as large as nations, full-scale war can ensue. Even smaller group clashes can produce bitter domestic strife, possibly civil war.

Group conflict can be especially intense when members of opposing groups develop strong emotional identities. In-group loyalties then lead to out-group hostility. The stronger the tie to one's own crowd, the more negatively one feels about competing groups. If the groups are competing over scarce resources, extremely high levels of conflict can result.

The rationalization of desire

The likelihood of severe conflict is exacerbated by a uniquely human tendency: *People need to justify their wants.* Think about it. Few people say, "I want your land because I'm selfish and self-aggrandizing, so I'm going to kill you and take your property." Instead, they say, "It's the national destiny of our glorious Freedonia to follow God's will and bring the blessings of liberty to oppressed North Saskatch." Or "Our glorious people need living space, and you decadent ones don't deserve the land that you once unjustly took from us." Or, "Our people have justly seized your possessions and reduced you to ruin in righteous rage against your insolence toward us and your blasphemous behavior toward God Almighty."

Even Adolf Hitler, one of the bloodiest tyrants of all time, saw himself directed from above. "I am acting in the sense of the Almighty Creator," he wrote in *Mein Kampf. "By warding off the Jews I am fighting for the Lord's work."*[18]

People develop rationales for every form of behavior. They end up believing that what they are doing is moral and makes perfect sense. When they find themselves opposed by others, they do not see the logic or merit in the others' position. Rather, they demonize their opponents. After all, "if we are acting properly, then they, in opposing us, must be acting improperly." This view of willful opponents acting outside the bounds of decency is sure to intensify levels of conflict between competing groups.

In fact, very few people, even our toughest competitors, resemble the sinister villains of traditional melodrama. Very few human beings chuckle happily while doing evil deeds in dark alleys. Life would be much simpler if that were the case. We could quickly identify the sick deviants and isolate them from society.

Instead, most conflict consists of people who are clashing in part because their competing interests have collided (they both want to control a particular land, they both want to open a particular market), but in part because *they both deeply believe in the rightness of their cause,* in the divinely chosen nature of their group, or in the inherent evil and immorality of their "enemies" (that is, their competitors). *Many of our deepest beliefs are more or less elaborate justifications for, or rationales of, our own interests or the interests of our particular group.* These beliefs exacerbate the natural antagonism that results from the inevitable competition over scarce resources.

Personal interests

It is, after all, fairly easy to compromise on resources. "Let's draw the boundary here—right along the top of this mountain range between our two countries." Or, "You want our support to lower taxes by 2 percent? Turns out we need a new highway across our district. Do we have a deal?" It is much harder to compromise on beliefs. "Let's see—you guys trying to kill us are Protestants. We Catholics are trying to kill you. Why don't we compromise and all become Muslim?" It is not likely to happen.

So the beliefs that we develop to justify our interests make conflict-resolution difficult. This perspective should not be taken as pure cynicism. Not *all* our beliefs are rationalizations. We believe many things that are objectively true (the earth is round, whales are mammals, education enhances earnings potential). Furthermore, we often hold beliefs that *do not* enhance our interests and may even hurt them (like the conviction that we should give money to help sick children in distant lands).

We must also acknowledge that few people consciously develop their beliefs *in order to* rationalize their interests. That would be hypocritical, and few of us are out-and-out hypocrites. Rather, most of us believe that we are honest people of good will. We are often not aware of the frequent congruence between our interests and our ideas. We sincerely, even zealously, believe in the values we espouse, certain that they are literally true. If pressed, we may fervently *deny* any connection between our beliefs and our interests.

Still, it is rare to find people arguing for principles that would seriously hurt them or their group. To illustrate the connection between interest and belief, think of people who hold strong convictions that run diametrically counter to their interests. You won't find many.

Take doctors, for instance. Over the decades, physicians in the United States developed an elaborate rationale for opposing "socialized medicine." That negative term was the one they used for a system in which government regulates health care with the aim of providing inexpensive service for the great majority of citizens. Doctors claimed the goal was impossible. Government intervention would produce nothing but bureaucracy and poorer healthcare.

This argument may (or may not) have been correct, yet somehow one never heard it trumpeted by people who were poor and sick. Sound it may have been, but it also happened to coincide neatly with doctors' interests. With more government control, they could expect to make less money and work under increasing restrictions. Naturally, they found reasons to criticize any change in the existing system, a system allowing them to work with lots of freedom and earn substantial incomes.

Other examples abound. Lawyers everywhere tout "the majesty of the law." Lawyers would have fewer clients if they decried "the futility and corruption of the law." Religious leaders of whatever stripe in whatever place bemoan "the increasing decadence of society" and call for "a return to traditional values." If everyone were already religious and moral, why would we need leaders to help us "find the true path?" Teachers stress the value of learning and the role played by a strong system of education in fueling economic progress. Just coincidentally, the more importance society places on education, the better teachers get treated.

In these and similar cases, the arguments may be sound (although they can also be disputed), but there can be little doubt of one thing. If the public accepts these arguments, the advocating groups end up better off. They retain social status, they gain supporters, they make money.

Political party affiliation

Arguments about politics and parties illustrate the point even more clearly. In the 1970s, Democrats were quick to find reasons to justify the impeachment of President Richard Nixon. His fellow Republicans, on the other hand, took a more judicious tack, warning about the "damage to the institution of the presidency" that "hasty and premature" talk of impeachment could produce. In the 1990s, the two parties reversed themselves. Republicans found reason after reason to bring impeachment proceedings against a Democratic President, Bill Clinton, while Democrats found no persuasive evidence suggesting a need for that action.

Each side justified its position with weighty constitutional arguments. This change in attitude toward the impeachment process is hardly a coincidence. It is much easier to justify impeaching a president of the opposite party than to explain removing your own leader.[19]

The term-limits debate provides a particularly dramatic illustration of how we rationalize our interests. In the 1990s, American supporters of this idea pressured state legislatures and Congress to pass laws limiting the number of terms that legislators could serve. They also sought pledges from nonincumbent candidates that, if elected, they would step down after just a few terms (typically, three or four), even if no law obliged them to do so.

As you might expect, new legislators and especially challengers to incumbents found this position remarkably persuasive. Term limits could force popular incumbents from office, thus opening up space for newcomers who would otherwise have difficulty winning a seat. Newer legislators might also support term limits; its implementation would force senior politicians into retirement, thereby opening up powerful leadership positions and committee chairmanships that they could claim for themselves.

Naturally, incumbents, and especially senior incumbents, derided the idea of term limits. They spoke of the need for a legislature composed of seasoned, experienced, and knowledgeable members. They argued that if legislators lacked long years of policy experience, they would lose power to the executive branch or to interest groups. They claimed that "the people's branch of government," under term limits, would lose power to unelected bureaucrats and lobbyists. These arguments carry a certain persuasiveness. They sound especially persuasive, no doubt, to the legislator whose entire career rests upon the acceptance of this reasoning.

The connection between one's stand on term limits and one's seniority in the legislature is vividly illustrated by the data in Table 2.1, which provides

Table 2.1 The connection between interest and issue position: support for a term limits amendment in the US House of Representatives as a function of house terms served.

Number of terms served	Supported term limits (%)	Opposed term limits (%)
1st term	83.5	16.5
2nd term	59.1	40.9
3–5 terms	52.0	48.0
6–8 terms	33.8	66.3
9 or more terms	30.7	69.3

Vote on a constitutional amendment to impose a 12-year lifetime limit on service in each chamber of Congress. Vote taken March 29, 1995. Data provided by Michael Corbett, *Research Methods in Political Science: An Introduction Using MicroCase*, 2nd edn. (Bellevue, WA: MicroCase Corporation, 1996, Instructor's Manual, p. 44).

evidence from a vote taken by the US House of Representatives in 1995. As we can clearly see, the more time that Representatives had served in Congress, the more likely they were to have found term limits abhorrent. At the ends of the spectrum, nearly all first-year legislators favored term limits, while over two-thirds of the longest-serving members opposed it.[20]

There are solid arguments on both sides of the term-limits debate.[21] We do not have to take a position to see the general point: *People have little difficulty rationalizing their interests, even when their arguments seem shallow and self-serving to outsiders.*

This point is central to understanding politics. That human beings pursue their interests is trivial. Much more important is that they pursue their interests all the more zealously because they develop complex and deep-seated rationales for those interests. These justifications often blind them to what they have done. They mistake pursuit of their own interests for proper and moral behavior. They see those who oppose them in a darker light. Opponents become not just legitimate competitors, but evil-doers or ignoramuses who oppose "well-reasoned and principled" policy stands.

Economists see us all as self-centered creatures bent on maximizing our economic well-being. In actuality, we rarely define ourselves that way. We prefer to imagine that we are just and ethical, trying to live up to the values of our God or the ideals of our culture.

"Us" versus "Them"

Our interests lead us to develop complex rationales that help us justify (and disguise, even to ourselves) our self-interested behavior. Unfortunately, it is these well-constructed justifications that make conflict between opposing groups especially difficult to resolve. The normal competition between groups over scarce resources is exacerbated by the existence of differing beliefs and values. We demonize those who hold ideas at variance from our own. Seeing members of competing groups as immoral, evil, and possibly inferior, we find it easy to justify hurting them. It becomes harder to exercise restraint in our judgment of those degraded creatures.

Of course, since people in other groups see *us* in just this same way, a formula for intense conflict develops. Social psychologists call this the **mirror-image misperception** problem.[22] Take two groups with opposing interests. Both work to benefit themselves while justifying as morally proper their harmful action toward the other group. In extreme cases, both groups claim that their behavior is dictated by transcendent or divine powers.

The extra zeal produced by a deep-seated sense of moral superiority makes compromise difficult. You cannot make deals with Satan. That is why wars of religion are especially brutal. Just before ordering his troops to wipe out an entire city of 20,000 people in a medieval religious war, a French general was asked by his soldiers how to recognize those citizens within the city walls who were *NOT* heretics. The general replied, "Kill them all! God will recognize his own."[23]

Opposing interests and divergent values are not the only causes of group conflict. *Conflict between groups is further exacerbated by any obvious, surface difference between members of the opposing groups.* Differences between people can take many forms. The most obvious differences—those that have led to especially unpleasant forms of violence—involve language, race, religious practice, and general appearance (skin color, dress, body type).

Religion

Religious differences have produced some of the highest levels of conflict in human history. Germany tore itself to shreds during the Thirty Years War in the seventeenth century. The issue: whether the one true faith was Protestantism or Catholicism. At the end of the slaughters (Peace of Westphalia, 1648), the population of the warring territories had been reduced by *one-third*. (That would be comparable with a present-day America reduced in population by *one hundred million* people.) After this disaster, the weakened Germany remained a secondary player on the European scene for over 200 years.

Group conflict has frequently been exacerbated by religion. Muslims and Hindus have fought viciously for over 1,000 years on the Indian sub-continent. Even today, their religious differences are mirrored in the tensions between the two major states of that region. India and Pakistan, flag-bearers, respectively of the Hindu and Muslim religions, have armed themselves to the teeth, fought border skirmishes, and developed atomic weapons, all in reaction to the other country's hated religion.

Late twentieth-century Bosnia provides an intriguing example of the intensity of loathing that divergent religions can provoke. The people of that small region of south-central Europe (formerly part of Yugoslavia) look alike, speak the same language, and have lived cheek-by-jowl for centuries. Still, bloody violence broke out among three Bosnian sub-groups in the early 1990s. Croats, Serbs, and Muslims, indistinguishable to outsiders, behaved toward each other with unimaginable ferocity. In less than a decade, hundreds of thousands, out of the few million Bosnians, died. A like number were wounded, maimed, or raped, and the lives of all suffered radical upheaval.

What prompted this unmitigated brutality? Religion played a major role. This land had been inhabited for centuries by nearly equal groups of Muslims, Catholics, and Eastern Orthodox believers. Each group hated the other two and struggled against them for dominance.

Of course, other interests beyond religion divided these groups. We have already noted that intellectual rationalizations intensify normal hostilities based on interest. Religion is the most deeply-implanted set of ideas that justify our behavior. Religion tells each of us not just how to behave; it leads us to condemn all those who think and behave differently. Most religions see non-believers as people acting outside the one true faith. Having rejected God's commandments, they may be agents of evil. This harsh perspective toward outsiders makes it easy to see them as less than human. Clearly, they merit punishment. Why shouldn't we be the ones to dole out that punishment?

Religious differences often reinforce social divisions. Cleavages between urban and rural people, upper and lower income groups, or business-owners and workers intensify if religion also divides them.

Thus, religious differences alone can cause group tensions, but when combined with differences based on interest, they can exacerbate those tensions to the point of violence. We are all the more likely to pursue our beliefs if doing so could lead to an improvement in our life circumstances. Wiping out a group of people whose property you can then confiscate makes the argument for wiping them out all the more compelling.

As with religion, other factors that differentiate one people from another intensify their normal conflicts. Humans are extremely sensitive to personal variation. Consider how people in your own circle denigrate someone you all know who looks or talks or acts just a little bit "different." Fear and suspicion of "the other" seems as built-in a human characteristic as any that one can name.

Conclusion

Humans are sensitive to individual differences, even superficial ones. When surface differences move from modest to dramatic (dress patterns, language, skin color), those who share one characteristic and those who share another may start looking at each other with extreme mistrust, even loathing. When those surface differences are combined with profound material differences (one race is richer than the other, one ethnic group owns factories while the other works in them, one language group owns land and another works on that land), we have a recipe for potential violence.

Dealing with that potential for violence is central to the human endeavor. It lies at the heart of politics. Because of politics, not all situations ripe for violence end in violence. Not all conflict is adjudicated by arms. In fact, one way or another, most conflict gets resolved peacefully. Conflict may be endemic in human affairs, but violence is sporadic. People have many ways of deflecting and channeling and dealing with conflict. They do not always come to blows. Conflict is inevitable, but violent conflict is not. It's time to explore methods for confronting conflict that avoid outright brutality.

Questions for discussion

1 Have recent presidents like Ronald Reagan, George Herbert Walker Bush, Bill Clinton, or George W. Bush invoked the backing of God or religion to justify their political goals?
2 Taking major issues in the news for the past few days, can you find examples of groups making general arguments that have the effect of supporting their own narrow interests? Can you find any people arguing in a way that would actually hurt their own interests?
3 When Senators voted at Bill Clinton's impeachment trial, all 45 Democrats found this Democratic president innocent, while fifty of the 55 Republicans declared him guilty. How do you explain that result?
4 What exactly would a world without politics look like?
5 What groups in the USA are most at conflict with each other? What groups are most in harmony?
6 What groups in Iraq have been most at conflict with each other? Why has the conflict been so violent?

3

POLITICS AND COOPERATION

If you ever attend a political convention in the USA, you will be struck by the raucous tumult. You will gape at the disorderly hustle and bustle. Throngs of important-looking people will be scrambling about, some bedecked with television cameras and microphones, others with yellow pads and briefcases, still others with funny hats and strange outfits. Beyond this boisterous turmoil, you will also be struck by the joy and exuberance of those present. People will be slapping each other on the back, shouting hello across large rooms, laughing uproariously in big groups and small. You will not mistake this event for a gathering of morticians or accountants.

If you observe your state legislature in action, or your city council, or a committee on Capitol Hill, you will see a different side to politics. People will be discussing, usually in serious, civil tones, what they can do to resolve one social problem or another. These proceedings will seem tame, even boring, if you are expecting the dramatic confrontations that television reporters present to the nation every evening. Yes, moments of high drama do occur in government (shouting matches, even fist fights), but they are exceptions, not the norm.

If you feel that a government agency is mistreating you (withholding a pension, failing to certify you for a particular program, losing your court records), try this. Write a letter to one of your elected representatives. Depending on the government agency that's messing with you, you could write to, say, a city councilor, a state senator, or a US Representative. In most cases, you will be gratified at the speed with which that person—or at least a member of that person's staff—gets in touch. You will also be impressed at the willingness to work with you. You will normally get real help in pushing your case with the agency that's causing you grief. Your representative may not achieve what you want, but will usually mount a serious effort on your behalf.

What do these examples from the world of politics have in common? They illustrate cooperative behavior. People do work together in life—and certainly in politics. There is a good reason for these efforts at mutual assistance. *Cooperation is essential to human existence*. It produces enormous benefits for groups and individuals alike, and few people are more skilled at coopera-tive action than those socially-sensitive beings we call politicians.

This insight helps make sense of the examples above. They all illustrate successful human interaction. The warm socializing of party members at a convention provides an emotional cement that strengthens the organization. Members develop friendships and loyalties that bind them together.

There is also a social purpose to the calm, often dull, discussion of policy issues at public meetings. The sober presentations illustrate a norm of responsible concern. The serious tone of deliberation damps down conflict. People can work together on common problems (finding a new landfill site, funding road improvements, raising student test scores), while avoiding the accusations, the bickering, and the raised voices that turn public attention from issues to personalities.

The eagerness to help constituents in trouble can also be explained. Elected officials want to be re-elected. Keeping voters happy is central to that goal. That is why normally, if you contact an elected official, that person will make every effort to give you a pleasing response. Politicians assume—and rightly so—that this form of cooperative behavior (helping constituents solve personal problems) pays off in votes on election day.[1]

As we see, people do work together a great deal. They have to. No one gets far in life without learning cooperative behavior. United, we are more effective than on our own. From a purely self-interested perspective, it is rational to get along with people.

Stressing cooperation may seem out of place in a book on politics, an activity based on the inevitability of conflict. Still, even in the conflict-ridden world of politics, cooperative interaction is central to the process.

Connections among people are nowhere based entirely, or even largely, on conflict. Love, nurturing, friendship, and collaboration are essential to social life. Children need parents to reach adulthood safely. They need teachers to learn how to operate successfully in their culture. They need peers to learn social skills.

Adults need the help of other adults to be productive. They cannot farm, build homes, produce goods and services unless they join up with others. Most of the great accomplishments of humankind—magnificent cathedrals, efficient highway systems, symphony orchestras, modern corpor-ations, and space programs, to name a few—could have occurred only within an intricate network of human cooperation.

The conditions of cooperation

Here, then, is a key question for political analysts. Under what conditions will people cooperate *with* each other, as opposed to struggling com-petitively *against* each other? Although there are many circumstances that induce people to work together, three major conditions appear to be the strongest determinants of cooperative behavior. First, *people work together because they like each other.*

This liking may be the result of family ties, personal friendships, community connections, shared interests, or group identities. Thus, families farm together, friends start businesses or sports clubs together, neighbors join civic associations and work on projects for local improvement, and people join fraternal organizations to socialize with others of similar background.

A second reason for cooperation involves self-interest. *People work together because they have common goals that can be met only by united efforts.* No individual alone, for instance, could stop the Vietnam War or American involvement in Iraq. Still, all those eager to halt these military actions could together create formidable organizations of protest. A single doctor can do little to influence government health care plans, but thousands of doctors united in one organization (like the American Medical Association) can make a real impact. The old term, **enlightened self-interest**, seem especially useful for describing this form of cooperation.[2]

Very few lone individuals can have much influence on the political process. The occasional crusader or whistle-blower does appear and sometimes has an enormous impact, but people like Joan of Arc or Ralph Nader stand out as rare exceptions. Few of us alone can "save France" or force automobile companies to focus on safety issues. Only united with others who seek the same aims can one have any hope of shaping policy outcomes. Thus, cooperating with others for common purpose is an entirely rational (if self-interested) form of behavior.

Finally, *the fear of a common enemy* can encourage cooperation. People will work together when they perceive an outside threat to both their interests. Take the example of Russians and Americans. They have not often been the best of friends. Through 45 years of Cold War (1946–1991), the people of both nations feared, even hated, each other. More than once, they came close to a cataclysmic conflict that might have annihilated half the world. Similarly, for almost 25 years after the 1917 Russian Revolution that brought Lenin and then Stalin to power, relationships between these two nations were poor. In the 1920s and 1930s, many Americans loathed the "godless communists" who ruled Russia, while many Russians despised the "greedy capitalists" who dominated American society.

Despite this nearly unbroken record of animosity from 1917 into the 1990s, Americans and Russians were close allies during the latter years of the Second World War. From 1942 to 1945, they expressed only good will and mutual support for each other. The popular press in each nation portrayed the people of the other land with sympathy. Leaders worked closely together, exchanged countless communiqués, shared war plans. The two nations became military allies.

Enemies cooperating

What explains this short but dramatic interlude of friendliness? Both peoples feared an immediate and dangerous enemy more than they feared each other. That enemy, of course, was Hitler's Germany. The USA and the Soviet Union drew close to each other as they worked in tandem against this common foe.

In the early 1970s, the USA and China—hated enemies for the previous two decades—found it in their interest to cooperate against a third power (the Soviet Union) that was dangerous to them both. During the early 1990s, as Yugoslavia broke up, Croats and Serbs, usually enemies, cooperated in suppressing the nationalist aspirations of a third political group, their detested rivals, the Bosnian Muslims. In the USA, in the 1980s, an unlikely alliance of radical feminists and Christian conservatives collaborated to fight a common enemy, the producers of pornography. Conservative Christians saw pornography as "undermining traditional family values," while feminists saw it as "degrading to women" and "a threat to women's equality." Although they clashed on many issues (like prayer in school and abortion), these two normally-hostile groups worked together so well on this matter that they persuaded the city councils of two major American municipalities to pass anti-pornography legislation.[3]

Cooperation among enemies, then, is not at all uncommon. Remember the old saying: "The enemy of my enemy is my friend." While this dictum does not always hold, it does contain an important kernel of truth. *Groups of people can form unlikely alliances when they feel threatened by a common danger.*

It is clear that cooperation is a central element in human behavior. Social scientists have begun to stress important spillover effects produced by cooperative behavior. When we work with others and learn the benefits that can ensue, we start to develop attitudes of trust toward human beings in general. Successful collaboration also engenders a positive view of our social and political system. It even produces a willingness to participate in that system for civic or community improvement. Robert Putnam calls this set of attitudes **social capital**. He concludes that this learned ability to co-operate promotes democratic attitudes: tolerance toward others, willingness to allow divergent points of view, and eagerness to act in public life for desired goals. For Putnam (and many others), cooperative behavior lies at the heart of the democratic process.[4]

Political responses to conflict across time and space

Conflict and cooperation, we now know, are both central aspects of human existence. The degree to which societies stress one or the other of these forms of human interaction helps define the kind of political systems they produce. Let us take a look at three significant models of the political process.

Soon after Bill Clinton won the American presidency in 1992, he convened a national conference on economic policy. Sitting in a large conference room with Clinton and his top aides were dozens of invited guests. All held important positions in the world of finance, business, economics, or policy-making. For 3 days, these experts debated, argued, proposed, and discussed a range of ideas for guiding the government's economic policies. This televised conference ended with no decisions taken, but it allowed key representatives of America's business, academic, and labor communities the chance to express their views both to the American people and to the most powerful figure in the nation.

When Mutesa I came to power in the Kingdom of Buganda, Africa, in the 1850s, he "instantly put to death some 60 of his brothers by burning them alive," according to historian Alan Moorehead.[5] "This was apparently regarded," adds Moorehead, "as a perfectly normal precaution against rebellion."[6] Mutesa thus eliminated all potential rivals and ruled as undisputed leader of his people for nearly three decades. His terrified subjects learned to obey his every whim, and Mutesa was in turn able to indulge his every whim. During his many years in power he ruled both capriciously and brutally.[7]

Soon after General Slobodan Milosevic gained political power in 1990 in Yugoslavia, his strident pro-Serb rhetoric began to frighten the country's many non-Serb ethnic groups. Large numbers of them concluded that they would not be safe under his rule or under the dominance of his Serbian compatriots. Several ethnic groups began to arm, seeking to consolidate their control over that part of Yugoslavia where they were most entrenched. Eventually, some of these groups moved toward complete independence from Yugoslavia and Milosevic.

This tactic worked with relatively little bloodshed in the case of the Slovenes. They were able to branch off from Yugoslavia and create a separate nation, Slovenia. Likewise, the Croats seceded from Yugoslavia and created Croatia, and the Macedonians exited to create the Republic of Macedonia. It took just modest amounts of bloodshed to achieve these secessions.

The same strategy, however, proved disastrous to the group known as the Bosnian Muslims. When they tried to create a separate nation known as Bosnia, Milosevic provoked a bloody civil war pitting both Bosnian Serbs and Bosnian Croats against the Muslims. Milosevic himself provided a great deal of help to suppress the Muslim attempt at an independent Bosnia. The resulting conflict was bloody. Hundreds of thousands of people died, as ethnic hatreds promoted by ambitious political leaders produced horrific brutalities on all sides.

What do these examples tell us? First, politics varies dramatically from place to place. Behavior that is unthinkable in one setting may be perfectly normal in another. Instead of killing his 60 closest rivals, Clinton met with them for peaceful discussion. Instead of meeting his 60 closest rivals for discussion,

Milosewic sent troops against them but was unable to kill them. Instead, those rivals organized to fight, and a bloody civil war ensued. Instead of sending troops against his 60 closest rivals, Mutesa merely ordered his loyal soldiers to arrest and kill them. His troops obeyed him slavishly, and no one came to his rivals' aid. Mutesa's commands, no matter how brutal, were simply accepted and followed. Clearly, *politics in one place is not at all like politics in another.*

In a certain sense, the politics of each time and place is unique. Our particular moment is like no other that has occurred before or since. Nevertheless, commonalities do exist across time and place. A close look at politics in any setting today (and in the past) will show a pattern similar to one of our three examples. *Nations (and groups) will structure their politics in one of three ways. They will manage conflict (a) peacefully, (b) through harsh command-and-control structures, or (c) by means of armed violence between hostile groups.*

Peaceful resolution of conflict

In one pattern, conflict will be managed by agreed-upon procedures for deciding who gets to decide. Elections will stand at the core of this process. Widespread opportunities will exist for discussion and debate by all interested parties. Only after broad popular input will authoritative decisions be made that bind the polity to action on any given issue. Even then, binding policy decisions are always subject to reversal or amendment, depending on the dictates of popular will as expressed through the regular legal and political structures. The **rule of law**, as expressed within a set of democratic institutions, characterizes this type of polity.

Suppression of conflict

In a second political pattern, conflict will be resolved by imperious dictate. Issues will be decided by strong authority figures who govern by fear. Leaders will impose their will through brute force, while citizens, living under constant dread of disaster, will meekly obey. Terms often used for this system include **dictatorial, authoritarian**, and even **totalitarian**.

No resolution of conflict

In the third political pattern, conflict will be neither resolved nor suppressed. It will be exacerbated by intense social divisions within the culture. No single authority will be able to control or manage the tension. Various social groups will exhibit mutual suspicion of each other. Harsh accusations will mark debate among the groups. The fears, hatreds, and suspicions among society's sub-groups will often lead to extreme levels of violence. This violence will be all the more barbaric for being out of control;

no single force in society will have the dominance to impose solutions. In these cultures, any historical era unmarked by violence will represent merely a period of exhaustion and temporary armed truce rather than a true state of peace among competing factions. Societies like these are said to be dominated by **internal warfare** and characterized by the misrule of a **failed state**.

To summarize, the response to political conflict can take one of three forms:

1   Civil procedures that involve discussion, compromise, voting, and adherence to the rule of law
2   Authoritative decrees, backed by superior force, conjoined with a cowed population's submissive acceptance of those decrees
3   Continual, often bloody, disputes about the policies to be followed, the procedures for determining those policies, and even the very boundaries of the land in which those procedures and policies are to be articulated.

Most countries, at any given time, resort to one of these three styles as their defining method for dealing with conflict.[8]

For most of human history, only two of these patterns prevailed. Politics everywhere was a matter of brute force. In one pattern, a small elite exercised total control. It was often led by a dominant individual: Genghis Khan, Alexander the Great, Charlemagne. In a second pattern, elites were fragmented. Each set of leaders mobilized the social group it controlled, urging followers to fight the other groups. Since no group could dominate, struggles to rule were frequent, lengthy, and ferocious.

In both cases, the mass of citizens had no voice. They were not consulted about who should rule or what the rulers' policy decisions should be. Average people were, in essence, subservient pawns at the mercy of those with power.

Indeed, *most people throughout history have had no political power at all*. Historically speaking, most people have spent their entire lives just struggling to survive. To the extent that they took any political action, ordinary citizens provided loyalty, obedience, tribute, and military service to their rulers, the wealthy and the powerful.

The standard two political variations, both non-democratic, made little difference to the average person. If the elite was unified behind a dominant ruler, the masses would be called upon to provide food, taxes, and service to that elite. The men would be forced into the military to fight the ruler's wars of aggression or defense. Women played a subordinate role, working endless days at home or in the fields, usually both.

If the elite was divided and the land fragmented, then the average person was forced to provide food, taxes, and service to a particular *faction's* leaders. Again, the men of military age would be forced to fight for an elite that was striving to secure dominance. Again, women endured oppression and exploitation, along with high levels of terror and brutality resulting from the continuing civil warfare.

In either of these cases, life for most citizens was unpleasant—"nasty, brutish, and short," in the famous phrase of philosopher, Thomas Hobbes. Only the most assertive, powerful, or lucky members of society had any say in the political process.

Both of these patterns—authoritarian control and violent struggle among factions—dominate world history. They still remain entrenched in many places. As of 2007, nations with strong authoritarian rulers include Cuba, China, Iran, North Korea, Belarus, and Zimbabwe. Nations with violently competing elites include Bosnia, the Sudan, Iraq, Somalia, Colombia, Northern Ireland, and Afghanistan.

These two patterns may represent a fading phenomenon.[9] Some of the examples may already seem dated. Still, the patterns are hardly archaic. Neither authoritarian nor fragmented cultures will soon disappear from world history. They did not survive thousands of years for no reason.

Furthermore, change does not always proceed in what seems the "inevitable" direction. From the 1780s to the 1850s, the USA looked like a developing democracy. It was a moderately peaceful nation moving from a system of competitive elites toward a modest form of democracy. That is, it went from an era in which only a small percentage of its wealthier people had political rights to one where about forty percent did. (By 1850, nearly all white males could vote and run for office.)

One might have expected this trend to continue. After all, its neighbor, Canada, similar in many ways, followed a comparable course and kept moving on a slow, evolutionary path towards full democracy. Where Canada was something of an aristocratic oligarchy in the 1770s, it had moved with almost no violence to full democracy by the 1970s. The United States followed a different path. Led by rabidly opposed regional elites, it tore itself apart during the 1860s, entering a period of barbaric internal war in the best traditions of a fragmented culture.

Democracy as a system of cooperation and its potential for breakdown

Nothing in the current structure of democratic nations means that democracy is eternal. Open societies can break down in many ways. These include a failure of elites to abide by democratic rules, the growth of a tension-producing, non-compromisable issue, and the rise of a radical mass-movement with wide, popular backing. Developments like these (and others) can lead to a breakdown of democratic order. They can signal the beginning of a brutal, violent struggle to settle disputes by combat rather than by discussion. Even today in established democratic systems, some event (like an economic collapse) could trigger the breakdown of social order and lead to calls for dictatorial rule.

The breakdown of democracy is just what did happen in several nations during the Great Depression of the 1930s. Germany provides the most spectacular example. It was admittedly a weak, fledgling democracy after the First World War. A democracy in form it was, however—until economic upheaval led people to seek an authoritarian solution to their problems. In the election of July, 1932, more than half the German electorate voted democratically for non-democratic political parties. Communists received 14.3% of the vote, while Nazis garnered 37.1%. Soon thereafter, the Nazis peacefully maneuvered their way into political power, and democratic Germany gave way to 12 years of totalitarian rule.

Lebanon illustrates another pattern in the breakdown of democracy. It had been a relatively peaceful place with democratic structures (elections, free press, parliament) from 1943 until 1975, when its constituent subgroups (Sunnis, Shiites, Maronite Christians, Palestinians, Greek Orthodox, Jews, Druze, and numerous others) discovered that they could no longer work peacefully together. Since no one group could impose its will on the nation, each formed armed militias, and general chaos ensued. For the next fifteen years, almost total anarchy reigned. "By the end of the war," says one source, "nearly every party had allied with and subsequently betrayed every other party at least once."[10] The violence left a hundred thousand people dead and a largely destroyed infrastructure in a country once considered "the jewel of the Middle East."

Democracies are not guaranteed as eternal. They can be undermined or overthrown. Sometimes they transition to dictatorship, sometimes to fragmentation. But both developments are becoming rare. In the early years of the twenty-first century, democratic forms of governance constitute the dominant form of politics.[11] For that reason, we must examine this political form in some detail. *It is within democracies that one sees the clearest examples of political cooperation.*

Democracy, at its core, is a system of using cooperation for the purpose of restraining power. It allows masses of people to organize in ways that restrict the arbitrary will of military, social, and economic elites. In non-democratic regimes, power is always exercised by a few. That small minority need show no particular concern for the wishes of the many, largely because the many have no way of making elites listen to their desires. A democratic process fosters cooperating groups, and they in turn force elites to pay attention.

Democracy brings elites face to face with mass aspirations in several ways. A key device is the encouragement of expression. We are all familiar with the notion of free speech and a free press. These values underpin democratic activity. If citizens are speaking and writing and not being suppressed for what they speak and write, then elites cannot feign ignorance about what citizens want. Neither can they arbitrarily say what the masses "should" be thinking, because many in the mass will speak up forcefully to disagree, and elites will find it hard to ignore those clamoring voices.

But democracy goes much further than providing citizens a means of self-expression. It provides them a means of self-rule. *The most radical aspect of democracy is that citizens decide who gets to make authoritative social decisions.* That power was once reserved for the self-chosen few. Now it's in the hands of the masses, and it's the institution of **free elections** that stands at the core of this power.

Without elections, free speech would not necessarily restrain or even influence an elite, especially a rigid and closed-minded one. Leaders might hear the masses, but still do what they prefer. Faced with regular elections, however, elites will be much less arbitrary than they would be otherwise. Elections allow people not only to choose their leaders, but to oust them as well. That fact—and *primarily* that fact—is why leaders in a democracy pay attention to mass wishes. Elections are the ultimate source of citizen power. *Free, fair, and frequent elections practically define the democratic enterprise.*

The reasoning here is simple. We all do what those with power over us want us to do. If your boss says, "Get that report done by noon tomorrow," or "Get me an order of fries, pronto!" you do that report, or you fry up those potatoes. At least, you do if you want to keep your job, and most people do want to keep their job. Likewise, if your teacher says, "Hand in a three-page paper by Friday on Zoroaster," you'll be scrounging around the library or surfing the Internet on Thursday night looking for information on Zoroaster (whoever or whatever that is).

Democracy works in a precisely similar way. Politicians in a democracy are not necessarily better people than leaders in other political systems, but like all of us, they want to keep their jobs. They work to please those who can keep them in their jobs—that is, the voters. They know that failure to please voters can cause them unemployment.

Since everyone in a democracy can communicate freely, voters are likely to hear about politicians who do not provide what they want. And punishment at the polls, while not certain, is always a possibility.[12] Most politicians are not willing to take chances. They go to great lengths to find what voters want and give it to them.[13] Leaders who take an imperious "I'm right, you're wrong" stance do not last long. Voters will eject them at the first opportunity. When that happens, other leaders learn valuable lessons about keeping in touch with popular desires.

Conclusion

It is the cooperative connection between voters and leaders that lies at the heart of democracy. People work together to choose leaders they like, and leaders try to do what the voters want. For that reason, along the conflict-cooperation continuum democracies lie closer to the side stressing collaboration.

Of course, democratic politicians don't always *succeed* in pleasing the electorate. For one thing, finding out what people want is not easy. People do not always know what they want—or can't articulate their wants very well. Besides, say you as a leader do discover what people want. It is not necessarily easy to provide it. Other leaders may read the public's mind differently and oppose your efforts. You all end up blocking each other, and nothing gets done.

It is also true that people often want contradictory or impossible things. For instance, we would all like no taxes and lots of government benefits. Impossible. And we are often split on policy desires. Half of Americans in recent years have wanted to make abortion difficult or impossible; the other half approve of the procedure. How do we give Americans "what they want" on this issue?

Still, with elections as the whip and office as the carrot, democratic elites do make a strong effort to stay in touch with mass concerns. With masses cooperating to express their desires, and elites cooperating to find ways of satisfying those desires, the use of force and violence as devices to regulate social relations is diminished. Voters find that enough of their wishes are satisfied to deter them from violent action against leaders. Likewise, leaders find ways to gain and hold power that do not necessitate violence. Cooperative behavior of a peaceful nature is therefore much more likely to occur within democratic systems than in the other major forms of government we have discussed.[14]

Questions for discussion

1   Did antiwar organizations during Vietnam and Iraq really have any effect? Can people working together really influence government policies? Can you think of any other examples?
2   Most people think of politics as a world of conflict. What examples can you think of to illustrate political cooperation?
3   Is "the enemy of my enemy" really my friend? Beyond examples in the text, can you think of others where this seems to be the case?
4   Does democracy really vary from older systems based on "brute force," as the author claims? Doesn't the majority in a democratic system impose its will on the minority through force as well?
5   What exactly led to the breakdown of American democracy in the 1860s (the Civil War)?

4

THE DIVERSITY OF POLITICAL CULTURE

What can you do when the Supreme Court makes a decision you do not like? To put it broadly, can American citizens do anything to reverse a series of Court decisions they detest?

When I ask people that question, they come up with many answers, including:

- March up and down outside the Supreme Court building in Washington, waving signs and banners to demonstrate anger at the decision
- Write letters to newspapers, contact (or create) Internet blogs, call radio and TV stations, and contact political leaders to express disagreement with the Court's policies
- Join like-minded citizens to elect a President who will appoint different justices to the Court. Work also for the election of US Senators who support judicial appointees you like and oppose those you dislike
- Work to bring another lawsuit before the Court, one that makes the best possible case for changing the justices' past policy decisions
- Pressure Congress to rewrite the law—or more drastically, to begin rewriting the Constitution itself!

You can surely think of other options in this vein. American citizens can undertake a number of peaceful, civil, legal, and procedural activities to change the result of Supreme Court rulings. They do, in fact, undertake these activities on a regular basis. Furthermore, political action of this sort often works. Over the years, concerted group efforts have succeeded in changing Supreme Court policies on such key political issues as government intervention in the economy, racial integration, abortion, and prayer in the schools.

Most Americans would stop the discussion at this point. They would be satisfied at having explained how citizens can respond to Court actions they dislike. Yet disagreement with judicial policy can be approached in a radically different way.

Consider what happened a few years ago in Colombia. A group of citizens had become unhappy with the policy decisions of that nation's Supreme Court. On November 6, 1985, a stolen truck raced up to the Court building. Out poured masked men wielding submachine guns. Firing wildly, they raced into the building, seized control, and took 300 hostages, including 24 of the 25 Supreme Court justices. A few hours later, the Colombian Army rushed the building. In the ensuing firefight, over 100 people died, including all the rebels. They managed, however, to kill 11 of the justices before meeting their own deaths.

Now *that's* a different way of responding to political disagreement!

A third type of response is possible. In Russia during the decades of Marxist rule, courts simply ratified and reinforced the line of policy laid down by the nation's dictatorial oligarchy. Hardly to our surprise, justices were neither mowed down by thugs nor placed under the pressures of peaceful political protest. Instead, citizens simply accepted judicial decisions in the most docile way, no matter how much they disagreed with their impact.

To understand the political process, we must open our eyes to patterns that differ from our own. We in the West assume that political disputes will be settled in a *non-violent* and relatively *open* manner. Disputes will be resolved through discussion, negotiation, voting, and the rule of law, not brute force. All (or at least many) interested parties will *participate* in the discussion, negotiation, and voting, and these activities will come under the scrutiny of numerous mass media outlets. Politics just does not work that way in many places—and has rarely worked like that at any time in the past.

Fighting it out, literally, has been common in human history as a method for dealing with disagreement. Consider the African nation of Rwanda. Its two rival ethnic groups consist of the Hutus and the Tutsis. In late 1963, the Hutus launched an assault on their traditional enemy and wiped out 20,000 of them in a single month. In 1994, the Hutus undertook a systematic campaign of genocide against the Tutsis and massacred *one million* of them.

In El Salvador, a country not much larger than Delaware with a population less than the city of New York, 50,000 people died in a civil war lasting from 1982 to 1992. Nearly 70,000 people have died in a Sri Lankan civil war raging since 1983. And the USA has hardly been immune from domestic barbarism. The Civil War (1861–1865) was one of the more gruesome on record. It produced over half a million deaths in a nation of 35 million people. An outbreak of domestic hostility on that scale today would result in 4.5 million dead Americans.

Though perfected in Stalinist Russia, authoritarian rule has been the most common political pattern through the ages. For much of history, tyrannical governments simply imposed their will on cowed citizens. The ideal citizen in oligarchic systems is fearful and obedient. A docile population is kept in check by the use of terror and force. Citizens learn to follow slavishly the will of their rulers.

I once saw first hand how **autocratic** nations operate when I lived for a few months in Archangel, Russia, under communism. During a brutal winter, the streets were kept in appalling shape. Sidewalks were clogged with snow and ice. Walking, even in the center of town, was a constant gamble. Yet when I complained to friends about the dangerous state of city walkways, they replied merely with embarrassed smiles and half-hearted shrugs. No one expressed shock or anger, merely passive acceptance of the appalling conditions. The norm appeared to be: close your eyes to these social ills, bear them as best you can, and keep your mouth shut.

We can well imagine the reaction of Americans to these conditions. The Mayor's office would be deluged with angry complaints. Radio talk shows would be bombarded with telephone calls from irate citizens. Political rivals of the current city leadership would appear on television to bemoan this sorry state of affairs.

These publicly voiced criticisms would continue, growing in volume and number, until city officials provided relief in the form of snow removal, salting of streets, and similar measures. If city officials failed to act promptly, they might well suffer political defeat down the road. Other city officials in later years would then pay closer heed to complaints of this sort.

This scenario is commonplace in democratic nations. In fact, Chicago Mayor Jane Byrne actually lost her bid for re-election in 1983, a few months after a snowstorm immobilized her city. It took days to get life back to normal, and Chicago residents blamed her for the tortoise-like cleanup. Many thought her dithering and ineffectual leadership was responsible for the slow pace of snow removal. We cannot be certain about cause and effect here, but the affair clearly hurt the Mayor's image, and she did lose the next election.

What about popular reaction to government incompetence in countries like Lebanon or El Salvador? They are either violent or ineffectual. There are parts of Somalia or Sudan where the government cannot repair roads because work crews would be attacked by armed guerrillas. In Iraq, it is "insurgents" who blow up power stations and oil pipelines. Government shortcomings in violence-prone places allow this type of anti-system behavior. As a result, the government can do little to make incremental improvements to placate its critics, even if it wished to. Often it does not wish to, preferring to *wipe out* those critics.

Political patterns in context

Political actions never occur in isolation. They reflect society's deepest-held values. Political patterns cannot change overnight, because the entrenched norms and expectations of a culture are embedded in the people's consciousness. Only thoroughgoing sociocultural change can produce substantive political change in the life of any nation.

To understand a country's politics, then, we must first come to grips with its culture.

But once we do understand a pattern of politics, we are well placed for understanding both past and future patterns, since political change occurs only after cultural change, and cultural change occurs only slowly.

This perspective suggests the value of severe realism when viewing the world's political scene. One should not place strong hopes on the odds of quickly changing a country's customary mode of dealing with conflict. North Korea will not tomorrow become a peaceful democracy.[2] On the other hand, the news is not all bad. Britain will not tomorrow break down into violent, warring factions. Cultures are stable. So are the political processes that reflect them.

The three most typical political cultures

While cultures deal with disagreement in different ways, the number of ways is not infinite. Far from it. Just a small number of styles characterize political systems everywhere. The three most common of these are often labeled authoritarian, pluralistic, and anarchic.

The former Soviet Union, Mao's China, and Hitler's Germany all stand as prototypes of authoritarian politics. Most Western political systems are regarded as pluralistic. And a range of countries exhibit the chaotic anarchy we have already associated with Colombia, Lebanon, Somalia, Sri Lanka, Rwanda, and Bosnia.[3]

Within each style of politics, variations will occur. Within pluralistic systems, for instance, the French have several political parties, while Americans have only two. This difference is minor compared with their broader similarities. Both countries allow freedom of speech and press. Both encourage peaceful competition among diverse groups for the right to influence policy and control government. Both provide an extensive array of civil rights and liberties for their citizens. On the matters that really count, they closely resemble each other.

Anarchic systems too differ on the surface. Struggles in Bosnia reflect ethnic hatreds, conflict in Peru may reflect class, ideological, and regional divisions, and conflict in Iraq reflects religious differences. Still, the result of these various conflicts is the same. Thousands of people end up being murdered in a continuing armed struggle to dictate political outcomes.

Of course, these "minor" differences between similar countries will appear great to those who live in them. The closer you get to any phenomenon, and the more you know about it, the more it appears unique. Scholars have produced entire books to explain the differences between countries as similar as, say, Sweden and Norway—or the USA and Canada.[4] Yet an introduction to politics must start with the broadest distinctions. Only after we learn what the major political patterns look like can we go on to describe the subtle differences between similar nations within the same category.

We can begin to understand the range of patterns in the world by focusing on a simple question. What is a society's "normal" method for dealing with conflict? I have a short answer to the question. Societies today deal with conflict in one of three ways: through *negotiation, repression,* or *war.* Depending on which style they stress, they end up with **pluralistic, authoritarian**, or **anarchic** political systems.[5] Most modern cultures lean toward one of those political styles for dealing with conflict.

Of course, any categorization simplifies reality. Any nation is a complex entity, and its process will contain elements of all three styles. In the USA, for instance, where negotiation is the primary means of settling political disputes, violence is hardly unknown. We see examples of it every day: from confrontation between pro-life and pro-choice partisans at abortion clinics to clashes between police and minorities in urban ghetto areas.

Even repression is a political tactic that Americans have made use of. We all know about the rule of fear that kept African-Americans "in their place" in Southern states during the many decades from the Civil War to the modern civil rights era. As another example, groups defined as "subversive" have over the years had their mail opened and telephones tapped by the FBI, and they have also been harassed in a number of less subtle ways. Some argue that a strong dose of political repression can be found in our treatment of illegal immigrants, not to mention terror suspects.

Just as we can find exceptions to the normal American pattern of dealing with conflict, so too can we find exceptions to typical political behavior in other places. We could find non-repressive examples of dealing with political strife in even the most repressive regime. And no system operates entirely through anarchic clashes of armed citizens. Even in Lebanon at its worst, some groups at least some of the time tried to resolve differences through discussion and compromise rather than with guns. No nation stands out as some "ideal type."

Nonetheless, it will improve our understanding of world politics if we think of most nations as *tending toward* one operating style. That style can be considered their standard, or most common, method of dealing with the inevitability of social conflict. Yes, all nations use various means for dealing with disputes—but most nations stress one of those means over the others. It is useful, therefore, to categorize each culture by its primary means for dealing with conflict.

Pluralism

A society that stresses negotiation develops from a unified culture. Most citizens share a common identity, seeing themselves as members of the same group or nationality. Whether Swedish, Costa Rican, or Japanese, they share a "we-feeling," a perception of social connection to each other. It may be vague and difficult to explain (ever try telling an outsider what it means to be a member of your group?), but it is deeply felt for all that.

People in cohesive cultures tend to agree with each other on key social values: the work ethic, the dignity of age, the importance of discipline, the need for freedom. They are not clones of each other, they are separated by differences of all kinds. But these differences are modest, minor: whether some popular singer is "better" than another, whether school budgets should rise or fall by five percent, whether stores should be allowed to expand their operating hours. People in this culture see other citizens as much like themselves, fellow human beings to be respected and supported—or peacefully opposed when they turn out to be "wrong" on some of these modest dividing points.

Of course, arguments can get heated over anything. I have seen people fall out over which baseball team to support, so even "minor" disagreement can lead to serious disputes. And naturally, even in a cohesive culture, there will be extremists whose views stand far outside the "normal" range of most citizens. The point is simply that, compared with other cultures, the deepest values of most people in this one lie within a fairly narrow range.

A second trait of pluralistic culture is citizen activism. Its members take an aggressive role in shaping their environment. They are convinced of their ability to mold reality. They work regularly to influence the external forces that define their lives. They are *engagé*, as Sartre would put it: actively involved in positive life pursuits. They struggle to shape their environment and feel certain of bettering themselves over time. Their activist ethos springs from optimism about the chance for progress in this world. Both individuals and societies can achieve their ends, if they just keep struggling to improve.

In a circular chain of reinforcement, this activism produces additional optimism about the value of personal effort. Since active struggle toward your goals *is* more likely to help you attain them than other options (passivity, prayer, luck), people in active cultures learn that activism pays off. They do often achieve their goals. Thus, they have every reason to feel optimistic about the value of activism.

Optimism about the ability to improve one's situation leads to a corollary belief. If things are not as desired, one should work to improve them. This attitude produces a politically alert and periodically involved populace. When political, social, or economic circumstances bring unpopular results, citizens (imbued with the spirit of optimism, certain they can change this world for the better) will enter the political arena to produce "better" policies. No wonder reform movements of every type spring up regularly.

These **homogeneous-active cultures** see a wide range of citizens regularly involved in public affairs, working to achieve the passage of political policies they like and defeat policies they abhor.[6]

Explaining low levels of violence

Some analysts have worried that this continuous citizen activism could increase levels of political tension.[7] After all, they reason, as more people get involved in politics, they will represent a wider range of opposing aims and interests. Political issues are often charged with emotion, difficult to resolve. The more parties to a dispute and the more varied their perspectives, the more unlikely it is that those involved will be able to coalesce around peaceful and satisfactory resolutions of the argument. We might expect a continuing series of violent confrontations in a culture of political activism.

Widespread citizen activism *does* produce violence in many places. It rarely does, however, in homogeneous-active cultures. What violence does occur there, affects few people, is short-lived, and fails to put a dent in the rock-solid structures of society. That is because political disputes in this culture rarely cut deep or involve profound value differences. Hence, they can be resolved in relatively peaceful fashion.

These are generalizations—political violence can occur in any society. In Sweden, that quintessential example of homogeneous-active culture, Prime Minister Olaf Palme was shot dead on a quiet Stockholm street in 1986. Race riots have been frequent in the USA; Japanese students have been known to arm themselves with helmets and batons, then charge police lines in protests over government education policies; and French farmers regularly dump tons of tomatoes or peaches onto major roadways, then clash with police and clean-up crews trying to restore order. These events should not surprise us. Politics touches us all, in ways that are intense and immediate. Even in the calmest of settings, people will sometimes react violently to political decisions they detest.

Nevertheless, when politically-inspired violence does occur in homogeneous-active cultures, it rarely threatens the foundation of the regime itself, because only a few people, relative to the entire population, engage in it and never for very long. Most citizens can accept the agreed-upon methods for dealing with conflict, and those methods are civil, procedural, democratic, and peaceful.

Political peace in the homogeneous-active culture rests upon its underlying cohesion. Despite all the political activism, citizens agree on the basics. The similarity of outlook reduces political stress in two ways. First, their political disagreements rarely touch fundamental values. Opposing groups may want a little more or a little less of a particular program. They may even disagree on whether to start some new program or abolish an existing one. But they do not disagree on whether or not to continue working within the existing constitutional framework. And they do not disagree with the proposition that all parties to any dispute have the right to continue living.

In short, dispute in this culture centers on issues of incremental, not fundamental, change. Yes, the high level of citizen involvement does produce a continuing stream of disagreement and confrontation, but clashes occur at the level of policy, not values. People argue over a little more of this, a little less of that. They do not dispute each other on fundamental beliefs.[8] When citizens disagree, they form interest groups, not militias. They turn to lawyers rather than guns.

Political disagreement in the homogeneous-active culture rarely produces violence for a second reason. People acknowledge a common humanity in their political opponents. The reasoning goes something like this: Those who disagree with us on the issue at hand are, after all, very much like us in most other ways. We all believe in "the American way of life," or in "France for the French," or in "the specialness of the Japanese." We agree, in other words, with our political opponents much more often than we disagree. It makes no sense to treat them as knaves or barbarians. We should instead treat them with dignity and understanding. We oppose each other today, but we may be allies tomorrow on one of the many issues where we do see eye to eye. Besides, both we and they face truly serious enemies beyond our borders. Let us act in a manner that allows us to continue living and working together, even if we oppose each other today on one specific issue.

This perspective leads opponents to treat each other reasonably. They do not dehumanize adversaries through heated, overblown rhetoric. In an atmosphere of trust and civility, political competitors can seek accommodation and compromise. They thus live to fight (and cooperate with) each other another day. Opposing sides accept the necessity of "agreeing to disagree." This trait of disagreeing, often vigorously, on details while maintaining a profound level of agreement on essentials stands as the distinguishing feature of the pluralistic, homogeneous-active political system. Political scientists call this phenomenon *disagreement on goals but agreement on the rules of the game*. It produces an ability to sustain *moderate* levels of disagreement for long periods of time.

Anarchy

Other societies produce either *no* disagreement (a unified elite dictates policy) or exceptionally *high* levels of disagreement that lead to violence and instability. The latter situation prevails in an **anarchic or heterogeneous-active culture**. Here citizens are definitely active; they get involved in politics to promote their own goals, to improve their life conditions. Unfortunately, they find themselves in total disagreement with each other concerning basic life values.

Heterogeneous-active cultures are undoubtedly the most interesting. Alas, an old Chinese curse: "May you live in interesting times!" "Interesting" is the opposite of "dull"—but dull suggests stable and by implication, peaceful. Heterogeneous-active cultures, though interesting, are rarely peaceful. They produce high levels of internal violence, sometimes staggeringly high.

In these divided cultures, we find no widespread agreement on basic norms. Rules of the political game, the proper religion, views of justice, the ideal family, definitions of equality, progress, and freedom: name the subject, and each group leaps into angry argument with the others to prove the truth of its own perspective. These fundamental divisions concerning life's central values produce a society of fragmentation. Instead of basic unity punctuated by the occasional modest division, there is a basic *disunity* exacerbated by a continued series of *profound* divisions. It is a society of diverse, clearly-differentiated people, deeply suspicious of each other and fundamentally at odds over all the key issues.

We have seen what can happen when people feel murderously about each other. Bosnia, Colombia, Lebanon, Rwanda: these are places that fit the pattern of heterogeneous-active culture. Citizens disagree on fundamentals. They cannot even agree on what form their disagreement should take. Parliamentary debates, street demonstrations, hunger strikes, guerrilla warfare: what political actions are legitimate? There are no widely accepted rules of the game. In any case, opponents *do not see* politics as a game. It is deadly serious, aimed at protecting a way of life, or life itself, against adversaries who would destroy both.

Combatants under these conditions cannot risk accommodation and compromise. That would be consorting with the enemy. Besides, you couldn't trust opponents to maintain an agreement. Each side believes others will cheat whenever possible for their own benefit, taking advantage of "our" good will or *naïveté*. The only solution is total victory. We must destroy the enemy to insure our own security.

Politics in heterogeneous-active cultures, then, goes well beyond parliamentary speeches, interest group lobbying, and electioneering. It includes (as part of its normal process) street riots, mass demonstrations, illegal antigovernment activity, illegal repression by government of opponents, and pitched battles between armed paramilitary followers of various political movements. Violence is frequent and expected. It is not an occasional aberration, but an ongoing element in the political process.[9]

Even when periods of relative calm prevail, suspicion and distrust poison the atmosphere. Not only do political opponents fear and resent each other, but nearly all resent the government as well. It is seen as staffed by opportunists, who line their own pockets, hand out favors to allies, and repress their enemies. Cynicism abounds toward government and toward all politicians (except toward those of one's in-group, and sometimes even then).

Governments in this circumstance are weak. Since no one feels emotionally tied to the existing institutions, leaders can't rely on any groundswell of citizen support in time of crisis. When the French Fourth Republic was on the verge of military takeover in 1958, its leaders called on citizens to turn out in the street to support the regime. No one turned out. The regime fell.[10]

Heterogeneous-active cultures are typically led by weak, divided governments commanding little public support. Hence, they are subject to frequent takeovers: coups d'état, assassination of leaders, peasant or worker revolts, and the like. These events reflect the widespread degree of citizen distrust. First one group and then another will decide that it is more urgent to take power (and insure its own security) than worry about legal niceties. Each group reasons that to sit back and do nothing is to run the risk that another group will seize control and use the powers of government for its own ends and against ours. All groups *not* in government are therefore in a perpetual state of semi-rebellion. And groups *in* the government must perpetually act as semi-oppressors, because they cannot sit idly by while powerful enemies out there are hatching revolutionary plots against them.

Authoritarianism

A third type of culture behaves in nearly opposite fashion to the previous one. **Homogeneous-passive cultures** possess a citizenry that is both cohesive and profoundly inactive. The resulting political style contrasts radically with the type of politics found in such places as Sri Lanka, Somalia, and Afghanistan.

We have already encountered the phenomenon of social cohesion. In a unified culture, citizens look at life in reasonably similar ways and live more or less alike. They agree on key values. They think of themselves as one people, a group distinct from others, a nation. Citizens are proud of their common heritage. Internal disagreements are modest in scope; they rarely touch fundamental principles.

In this common identity, this "we-feeling" for others within the culture, the people of this third culture type resemble citizens in the homogeneous-active culture. They differ, however, in their complete lack of social activism. They are extraordinarily unwilling to form independent groups to work for common goals. When social problems arise, they sit on their hands. "Mind your own business" and "Do what the government says" are two deeply ingrained norms.

As a result, spontaneous citizen input into the decision-making process is rare. There is no sign of organized, independent groups struggling against each other for the power to influence government policy.

Explaining this passivity is easy. It makes perfect sense to avoid political involvement, when it will prove fruitless or dangerous. If governments always throw people in jail (or worse) at the first sign of political protest, citizens will abandon all but government-approved political activity. If criticism of government produces no substantive results and furthermore lands you in trouble, you are unlikely to become a government critic. Most citizens in this culture will avoid politics altogether. (It is too dangerous.) Those who do become active will staunchly support the ruling elite. Citizens in homogeneous-passive cultures end up either non-participatory or cheer-leaders for the regime.

A familiar kind of politics emerges from this culture of cohesion and passivity. We often use words like "dictatorship" or "authoritarian" to describe it. The word "totalitarian" was coined to describe its most extreme form. Since all think alike in this culture, a strong set of leaders, embodying the general ethos, will usually emerge. Since few citizens are active, few dispute this elite's claim to rule. Since the elite embodies the culture's core values in any case, few *wish* to dispute that rule. *Passive acceptance of leaders who embody the received cultural norms*: that is what the political pattern typically looks like in homogeneous-passive culture.

Refining the terms

Readers of this chapter have been exposed to some strained vocabulary. To categorize these cultures, I have used descriptively precise words. The phrase "homogeneous-passive," for instance, tells in a nutshell that citizens of that culture think and act alike ("homogeneous"), but do not participate much in politics ("passive"). This term avoids emotional overtones or partisan language, being almost clinical in its objectivity.

Despite the advantage of this terminology, these phrases are cumbersome and smack of social science jargon. They also commit a scholarly sin: they invent new words to describe already-labeled phenomena. Each culture type has long been familiar to students of political behavior—but under other names. For instance, the "homogeneous-active culture" sounds a lot like the American meaning of "democracy." And the homogeneous-passive culture sounds a lot like "dictatorship." Why not simply use those common, everyday words and avoid unnecessary, not to mention irritating, jargon?

The trouble with "democracy" and "dictatorship" is that the words are heavily value-laden. They raise emotional temperatures. Everyone knows that democracy is "good," dictatorship "bad." Consequently, every country in the world, it turns out, is a democracy. That is, rulers throughout the globe claim loudly that theirs is an ideal democratic system (no matter what form of government they actually operate). Not surprisingly, they also claim that the government of their worst enemies is clearly dictatorial. Even Fidel Castro, an obvious dictator, used to maintain that his Cuba was solidly democratic.

What we need in a science of politics are terms that are factually descriptive, but emotionally non-provocative. Terms that meet those criteria do exist for the culture types under discussion. These cultures have been investigated, described, and labeled by many researchers over the years. While agreement on the meaning of terms is notoriously lacking in the social sciences, many scholars have produced descriptive words for these systems that are widely in use and lacking in obvious emotional stimuli. I propose adopting these words in the interest of scientific objectivity.

From this point onward, therefore, let us re-label the three culture types:

- Homogeneous-active cultures will be called **polyarchal** cultures, or polyarchies
- Heterogeneous-active cultures will be called **fragmented** cultures, or cultures of **fragmentation**
- Homogeneous-passive cultures will be called **collectivist** cultures, or cultures of **collectivism**.

A fourth style for dealing with conflict occurs in **heterogeneous-passive, or parochial**, cultures. It is a style associated with traditional empires, but rare in modern times, so I give it slight attention here.[11]

Table 4.1 summarizes the argument. It shows that the culture categories derive from two key variables: homogeneity and activism. The terms I apply to each culture are in wide usage. Social scientists know them and tend to agree on what they mean. It is therefore worth our while to make use of them.

One of these terms—**polyarchy**—is closely associated with a single scholar, Robert Dahl. He invented the term and made it well known through his prolific and seminal writings.[12] The word seems especially appropriate for the dispassionate description of some real-world political systems.

Polyarchy means, literally, "many rule." Dahl uses the word specifically to describe political systems in which *many participants are allowed to contend publicly for political power*. Note the relative objectivity of this statement. Dahl argues, and I agree, that we should avoid the word "democracy" as a description of any existing political system. The word carries too much emotional baggage. Besides implying some ideal state of affairs in which everyone is happy, it also suggests a system in which *all people share equally in political power*. That situation has never existed. Indeed, it is doubtful that power can ever be shared equally by any group of people numbering more than a few dozen. So the word democracy, beyond the ideological and emotional difficulties it presents, makes no sense as a description of any large-scale political system in the world today.[13]

Dahl argues, in essence, that we should jettison democracy as a descriptive term and adopt the practical and non-emotional word, polyarchy. Polyarchy does, after all, describe the way some real-world political systems work. Nations do exist wherein (1) competition for power occurs; (2) many people can participate in that power struggle without fear for their lives; and (3) responsibility for public policy-making is shared by a large and diverse set of actors. Those are the systems that Dahl calls polyarchies.

The fit seems obvious between the homogeneous-active culture and

Table 4.1 Types of political culture.

		Citizen agreement on basic values?	
		Yes	No
Citizens hold activist outlook?	Yes	Polyarchal culture (Example: Sweden)	Fragmented culture (Example: Rwanda)
	No	Collectivist culture (Example: North Korea)	Parochial culture (Example: Roman Empire)

polyarchy. Only in a culture of participants, will a large number of citizens get involved in the political struggle and achieve some influence. Only in a homogeneous culture will the conflict resulting from this participation be moderate and restrained, so that competition can occur in a nonviolent atmosphere. Majorities will get their way, but will not ride roughshod over minorities. Polyarchal culture, homogeneous-active culture: come to the same thing. We will use the simpler term.

The idea of a fragmented culture is found widely in the literature of political science. The terms "plural society" and "segmented culture" are also used to describe deeply-divided nations, and words like "anocracy" or **failed state** have been applied to their political systems. This concept of a fractured, conflict-ridden culture is not associated with a single author. A number of scholars have pointed to this phenomenon.[14]

I find the word "fragmentation" powerfully descriptive. It suggests a fractured society, torn by clashing sub-groups. In a culture of social fragments, each isolated sub-culture has little in common with the others. Trust levels are low, conflict levels high. The literature of political science has frequently described this pattern of deep social cleavage, a pattern presented above under the rubric heterogeneous-active culture. Let us henceforth use the straightforward term "fragmented" to describe this society.

Collectivism is also a common term in the discourse of social science, and again associated with no particular scholar. It implies a society in which people are unified: they think alike and hold similar values. The word also suggests a certain passivity, a follow-the-leader mentality. Some analysts prefer words like "**authoritarian**," "dictatorial," or "**totalitarian**" to describe this culture, but those words are as emotive and value-laden as "**democracy**." Collectivist has a neutral, non-pejorative ring to it.

Besides, to label this type of culture dictatorial would be misleading in two ways. First, it is not the only culture that can produce autocratic leadership. Dictators will often be found in parochial/imperial cultures. Empires have their emperors, after all.

Fragmented cultures also produce the occasional autocrat. In the latter case, dictatorship occurs when one of the conflicting subgroups wins temporary dominance and imposes its leader over the rest of society. That leader may then proceed to repress or even wipe out his group's internal enemies. (Saddam Hussein represented this phenomenon. He was a dictator promoting Sunni interests over those of all other groups in the fragmented culture of Iraq.) Labeling the collectivist culture as "dictatorial" would create the misleading and erroneous impression that only this particular culture is likely to produce repressive, one-person rule.

Furthermore, the use of words like "totalitarian" and "dictatorship" suggest that the people within that system are being ruled against their will. That too creates a false impression. Indeed, in collectivist nations, most people *accept* the regime willingly. Its leaders and those who staff the various institutions of the system are just like everyone else. It is a homogeneous society, remember. Most citizens in this culture do not feel any great desire to revolt and would not describe themselves as living under a dictatorship. Living in a homogeneous culture that stresses social harmony, they may well feel that one party expressing the general will makes perfect sense. The term collectivism, implying submission of the individual to the will of the group, perfectly captures this outlook.

Parochialism (a footnote)

The fourth culture type, heterogeneous-passive, is well described by two words: "imperialist" and "parochial." It is an imperialist culture from the point of view of its leaders: strong autocrats ruling a far-flung patchwork of disparate regions and nationalities. It is a parochial culture from the point of view of the populace. Most people within the system live in a narrow world of family and village, scarcely even aware that they form part of a larger political community.

In this culture, one group imposes its will on a large and diverse set of people, keeping them passive, obedient, and uninvolved with each other. Although the term "imperialist" has been in common usage since at least Roman times, the very notion of empire seems antiquated today. Imperial states have disintegrated after experiencing a growth of activism among their diverse but no longer inert sub-cultures. The result is a large number of mini-states that serve as springboards for the many new, if minuscule, nationalisms. It is safe to say that the decline of the imperialist (or parochial) culture is in full swing.

Conclusion

Our four cultures differ significantly from each other. As we would expect, they produce four distinct political systems. The political process within each culture can be clearly differentiated from the others on the basis of four variables. Specifically, each system produces a different answer to the following questions.

1 What is the attitude of people in the culture to the inevitable set of **social divisions** that exists in their society?
2 How exactly does society deal with the **conflict** that springs from these social divisions?
3 What is the citizenry's general **attitude toward the state**?
4 How do state institutions operate? What is the typical structure of **government**?

Each culture provides a unique answer to these four queries. Table 4.2 summarizes those answers and, in doing so, illustrates the four basic political patterns of our time.

Table 4.2 presents a clear and easy-to-understand **typology** of culture types. Typologies represent generalizations about reality. They can be

Table 4.2 Overview of the four political cultures: The major characteristics.

Polyarchal culture

1	Attitude towards social divisions?	Relative trust prevails between people in different groups; an ethos of tolerance predominates, allowing for expression of differing social, religious, and political values.
2	How does society deal with conflict?	Low levels of political conflict lead to the acceptance of civil procedures and democratic norms to resolve disputes ("rule of law," open debate, elections, etc.).
3	Attitude towards the state?	Moderately strong state loyalty, which falls short of blind obedience, but overrides local and parochial ties.
4	Typical structure of government?	Long-lasting, stable, popular regime; elections determine which elites rule; peaceful governmental turnovers; high participation rates.

Fragmented culture

1	Attitude towards social divisions?	Social groups deeply mistrust each other; they do not acknowledge the legitimacy of the aims of opponents (nor, sometimes, even their right to exist); conflict levels are high, violence common.
2	How does society deal with conflict?	No widely accepted procedures for resolving disputes; the basic decision rule to determine who governs is: "rule of the strongest."
3	Attitude towards the State?	State viewed with alienation and hostility; occasionally seen as a means to an end (seizing control of the state allows promotion of one's own interests), but more often seen as a means for enemies to carry on their own nefarious plans for self-aggrandizement and oppression.
4	Typical structure of government?	National governments are unstable in form and duration.

Collectivist culture

1 Attitude towards social divisions? — Citizens deeply fear disagreement and dis-harmony. They deny or turn a blind eye toward social divisions. Calls for suppression of socially dissident behavior will be widely supported.

2 How does society deal with conflict? — Social divisions are artificially suppressed by a dominant elite. Remaining disputes are resolved by unquestioning (and fearful) acceptance of authority figures' decisions.

3 Attitude towards the state? — Strong attachment to state, amounting at times to blind loyalty and unquestioning obedience.

4 Typical structure of government? — Long periods of stable, authoritarian (usually militaristic) government, alternating with revolutionary turnover and short periods of political chaos.

Parochial culture

1 Attitude toward social divisions? — **Ethnocentrism** prevails; people live within the culture of their own subgroup, hardly aware of other subgroups; when made aware of them, they express fear and hatred.

2 How does society deal with conflict? — Major disputes resolved by fiat from a unified elite in control of the state apparatus; these central rulers delegate decision-making on "minor" matters (i.e., those that do not affect their power base) to traditional sub-group (ethnic, regional, religious) leaders.

3 Attitude towards the state? — State hardly acknowledged by those living inside its borders; local and parochial loyalties paramount; sub-group leaders recognize and support the state apparatus, in exchange for modest rewards.

4 Typical structure of government? — **Oligarchic** rule of a unified elite; disputes occur from time to time among members of the elite, but are usually resolved within the elite by intrigue or low levels of violence (e.g., assassination).

---

intellectually useful, even stimulating, yet all generalizations inevitably distort some aspects of the real world. No society perfectly exhibits all the hypothesized traits of a single culture type. The best we can say is that many real-world societies *tend toward* exhibiting the characteristics of *one* of these types.

Some societies may fall between the cracks. Either they have characteristics of more than one type, or they are in transition between two of them. As an example of the former, the old Soviet Union, in the Brezhnev era, had many traits of the collectivist culture—especially within Russia, an extremely homogeneous place at the time—but it bore significant resemblance to imperialist culture as well, given the diverse set of people living under the regime's control. Current Japan, on the other hand, illustrates the transitional case. It looks like a collectivist culture and surely was until recently, but it appears to be moving, even if slowly, toward a polyarchal one.

Given the uncertainty of life and the inevitability of change, these categories must not be seen as rigid absolutes. They provide helpful, suggestive ways of ordering a complex reality.[15] The good student of politics maintains an openness and a common sense in using intellectual constructions. Not all societies will be perfectly described by these four terms. Let us use them where they illuminate the political process, but look for other ways to make sense of the world when these terms show an inability to explain political realities.

Questions for discussion

1 In the wake of the 9/11 terrorist attacks, has the USA become less pluralistic and more authoritarian? (That is, less willing to resort to discussion and more willing to use force to resolve disputes.)

2 Is it fair to compare civil wars in Rwanda, Lebanon, and Somalia to the American civil war in the 1860s? What are the similarities and differences between these different conflicts?

3 Why are citizens passive in authoritarian systems? Is it because rulers are repressive or because citizens just refuse to act to protest government excesses?

4 Sinclair Lewis wrote a novel in 1935 with the ironic title, *It Can't Happen Here*, in which he showed American government indeed succumbing to dictatorship. Could that happen today? Why didn't it happen during the Great Depression of the 1930s?

5 What are the long-term prospects for fragmented cultures like those of Iraq, Colombia, and Rwanda: more of the same, authoritarian rule, or democracy?

5

THE ORIGINS AND PERSISTENCE
OF POLITICAL CULTURE

If radically different political cultures exist, a logical question arises. Where do these differences come from? Why exactly are people alienated from politics and cynical in southern Italy, Colombia, and south central Los Angeles, while they are imbued with a reasonable degree of trust in governmental processes and a participatory spirit in Sweden, Switzerland, and Minnesota?

Answering these questions is not easy. Obviously, if we knew how to create stable, peaceful, and participatory societies, we would jump to do so. For more than a century, democratizing the world has been a central goal of American foreign policy and a strong desire of the American public. If the task were simple, we would have a world of peaceful polyarchies by now.[1]

In fact, the conditions that give rise to a culture supporting polyarchal politics are complex. They take ages to develop and have a life of their own. They appear immune to outside manipulation. Accidental occurrence, as much as rational planning, seems to account for the values embedded in any given culture.

Why cultures develop

A government's method of tax collection, to take a simple example, can have enormous consequences for cultural values and the overall political system. In his study of France before the revolution, Tocqueville showed how a government can lose the loyalty of its citizens and reduce their level of social trust, simply by failing to think through the implications of its tax-collection process.[2]

Every year, bureaucrats in the French Finance Ministry would arbitrarily decide a tax due from each village in the country. This sum varied from one year to the next, so no town could ever be sure just what its tax bill was going to be. Regularity, stability, and planning all became impossible, and villagers knew they could blame the government for this chaotic state of affairs.

Worsening the situation was the fact that there were no regular tax collectors. Each year, a regional official randomly chose some village resident to collect taxes from his unhappy peers, and, over time, the burden of this task would reach every household in a small village.[3] It is no surprise that each person in the village came to be heartily detested by everyone else.

Since these temporary officials were unschooled in tax law, had no official records to help them, and could neither read nor write, their decisions about who owed what to the government were even more arbitrary than the government's decision about how much each village owed as a whole. Human nature being what it is, their decisions would reflect not "ability to pay," but the connections and animosities of local life. A cousin might pay little tax; a village rival would be gouged.

Since no one could tell who would become tax-collector (or when), villagers learned over the years to be secretive, to remain aloof from each other. After all, if someone knew you well and realized that your affairs were thriving, he could tax you outrageously when his turn came to collect taxes. Unlike the American pattern of conspicuous consumption, French peasants feigned conspicuous poverty. They learned to let no one inside their homes, in order to avoid the possibility that word of their comfortable circumstances might leak out to the tax collector of the day.

Many of the patterns set up by this absurd system endured for centuries. The French hatred of taxation is legendary; so is their cleverness at evading tax payment. Their wholehearted suspicion of government also dates from this era. Finally, the French villager's distrust of "the others"—that is, peers and colleagues in the community—is also legendary and derives, at least in part, from the pre-revolutionary tax system.

In all countries, as in France, one can find key historical developments that shaped current values and outlooks. *Cultures don't develop overnight, nor do they change overnight.* They are the product of unique historical developments that occur over centuries and reflect unplanned, accidental events.

Causes of polyarchy

Robert Dahl has for years explored the conditions that make polyarchy more or less likely. His studies clearly show that certain key variables play a vital role in shaping the political values of people in any given place. His work (and that of others) points to a small number of variables that help determine a nation's culture.[4]

Level and distribution of wealth

Political scientists rarely speak with one voice. If there is a single point on which most of them agree, however, it is this: impoverished nations are unlikely to develop stable, free, and competitive institutions. Not all wealthy countries become polyarchies, but most do. Not all poor countries are non-polyarchal, but most are. These assertions can be easily demonstrated.

However we choose to measure national wealth, we find that richer lands are likely to be polyarchal, poorer ones less likely.[5] A few facts will quickly illustrate this point.

Let us take some well-known data put out by Freedom House, an internationally respected organization that tracks the level of freedom for all countries. Each year since 1972 Freedom House has compiled "freedom scores" for each nation on the globe. These range from 2 ("most free") to 14 ("least free").[6] Countries are categorized as shown in Table 5.1.

For our purposes, we can use the "Free" label as a stand-in for polyarchy. Countries in that category all have competing parties, free elections, protection for political and civil rights, and other structural features standard in stable democratic systems. And countries with higher scores in the other two categories show those elements of chaos or authoritarianism associated with fragmented or collectivist cultures. If the wealth–polyarchy connection holds, countries labeled "free" should be wealthy, and the "not free" countries should be poor. In the same vein, wealthy nations should be "Free" (i.e., democratic or polyarchal) and poorer nations should not be.

That's exactly what the evidence shows—dramatically. Start with Table 5.2. The median freedom scores of rich countries stands at 2 (most free), while scores of the poorest nations are much higher (i.e., tending toward the "not free" levels).

Indeed, 23 of the 30 richest countries were rated 2 in each of the three

Table 5.1 Freedom House typology of the world's nations.

"Freedom score"	Nation considered as:
2–5	"Free"
6–10	"Partly free"
11–14	"Not free"

Table 5.2 The connection between wealth and freedom.

	"Freedom scores" (median)*		
	2002	2003	2004
30 richest countries	2	2	2
30 poorest countries	9	8.5	8.5
20 richest countries	2	2	2
20 poorest countries	8.5	8	8
10 richest countries	2	2	2
10 poorest countries	10.7	10	10

* Scores range from 2 (freest) to 14 (least free). For the sources of data in this table, see the text and Notes 6 and 7.

most recent years for which data is available, 2002, 2003, and 2004.[7] Two other rich countries had scores of 3 in each of these years. Only five of the 30 richest nations of the world in 2005 were "Partly Free" or "Not Free."

In contrast, only four of the 30 poorest countries were considered "Free" by Freedom house, and three of those countries had scores of 4 or 5 (not 2 or 3) during this 3-year period. Only one of these poor countries gained Freedom House's highest rating for freedom (2) in each of these years, and that nation must be considered a bit of an oddity: it is Tuvalu, the smallest member of the United Nations. Consisting of some 11,000 people scattered over nine little islands in the Pacific, half-way between Australia and Hawaii, Tuvalu can hardly be seen as typical of the world's poor nations. Most of them, it turns out, are far from democratic.

We can see this polyarchy-wealth connection from another angle. If we compare countries labeled "Free" or "Not Free" by Freedom House, we see that the free nations are much richer than those lacking freedoms. Take the 45 countries considered "Not Free" in all 3 years from 2002 to 2004. Table 5.3 shows that their median level of wealth came to US$3,350. That compares with a median level of US$21,572 for the 46 "freest" countries (those that scored a 2 in 2004 and no lower than a 3 in either of the other 2 years of our time period).

For perspective, the median wealth of the 192 nations in this study came to a little more than US$6,000. Thus, most "unfree" countries were poorer than average, while most free nations were *much* richer than average. In fact, among the 45 least free nations, only seven showed a median level of wealth above US$10,000, while only eight of the 46 freest nations came in *below* US$10,000. In short, just 15.6 percent of non-democratic nations might be considered reasonably well-off, compared with 82.6 percent of democratic countries.

The differences are dramatic. No matter how one manipulates the numbers, wealth and freedom go hand and hand. As Dahl puts it, "The higher the socioeconomic level of a country, the more likely it is to have a competitive political regime."[8] He wrote those words decades ago, and they have held up in study after study over the years.

Just why wealth correlates with democratic or polyarchal behavior is not

Table 5.3 The correlation between freedom and wealth.★

	Median wealth per capita (US$)
The 46 freest countries, 2002–2004	21,572
The 45 least free countries, 2002–2004	3,350

★ Wealth is measured by GDP (2005) *per capita* in international dollars, taking account of purchasing price parity (PPP). For the sources of data in this table, see the text and Notes 6 and 7.

entirely clear. The process linking the two variables is surely complex, but two reasons quickly suggest themselves. First, wealth produces satisfaction, or at least some degree of contentment.[9] People in comfortable situations do not rush from their homes to riot in the street. They do not hunt down and kill their neighbors. They do not risk their lives trying to topple governments. In short, people who are even moderately well-off seem unlikely to act in ways that produce political instability.

Second, wealth must be spread equally or reasonably equally to insure the survival of polyarchy. If many people are fairly well-off, no one has a reasonable claim to special privileges. If few are badly off, no one can make a legitimate case for disenfranchising "the lower orders," "the peasants," "the slaves," "the great unwashed," or whatever term might be in vogue to denote a society's poorer citizens. When all citizens are reasonably equal in wealth, you rarely find elite rule or mass rebellion (both of which are incompatible with polyarchal culture).

Thus, in any society *equality of wealth* is as important as wealth itself in laying the groundwork for polyarchy. If many people are well-off and few impoverished, a sense of general contentment will combine with feelings of social equality. Wealth *and* equality: these two factors lay the groundwork for mass participation in non-extremist political activity, a political style that practically defines polyarchal politics.

Remember that five of the richest countries were "Not Free," despite their wealth. Three of these wealthy lands were the oil-rich nations of Qatar, the United Arab Emirates, and Brunei, where money is very unevenly distributed. It ends up in the hands of a few powerful families. The prospect for democracy in places like these, with their huge class divisions, has always been shaky.

The class system

A second variable affecting the chances for polyarchy is the class system. If clear and strong social divisions exist, creating enormous barriers to those wishing to rise from one class to the next, distrust between socioeconomic groups will be high. Conflict levels will be intense preventing the development of social harmony. People in different groupings will not see each other as equals, to be respected and given equal rights. They will never develop that all-important sense of connection that is crucial for stable polyarchy. The longer the period in which these feelings of class difference exist, the more likely they are to instill social tensions that make a cohesive culture difficult to achieve.

The beliefs of political activists

The most active members of any group will gain the most power and have the most impact on group structures and policies. Wasn't that true of the "in-crowd" at your high school? The same holds with political systems. Political activists, those who spend large amounts of their time on political affairs, will have an inordinate impact on the political life of their country.[10] These participants can vary dramatically in behavior. In some places they seem shrill, rigid, vengeful. Politics there is unlikely to develop the key norms associated with polyarchal systems: tolerance, compromise, respect for majority rule and minority rights. Where political activists exhibit traits congruent with democratic processes—respect for those you disagree with, support for widespread citizen participation, acceptance of the legitimacy of government decisions you dislike—then the entire society's commitment to polyarchal methods of resolving conflict will grow.[11]

Number of distinct and antagonistic sub-cultures

We have already made much of this point in preceding chapters. In a nation racked by ethnic, racial, and regional hatreds, one hardly expects to find citizens thinking of each other as equals, respecting each other's viewpoint, accepting with equanimity the possibility that members of a competing political group may gain power. In short, the growth of polyarchal norms won't develop where inter-group animosity is high. Few nations with large, cohesive, and dramatically differing sub-groups have remained polyarchal for long.

Historical developments

The events of a nation's past hang heavy over its present and future. Three types of historical occurrence are especially crucial in determining the likelihood of a nation becoming polyarchal.

Independence or foreign control?

Foreign domination, especially over a prolonged time, seems especially unfavorable to polyarchy. If you have not experienced freedom, you cannot easily learn the norms and habits of polyarchy. Citizens used to fearful obedience do not gain practice in give-and-take methods of resolving conflict.

Russia offers a prime example of this pattern. For 200 years (approx. 1240–1450), Russians lived under the control of a brutal Tatar (or Mongol) empire. Most Russians, by necessity, survived this period by behaving as servile subjects. Their attitude of abject obedience endured long after the end of the Tatar reign. The few Russian leaders whom the Tatars allowed to operate adopted the attitude of cruel arrogance exhibited by their masters from the East. Thus, Russian citizens came to think of themselves as obedient subjects, while Russian rulers defined themselves as ruthless demigods.

Those norms, set firmly by the year 1500, have shaped Russian politics ever since.

Life under the domination of another people will often produce these feelings of fear and servitude that are wholly incompatible with the participationist ethos of a polyarchy. It undermines polyarchy in other ways too. Domination by outsiders can bring those feelings of alienation and distrust that are characteristic of fragmented cultures. In a few special cases, foreign domination may *not* undercut the chances for polyarchy and may even enhance them. That situation occurs when the foreign power itself is a polyarchy of some kind—or developing toward polyarchy. The USA, Canada, Australia, New Zealand, and other former British colonies were once under "foreign domination," but have clearly today become polyarchies. The same might be said (perhaps with less conviction) for Puerto Rico, the Philippines, Japan, South Korea, and other lands formerly under US control. Foreign domination, it appears, does not *have* to prevent polyarchy.

These examples may represent special cases, since the foreign power encouraged the development of competitive elections, parliaments, and other trappings of the polyarchal system. Nevertheless, they teach us that foreign domination *alone* does not undercut the conditions suitable for polyarchy. What counts is *foreign domination as a militaristic-autocratic phenomenon.* Britain, for instance, (polyarchy or not) behaved much more tyrannically in Africa than in North America. Partly as a result of their harsh colonial experiences, the former colonies in Africa found it much harder to evolve toward polyarchy than did British colonies in the Western Hemisphere, which had developed under relatively benign rule from Britain.[12]

It seems safe to draw this conclusion: Nations that experience a long period of oppressive rule, whether from foreign or domestic tyrants, will find it difficult to develop a polyarchal culture.

Historical accidents and singular events

Chance plays a greater role in our lives, and in the development of nations, than we usually care to admit. How different the history of Europe might have been, for instance, had the winter of 1812 been mild instead of brutally cold. Napoleon's army might *not* have been wiped out during his invasion of Russia. What if it had instead survived to keep him master of the Western world? Would that occurrence have impeded the growth of those conditions favorable to polyarchy that developed in Western Europe during the nineteenth century?

In a similar vein, what if the Battle of the Spanish Armada in 1588, which gave Britain supremacy of the seas for generations, had *not* occurred during a violent storm that handicapped the bulky and hard-to-maneuver ships of the Spanish fleet? A Spanish victory there might have led to Spanish, not English, colonization of North America. Think what a different world we would live in today. North American politics might then have developed along the lines of the current political system in Colombia.

And what about the impact of discovering gold in California in 1848? Many historians believe that the American North could not have won the Civil War without the financial benefits of the Gold Rush. It gave the North money to buy weapons and supplies, as well as funds to pay men to fight. It also gave New York bankers enough confidence in the future that they were willing to make loans to Lincoln's government for prosecution of the war. The influx of that gold into the Northern economy kept it humming along during the war instead of faltering, as many had expected. One could argue that this chance discovery kept the USA united in fact and allowed the abolition of slavery, one of the great impediments toward the development of polyarchy in North America.

In short, the unforeseen consequences of unplanned and unintended events can have enormous historical repercussions for the shaping of a nation's political culture. Chance events from long ago help explain why one culture today differs dramatically from another.[13]

The timing of mass political participation

The studies of Dahl and others show that one variable makes an extraordinary impact on the likelihood of polyarchal development: the conditions under which a majority of people enters political life. To summarize simply, if *suddenly* the mass of citizens in a given nation enters politics, the chances for that nation to become a stable polyarchy diminish.

This point is easily illustrated. Imagine that the USA were to "liberate" North Korea tomorrow. Our President would surely announce that North Koreans now had "their freedom," and he would urge them to move quickly toward fair and competitive elections. Yet even if we (or the UN) *guaranteed* them a free election, one would hardly expect to see North Korea operating in the democratic fashion of Norway, say, or Luxembourg in the next year or two—or even in the next 20 years. In the same manner, if the USA decided to "free" the people of Libya by toppling their long-time dictator, Moammar Qaddafi, that country would not overnight become a model of pluralistic competition.

There's no need for hypothetical examples. The USA *has* actually intervened in a number of places to "free" various people from their tyrannical rulers, practically forcing them to hold "democratic" elections. American Marines invaded a number of Latin American countries during the early decades of the twentieth century, with "democratization" as the prime rationale. In most cases the cure did not work. The fragile democratic institutions we set up were toppled within a few years (sometimes months), as the typical local pattern of strong-man rule or civil war reasserted itself after the departure of American troops.[14]

Polyarchy does not spring up overnight. Illiterate people used to obeying autocrats or habituated to following sectarian zealots into deadly warfare do not suddenly behave like members of the League of Women Voters just because someone out of the blue tells them they are "free" and have the right to participate in "fair elections."

People everywhere continue to act as they always have. If they are used to obeying dictators or using violence against enemies, they won't suddenly stand up to tyrants or show tolerance to foes the moment they are allowed to vote. People in a collectivist culture, if suddenly given the vote, will likely choose an authoritarian leader who will behave like any dictator and make the cancellation of future elections his first priority. In a fragmented culture, first-time voters will be swayed by vocal sub-group leaders. The electorate will proceed to choose demagogic representatives who promise to annihilate each other.

As a result of the sudden influx of the masses into politics, elections will produce another dictatorship or another civil war, depending on the culture in which the elections occur. In either case, polyarchy perishes.

Polyarchies do not develop when an uninformed mass of citizens, not schooled in the habits, norms, and ideals of democracy, are suddenly given the vote. Three historical traditions seem necessary to ensure the stable construction of polyarchy: (1) a history of political competition; (2) a gradual enfranchisement of the citizenry; and (3) a tradition of mass education.

A tradition of political competition

This point is crucial. One of the hardest things for anyone to accept, it would appear, is the existence of legitimate rivals. Over the ages, most political systems have tended toward anarchy and fragmentation (as rivals for power tried to kill each other) or dictatorship (as one set of competitors triumphed and imposed its will on everyone else). One of the latest ideas to develop in the history of political systems was the concept of the **loyal opposition**.

The fact that a rival faction could oppose you and your group and your interests and *still* be allowed a fair hearing, still be treated as an honorable equal with the same rights and privileges that you have: that alone was a radical concept. Even more radical was the idea that that group *should be given every opportunity to expand its political powers so as to supplant you and your group and your interests,* allowing these outsiders to control the powers and resources of government that had traditionally been in *your* hands. Such an idea had been virtually unknown for most of human history. Not until the eighteenth century did this notion of a legitimate opposition slowly take hold—and it developed only in parts of western Europe and a few other places populated by the descendants of west Europeans.

The idea that non-ruling groups have the right to compete for *and take* power peacefully is historically radical. Open competition in which you can actually lose power is not a popular idea for ruling elites. And it is those elites who most help to build and sustain political institutions. It is they who must accept the value of competition if they are to create institutions that foster it (free, fair, and frequent elections, free speech, free press, right to assembly, and so forth).

We must, in fact, use stronger terms than "accept the value of competition." Support for the idea of competition must be *embedded* in elite value systems. In stable, long-term polyarchies political activists must actually *defend* their opponents' right to compete. One of the most famous aphorisms about democracy nails this point. Voltaire is reputed to have said to an opponent: "I disapprove of what you say, but I will defend to the death your right to say it." Whether Voltaire made that statement or not, its sentiment lies at the heart of values that must be widespread for a polyarchy to thrive.

Gradual enfranchisement of the citizenry

If the idea of legitimate competition is difficult for elites to accept, it would appear even more difficult to accept by people unfamiliar with the political process. In nearly all countries today where the right to rule is determined by free and fair elections, the tradition of legitimate competition developed first at the elite level, then gradually spread to the masses as they were slowly admitted to full political rights and then socialized, so to speak, into the norms of the polyarchal political process.

In other words, if you want to move toward democracy, start slowly. Teach a small number of leaders—society's most active political participants—the idea of competition. Encourage them to try it out, make sure they understand it and learn to abide by its rules: losers leave office, winners get power, no one wipes out the other. Then after a few years expand the political class a bit, and then some more, and finally open it to all, but open it only after the broader culture has accepted this general habit of competition, only after most people have come to accept that their group will not win every election, that elections must be held regularly, and that deference to the electorate's wishes in each election is absolutely mandatory.

Dahl summarizes this process in a simple and powerful way. In the historical sequence most favorable to the development of polyarchy, he says, "*competition precedes inclusiveness.*"[15]

Unfortunately, in this age when mass democracy is seen everywhere as "a good thing," it is impossible to carry out this dictum in the real world. Imagine telling the people of East Colombistan, e.g. that only 10 percent of them can vote in the election following the popular overthrow of their hated tyrant. "It's OK," you announce. "In another 20 years, another 10 percent of you will be allowed to vote, and at this rate, in just three or four generations nearly all of you will be granted the franchise. Be patient."

This plan will not work. The trend toward mass voting evolved slowly over decades in the 1800s. It would be impossible to reconstruct this pattern in the twenty-first century. People everywhere "can't wait," in the words made famous by Martin Luther King. Whenever dictators fall, the masses today will demand to be consulted.

That makes the development of polyarchy somewhat more difficult, but not impossible. First, this phenomenon, the slow introduction of the masses into political life, is just one of many variables that make polyarchy likely. Its absence hinders, but by no means precludes, the development of polyarchal culture. Second, its absence can be partially overcome by two other factors. One might be called **the demonstration effect**. Citizens in many places today with no polyarchal traditions can see how polyarchies work in neighboring countries or through the global communications network. They may absorb polyarchal norms vicariously, so to speak.

The fact that polyarchies are not only internally peaceful, but also wealthy, may further induce citizens in non-polyarchies to imitate the behavior patterns of these seemingly successful systems. That is, to gain the apparent benefits of polyarchy, they may demand elections, form parties, and speak out for their beliefs while refraining from killing others who speak out for opposing beliefs. One sees this trend in numerous central European nations such as Slovenia, Slovakia, Croatia, and Macedonia.

Furthermore, countries moving rapidly toward polyarchal institutions may benefit from rapid increases in the education level of their citizens. Education, a key variable that goes hand in hand with polyarchy, may help overcome a population's lack of real-world experience with polyarchal patterns. Note some of the countries that violated Dahl's "rule" about the desirability of slow popular involvement. Spain, the Czech Republic, and Estonia, among others, allowed rapid mass input after dictatorships fell and become polyarchal anyway. What characterized these nations was a well-educated citizenry at the time when the political system suddenly moved from dictatorship to mass voting. This variable, education, is so important that we need to examine its effects in some detail.

An educated populace

Polyarchy and education go hand in hand. Countries with illiterate citizens seem unable to build a long-term system of pluralistic competition. True, a well-educated population does not *guarantee* polyarchal politics. Germany in the 1930s, supporting a Nazi dictatorship, had citizens as well educated as those in democratic Britain, France, or Norway. And India looks like a major exception in the other direction. Even though nearly 90 percent of all Indians could neither read nor write at the time of independence (1947), India has operated a reasonably strong democratic system for most of the past six decades.[16]

As we know, there are exceptions to every rule. Nevertheless, in most cases polyarchies need an educated mass base to stand any chance of long-term survival.

To verify this proposition takes little effort. Look around the world. The vast majority of highly-educated nations are polyarchies or nations moving toward polyarchy. The vast majority of countries with poorly-educated citizens are non-polyarchies (fragmented states or dictatorships). The correlation between level of education and likelihood of stable political competition is clear and strong.

To illustrate, let us compare education levels in countries that are clearly polyarchies to levels in countries that are clearly *not* polyarchies. In Table 5.4, I have constructed a comparative list of nations. In the left column are clear examples of strong, stable polyarchy. Countries in this column meet these strict criteria: *For 30 years (1976–2005) they have been:*

- *independent nations* (never part of some larger entity, as Belarus, East Timor, and many others were, a situation that can strongly impact the pattern of a country's political culture)
- *with more than a million citizens* (to avoid tiny anomalies like Andorra and Vanuatu)
- *rated "Free" by Freedom House for at least 25 straight years*, 1981–2005 (and never rated "Not Free" during this time period).

In fact, nearly all the countries in the "Strong Polyarchy" column were "Free" for the entire 30 years under consideration.

The strictness of our definition leads to the omission of several countries that would seem to belong here. India, for instance, is omitted because it was rated "Partly Free" for 8 years at different times during this era. (Turkey, Chile, and others missed the list for the same reason.) The Czech Republic, Panama, Taiwan, and South Africa were omitted from the group, because they have not operated democratic institutions long enough, even though these states and several others seem well on their way toward membership.

In other words, countries on this list are the clearest examples of strong, long-lasting polyarchy. If there is a difference between polyarchy and other forms of politics, then this group should illustrate those differences in the strongest way possible.

In like manner, countries in the right-hand column represent the clearest examples of "non-polyarchy." They too were selected from among those nations with a million citizens that were independent over this entire 30-year period (1976–1981), but in their case they were rated "Not Free" by Freedom House for 25 of the 30 years under consideration (and never rated "Free" in any of those years). The strictness of this test forces us to omit an obvious candidate like Iran, which was rated "Partly Free" for six of these 30 years—just enough to keep it off the list. Other obvious possibilities like

Eritrea or Turkmenistan missed the cut because they have not been independent long enough. We cannot be sure that their brutal, undemocratic patterns have long-term durability.

With this chart, we can see two groups that represent precisely opposite patterns. (By pure chance, there turn out to be 26 countries in each category.) One group of countries can only be described as strong, stable democracies (Sweden, Japan), while the other set consists of countries with no democratic features of any kind. These places are either near-anarchies (like Somalia and Rwanda) or long-term dictatorships (like Syria and North Korea).

As expected, we see dramatic differences between these two groups. See Table 5.5 for which nations are well-educated. From the many indicators of educational achievement, I chose a statistic that UNESCO provides for most nations of the world: the number of students in higher education per 100,000 inhabitants. If an educated populace is essential to polyarchal culture, we would expect to find many more students in higher education in

Table 5.4 Polyarchies and non-polyarchies, 1976–2005.★

Strong polyarchy for entire period	Clear non-polyarchy for entire period
Australia	Afghanistan
Austria	Algeria
Belgium	Angola
Botswana	Brunei
Canada	Burma (Myanmar)
Costa Rica	Burundi
Cyprus (Greek)	Cambodia
Denmark	Cameroon
Finland	Chad
France	China
Germany	Congo-Kinshasa
Greece	Cuba
Ireland	Equatorial Guinea
Israel	Guinea
Italy	Iraq
Jamaica	Laos
Japan	Libya
Netherlands	Mauritania
New Zealand	North Korea
Norway	Oman
Portugal	Rwanda
Spain	Saudi Arabia
Sweden	Somalia
Switzerland	Syria
UK	Togo
USA	Vietnam

★ See text for definitions and data sources.

polyarchies than in other political systems. And this statistic does vary dramatically. In 2002, it went as low as *the single digits* in places like Tanzania and Malawi, while rising to as high as 5,708 in the USA and 6,888 in Libya (which comes in first on this indicator, for some strange reason).

It takes little more than a quick glance at Table 5.5 to confirm our hypothesis: polyarchies are much better-educated places than non-polyarchies. Tables 5.6 and 5.7 make this point in as strong a fashion as possible. Table 5.6 shows that if we take 2,000 students in higher education

Table 5.5 Regime type and support for higher education.*

Strong polyarchy	Support for education	Clear non-polyarchy	Support for education
Australia	5,179	Afghanistan	165†
Austria	2,833	Algeria	2,184
Belgium	3,638	Angola	95
Botswana	478	Brunei	1,262
Canada	3,844	Burma (Myanmar)	1,151
Costa Rica	1,888	Burundi	180
Cyprus (Greek)	2,555	Cambodia	313
Denmark	3,776	Cameroon	517
Finland	5,612	Chad	77‡
France	3,541	China	1,173
Germany	2,833	Congo-Kinshasa	680**
Greece	5,118	Cuba	2,094
Ireland	4,642	Equatorial Guinea	226‡
Israel	4,780	Guinea	108††
Italy	3,329	Iraq	1,333
Jamaica	1,743	Laos	509
Japan	3,126	Libya	6,888
Netherlands	3,279	Mauritania	328
New Zealand	4,806	North Korea	1,300**
Norway	4,706	Oman	739
Portugal	3,989	Rwanda	247
Spain	4,492	Saudi Arabia	2,234
Sweden	4,676	Somalia	Very low‡‡
Switzerland	2,593	Syria	1,769†
United Kingdom	3,872	Togo	343‡
United States	5,708	Vietnam	993

* See text for definitions and data sources. The data on higher education comes from the years 2001 or 2002, unless otherwise indicated.
† Most recent data from 1990.
‡ Data from 1999.
** Calculated from data on the website of the US Department of State: http://www.state.gov/r/pa/ei/bgn/2823.htm (accessed in October, 2006).
†† Most recent data from 1995.
‡‡ No data available (as of October, 2006, UNESCO, the US State Department, and the CIA's *Factbook*, provided no data on higher education in Somalia.

Table 5.6 Connection between regime type and support for higher education, 1.

The 26 most polyarchal nations	88.5% (23 of 26) provide higher education for 2,000 or more citizens for every 100,000 inhabitants
The 26 least polyarchal nations	19.2% (5 of 26) provide higher education for 2,000 or more citizens for every 100,000 inhabitants

Table 5.7 Connection between regime type and support for higher education, 2.

	Median number of students in higher education for every 100,000 inhabitants
The 26 most polyarchal nations	3,810
The 26 least polyarchal nations	599★

★ Data for four of these nations is estimated (see footnotes to Table 5.5); it seemed a safe bet to assume Syria would be well above the median and Afghanistan, Guinea, and Somalia well below. Leaving these nations out of the calculations puts the median for the 22 remaining non-polyarchies at 710.

per 100,000 inhabitants as a cut-off point, then we find that nearly all poly-archies (88.5 percent) are above that number and most non-polyarchies (80.8 percent) are below it. Table 5.7 shows that the median number of university students per 100,000 inhabitants is 3,810 in polyarchies and 599 in non-polyarchies. These differences could hardly be clearer.

Thus, an educated citizenry and polyarchy go hand in hand. The reasons for this correlation are complex. The connection may derive from a fact we have previously discussed: allowing those you hate to compete for the right to gain power is not an easy idea. Education may help make it acceptable. Education, after all, expands one's horizons. It opens one's eyes to other ways of thinking and acting. It may lead to greater tolerance for the rights of the people who hold those other viewpoints.

In addition, education helps one understand the rationale underlying the very idea of peaceful competition. If you allow others to seek power without trying to kill them, they may reciprocate, allowing *you* to seek power without fear of being killed. The personal benefits of this system are obvious.

Education also improves one's mastery of the environment, enhances one's life chances, and increases one's overall self-confidence. Self-assured people, compared to the insecure, may be less threatened by those who are different from them, better able to let others share power without fearing obliteration of self as a consequence.

Finally, education may enhance the possibilities for polyarchal politics by producing higher levels of cultural homogeneity. Most educated nations

75

develop a reasonably unified system of education; thus, their schoolchildren learn the same perspectives and absorb the same values. This agreement on values, as we know, is a key requirement for polyarchal culture.

These are all speculations. One can conjure up other reasons to explain the correlation between education and polyarchy. This is not the place to work out a complete theory. We stress here the fact itself and its causal significance. If you want a polyarchy, you need to provide your citizens with mass education of high quality. Without it, the task of sustaining peaceful political competition is daunting.

Why cultures persist

Compare these two comments about Italy that once appeared in the *International Herald Tribune*.

> Almost every day, new disclosures link Italy's political and business leaders in a vast web of organized corruption. The scale of wrongdoing has outraged even the famously cynical Italian public, feeding demands for fundamental changes . . .
>
> The situation in the Italian Parliament is becoming graver, and the [Cabinet] continues to oppose the inquiry into the Banks Scandal . . . We live in an age when the people have lost all confidence in those who represent them . . . They want honest men.

Both comments describe a key element in Italian politics: widespread corruption among political elites. Both argue that this pattern has led to high levels of voter cynicism and an unstoppable demand for radical reform.

Despite their similarity, however, the comments differ in one dramatic aspect. They were written 100 years apart!

The first comment appears on page four of the *Tribune's* edition of March 4, 1993. It represents the lead editorial. The second comment appears *on the same day and on the same page*, but with this difference: it is found under the rubric "In Our Pages: 100, 75 and 50 Years Ago," and it is subtitled "1893: Italian scandals." In other words, it is a 100-year-old quote from the same paper.[17]

It would appear that nothing has changed in the broad pattern of Italian politics—except the names of the players.

The same could be said of many countries. Go back 100 years, and you will find people in the USA complaining about the "obscene" power of "petty tyrants" in Congress who wield "excessive" power in committee through the "archaic and irrational" seniority system. Political moralists have been demanding "reform" of Congress to "better reflect the people's will" for a long time.

Political patterns, in other words, persist. Take any group of astute political

76

observers. Transport them one hundred years back in time within their own country. Once they make allowance for obvious technological differences, they will feel right at home and understand perfectly what is going on.

We can predict the same would be true if we transported them 100 years into the future. If we could leap ahead to the twenty-second century, what would we see in the USA or Italy? Some American reformer will be denouncing the excessive power of some "congressional dictator" ensconced at the head of some obscure subcommittee. Meanwhile, some Italian reformer will be denouncing the continued scandal of corrupt Italian legislators, pointing out that the people are "fed up" with the old system and wish for its immediate transformation.

Obviously, change is possible; these predictions could be wrong. Yet pattern persistence is the most common expectation. Bet on things continuing to happen as they have in the past, bet on people continuing to behave as they have in the past, and you are unlikely to go broke!

There's a good reason for this stability. *Political systems change slowly*, because they are based on deep-seated cultural norms, values, and expectations. These learned outlooks are ingrained in us all from earliest days, and early learned values are the most likely to persist. The culture that passes on these values took decades, even centuries, to develop. It *can* change over time, of course, but this change will normally occur incrementally, at the margins—just as our deepest values change but slowly.

In any person's lifetime, then, most culture change will seem modest, barely recognizable. And the more deeply ingrained the cultural attitude, the less likely it is that time and events will affect it. *Only dramatic, powerful, long-lasting historical developments will affect the core of a cultural outlook*, and events with that type of impact on a nation occur rarely. Japan's devastating loss in the Second World War, for instance, wrought a modest change in that nation's culture. A lesser historical event, like the Oklahoma City bombing, had almost no impact on American political culture. Even the disaster of September 11, 2001, has done little to change the deepest values and typical behavior patterns of most Americans.

We can test the truth of this position by looking at history. Has American culture changed seriously in the last 100–200 years? Our first reaction is to say, "Of course!" Dramatic developments have occurred since the times of Washington, Lincoln, and even Wilson. We have gone from an agrarian to an urban society. We have become more tolerant and egalitarian in matters of race, ethnicity, and gender. Many Americans have become less religious and nearly all less puritanical than we once were. But in many essential elements, American culture has changed little since foreigners began describing it 200 and more years ago.

The most famous observer of American mores was the French aristocrat, Alexis de Tocqueville. After an 1831 visit to the USA, he returned to Europe and wrote his brilliant social analysis, *Democracy in America*.[18] The book became a runaway bestseller and has been continuously in print ever since. Delving into this work from time to time, I am always amazed at its contemporaneity. Do a modest update of the language, and the text reads as if written yesterday.

Tocqueville's pithiest observations could be uttered by any pop psychologist on television. American character, says Tocqueville, exhibits "a restless spirit, immoderate desire for wealth, and an extreme love of independence."[19] He goes on: "The passions that stir the Americans most deeply are commercial and not political . . ."[20] As a result of these traits, says Tocqueville, Americans have become the richest people on earth. Yet even so, the apple contains a worm. Americans "find prosperity almost everywhere, but not happiness. For them desire for well-being has become a restless, burning passion which increases with satisfaction."[21]

How often have we heard Americans described in these terms? We are a driven, ambitious people, worshipping the false God of Mammon ("the almighty dollar"), never satisfied despite all our wealth. When you hear people today intoning these somber clichés, deploring the loss of "traditional American values," just remember: Tocqueville was saying the same thing in the 1830s. And he was hardly the first to make those observations.

There is another instance in which Tocqueville captured something enduring in American culture. Imagine the way new immigrants to the USA feel when they arrive today, especially those used to orderly or oppressive regimes. Would their reaction be different from that of Tocqueville in 1831?

> No sooner do you set foot on American soil than you find yourself in a sort of tumult; a confused clamor rises on every side, and a thousand voices are heard at once, each expressing some social requirements. All around you everything is on the move: here the people of a district are assembled to discuss the possibility of building a church; there they are busy choosing a representative; further on, the delegates of a district are hurrying to town to consult about some local improvements; elsewhere it's the village farmers who have left their furrows to discuss the plan for a road or a school. One group of citizens assembles for the sole object of announcing that they disapprove of the government's course, while others unite to proclaim that the men in office are the fathers of their country.[22]

The chaos and color of American life have always played a large role in this culture. Like most social patterns everywhere, the unruly nature of American society did not spring up just last week.

The America that Tocqueville observed sounds familiar in a hundred ways, right down to mundane aspects of everyday life. Note, for instance, how he described something as ordinary as the format of an American newspaper:

78

> In America three quarters of the bulky newspaper put before you
> will be full of advertisements and the rest will usually contain polit-
> ical news or just anecdotes; only at long intervals and in some
> obscure corner will one find one of those burning arguments which
> for us [in France] are the readers' daily food.[23]

Have American newspapers changed in essence since this description? Most
space is still devoted to advertising. Most of the writing is chock-a-block
with unrelated anecdotes interspersed with major political stories of the day.
And pieces devoted to political opinions (Tocqueville's "burning arguments") are relegated to some difficult-to-find middle section of the paper
known as the editorial page. (And they are still on the front page of French
newspapers.)

Tocqueville goes on to observe that "the number of periodical or semi-
periodical productions in the United States surpasses all belief."[24] If you
have ever stood before an average American newsstand, you would never
dispute those words—yet they were written over a century and a half ago.

Tocqueville's account of culture, society, and politics in the USA has endured for generations because he caught the essence of the American value
system. He was the first to explore the relationship between American
beliefs and the American form of government. For Tocqueville, American
values underpinned a working democracy: "It is their mores . . . that make
the Americans . . . capable of maintaining the rule of democracy."[25] By
"mores," Tocqueville meant what social scientists today call "cultural values."
He was among the first to study the effect of beliefs on social behavior.

To summarize Tocqueville's argument, Americans in 1831 were capable
of maintaining democracy because they deeply believed in values congruent
with democracy. The values included:

- a love of freedom
- a spirit of independence and individualism
- an orientation of common sense and a concern for the practical
- a restless desire to better oneself, to get ahead, to acquire wealth
- a deep-seated belief in the need for education—especially education for
  all and not just for an elite
- an informality of spirit, an ease of interacting socially with people of all
  ranks and statuses
- a "joiner" orientation (not Tocqueville's term); that is, a readiness to join
  existing groups or get together with others to form new ones
- a strong belief in the legal equality of all citizens and, following from that
  belief, a zealous attachment to the ideal of "the will of the majority"
- a tolerance of minority perspectives
- a deep belief in God and a strong commitment to religion and religious
  values.

Do these perspectives sound familiar? A century and a half after Tocqueville, contemporary observers of the USA use similar words to describe American culture. Of course, one must not conclude that change never occurs. Reviewing Tocqueville's list of "mores," modern observers will add here, subtract there, and modify the emphases. Religious commitments, for instance, no longer seem as solid as they once were, while Tocqueville saw American dedication to religion as perhaps its foremost characteristic. Yet even after years of decline in religious fervor, Americans still hold a wide lead over the citizens of other democratic nations when it comes to "belief in God." They also surpass similar nations on all indicators of religious activity.[26]

Looking at American values today, some analysts might want to stress an increased focus on commercial materialism, and yet throughout *Democracy in America* Tocqueville made clear that an eagerness to gain wealth was rampant in American society. One great change that *has* occurred in the last century and a half is the way Americans define "citizen." They still believe in "the legal equality of all citizens," but "citizens" now include women, people in the age group from eighteen to twenty, non-landowners, and minority groups of every type—especially African-Americans, most of whom were slaves in Tocqueville's day.

Change, in short, has occurred, but perhaps more dramatic is how little has changed in the basic spirit of the country, the outlook of the people, and the workings of American political institutions. Does anyone doubt that Tocqueville, returning to the America of our time, would recognize the scene?

The USA is not unique. In the institutions of all countries, one sees this persistence of social and political patterns. Discussing China, Lucian Pye argued decades ago that "two thousand years of Confucian government was an uninterrupted era of authoritarian rule."[27] The non-democratic China of today is hardly an aberration.

Similarly, Robert Putnam shows the persistence of culture in Italy. He demonstrates that historical developments occurring about the year 1100 helped produce the famous division of Italy into two regions, North and South, with the former developing a tradition of popular self-rule and the latter a tradition of corrupt, authoritarian governance.[28] Even today, as Putnam shows, the alienated **fatalism** of the southern peasant and the participatory involvement of the northern worker persist, reflecting generations of cultural tradition.

Cultural patterns persist and insure the persistence of political patterns. Great Britain illustrates well this weight of cultural heritage. Everyone is familiar with the centuries of British support for the idea of limited monarchy. It was first enunciated in 1215 and reinforced numerous times since, most prominently during the Glorious Revolution of 1688. Colombia and Russia are two other countries that illustrate the persistence of cultural and political patterns. Any would-be Tocqueville visiting those countries in 1831 could return today and understand perfectly the current society and contemporary politics of each place.

Colombia is well known in our time for its social violence, a violence that spills over into the political process. Current observers often link Colombia's violence to its infamous drug traffic. That approach would appear faulty, however. Colombians have never needed the excuse of drug wars to engage in political violence. The country has rarely known non-violence. Back in 1968, James Payne described Colombia as "a system which for a century and a half has been characterized by frequent fighting."[29] He goes on to point out:

> On a scale of political deaths per generation, Colombia has one of the highest levels of political conflict in the world. In nearly 150 years since independence the country has been racked by ten national civil wars . . . In addition there have been countless local revolts and flare-ups . . . Political conflict has never been low . . . The civil wars have not represented abrupt breaks with a prior period of tranquility. Instead they were seemingly natural extensions of an always heated politics.[30]

Payne's work was written long before Colombia's brutal drug cartels began their notorious operations.[31] Intense conflict among citizens is a longstanding trait of Colombian culture. A perpetual politics of armed violence is the natural result of this culture of incivility.

In Russia, too, observers over the centuries have noted the continued reoccurrence of deeply-ingrained political patterns. These patterns reflect neither the American tradition of peaceful citizen influence on the political process, nor the Colombian tradition of violent and perpetual struggle for control of power. The Russian political tradition stresses hierarchy and order, submission to authority, and unchecked rule of the few.

This tradition of autocracy goes back centuries. It did not suddenly arise in 1917 via Vladimir Ilyich Lenin. One can trace its origins to the devastating Tatar invasion of old Russia around the middle of the *thirteenth* century. As the warriors of Genghis Khan and his successors swept westward,

> the Russian land was conquered and covered with blood. Every Russian town [was] sacked and burned.[32]

Thus began a period during which Russians learned to endure absolute rule and enforced submission to superior strength.

> For two hundred years Russian principalities and city republics survived only by total, humiliating subservience to their Asiatic rulers.[33]

The barbarous behavior of Russia's Tatar rulers strains credulity. In one battle alone (Moscow, 1571), the Crimean Tatars were said to have killed 200,000 people and carried another 130,000 off into slavery.

The succeeding centuries saw a continuing procession of autocratic Russian rulers. Peter the Great killed hundreds of thousands in his various wars. Thousands died following his quirky decision to build Saint Petersburg in the middle of a pestilential marsh. Catherine the Great also killed tens of thousands while fighting wars and smashing peasant rebellions. Most of the succeeding tsars also behaved in despotic and tyrannical fashion. The pattern continued down to the last tsar, Nicholas II, whose unwillingness to share power with even a puny version of a democratic legislature (the Duma) and whose insensitivity to the enormous casualties suffered by his people in the First World War, insured his downfall and the triumph of communism.

The communist leaders who seized power in 1917 behaved exactly in the Russian tradition: with brutal absolutism. Lenin, Stalin, and later communist leaders up to Gorbachev (1985) brooked no opposition, used terror to insure a submissive population, and forced enormous sacrifices from a cowed citizenry. Obviously, differences existed between monarchical and communist rule, but the essential Russian pattern of imperial command and fearful obedience continued.

It is of course impossible to predict the next stage in Russian politics, but given this dismal background it would take a brave seer to predict a smooth or rapid transition to polyarchy.

Conclusion

Nations, like people, hold fast to their traditions. Once set in place, cultural norms exert enormous impact on thought and behavior. Change can occur, but short-run change will almost always occur within the confines of the traditional pattern. Thus, particular leaders do change frequently in places like Bolivia and Somalia. What does not change is the long-term pattern of violence and anarchy.

In the same vein, the increasing enfranchisement and empowerment of more and more groups in American society over the decades fits perfectly into the polyarchal pattern that was firmly in place by the late eighteenth century. What *would* be a change in the American polyarchal system would be the establishment of a 20-year dictatorship, say, or the occurrence of several military coups over the next decade. One hardly expects either development to come about.

It may be possible to produce rapid, substantive change in a culture, but only under highly stressful conditions. The destruction and dismemberment of Germany in the 1940s helped revamp the culture of West Germany—to the point where it could sustain competitive politics for several decades.

Such traumatic events as the Second World War, however, occur rarely in a nation's history. Normally, change of the deep-seated variety necessary to alter the essential pattern of a country's culture will occur only slowly, over decades or even centuries.

Questions for discussion

1 Why is democracy harder to develop in lands where wealth is concentrated in the hands of a few and where most people are poor?
2 The USA came into existence after a tax revolt in the 1770s. It is today one of the lowest-taxed countries among industrialized nations. Do you see any long-term cultural connection here?
3 If education and democracy go hand in hand among nations, is it also true among individuals? Are more educated people also better citizens?
4 Is restlessness, a continuing anxiety about the need to move upward, a natural element in any pluralistic culture—or is it particular to American culture?
5 Does the author make too much of "pattern persistence?" In what ways has the USA (or other countries that you know of) changed since the nineteenth century?
6 How about you personally—have any of your deepest values changed in, say, the past 10 years?

Part II

INDIVIDUALS IN POLITICS

6

WHO BECOMES POLITICAL?
WHO DOESN'T?

Once as an Army private, I casually mentioned some recent political event to a barracks mate. He cut me short. "Drop it!" he growled. "I never talk about politics." I was stunned, never having encountered such willful apathy toward the most fascinating subject on earth. (I was young, remember.)

Think about it for a minute. Some people will always be focused on politics. They will be so intrigued that they will forego other activities to read about politics, listen to radio talk shows, watch TV news programs, contribute to blogs, and discuss politics with all and sundry. They will write officials, join political groups, go to meetings, work for candidates, and even run for office.

We all know someone like that. We also know people with only the barest interest in politics. They cannot imagine spending an evening at City Hall watching politicians debate the zoning law. They skim past public affairs channels as if they were eye poison. They know next to nothing about politics. Maybe they can name the current vice-president, possibly one of their own Senators (but not both), and certainly not the current Speaker of the House.

So at one extreme, we have political junkies, and at the other, political know-nothings. Most people fall somewhere in the middle, with some interest in politics and a modest knowledge of it. Is there any difference between these groups? Does each have a particular set of social, economic, or psychological traits?

The question is crucial, because the know-nothings will have little impact on public policies. The junkies will. Generally speaking, the more politically involved you are, the more power you are going to attain. You cannot affect outcomes if you keep your mouth shut and sit on your hands. What distinguishes political activists (who *will* gain influence) from the rest of us (who will not)? Are they different from us in major ways, or are they representative of citizens as a whole?

If there is one thing social science knows, it is the answer to this question. Literally hundreds of studies have traced the variables that induce political involvement (or apathy). The results are complex, but they do show a definite difference in the kinds of people who love or hate politics.[1]

Deciding to be political

We will focus on the two central choices that free citizens can make about politics. First, will they get involved? Second, how deeply will they get involved? These decisions do not occur randomly. Different groups of people answer these questions in very different ways.

If, for example, 10 percent of Americans are seriously interested in politics (as studies suggest), that does *not* mean that 10 percent of workers and 10 percent of Asian-Americans and 10 per cent of Mississippi residents are politically involved. Likewise, if 3 percent of Americans donate money to political campaigns, it does not follow that 3 percent of doctors and 3 percent of mill workers and 3 percent of Methodists donate money.

People with different personalities and social statuses do not behave alike. Some will be more politically focused than others. We need to know who the politically involved are, because it is their ideas and interests that will carry the most weight in directing the affairs of state.

Social cleavage occurs in all societies. People everywhere define themselves, or are defined by society, as belonging to certain groups and not belonging to others. People everywhere have differing life experiences and different lifestyles. Take religion for example. In America, few Easterners and few bankers will be found handling snakes or jumping into water over their heads for baptism.

Likewise, dress patterns vary. Few people in Idaho will wear three-piece suits; few people in Washington, DC wear boots. Attitudes on key social issues also vary. Most workers oppose free trade practices; most big business leaders support them. It should not surprise us, therefore, that *political* ideas and actions also vary from one group to another.

To understand politics anywhere, start with group difference. No society is perfectly homogeneous. At a minimum, people are divided by age, ethnicity, race, class, region, religion, and gender. The impact of group affiliation and shared experience is strong enough to create patterns of behavior that distinguish most people in one situation from most people in another. To know how politics works, we must familiarize ourselves with *group* political tendencies.

Let us start with the most consistent finding in political science research. *Most people are not interested in politics most of the time*. "How can this be?" ask political junkies, but let us be realistic. Most people focus their attention away from politics. They are wrapped up in the day-to-day realities of life: family, relationships, job. In their spare time, people watch television, work at hobbies, indulge in sports, cruise the mall. The idea of voluntarily attending city council meetings or choosing to watch legislative committees at work, strikes many as odd behavior—even bizarre.[2]

Politics for most citizens ranks low on the interest scale. Paraphrasing Lincoln, we might say that politics interests all of the people some of the time, and some of the people all of the time, but never all of the people all of the time. Most of the time, in fact, politics involves just a small percentage of the population. Who are these people and what are their characteristics?

Participation: the key variables

Education stands as the single best predictor of political involvement. Every study of political participation has shown that, whatever the setting, the more years of formal schooling people have, the more likely it is that they will engage in political activity.

This finding should hardly surprise us. Think about it at the extremes. It seems reasonable to suppose that people with PhDs or law degrees will be more politically involved than people who stopped all formal schooling at age 12. But it turns out that education is such a powerful force that even *one* more year of schooling will make you more attuned to politics than someone with one less year. If you take a group of 50-year-old white male welders living in Sioux City, Iowa, for example, you will find that those who made it through the 11th grade of high school (some 30 years ago) are slightly more likely to show an interest in politics, vote, and go to meetings than those who left high school after completing only 10th grade.

In other words, hold everything else constant, add a little more education, and you get a little more political involvement. It follows that a lot more education produces a lot more political involvement. If you want politically active citizens, support educational opportunities for the many.

Class is another variable that affects political involvement. Other things being equal, the lower you are on the totem-pole of life, the less politically active you will be. Unskilled workers are less likely than business executives to read about politics, talk about politics, vote, or run for office. Middle-class professionals will be more active than people on welfare.

The implications are clear for those who wish to raise the level of mass involvement. Develop a dynamic, growth-oriented society that spreads wealth to the many. Before you know it, political activity will be booming. On the other hand, if you are a dictator and want to keep people quiet, make sure they stay poor and barefoot. You will insure their passivity for years to come. Poverty-stricken people do not participate in politics, so they will not be out in the streets trying to topple your regime.

Gender is a powerful variable affecting political activism. Gender differences are especially marked at the higher levels of the political process where everywhere, women are in the minority, usually the extreme minority. Wherever we look, we find few women heads of state. There are also few women in national cabinets or other powerful leadership positions. *Women remain in the minority at every political level of every nation*—right down to school boards and town commissions.

Women are also less likely than men to engage in ordinary political activities. Men more than women will read newspapers, gather in public to discuss government affairs, state an interest in politics, join political organizations, and vote.[3]

It is important to note that this pattern is hardly uniform. The more "modern" the country, the closer women come to political equality. That is, in most nations with advanced, post-industrial economies, women participate in most aspects of politics at nearly the same level as men do, and sometimes at higher levels. For instance, in the USA women *vote* at higher rates than men, making up 52–54 percent of voters in most elections.

It is also true that in the segments of society that represent the future (professionals, young people, the highly educated), the participation gap between men and women practically disappears. Given the direction of history—toward postindustrial societies of educated professionals—one expects this male-female variation in political involvement to diminish with time.[4] For the moment, however, the evidence is clear. Politics is still largely a man's world, as it has been for all of human history, and that pattern has clear policy consequences. Imagine, for instance, how defense and welfare policies might differ if women instead of men made up 85 percent of Congress.[5]

Two other factors, **religion** and **ethnicity**, are often thought to bear on the likelihood that people will become politically active. Certainly, they both affect our *social* behavior in a variety of ways. Their impact on political engagement is complex, however, and can only be suggested here.

Perhaps the main impact of religion and ethnicity springs from their effect on social status, or **class**. What counts is NOT your specific religion or ethnic group. Rather, it is the *relative social standing* of that religion or group within the culture of which you are a part. Thus, American Catholics were less politically active than Protestants during much of the nineteenth century, but that was not simply because they were Catholic. It is because Catholics then were recent immigrants, working-class, and poor. *Most people* in those circumstances would be less politically active than average, whatever their religion. Where Catholics are in fact the dominant group (as in France), they have had no trouble getting deeply involved in politics.

Likewise, **minority ethnic** and racial groups, of whatever kind, especially those clearly despised by the majority, will be less politically active than average, mainly because most minority groups are poorer and lower in social status than average, and groups toward the lower end of the socioeconomic spectrum are usually not politically active.

Upon further investigation, many ethnic and religious minority groups are *more* active than one would expect—*if* one holds other variables constant. Thus, African-Americans vote in relatively low numbers, and one might at first glance attribute this to something in Black culture. On closer inspection, we find that Blacks are *more* likely to vote and in other ways participate in politics than are white Americans, if the variable of class is held constant.

That is, Black working-class Americans vote in greater percentages than do white working-class Americans; and Black middle-class Americans vote in greater percentages than do white middle-class Americans.

Why, then, does it *appear* that Blacks have a poor turnout rate? It is simply that the majority of them are working-class or lower on the social prestige scale, and working-class people everywhere do not participate much in politics (unless they are encouraged by strong unions and strong political parties, neither of which exist in the USA).

So the participation rate of African-American voters is weak because most of them are poor, not because of their culture or skin color. The real question is why their involvement is *higher* than average compared to typical white poor or working-class people. The reason has to do with **social identification**. Blacks (and minority group members in all cultures) are extremely conscious of their group identity. Most white Americans do not go around all day aware of their whiteness. Black Americans can hardly help but think regularly about their skin color. In like vein, Turks in Germany are constantly reminded that they are Turks, because they must routinely deal with discrimination—as do Kurds in Iraq, Koreans in Japan, and so forth.

Any kind of group identification makes you attuned to the way society, through its political mechanisms, can impinge on the daily life of your group—and on you. If you belong to the unchallenged majority, you take your condition for granted. Your status most of the time will affect your social and political choices only subliminally. Things are clearly different for minority group members. African-Americans (and German Turks and Iraqi Kurds) *know* that politics affects them frequently and seriously. Hence, compared to complacent and apathetic majority group members, they will be better informed about politics, more ready to get involved to defend themselves, and more willing to fight for improvements in their social condition.

These facts show the tremendous importance of social consciousness, **social identity**, in producing political participation. External circumstances alone (your class, e.g.) cannot explain everything about your likely behavior. It is also crucial to know what is going on in your head—how your consciousness processes the objective circumstance in which you find yourself.

Thus, if you are poor but do not particularly identify with any group, your social isolation usually leads to apathy and non-involvement. But it is different if you are poor with a strong group identity. Now you are more aware of your social situation, and you interact with people who provide suggestions for social and political action that could improve your lot. You might at least go vote for the candidate promising benefits to your group.

This line of reasoning helps explain why religious affiliation, like class, race, and ethnic identity, can impel people to political involvement. It is not

91

the specific religion that counts, but the degree of attachment to that religion. If you go to church, mass, synagogue, or mosque only once a month and that's it, your religion may have little impact on your behavior.

Things are different, however, if you are devoted to your religion, attend services regularly, try to follow its precepts, and organize daily life around its rituals. Then much of your behavior will reflect your religious creed. You will see connections between your beliefs and political issues of the day, and you will be more likely than other citizens to take political action on behalf of your religion's ideals. You will certainly show up on election day to vote for the "right" candidates.

This pattern, a deep connection to one's religion that leads to social action, is called **religiosity**. It has special impact on the *direction* of one's vote, the party and candidates that you will support. As we shall see in Chapter 7, religiosity usually produces conservative political action. Taking two people alike in every other manner, we'll find that the more "religious" citizen will also be more conservative.

Religiosity also affects the likelihood of political *involvement* (our topic here). The more pious members of society will also be more politically active.[6] It is hard to tell, unfortunately, just why that is the case. The most likely explanation stresses group connections. Strong identities of any kind induce social action, and some of that action will spill over into politics. All social connections lead us to develop ties to respected others and to group leaders that could ultimately involve us in social and political activities.

The importance of social ties

The richness of a person's group or social life has a huge impact on political activity. A way to summarize this complex variable is through the term "social rootedness" or **social connectedness**. Its effect on one's likelihood of political involvement is powerful.

It turns out that the more groups you belong to and the deeper your involvement in these groups, the greater will be your awareness of politics, your interest in politics, and your involvement with politics. Social activity has a carry-over effect. The more social you are, the more political you are. This finding makes sense, since politics itself is a social activity. Involvement in the political process grows naturally out of other social activities, even if they do not appear at first glance to have political implications.

It is easy to illustrate this link. Start with social isolates. They are among the least likely members of society to be politically active. In the extreme case, hermits will always be uninvolved in politics. Shy and introverted people won't become active either. Those with few social connections, who belong to no groups, who have few family ties, who live in isolated places, who are unemployed, who work with just a few others or by themselves: these people won't be much involved in politics either.

Group joiners, on the other hand, will be. The man or woman who belongs to the Kiwanis Club, the Chamber of Commerce, and the Literary Guild, who raises money for the United Fund, who volunteers for the Cub Scouts or Brownies, who coaches children in Little League sporting events—that person is much more likely to have political interests than the couch potato whose spare time is spent channel surfing.

Groups work in a variety of ways to channel people toward politics. Often, it is indirect. The more groups you are in, the more people you meet. The more people you meet, the more conversations you have. The more conversations you have, the more likely it is that a subject with political implications will arise.

While having coffee with friends, for instance, someone will mention that her car's front end was just jolted out of alignment after hitting a pothole in the street. Someone else will blame the "do-nothing" Mayor for "letting city streets go all to hell." A third person may chime in that it is not the Mayor's fault; "those cheap city councilors are to blame." Before you know it a full-fledged political conversation is under way.

In addition, socially oriented people, as a matter of course, discuss events of the day as reported by the local newspaper and the electronic media, and many of those events are politically charged. Hence, the socially active person is much more likely than the social isolate to be drawn into discourse that bears on politics. That stimulus will get most social joiners interested enough in politics at least to vote. For some, the frequency of talk about politics will lead them to discover an abiding personal interest.

Groups can have a direct, as well as indirect, effect on political involvement. The more people you know, the more likely it is that someone will think of you when a vacancy occurs on the neighborhood planning commission. Join enough groups, or stay in one long enough, and someone will inevitably ask you to help in the campaign of their cousin's daughter-in-law, who's running for School Board. People may even appreciate your qualities enough to suggest that you run for office yourself. Join lots of groups, in other words, and sooner or later you will get into politics.

Some groups are much more clearly oriented toward political issues than others. If you belong to one of those groups, you are much more likely than average to become politically involved. If you belong to a local hiking group, you *might* get drawn into politics. If you belong to an environmental organization, on the other hand, politics would impinge on your consciousness much more frequently. That would apply even if you joined for no political reason, but simply because of your desire to "clean up the environment" or "save the whales."

Other social groups take you even closer to politics. Labor unions and business associations (e.g., the Chamber of Commerce) are perhaps the best examples. You might belong to them originally for non-political reasons, but they will quickly raise your political consciousness. Union members are much more likely than non-unionized workers to show an interest in politics, to vote, and to engage in other political activities. Where labor unions are strong, working-class people are more involved in politics, better represented, and hence better treated (better working conditions, higher pay, longer vacations) than in places where unions are weak. (After all, people who are active in politics get attention from politicians.) In this regard, Swedish workers (85 percent unionized and politically active) are much better off, relative to the rest of their society, than are American workers (13 percent unionized and politically weak).

The ultimate example of the impact of groups on citizen involvement is the political party itself. Parties are social organizations, and their main purpose is precisely to spur political participation. It stands to reason that the stronger the party organization in any given place, the more citizen political involvement will occur. Conversely, places with weak parties will have low levels of citizen involvement.

Other factors in participation

The link between social connectedness and political activity can show up in roundabout ways. Certain objectively measurable aspects of life make you more or less likely to feel like an integrated, connected member of your society (hence, more likely to be political). The easiest of these variables to understand and quantify is **age**. The younger you are, the less likely you are to be a settled member of society with an investment in it and a sense of responsibility toward your community. Hence, you are less likely than older citizens to see reasons for political involvement.

Younger people, too, are less likely than middle-aged or older people to be group members. Think about it: Who joins the Elks, signs up to run the church auction, or volunteers to collect funds for the local hospital? It is usually people who have finished their education, have a steady job, settled down in a community, are married, and produce children. On the whole, young people escape the pressures and inducements toward political activity that social group membership provides.

Other things being equal, young people will participate in politics much less frequently than middle-aged or older people. In any typical American election, the voting rate of older people is often *twice* as high as for young people. In the election of 1996, for instance, under one-third of Americans aged 18–24 turned out to vote, compared with about two-thirds of those over 65. In the high-stimulus election of 2004, the percentage of citizens under 25 who voted rose to over 41 percent but still fell far short of the *70 percent* turnout rate among those 65 and older. In mid-term congressional elections, the age discrepancy becomes even more dramatic. Well under 20 percent of young people vote for their representatives in Congress during mid-term elections, while 60 percent of the elderly do.[7]

Purists find the voting rates of young people scandalous. How can they be such poor citizens, so unconnected to public life! To political scientists, the pattern makes sense. Young people do not participate much in politics, because their lives aren't as embedded in society as they will become in later years.

In the same way, *married people* and *homeowners* are also more involved in politics than single people and renters. The principle is clear. The bigger stake you have in society and the more conventional your ties to mainstream culture, the more you will develop those social connections that lead to political awareness and involvement.

This point leads to one of the fascinating findings of social science, one that has been characterized as "the more, the more" thesis.[8] Each variable affecting participation has a *cumulative* effect. In most nations, as we have seen, men are more likely to be politically active than women. So too will educated people be more active than less educated people, and upper-middle-class people more active than (non-unionized) workers. As individuals gain more of these participation-inducing traits, they become *much* more likely than average to exhibit political interest and get politically involved.

Thus, an *educated* **male** (two participationist attributes) is more likely than either the average male or the average educated person to show political interest. Similarly, the *educated, wealthy* **male** (three factors associated with participation) is *extremely* likely to become politically involved. Add a few other traits—an educated, wealthy male who is married with children, has owned the same house in the same community for three decades, and who belongs to a local business association—and you reach a near-statistical certainty that that person will be participating in politics well above the level of the average citizen.

The opposite principle holds true. The fewer you have of the characteristics associated with political involvement, the less likely it is that you will develop any connection to the world of politics. A poor, illiterate, rural, minority woman is one of the least likely people in the world to get involved in the political process. By no coincidence, this person is precisely the least likely everywhere to benefit from the output of that process. Governmental policies from Georgia to Ghana treat poor rural women as invisible. Politically speaking, that is exactly what they are.

Circumstances, too, affect participation

Education, class, gender, social connectedness are a few of the variables that explain why some people are more likely than others to develop an interest in politics and even become politically active. The really interesting question is: *why* do these variables have the effect they do? To answer that question, we must move into the realm of psychology.

We have already learned through the **B = f [OE] theorem**[9] that behavior is a function of not just our psychological predispositions, but also our external circumstances. To understand people's behavior in any given situation, you must understand their attitudes, values, personality traits *and* their circumstances. You cannot ignore either the psychological aspects of behavior (what's in the mind) or the social-economic-political circumstances (what's in the environment).

We know that a college-educated, middle-class professional is more likely to vote and attend political meetings than a high-school-educated factory worker. But what if the educated person lives in a dictatorship? What if the factory worker belongs to a strong union in a democracy? Other things are no longer equal. The dictatorial environment will discourage political participation by all but ardent supporters of the regime. The union environment will encourage participation, producing involvement by many who would otherwise remain on the sidelines.

Both situation and psychological predisposition affect behavior. To know why people act as they do, learn what they are like, but learn also the social setting in which they operate.

Personality factors

Education, class, gender, and social life connections all affect the likelihood of political involvement in two ways. First, they structure our environment. They help determine the community we live in, the messages we hear, and the people with whom we interact. Second, they exert a psychological impact. They influence the way we think about ourselves and the world. They do so for many reasons, but one stands out as vital. These forces affect our sense of "self-worth." Every study of political participation shows that those with self-confidence, a strong self-image, and a positive view of their own potential are the most likely people to become political participants.

Self-confidence derives from many sources. Genetic factors beyond the scope of political science surely play a role. But so do the variables we have been examining. Education, for example, provides the knowledge needed to understand politics. As a subject becomes easier to grasp, you are more apt to talk about it, read about it, get involved in it. Education increases your sense of **self-esteem** by giving you more knowledge and better reasoning powers. It helps you understand the world, thus enhancing your sense of competence and worth.

Education affects your self-image in other ways. For one thing, it helps you understand how public policies affect the circumstances of your own life. You can then act in public ways that might lead to improvement of your private conditions. Even for those who do not undertake specific political acts, increasing education leads to an improved sense of control. Simply understanding your environment makes you feel more competent, more self-confident.

Finally, education is linked to social status. The more education one has, the more money one makes, and the higher one's place on the social ladder. Naturally, increasing amounts of money and status enhance self-esteem. Better-educated people feel competent enough to jump into complex, conflict-ridden activities like politics that might confuse or frighten the less educated and less self-confident.

Social connectedness, like education, also makes one feel better about oneself and increases the likelihood of becoming politically effective. Involvement in a series of groups is apt to produce friends and supportive relationships. The more social ties you have and the more friends, the higher your self-esteem is likely to be. Group connections produce a sense of **social competence**—a psychological variable always associated with high levels of political interest and involvement.

Social connections also increase our capacity for **political efficacy**. The more people you know, especially the outgoing types you meet in voluntary community groups, the more likely it is that you will come to know political movers and shakers. At the least, you will get to know people who do know the politically influential. And there is nothing like knowing the Mayor, or a friend of the Mayor, to give you a sense that you possess some potential clout.

Social connectedness also helps you understand politics by providing realistic experiences about how social groups work. Loners do not get day-to-day experience in give-and-take, argument and debate, conflict and compromise. Socially active people gain skills in connecting with others, skills that are useful in political interactions. They also gain social knowledge and leadership skills that carry over naturally to political activity.

Of course, these variables work in the opposite direction as well. The less education you have and the fewer social ties, the lower your sense of self-esteem and political efficacy. Hence, the less likely you are to be politically active.

The point suggests why class and gender affect political activism. They strongly influence one's sense of self-worth. In most places throughout history, most men in the lower social rankings and nearly all women, whatever their status, have been taught to think poorly of themselves. Indeed, even today poor people and women in most societies learn in a thousand ways that society looks down upon them.

If others treat you with relentless negativism, it must have an impact. Humans are social beings. They develop images of themselves based on the way others see them. A constant barrage of criticism weakens the ego of all but the strongest personalities. Those subjected to a steady diet of scorn can hardly avoid the development of a negative self-image. If society has castigated you for much of your life, you normally won't develop the self-confidence needed for political involvement. Rather, you will develop a cynical, alienated view of society, and that outlook will produce withdrawal from social commitments, not entry into them.

An illustration

We now know a good deal about political participation. We will now apply our newly-gained knowledge to the real world. We should be able to figure out just where on this planet citizens will become activists and, equally interesting, where they will not.

Places of political activism are easy to predict. Participation will surely be high in countries (or sections of countries) that produce a well-off, educated citizenry. It will also be high in places that encourage tolerance. Where gender, race, religion, ethnicity and other artificial social distinctions are *not* used by some citizens to oppress others, the number of citizens with a severely negative self-image will be reduced and the chance that people will feel good about committing themselves to social action will increase.

Activity levels will also be high in places characterized by a wide variety of active, voluntary social groups. Especially where strong labor, farm, and business associations exist, we expect to find significant citizen involvement in politics. Where political parties are strong and employ aggressive mechanisms of social recruitment, we will also find high levels of citizen activism. Finally, we will expect to find high levels of political participation in places where citizens are older than average (preferably over 30) and reasonably stable in their habits (married, own property, do not move often).

Correspondingly, citizen political involvement will be lower in places inhabited by poor, uneducated people hampered by a host of discriminatory social distinctions, especially those based on gender, class, religion, race, and ethnicity. Activism will also be muted where social organizations are weak to nonexistent, including the absence of economic and political organizations such as unions and parties.

These, of course, are general rules. Exceptions always exist. They tease our minds as we think of them, and they lead us to expand or revise the general rules. It turns out, for instance, that participation in politics has always been high in the American state of Maine, where I live, even though it does *not* rank high on several of the variables which appear necessary for high levels of citizen activism. For instance, Maine has never ranked very high on national indicators of wealth and education.

To understand the high levels of citizen involvement in Maine, one must add one more factor to the equation. Social scientists often call it a **sense of civic duty**. This phrase delineates an attitude of obligation, of responsibility for getting involved in public affairs. People with this outlook will argue that "good citizens are supposed to take part in the life of their community." To the extent that you believe in this precept, to the extent that it has been hammered home in your family, in your school, in the town where you grew up, you will act on it as an adult. At the very least, you will vote regularly, show up for the occasional public meeting, and perhaps communicate from time to time with your mayor, governor, or senator.

The opposite of civic duty is cynicism and distrust. Political scientists often label this attitude **political alienation**. If officials are stupid, corrupt, and uncaring, states the cynic, what is the sense of activism? It does not matter who gets into office, they will all be concerned with lining their own pockets, not representing us or doing what's right. Why bother to vote or make an effort to influence these crooks? You cannot have an impact (unless you are willing to play by their dirty rules), so why waste your time?

Where citizen alienation is high, one expects less political participation than in places where a strong sense of civic duty prevails. An ethos of citizen responsibility, plus a trust in the motives of public officials, predominates in Maine, a state with a strong moralistic tradition inherited from early Pilgrim settlers.[10] By no coincidence, Maine led the nation in voter turnout at the 1992 election. (Of all adult Mainers, 72 percent voted, compared with 55 percent of all Americans.) Maine came in third (behind Minnesota and Wisconsin) in 2004. For any given election, it usually ranks in the top five states for percentage of eligible citizens who go to the polls.

By way of contrast, turnout rates are much lower in Maryland, a state much wealthier and better educated than Maine and therefore "objectively" one that should produce higher turnout rates. This state, however, is characterized by widespread levels of citizen cynicism, feelings that government officials do not care about average citizens, and a belief that most politicians are corrupt and self-serving. These attitudes reflect, in the terms of Daniel Elazar, an "individualistic" sub-culture.[11] Holding political attitudes of cynicism and distrust, many Marylanders do not bother to show up at election time. Psychological factors thus weigh heavily in explaining the Maine–Maryland differential in turnout rates.

Table 6.1 shows clearly that Mainers are not only much more participatory than people from Maryland, but also more active than New Yorkers and Californians, two other sets of people wealthier and better educated than residents of Maine. In 1993, I published a comparable table for these same four states, using data for the 1980s.[12] The results were exactly the same. Maine, while poorer and less educated than the other three states, had significantly higher turnout rates in both presidential and congressional elections. Once embedded, cultural norms have long-lasting effects.

Social life turns out to be highly complex. Those looking for single-variable explanations will always be disappointed. We need many variables to explain any sociopolitical pattern. There's an up-side to all this. For those trying to make sense of the political process, solving the puzzle of cause and effect provides an endless source of fascination.

Table 6.1 The effect of political culture: Selected data comparing Maine to three other American States.*

State	Median household income, 2003 (US$)	Education level, 2000 (%)†	Voter turn-out, 2004 (%)	Voter turn-out, 2002 (%)
Maine	39,212	22.9	73.4	50.8
MD	54,302	31.4	63.7	46.3
NY	44,139	27.4	57.5	36.1
CA	48,440	26.6	60.0	36.1
US	43,318	24.4	60.9	39.5

* Data on income and education for this table was gathered from the US Census Bureau (see, in particular, their website: http://quickfacts.census.gov/qfd/states/ (accessed October, 2006). Data on voting turnout was gathered from the US Elections Project, an excellent database overseen by political scientist Michael McDonald; see: http://elections.gmu.edu/voter_turnout.htm (accessed October, 2006).
† "Education level" equals the percentage of the adult population aged 25 and older holding a college degree in 2000.

Conclusion

Objective social variables (e.g., class, gender, race) affect political involvement by inducing or undermining the *subjective* self-confidence needed for that quintessentially social action: political participation. Those on whom society smiles most brilliantly (well-educated, successful, majority-group males) develop the inner self-confidence *and* the social connections that make political involvement easy and natural.

For others, people who are *not* told daily by society to think highly of themselves, social connectedness can help produce the same results as high social status or a good education. Close friends and group leaders stroke the ego and make one feel good about oneself. They induce those feelings of self-esteem without which political activity becomes daunting, something to avoid.

Figure 6.1 sums up what we have learned about the factors likely to encourage or inhibit political participation.

Questions for discussion

1   What difference does it make who gets involved in politics? (*Hint*: Why are government policies so generous for the elderly and so stingy for students?)
2   Since education levels have been increasing for years, shouldn't we expect participation rates to be correspondingly rising?
3   Why are women more likely to participate in politics in wealthier than in poorer countries?

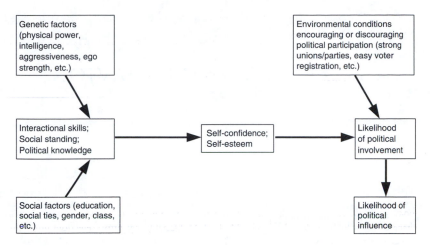

Figure 6.1 Simplified schema for understanding the causes of political participation.

4 The author states that alienation leads to non-involvement. Why
   wouldn't it lead to someone being mad at the world and therefore eager
   to get into politics to change things?
5 The author argues that Maine is more participatory than it "should be,"
   given its socioeconomic circumstances. What other states or regions
   would you expect to be more activist than average—and why? What
   places would you expect to have low levels of citizen involvement?

7

CITIZEN VOTING BEHAVIOR

Whether to participate in politics is one question. Once you decide to enter the political arena, you face another issue. *How* are you going to act?

In theory, one can imagine a host of activities open to the political participant. You can merely *discuss politics* from time to time with your friends. You can move on from there to pay serious attention to politics and to *vote* regularly. A step past discussing, information-gathering, and voting is *persuasion*, an active effort to bring others to your point of view.

Persuading activity can take lots of time. You can write letters to your local newspaper, to the mayor, even to your senator and the president. You can go on from there to join political groups, attend political rallies, and help candidates for office. At the deepest level of commitment, you might run for office yourself.

Although we can imagine many different political acts, most of them take place at one of three levels.

1   At its simplest, at the level typical of most **citizens** everywhere, politics occurs only in the occasional conversation and in the period around elections. Average citizens do talk about political matters from time to time—when the subject comes up—with friends, neighbors, and colleagues. They will also express their attitudes toward current political events in that formal societal rite we call an election. Once in a great while, usually during a crisis of some kind, they may get briefly caught up in more extended political activity. Then they may attend a political rally or write a letter to some political figure. But most of the time most citizens think and do little about politics.

2   It takes a serious commitment to move past this simple talking-voting activity to a higher level of involvement. It is no surprise, then, that the number of participants drops dramatically at this stage. Here we find the **political activists**. These people spend huge blocks of time following politics in the media, discussing it in detail with like-minded friends, going to political meetings, joining organized political groups, attending

rallies, and donating time and money on issues they support and candidates they admire.

Political activists vary enormously. Some are the stereotypical "good citizens performing their civic duty." Some are the stereotypical "opportunists hoping to enrich themselves." But simplistic images like these distort reality. Like most people, those interested in politics display a mix of motives and a range of personalities.

Activists enter political life from desires as basic as wanting a job to interests as abstract as wanting to promote a political philosophy. Some are seeking to make friends, some want to change a given policy, some hope to promote their careers, and some just love the political "game." In all cases, the action of citizen participants is supremely "political." That is, like most human behavior, it is self-interested and likely to promote conflict with others who hold differing aims and interests.

3   At the highest level of political involvement are **political leaders**. The intensity of their commitment goes beyond the efforts of political activists. Leaders devote most of their lives and most of their resources to politics. It is not something they do on a part-time, in–out basis. For years, they spend many of their waking hours in political endeavors. It is a career for them, their life's work. People at this *leadership* level have a passion for politics that sets them off from the garden-variety political participant.

When George H.W. Bush left politics (unwillingly) in January, 1993, it had been nearly three decades since he began full-time political work by running for the US House, from Texas. Lyndon Johnson left the Presidency (again, unwillingly) in 1969; he had first been elected to Congress in the late 1930s. A gentleman named Carl Hayden represented Arizona in our nation's capital from the time his state was admitted to the Union in *1912* until he finally retired in 1968 at 91 years old.[1] Robert Byrd was first elected to the West Virginia legislature in 1946; he has been a US Senator from that state since 1953, having held elective office continuously for 60 years. (He is still a Senator as I write these words.)

These examples only scratch the surface. At this level (the political elite), we find people who spend decades in public life, who live (and sometimes die) for political causes. Existence holds little meaning for these individuals outside of politics.

Given their intensity of commitment, these elite activists are going to find their way to power. They will assume leadership positions at every level, from town councils to presidencies, from local citizen groups to international lobbies. Their single-minded focus insures that they will gain power and influence far beyond their numbers in the population. This group of **Influentials** is so important that I later devote several chapters to their ideas, personalities, and behavior patterns.[2]

Participation levels in perspective

To recapitulate, political activity can encompass:

- no action or next to no action
- a modest level of involvement (occasional discussions, voting)
- a serious level of commitment, involving a regular set of political actions either for conventional aims or for radical system change
- a deep and intense lifetime commitment to gaining political power and influencing political outcomes.

Figure 7.1 summarizes the argument. It makes clear that participation in politics occurs at several levels. Each level of involvement requires a much greater voluntary output of energy and much greater use of personal resources than the preceding level.[3]

At the lowest level of involvement are citizens unwilling to invest even minimal effort to the political enterprise. They have, for whatever reason, no interest in politics. This lack of interest is closely related to a lack of political skill.[4] These people often have few of the resources (knowledge, money, connections) needed to make an impact on politics. They are usually not just political isolates, but social and economic isolates as well.

At a level of energy somewhat beyond these political **apathetics** stands a vast group of marginally involved **citizens**. They will, in most countries most of the time, include the majority of the population. These people have some idea of what is happening in politics, pay some attention to political events, and invest a modest level of energy in political action. Those acts consist primarily of occasional political discussions, paying some attention to political developments during election campaigns, and tuning in to the discussion during other critical moments in their country's history. *Their most important act is to vote.* In so doing, they distribute power among the deeply-involved activists and the political leaders of their society, thereby determining policy outcomes for everyone.

At a much more intense level of activism, we find that set of committed party workers, campaign volunteers, interest group members, and all-around political junkies who constitute the core membership of political groups everywhere. Depending on how liberally we define intense political activity, these **participants** will normally include 10–20 percent of any country's citizenry.

Finally, at the top of the ladder, we find those activists who form society's leadership pool. These **Influentials** are the people who devote their adult lives to politics and who, as a result, gain a disproportionate share of the power positions that allow them to influence policy outcomes. All existing evidence suggests that these people will always form a tiny percentage of the population—probably about 1 per cent but possibly 2–3 percent, depending (again) on how liberally we define full-time political activism.

Estimates of the number of people in each category (see Figure 7.1) are based on a wide range of data. The numbers are not (and cannot be) precise. They represent a range of possibility. That is because political involvement itself is not stable. Participation will vary from era to era, country to country.

In a period of stability, such as the USA experienced in the 1950s, the number of people found toward the lower end of the pyramid (the inactive and the marginally active) will be larger than it will be in a period of upheaval and activism such as the late 1960s. Similarly, the number of active citizens will be larger in countries that encourage participation and provide the resources for participation than in countries that discourage participation and fail to provide the monetary and educational resources that make participation likely and possible.

Still, our conclusion stands. In all places and at all times, a serious minority of any country's population, at least a fifth and up to two fifths, will simply remain outside the political system, uninvolved other than as subjects. They will occasionally be touched by the effects of government policy, but will never influence that policy. I have labeled this group the **Apathetics**. (Some prefer the term **Disaffecteds**.)

A larger group in the population will be somewhat more active. People in this group talk about politics, vote, and occasionally take other political action. They will usually represent over half the population of any country. In straightforward manner, let's call them **Citizens**. When conjoined with Apathetics, they form the vast majority of people in any political system.[5]

Next, those people who work actively in politics (**Participants**) will usually make up one-tenth of any nation's citizenry, rising to perhaps one-fifth of the population in wealthy, educated countries or in countries undergoing serious levels of political turmoil. Though always remaining a minority, their impact should never be underestimated. For one thing, their actual *numbers* can be large. Just 10 percent of all adult Americans, for example, equals well over *20 million* people. No social analyst and certainly no politician will ever ignore a chunk of the population that large. In addition, people in this group are so much more active than Citizens and Apathetics that they have an enormous impact on political decision-making.

Finally, the number of people at the leadership level (Influentials) will always be tiny. Humanity is numerous, interests are diverse, and career options are many. Given the myriad ways to make your living and spend your spare time, only a small number of people will ever be attracted to *any* specialized career path. Every society produces artists and actors, bankers and bakers, mechanics and lawyers, astronomers and politicians, but no society produces a profusion of any of these. Human beings have varied interests, different tastes, and diverse skills. The number of people who both *love* politics and *excel* at it will always be small.

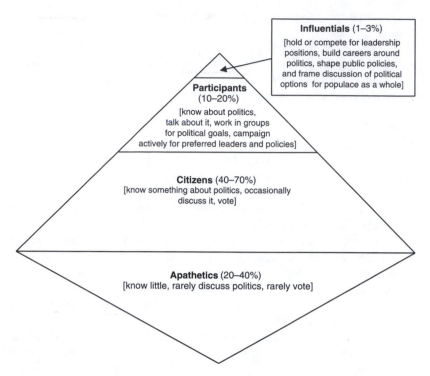

Figure 7.1 A schema for illustrating political participation: The typical distribution of a nation's citizens.

Existing evidence suggests that the number of Influentials will always be at least one percent of the population.[6] (You need about that number of people just to staff, and compete for, the major leadership positions in any society.) On the other hand, it will rarely get beyond the three percent level. For one thing, there is simply no need for that many full-time activists, so when numbers reach the 2–4-percent stage, many people will find themselves never attaining the offices they want or having the influence over outcomes they seek. They are likely then to slip back a level or two in political commitment (becoming Participants or just plain Citizens), while finding other ways to pursue a career and spend their free time.

A closer look at citizen types

We need to take a closer look at the groups sketched above. The least time will be spent on Apathetics. Being outside the political realm, these people have little impact on it. We can only note that most members of this group are already disadvantaged in many ways. They are poor, poorly educated, often members of disliked minority groups, and more likely than average to be women. They often live in poor, rural areas or in the worst slums of big cities.

Apathetics

These people are already hurt by the normal processes of their society. Their lack of political activism hurts them all the more. If they did get involved and pushed for beneficial policies, they could end up better off. Still, they are unlikely to do this. They have few resources that could prove valuable in the political realm. Remember, they lack money, social skills, and education. They also lack motivation. With no interest in politics, they simply pay no attention to it. Certainly, they do not organize and act on political matters.

As concerned human beings, we can feel sorry for people in this category. We can hope that they will find ways to move competently into the political sphere. We can go further and undertake policies to diminish their numbers (improve education, reduce poverty, eliminate discrimination). But as political analysts, we can do little but ignore this group. It does not act politically, and it has little impact on political life. We must move on to examine people whose behavior does impinge on the political process.[7]

Citizens

These people, too, remain inactive for extended periods of time, but their numbers alone keep us from ignoring them in our effort to grasp how politics works. Beyond that, we *must* pay close attention to their behavior, because when it does occur, it comes at momentous moments in a nation's history and produces policy and personnel decisions of the greatest significance. One thinks, for example, of the French Revolution, American support for the New Deal in the 1930s, and the overthrow of the Shah in Iran in 1979. All these events occurred because previously-passive citizens became mobilized to action.

Can we draw any hard and fast conclusions about how that 40–70 percent of society behaves when it does enter the political arena? To simplify our response, let's restrict the focus to a single action: voting. Although most Citizens occasionally engage in other activities, voting is the one act they all undertake regularly. It is their one action with collective impact on the political system. What factors determine the way this large and crucial group will behave in any election?

To answer, we must recall our old friend, the $\mathbf{B = f\ [OE]}$ equation. People's behavior results from their psychology (what's in their heads) *and* from the situations in which they are called upon to act. We will begin with the psychological or attitudinal side of the equation. Why do people develop the attitudes toward politics that cause them to vote as they do?

107

We know the power of early-learned norms and deeply-ingrained cultural expectations. Those attitudes we absorb while young, almost by osmosis, through unquestioning acceptance of the outlook of everyone around us, will have the deepest impact and the longest influence on our way of thinking. What forces will have a special power to shape our world outlook?

The number of influences on our attitude toward life could, obviously, be large. It turns out that *a handful of factors have special influence on the way people understand politics*. These influences can be summarized in the key words: *culture, class, religion, race, ethnicity, gender, region, and age*.

Sociologists usually call these **demographic variables**. Each term implies a set of common experiences that people within the category have undergone. These experiences have a formative impact in shaping world outlooks.

To illustrate, few would dispute that gender has a lot to do with how you think and behave. Imagine how different your life would be if you woke up tomorrow as a member of the opposite sex. If your imagination is weak, go to your local video store and rent *Tootsie, Yentl, Switch*, or *Victor, Victoria*, among many other films on this theme. You will quickly see how people get treated differently, and then start acting and thinking differently, when they are believed to be male instead of female, or vice versa.

Likewise, imagine how different your life would have been, had you been born into a different racial group, or into a different class, religion, or region. Even age has a serious impact on our perspectives. As a youth, I scoffed at the idea of buying insurance, getting tied down to a mortgage, and putting money aside for retirement. Those ideas make a lot of sense to me now.

These variables, while not the only influences on our world outlook, have all played key roles in shaping our central values. They are especially powerful in determining our political preferences. They help explain where most of us will be located along a continuum of political belief known as the traditional **Left–Right spectrum**.

The political spectrum

This concept plays a central role in the study of politics. What exactly does it mean? In the next two chapters, we explore questions of belief and ideology in detail. They are vital for understanding how Activists and Influentials think. Here we need give only a brief summary of the concepts, because most Citizens do not particularly think in the ideological terms associated with **Left** and **Right**. However, when they take their most common political action and *vote*, they are forced to choose from among options presented them by political participants who *do* deeply believe in the Left–Right spectrum. Thus, the *effect* of most voters' actions is to dole out policy-making power to Influentials and their backers (Participants), who *do* think of themselves as situated somewhere along this continuum. Knowing about it, then, is vital for an understanding of politics in the modern world.

The words Left and Right—along with supplementary terms like Center, Extreme Left, Center–Right, and so on—constitute a common language, a shorthand, for political activists everywhere. They help participants situate themselves in the political arena. They allow politicians to identify friends and enemies. And they help observers make sense of the Byzantine world we call politics.

Knowing the origin of these terms helps clarify their meaning. The words "Left" and "Right" came into usage during the French Revolution, that cataclysmic event which, in many ways, signaled the birth of the modern world. When Louis XVI called parliament into session in 1789, that body (the Estates General) had not met for over 100 years. It had no established traditions and few precedents to guide its operations. One of the many questions it had no immediate answer for was: "Who will sit where?" As it turned out, the more radical members of the assembly, those most eager to upset the old social order, began sitting (purely by chance) on the left side of the hall—that is, to the Assembly President's left as he looked toward the chamber from his central podium.

Now where would you sit if you supported the status quo? If you backed the king and aristocracy, accepted the entrenched power of the Catholic Church, scorned the "upstart" middle-classes, and feared the "unenlightened" peasantry, where would *you* sit? Naturally, you would put some distance between you and the "radical loonies" over there on the *left* side of the meeting-room. You and your like-thinking buddies would move far away, to sit the *right* side of the hall, in fact—as distant from the radicals as you could get.

That is exactly what happened. **Radicals** sat to the Speaker's left, **Reactionaries** to his right. Naturally, **moderate** legislators had little choice but to sit somewhere between the two warring factions. They ending up taking the center seats and quickly became known as **Centrists**.

These seating arrangements occurred first by accident, then by choice. Finally, they became a long-established tradition. For decades in French politics you could pinpoint any legislator's exact degree of radicalism or **conservatism** by observing just where in the legislative chamber that person ended up sitting.

Beyond France, the power of the French Revolution was amazing. Not only did these terms, specific to the French case, sweep around the world at the time, they still retain their significance in the political discourse of most countries today. Indeed, many assemblies around the world even retain the seating arrangements adopted by the Third Estate in 1789 (a semicircular hall with parties seated left to right to indicate their degree of radicalism). Parliaments with an Anglo-Saxon tradition (Britain, Canada, Australia, New Zealand) provide an exception to this rule. There, governing and opposition parties face each other across an aisle. In both houses of the US Congress, the semi-circle arrangement holds, but a wide center aisle separates Democrats from Republicans, and (oddly) Democrats (the more Left party) sit on the right side of the presiding officer.

So much for history. What do these terms mean today? To answer, we must recall what they meant at the time of the French Revolution:

LEFT	**A radical change in the status quo** ("Off with their heads!")
RIGHT	**A rigid adherence to the status quo** ("Keep the masses in their place!")
CENTER	**Modest reforms within the existing system** ("Can't we all sit down and talk about this?")

Their meaning has changed little in the intervening 200 years.

The simplest way to understand the Left position is to see it as advocating a **redistribution of values**. In every country, Leftists want to provide more to the "have-nots," usually at the expense of the "haves." At its most radical, the Left wants to overthrow, abolish, or even kill the "haves." In less radical formulations, Leftists are content simply to narrow the gap between those who have and those who do not. In all cases, their sympathies lie with the disadvantaged, with those folks who have less, usually a lot less, of the goodies that society has to offer.

Rightists, of course, take the opposite perspective. They usually believe that the current structure of society represents an ideal set-up. It may be the product of wise, rational, and benevolent decision-making by legendary historical figures. It may derive from the successful social evolution of a sensible society. It may represent God's will for humankind. For whatever reason, conservatives generally approve of society in its current form and would change it little.

Centrists stand somewhere between these two perspectives. They are willing to accept some change in the status quo, but they do not want to go too fast or too far. They will accept incremental, marginal reforms to help the disadvantaged. They may be willing to chip away at, but they do not want to destroy, the position of the well-off.

Even in socialist and communist countries, these terms retain some of their original meaning. Lenin, that ultimate "Far-Leftist," lashed out at various times in his career against "Right-wing" Marxists (e.g., the Mensheviks) and "Left-wing" Communists (whom he called "infantile"). For Lenin, even some Marxists were too accepting of the status quo (too conservative, too "Right"), while some were too revolutionary (so far "Left") as to be unrealistic about what could realistically be achieved.[8]

One cannot emphasize enough the depth of the Left–Right schism over the *redistribution of values*. Values can refer to anything a given society holds in esteem: honor, piety, power, wealth, land, or cows. In every society in every era, some people have more than others of what society treasures. Leftists want to redistribute those treasures: more to the many, less to the few. Rightists want to keep the existing distribution intact.

This concept of the redistribution of values is a powerful one. It explains the difference between Right and Left on a vast array of issues in our current age. Take, for example, that salient topic, the treatment of women.

What has the **Feminist movement** been all about? Simple: it has supported a redistribution of social values—*from* men, *to* women. Until the last decade or two, men (compared with women) had vastly more power, status, money, legal rights, and even the psychological self-confidence that goes with the knowledge that you are favored. At first feminists alone (one segment of the Left), and then nearly all Leftists, came to decry that lack of balance as unfair and unjust. They wanted to redistribute values, so that women could make more money, have better jobs, and gain better treatment all around.

Rightists, of course, reacted angrily to any suggestion that the status quo (from about 1950, when women supposedly stayed at home and managed families) was anything other than moral, just, natural, and a product of God's will. Women were *supposed* to stay home, make no money, and change diapers all day. Separate and unequal gender roles were what nature (and the Lord) intended.

We all know the arguments on both sides of this issue. This is not the place to rehash them. Rather, you should see them in a new light. They reflect the debate between Left and Right, between pro-status-quo and anti-status-quo forces, between those seeking to redistribute values and those opposed to a redistribution.

Once you understand the Left–Right continuum and the principle on which it is based, you can see that a large number of issues that previously stood by themselves in your mind, needing individual explanation, can now be placed in a context and given perspective. For instance, you should now have no trouble understanding what Rightists and Leftists think of labor unions or the civil rights movement—and why.

As a general rule, any group challenging the status quo for rewards it claims to deserve will be considered as somewhere on the Left side of the political spectrum. Such groups would include handicapped people, gays, ethnic minorities, feminists, and union members. Any group resisting change and defending a currently held advantage will be considered as occupying a Right-wing political position. Business leaders, landowners, and church hierarchies would typify these groups.

The diagram in Figure 7.2 provides a simple summary of the Left–Right spectrum. Well-known political groupings cluster at various points along this continuum. Of particular interest to American politics, liberals are found in the Center–Left position, conservatives in the Center–Right.

Of course, the world of political ideology is more complicated than we can show here. (Chapters 8 and 9 address some of these complexities.) Still, we cannot leave the topic without adding one or two additional points. First, things are never as simple as just saying that there is a Right and a Left side to all issues. Remember that Right and Left exist on a continuum. People shift along that continuum, depending on the issue and their own circumstances. Often they fall into a gray area toward the center. Few people take extreme positions at one end or the other.

In most stable systems (especially the polyarchies), people cluster near the center, moving from there mostly to the moderate Left or moderate Right. In these centrist-oriented systems, debate takes place among moderates, Center–Rightists, and Center–Leftists. Policy proposals with the most serious chance of adoption will fit somewhere in the space between the moderate Left and the moderate Right.

Finally, this Left/Right perspective on politics does not explain everything. Some issues cannot easily be placed on this continuum. The intergroup hatreds and conflicts that arise from religious, ethnic, and racial differences may be related to redistribution matters (usually one group resents another for having more), but they are also deeply rooted in the kind of psychological bias we have already examined. People who are different are automatically distrusted. This distrust leads to resentment on both sides, and conflict is sure to follow, regardless of anyone's ideology. The ideas of Left and Right have little to do with intergroup hatreds.

Other issues too fail to fit neatly along the Left–Right continuum: the ethics of public officials; questions of war and peace; some policies involving public goods, such as a national system of parks and campgrounds, along with environmental issues; and "lifestyle" questions, such as the legalization of marijuana. Chapter 9 introduces a more sophisticated way of categorizing issues and participants that takes account of policy disputes outside the traditional struggles over economic distribution.[9]

We can learn much, however, by working with the standard Left–Right spectrum. It helps a great deal to know that when Citizens go to the polls, they are choosing from among a set of parties that *see themselves* as aligned somewhere along a straightforward ideological continuum. Depending on which parties they select, voters will get policies that are either more conservative or more liberal. The big question now becomes: What exactly causes people to choose parties on the Right, the Left, or the Center?

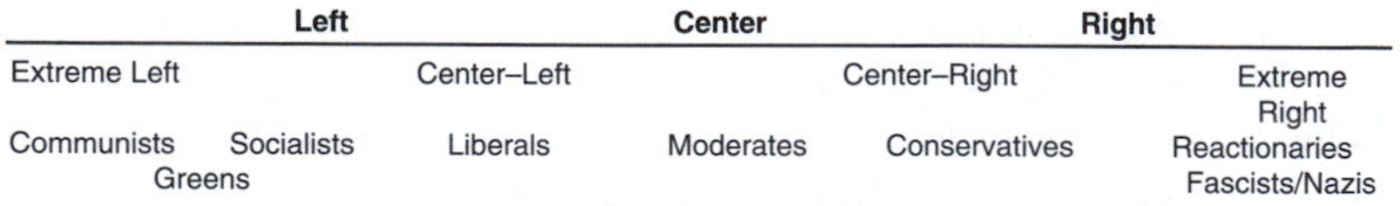

Left		Center		Right
Extreme Left	Center–Left		Center–Right	Extreme Right
Communists Socialists Greens	Liberals	Moderates	Conservatives	Reactionaries Fascists/Nazis

Figure 7.2 The Left–Right spectrum: A diagram for understanding political positions in the modern world.

Who votes how—and why?

My wife and I attended a convention in Chicago a few years ago. At the end of a cold, February day, we dressed up, donned our good winter coats, and left the hotel to find a restaurant. Just outside the lobby stood a ragged black man seeking handouts. We ignored his pleas for "spare change," but before we could move far down the sidewalk, he tried a different pitch. "Please," he called after us. "I'm a Republican!"

Class and voting behavior

What is so telling about this story? Put simply, it supports a basic myth: social standing determines political preference. To this poor man, we looked rich. Therefore, we must be conservative.

Like all myths, this one is based in reality. Right-of-Center conservative parties *are* closely aligned with people in the higher-income brackets. These parties do not want to upset the status quo. They also believe that wealthy people should be allowed to keep their wealth intact. If you were well-off, wouldn't these ideas appeal to you? It seems, at first glance, that citizens with more money than average should be ardently supporting conservative political parties.

On the whole, this expectation holds. *The higher one's position in society, the more likely one is to take a conservative, or Right-of-Center, political stand.* Thus, a middle-class person might be a moderate, while someone in the upper-middle-class would be conservative, and an aristocrat reactionary.

The same line of reasoning leads people who are less well-off to line up with Left-of-Center parties. Those parties, after all, advocate a redistribution of resources *from* the better-off *to* the indigent. They want high levels of taxation on the rich, low or no taxes for the poor, and social policies that help working citizens rather than business owners. It makes perfect sense, then, to postulate that *the lower one's socioeconomic standing in any society, the more likely one is to vote for parties of the Left.* Under this logic, better-off workers will support liberals, unskilled workers will vote socialist, and the poorest people will lean toward communism.

These patterns hold true, in general. Of course, life is never this tidy. Spock in the *Star Trek* series never tires of noting that "humans are not logical." Some people just do not behave as, in theory, they "should." One finds many rich liberals; one finds even more poor conservatives. The connection between social status and political loyalty is a tendency, not a law.

This tendency, however, does hold up well in most places. In nearly any nation that allows free elections, you will make money betting that rich people vote to the Right and poor people to the Left. Just do not be surprised to come across numerous exceptions.

The tendency is further complicated by different historical developments in one place or another. As a result, the meaning of "voting Left" or "voting Right" can vary from country to country. Where class sentiment is strong and party options are many, there may be a dozen serious parties providing nuanced alternatives across the spectrum. France has traditionally been a country with many political options. The poorest workers there did vote communist, while the better-off workers voted socialist, and so on, up the ladder. That's because many parties existed, filling spaces all across the traditional Left–Right continuum.

In the USA, we see a dramatic contrast. Since the 1860s, Americans (for a host of reasons) have had just two parties with any chance of gaining power: Democrats and Republicans.[10] These parties face a generally moderate electorate, with voters grouping mostly in the Center. Since both parties must attract centrists to win elections, neither moves far to the Left or Right. Thus, when American workers decide to vote "Left," they have only one practical choice: the moderately liberal Democratic Party.

In the same vein, when business people choose to vote "Right," they must opt for the moderately conservative Republican Party. The worldwide pattern does hold true for the USA—wealthier people vote Right and poorer people vote Left—but the meaning, and the political impact, of those choices is quite different in the USA than in France, where one can vote for a range of parties from Far-Right to Far-Left.

Americans have a restricted set of party choices, while the French have a much broader range. It turns out that the French pattern is much closer than the American to typifying the situation in stable polyarchies around the world. *The general rule for democratic societies is this: At election time, voters can choose from among several parties, and at least four or five of those parties have a reasonable chance of participating in the next government.* The USA, often an exception, proves once again unique. No other polyarchy provides citizens with just two "serious" options.[11]

Whether a country has 2 or 20 parties, however, our general point holds everywhere. Class affects voting behavior; the lower one's socioeconomic status, the more likely one is to vote for Left-oriented parties, and the higher one's status, the more likely one is to vote to the Right.

Examples of this rule are abundant. In the 1992 election, 59 percent of those whose family income was under US$15,000 voted for Clinton, while only 36 percent of those in families making over US$75,000 voted for him. To reverse the point, 48 percent of voters in wealthy families (over US$75,000) voted for Bush, but only 23 percent of the poorest voters (from families making under US$15,000) did so.

Indeed, if voting in the USA in 1992 had been restricted to people from families making at least US$50,000 a year, George Bush (senior) would have been re-elected handily.[12] In the same vein, if only citizens making under US$50,000 a year had voted in 2004, John Kerry would have become president.[13] One major voting study puts it clearly: "High-income Americans have consistently . . . been more prone to identify with and vote for the Republican Party than have low-income Americans, who have sided with the Democrats."[14] And another study concludes that "income divisions [in American politics] are more important now than in earlier decades."[15]

The class factor can be seen even more dramatically in the UK. There, 54 percent of working-class voters opted for the Labor Party in the 1983 election, but only 28 percent of them voted Conservative. In France, 72 percent of the working class voted for one Left-wing option or another during the 1981 Presidential election, while only 17 percent voted for a Rightist candidate. These are merely examples. The same pattern can be found nearly everywhere one looks.[16]

Further considerations on class

Class is by no means the only variable needed to explain voting behavior. For one thing, recalling the $B = f [OE]$ equation, we know that the *environment* within which an election takes place also affects how people vote. One element of that environment is the number of parties and their positions on the ideological continuum. Disadvantaged voters in America vote only as far "Left" as Bill Clinton, Al Gore, John Kerry (or in a few cases, Ralph Nader), whereas disadvantaged voters in Bologna, Italy, have frequently voted much further Left—for Socialists and even Communists. The less-well-off in any society will vote Left, but just *how far* Left will depend on the available political options.

American culture is so centrist and moderate that proponents of even the mildest form of socialism have little chance of gaining votes.[17] In some cultures, however, socialism and communism have been perfectly respectable options and able to garner widespread support.

So a "Left" vote in the USA means something entirely different from a "Left" vote in France, say, or in India. Still, the basic axiom holds: Wherever elections take place, the lower your social status, the more likely you are to vote Left, *whatever* Left happens to mean in your particular environment. As a corollary, the lower your status, the *farther* to the Left you will vote—*if* you have options among several plausible Left-of-Center parties. Thus, well-paid, skilled workers in Europe are likely to vote Socialist, while poorly-paid, unskilled workers are more likely to vote Communist.

A second *caveat* is needed to put class influence into perspective. Remember that in discussing the variables that induce or inhibit participation in politics, we began with objective factors (gender, level of education) and found it necessary to move on from those to *subjective* ones. Similarly, when it comes to ideology, choice of political position depends on subjectivity as much as objective social circumstances.

Remember that "ideas believed to be true will have true consequences." A sociologist's flat assertion that based on their jobs and income, Jacques is a member of the "working-class," while Gertrude is "middle-class," means little for understanding the behavior of Jacques and Gertrude if *they* do not define themselves that way. It may turn out that Jacques, the worker, is a conservative, admires business acumen, and votes Right-wing in each election, while Gertrude, the rich man's daughter, sympathizes with the underdog, reads Marx regularly, and travels around the world organizing demonstrations for Greenpeace. To understand how people will behave, we must focus not on "reality," but on how people interpret reality.

For example, we know that people in working-class circumstances will normally vote Left—that is, in a radical, anti-business direction. In France, this pattern holds quite well, until one comes upon workers in the industrial areas of Alsace-Lorraine. These laborers, it turns out, have a long tradition of voting for Gaullists and other conservative politicians. Why?

It appears that these workers are deeply religious Catholics, people who live in an area that has long accepted Church ritual and teachings. One of those teachings stresses humility and submission to secular authorities, including one's boss. Workers raised in these beliefs are unlikely to be attracted to the radical anti-system doctrines pushed by parties of the Left.

Thus, for psychological rather than economic reasons, one finds conservative workers. Likewise, we can find liberals and radicals who are affluent. Lots of middle-class (or higher) citizens identify downward (in a sense) and vote Left. They act politically as if they were members of the working-class.

Intellectuals are perhaps the best illustration of this pattern. Think about the people who make their living through the written or spoken word (teachers, professors, journalists, writers, media personalities). What is the best way to describe the socioeconomic circumstances of these well-educated, white-collar, middle-income people? **Middle-class professional** is the usual term, a phrase that groups these thinkers and writers together with lawyers, doctors, accountants, insurance executives, computer experts, and other such worthies of our postindustrial age. And since middle-class professionals in modern societies make better than average incomes—indeed, they make out quite nicely compared to the average citizen—we would *objectively* expect to find most of them over on the Right, or at least Center–Right, of the political spectrum.

The evidence generally upholds that modest assumption. Yet middle-class professionals who *think of themselves* as "intellectuals" behave in quite different ways politically from those middle-class professionals who think of themselves, in fact, *as* middle-class professionals. Those who see themselves as intellectuals sympathize with workers—and with the less well off in general.

These "downward-identifiers" even develop a self-image congruent with the normal expectation for a lower-status person. That is, they resent their supposedly scorned social position, believe they are not appreciated enough (especially in monetary terms), and support policies that would redistribute values (especially income and prestige) from those who currently have them to those who do not (in which number they include themselves). Needless to say, they will vote Left much more often than one would expect on the basis of their actual income or social status.[18] It is clear, once again, that to understand social behavior, we must look beyond objective social facts to subjective interpretations

Gender and voting

When we move from class to the next key variable, **gender**, we see even more dramatically the profound effect of the subjective on political behavior. The impact of gender on political orientation should, in theory, be obvious. In all societies throughout history, women have had less of what is valued than men. That is still true today. Women everywhere get worse treatment from society than men do.

In short, here is a group that is everywhere disadvantaged by the status quo. A redistribution of values (in the direction of more respect, more money, and more rights) would benefit women in all nations. One would surely predict that women around the globe will be much stronger advocates of Left positions than men.

That prediction would be wrong. When it comes to gender and politics, women generally have been somewhat *more* conservative than men. Even more important, men and women actually differ little from each other on most political and social issues.

This pattern occurs because (a) people marry those who are like themselves, and (b) people who live together and share similar experiences come, in time, to share similar views, including political views. Most of the difference in male-female voting patterns derives from the separate voting tendencies of men and women *who live apart* from each other. Women living alone (never married, separated, divorced, or widowed) are significantly more Left-leaning than men living alone or than women living with men. Married men are the most conservative group of all.[19] Since one finds an ever-increasing number of women living alone in modern societies (where divorce and separation is common, and where women live longer than men), the **gender gap** is greatest in the most advanced cultures. That is, in the wealthiest polyarchies, women vote more to the Left than do men—and by wider margins than in other societies.[20]

Still, the dramatic difference that we might have expected in male-female political behavior does not occur. Objectively, women should be far to the Left instead of just slightly more Left-leaning than men. How can we explain their lack of radical orientation? The answer lies in subjective factors, inside people's heads. For any number of reasons over the centuries, women have learned to take a conservative outlook on life.

To begin, women suffered more than men for any nontraditional, aggressive, or risk-taking behavior. Women who refused the standard female role of looking for male protectors (fathers, brothers, husbands) were open to various forms of male violence (rape, beatings, forced prostitution, and even murder). Women who accepted the standard role of mother and child-rearer were rewarded with at least a modicum of social respect. At least some of the time they were protected from the worst forms of male savagery. (Why only "some of the time?" Because even those women who accepted the traditional role were not always protected; individual husbands could and often did beat their wives with legal impunity.)

Women learned quickly that the hurts they suffered from the status quo were nevertheless better than the devastation they would suffer from any attempt to change that status quo. This made them natural candidates for the conservative position. Remember too that people come to internalize beliefs that suit their interests. Declaring your pride in being a wife and mother helps you feel better about yourself; it allows you to do your job with a better attitude. As a result, others *may* (though not always) treat you better, as they see you play your assigned (if low-prestige) social role at a high level of competence.

Another reason why women are often conservatives is that society has dictated their role as bearer of the traditions and conserver of the culture. Like all human beings, women psychologically absorbed the roles they were expected, even required, to play. They have, in overwhelming numbers, been the teachers of children. They raise and shape young people from the day of their birth until some time after puberty. They pass along their culture's values to the next generation.

Naturally, someone in that vital role, conserver of the past and teacher of the traditions, will absorb the outlook and perspective of that role: namely, that the way things have always been done is the best way to carry on. Women will be strong supporters of the status quo, then, and that should make them Right-of-Center advocates.

A final conservatizing effect on women is religion. As we know, level of religious devotion correlates with degree of support for conservatism. And everywhere, women are more religious than men (no matter what the religion). Thus, religion combines with gender to reinforce the conservative political outlook of women.

This pattern is so strong that what must now be explained is why many women in advanced industrial countries have dropped their conservative outlook and become more radical, more Left-oriented than their male counterparts. The answer is complicated, but we can start to understand by returning to the causes that made most women conservative in the first place.

Life in the USA or UK or Sweden is no longer dangerous (or at least not nearly as dangerous as it used to be) for those women who try to break out of the traditional mold and compete in society *without* male protectors. In addition, society no longer forces all women to spend the whole of their lives at home. The reasons have much to do with scientific advances. Society no longer needs women to be pregnant all the time to insure that they produce at least two or three children who will grow to adulthood, replenish the race, and support parents in their old age. Raising the one or two children that most women are now likely to have is hardly a full-time activity, let alone a lifetime's occupation. And many women in modern countries never have any children. Add these facts to a huge increase in life expectancy, and suddenly the things that women were always expected to do don't take a large percentage of their adult years.

Concurrent with that development, the things that men traditionally did (hard labor, hand-to-hand combat) that women supposedly could not do have also changed. There is no longer any culturally-supposed genetic reason why women cannot do the jobs that modern society demands and rewards. Women can be lawyers, computer programmers, accountants, and business executives as well as men. They can sell insurance, issue junk bonds, and give political speeches as well as men. In other words, there is no longer a physical or biological argument against women doing the work most valued in a modern, postindustrial society.

And once women start doing that work, they will start asking why their contributions to society, now exactly the same as men's, continue to be valued at a lower level. *That* is the point at which the radicalizing, Left-oriented outlook of modern woman begins.

Societies moving toward gender equality will inevitably arrive at the phase that economically-advanced nations currently occupy. In developed countries, women are no longer treated as second-class citizens, kept from even imagining that their status could improve. On the other hand, they are not treated exactly the same as men, either. They are not given the same opportunities, and they do not gain the same level of money, respect, and status. That leads many women in modern countries to behave as we originally conjectured. They see themselves in less-than-equal circumstances, see that a change in the status quo toward a redistribution of values would benefit them, and adopt positions consistent with support for redistributionist (that is, Left-oriented) political policies.

Not all societies, of course, will advance toward gender equality at the same rate. Again, the subjective factor plays a major role. Where the culture of a place strongly promotes a traditional relationship between the sexes, women's likelihood of bursting forth toward some reasonable level of equality with men remains low. Take Japan, for instance, an economically advanced society if ever there was one. That country lags far behind the nations of northern Europe and North America in its views on gender equality. Women there, for instance, are not expected to continue in the paid labor force after the age of about 28. Many are simply fired after a few years of work, if they haven't already quit the job on their own to get married and become full-time homemakers.

Japan's culture, in short, inhibits the seemingly inevitable development of gender equality in a post-industrial age. In like vein, countries with an Islamic tradition or a Hispanic "macho" culture also are moving at a snail's pace toward a semblance of male-female equality in social relations.

We can predict that *the more traditional a country's culture, the more likely it is that women will take a conservative attitude toward politics.* As women shed traditional roles and enter the paid labor force throughout the world, they will become radicalized and move Leftward. We can further predict that this development will happen more slowly in countries where current cultural norms strongly enforce traditional gender-role expectations.

This same principle applies within countries as well. There will be certain regions or sub-cultures within each nation where traditional attitudes remain strong. There, we will find the greatest number of conservative, as opposed to liberal or radical, women. It will not surprise us, then, to find large numbers of conservative women in Southern and rural areas of the USA, whereas women in the North, in the West, and in urban areas exhibit more liberal orientations.

Religion and voting

Religions are among society's oldest and most influential institutions. We saw in the previous chapter that religious attachments affect political behavior by leading to increased levels of activism in the devout.[21] These attachments also affect the political *direction* of that activism. Religious leaders represent and preach the perspectives of ancient teachings and deeply-entrenched interests. No wonder religious adherents accept conservative perspectives like "doing things the way we've always done them" and "living by the traditional values."

Beyond this simple correlation of religion and conservatism is a related phenomenon. The more zealously you adhere to your religion (no matter what religion), the more conservative you are likely to be in politics. To put it another way, *the more religious you are, the more likely you are to support political conservatism.*[22] We can see the power of **religiosity** in the fact that *Americans who attend church regularly are more likely than occasional attenders to vote Republican and much more likely than non-attenders.* The same pattern holds true in all other polyarchies. Regular church-goers will vote to the Right more frequently than other citizens.[23]

This rule, as with all generalizations about social behavior, must always be preceded with that famous phrase, "other things being equal." In other words, if you hold all other variables constant and take two people who are exactly the same in all other respects, it will turn out that "most of the time," the more religious person will also be the more conservative one. Obviously, there will be exceptions, but if you look at thousands of people, the religion-conservatism link will consistently prevail.

120

"Other things," of course, are not always "equal." Take the well-known phenomenon of Catholicism and politics. In most countries where Catholics exist in any number, they are more conservative than people of other religions (Protestants, Jews), and much more conservative than non-believers. One sees this pattern clearly throughout Europe. For instance, in those parts of France and Italy where the Catholic Church is strong, so too is there strong support for conservative parties. The most Catholic section of Germany, Bavaria, is famous for its political conservatism. In contrast, the Protestant city of Berlin has always been known as a hotbed of Leftist radicalism.

That is the standard pattern. However, the USA defies this expectation. Historically, American Catholics have voted Democratic (that is, Left) in much larger numbers than Republican (Right). Catholics also supported Democrats in *much* higher percentages than members of the supposedly more liberal religious group, Protestants. In fact, throughout most of American history if only Catholics had been allowed to vote, Republicans would hardly ever have won an election.

Does this pattern undermine our hypothesis that Catholics should be conservative? No. We must remember our note of caution, "other things being equal." It is not hard to figure out why American Catholics have traditionally supported Democrats and not Republicans. Up to about 1950, most of them came from three major ethnic groups: Irish, Italians, or Poles. In small percentages, they also sprang from French or Hispanic origins. (Lately, Hispanic numbers have dramatically increased, but until the 1970s, they were a tiny group.)

What do all of these American Catholics have in common? They are today or were in the past what sociologists call "under-privileged ethnic minorities." At a minimum, they were known as "working-class ethnics," but the dominant (Protestant) majority had worse names for them. (You know what they are.) In other words, the population already in place, with its value system shaped by British culture, despised these newcomers because they were not English, not Protestant, and definitely not middle-class.[24]

Catholics were treated as second-class citizens. What do we know about people who are scorned by society, have few of the values that society esteems, and would benefit from a redistribution of those values? They turn to Left-oriented solutions, to people and parties advocating redistributive policies.

American Catholics have been Left-leaning, then, because they have traditionally been ethnic minorities in the working class. Devout Catholics in Ireland, Italy, and Poland, in France, Spain and throughout Latin America, do *not* find themselves in the minority. Neither are they Left-oriented in those countries. The theory linking religion to conservatism holds generally, but *class and ethnic minority status can sometimes combine to overcome the impact of religion*. Religion is not the only variable affecting human behavior.

Besides, *the degree of religious commitment* must also be taken into account. Catholics in the United States have never been as conservative as Catholics in other countries, because they have inevitably absorbed, over time, the dominant values of the broader liberal American culture in which they find themselves. That constitutes another reason why American Catholics are not as conservative as their counterparts elsewhere.

Race, ethnicity, and voting

We know by now that people everywhere take group identities seriously. *People identify with people like themselves.* Among the strongest group forces are *racial and ethnic ties.* As humans, we seem to distrust people who differ from us—and the more different they are, the more we invent reasons to dislike and even fear them.

People in different ethnic and racial categories automatically bring negative perspectives to bear on each other. They often talk differently, sometimes speaking entirely separate languages. They usually look different from each other. It may simply be a question of different clothing. Or body type differences can be dramatic. Average members of group A may be short and pudgy, while Group B members will, on the whole, be tall and lean. Often, skin color clearly sets group members off from each other.

Ethnic differences exist in every nation on earth, and they always have political overtones. Everywhere, some groups will be part of the dominant element in society, while others will be less powerful. Weaker groups will be discriminated against in various ways. They will come to think of themselves as "disadvantaged minorities," developing a set of resentful attitudes that will affect their political behavior.

Remember that the more you desire a change in the status quo toward a redistribution of values that will benefit *you,* the more Left a position you are likely to take. Thus, disadvantaged minority group members will usually find themselves on the Left side of the political spectrum. To illustrate, African-American voters have for decades supported Democrats over Republicans in overwhelming numbers. In any given election the Democratic candidate starts the race by assuming that at least 75 percent of the Black vote is secure. That number often moves higher by election day.

Of course, we must never forget the "other things being equal" warning. Yes, most of the time ethnic and racial minorities will lean Left, but other variables will occasionally intervene. A particular religious minority, like Shiites in the Middle East, may incline more to the Right than to the Left of the spectrum. Their strong religious conservatism plays a major role here. Or a minority group that happens to be reasonably satisfied with the status quo (Chinese-Americans come to mind) may show little sympathy for the Left. Like all variables, the race/ethnicity factor alone cannot alone explain political behavior. Still, when other forces are held constant, we can expect to find a strong correlation between minority group status and Left-leaning political behavior.

Geography and voting

Another variable with political impact is **geography**. Where people live has a decided effect on how they think about politics. We have already seen that place of residence affects *whether* one will participate in politics.[25] As for the impact of geography on *how* people participate, things get complicated.

A traditional way of dividing people by **region** is to postulate an **urban–rural split**. Life on farms or in small towns is clearly different from life in the urban metropolis. Social scientists hypothesize that *rural people will be more conservative than urbanites*. Generally speaking, this conclusion holds. Why it does is not entirely clear. It violates our expectation that those who have less of life's desired outcomes will want a rearrangement of the status quo in a redistributionist direction. Rural people are usually among the poorest in any society. Why aren't they also among the most Left-leaning?

Is there something inherently conservatizing about living on or near farm-land? Perhaps. The explanation may lie in the lack of exposure to innovation and renewal that city residents are constantly exposed to. Or conservatism may derive from a necessary adaptation to the ever-repeating rituals of farm life imposed by nature and the flow of the seasons. Whatever the reason, if you compare farmers (and rural residents generally) with their exact coun-terparts in urban areas, holding income, gender, religion, ethnicity, and so forth constant, you will find that city-dwellers vote more to the Left and hold more radical viewpoints than do rural folk.

As always, exceptions can be found. Peasants can be radicalized, as the Viet Cong discovered to their advantage. And North American farmers whose land is about to be taken away can be radicalized pretty quickly. Leftwing "prairie parties" have played significant local roles in both Canada and the USA. The Non-Partisan League in North Dakota, the Farmer-Labor Party of Minnesota, and the Cooperative Commonwealth Federation in Saskatch-ewan (all well to the Left-of-Center) became powerful forces in the 1930s and remained strong for decades. Despite exceptions, however, the general rule holds: Rural areas tend toward conservative traditions, urban areas toward liberal or radical ones.

Suburbia and politics

A new factor in this equation, the growth of **Suburbia**, entered political life some time after the Second World War. It was symbolized by the large planned community of Levittown, New York.[26] Just as people from rural areas everywhere flock to the city to improve their miserable for-tunes, so eventually do many urban people, especially from the middle and upper-middle strata, leave the city for the country. They are not returning to the traditional, poverty-stricken countryside, however, but to an artificial, carefully-controlled, "country-like" kind of place, with grass and trees and bushes and sometimes even minuscule, artificial farms ("gardens"). The situation seems ideal for those who can afford it. People gain the benefits of country living (fresh air, safety, beauty, community), while suffering few of its drawbacks (grinding poverty, difficult working conditions, insecurity, and an unsanitary lack of modern conveniences).

This artificial safe haven—outside the city, yet wholly dependent on it—came to be known as "suburbia." Lately, the invention of the enclosed shopping mall, the development of superhighway systems, and the computerization of the world economy have freed suburb-dwellers from any dependence on a nearby city. Postindustrial suburbanites simply do not need cities as once they did—for work, for shopping, for entertainment. Or if they decide that they do need cities, they can build their own from scratch. Joel Gaveau coined the term **edge city** to describe this latest social development: the shifting of wealth, power, and population from the traditional urban centers to the green ring areas beyond the old city boundaries.[27]

At first all, these developments were quintessentially American. They were based on a culture of individualism, wide-open space, and widespread automobile ownership. Now they have spread around the globe. In the USA, ever at the forefront of world social development, the largest bloc of Americans lives not in the city and certainly not in small towns or the countryside, but in suburbs.

What political consequences arise from this phenomenon? It creates a host of problems that we cannot begin to examine in this introduction to politics. Not the least of these problems is the enforced separation of the various segments of society from each other. People in the suburbs live radically different lives from those in the cities, where poorer people and ethnic minorities cluster. Middle and well-to-do people wall themselves off from the problems of poor, giving them less perspective on those problems and making them less sympathetic to redistributionist proposals. Those in the suburbs see themselves and all around them as doing all right. The status quo looks good. City-dwellers are more likely to face bitter economic problems. They may look favorably on people running for office who promise to redistribute economic benefits. The satisfied suburbanites, in contrast, should vote in a more conservative direction than urban-dwellers. In short, rural *and* suburban residents, for somewhat different reasons, will be more conservative, more oriented toward the Center–Right or Right, than city residents.[28]

It will not have escaped your attention that the rural–urban–suburban cleavage may owe little to geography and more to class, or socioeconomic status. Certainly, the political difference between urban and suburban follows the expected differentiation of middle-income (and higher) citizens

124

from those in the lower-middle to working (and lower) classes. It is hard to untangle the exact cause-and-effect relationship. Does place of residence have an independent impact on voting behavior, or is it simply an artifact of class? We cannot answer that question here. Let us simply bear in mind that a nearly-universal pattern does exist (for whatever reason), and politicians everywhere absorb this knowledge with their mother's milk. To find conservative voters, go to the suburbs, towns, and farms of the nation. To find liberal or radical voters, head to the cities.

The distinctive region

Beyond the rural–urban split, it is difficult to generalize about political patterns based on geography. One can *not* simply say, for instance, that those citizens living in "the South" of their country (any country) will usually be conservative (or liberal). One country's South may be conservative (the USA, UK), another's may be radical (France), and in still a third the term may not even have a meaning (Canada, where "everyone" in effect lives in "the South"—three-quarters of Canadians live along a narrow strip of land within 100 miles of the USA). Attempting political generalizations based solely on geographical location is, on the face of it, absurd.

Despite this point, we must still recognize that geography plays a role in politics. It turns out that *nearly every country contains at least one distinctive region*. The political process there follows its own rules. It produces special practices that strike citizens in other parts of the nation as odd, if not incomprehensible.

The distinctive **region** of the USA has been the South. There, people supported Democrats for 100 years after the Civil War—from the 1860s to the 1960s and beyond. White Southerners voted Democratic for all offices, whether or not they liked the national Democratic Party's stand on major policies. (In fact, much of the time, they did not.) In a small part of the UK, Northern Ireland, Protestants and Catholics are still fighting the Wars of Religion, a struggle long forgotten by the rest of the population. In Sicily, a minor area of Italy, the most powerful local leaders are not government officials, but members of the Mafia. And on it goes.

Each distinctive region has a flourishing subculture, one whose patterns clearly differentiate it from dominant national trends. Each regional subculture reflects a complex set of historical developments unique to that nation. One subculture will produce conservative effects (the American South), another radical effects (Saskatchewan), and a third will produce high levels of intergroup violence (Northern Ireland). Under these circumstances, generalizations based on region prove next to impossible.

What we can underline, however, is *the inevitability of regional distinctiveness*. No matter how homogeneous and deeply-rooted the cultural pattern may be in any country, people in one of its sections will behave in some strikingly different manner from that of the dominant majority—and you will not understand politics in that country until you understand that dramatic regional exception.

For instance, the American political outlook is often said to exemplify the thinking of eighteenth and nineteenth century European liberal philosophers.[29] Yet clearly, "the mind of the South" (to use a phrase made famous by W.J. Cash[30]) must be sought in a different set of philosophical roots.[31] Daniel Elazar, an expert on American subcultures, saw in Southern paternalism a very different culture from that found in other parts of the USA.[32]

The British tradition is often said to exemplify a peaceful, compromise-oriented, incremental approach to dealing with the strife inherent in political interactions. Yet clearly, the way people work out their differences in Northern Ireland (through violence) forces us to note at least one glaring exception to that pattern.

Each country has its distinctive region. Politics there will differ from politics elsewhere in the land. Without understanding these regional differences and their impact on national patterns, one will never comprehend the overall political system of that nation.

The American South

To illustrate this point, let us examine a country that most readers of this text know well. The effect of the distinctiveness of the South on American politics can hardly be exaggerated. We will ignore the obvious effects: the Civil War, the decades of segregation, the Civil Rights Movement. We will just look at the South's effect on the political party system of America from 1865 to late in the twentieth century.

What voting patterns would we expect in a place like the American South after the Civil War? The answer is simple: support for conservative, Right-of-Center politics. The reason is also simple: *Where the majority feels its dominant position threatened by the demands of a minority group, it will support Right-wing, pro-status-quo, conservative positions. Two corollaries follow: (1) the larger the minority group and (2) the greater the status gap between minority and majority, the more conservative, even reactionary, will be the majority's political position.*

The reasoning here should be clear. Any majority that is better off than a disadvantaged minority benefits from continuation of the status quo. It will naturally take a conservative attitude toward redistributionist change. If it faces a large and poor (or despised) minority group that would benefit by major (even radical) change, this beleaguered majority will by natural reaction move far to the Right. That is, it will vehemently resist any change at all in the existing state of affairs.

These simple principles explain why white Southern voters for nearly a hundred and fifty years have consistently taken conservative political positions. So far no surprises. What does shock those new to this subject is this: Over that same period of time (from the Civil War to the 1980s), white Southerners overwhelmingly voted for the more Left of the two American political parties—that is, for Democrats. How can we explain this paradox?

The answer is easy for anyone who knows why the South is America's distinctive region. This is the section of the country that supported the worst form of racism—slavery—and lost a brutal civil war trying to maintain it. That loss matters a great deal. Remember the importance of psychology. It used to be said of Americans that they had never lost a war. Even after Vietnam, one can still say that the country has never been invaded by a foreign power, defeated, and occupied. Yet that statement too is untrue. The devastating psychological consequences of military conquest and foreign rule *did* occur to some Americans: precisely to whites who lived in the Confederate states between 1861 and (roughly) 1877.

The effects of foreign defeat and occupation on the white Southern psyche can never be underestimated. The burning hatred that white Southerners came to feel toward their Northern "oppressors" overrode all other attitudes that might normally develop in the course of a people's history: attitudes based on class or gender or age or similar variables. For decades, whenever white Southerners had a chance to express themselves politically, they chose to opt for a vehement rejection of that party associated with causing the shame and sorrow of their military defeat in the Civil War.

Their nemesis was of course the detested Abraham Lincoln's Republican Party. Naturally, white Southerners opted for the strongest alternative to this hated organization. Over the years, they voted Democratic at every chance. In a two-party system, they had no other option. The staunchness of their Democratic support was such that the entire region came to be known as "the solid South." One never had to ask how Southern states voted in any given election. Every one of them always voted Democratic.

Once again, we see the importance of psychological factors on political behavior. White Southerners "should" have been voting Republican all those years. That is, based simply on their objective characteristics, we would have expected them to vote for the more conservative of the two American parties. What went on in the heads of white Southerners, however, insured that they would never do that. They developed a clear and strong set of psychological identifications: *against* Republicans, *for* Democrats. This made no sense in Left–Right logic, but it made a good deal of psychological sense.

The major impact of Southern support for Democrats was two-fold. First, it diminished Republican strength at the national level. Even though Republicans dominated American politics from the Civil War to the Depression, they would have been even more securely in control of political power had the South voted for them. Second, it kept Democrats at the national level split in nearly schizophrenic manner, assuring deep Democratic divisions for decades both in Congress and in national party structures (especially at national nominating conventions).

Since the Democratic Party in all other sections of the country represented standard Left-of-Center liberalism, its members in Congress and at conventions felt themselves cursed to be saddled with that large and extraordinarily conservative minority of members representing the traditional South. Yet the party could not simply oust this faction from its ranks. That would have insured its minority status for decades. What liberals had to do for generations was to find accommodation with their conservative regional colleagues.

This necessity insured that politics within the Democratic Party was noisy and interesting; yet it also reinforced the accommodationist, minority-focused, compromise-oriented side of American culture. Major national policies couldn't be made without taking into account the wishes of that key minority group: white Southerners. Not until the 1960s, when another powerful minority, African-Americans (*also* within the Democratic Party) started becoming a vocal force on the political scene did Democratic efforts to reconcile the two wings of their party, liberals and white Southerners, come to a stunning and final failure.

White southerners now vote "rationally," and that development has wrought enormous change in American politics.[33] Slowly over several decades (starting as early as 1948), whites in the South moved from being a core element of the Democratic Party to being staunch Republicans. Partly for that reason Republicans improved their position nationally from being the clear minority party (1930s to 1980s) to being (albeit just barely) the majority party (1980s to early 2000s).

The South's impact on modern American politics makes a fascinating story.[34] We will not delve further into the high drama of this historical anomaly, but the point has been made. Regional subcultures within all nations play key roles in shaping national political systems.

Age and voting

One final variable often believed to affect political voting is **age**. Its impact, however, is less dramatic and more complex than usually supposed. Superficial observers assume that the younger you are, the more radical you are. The old saying goes: "If you are twenty and no radical, you have no heart; if you are forty and no conservative, you have no head." This suggests that young people everywhere will be Leftists and old people Rightists.

That supposition simply fails for lack of evidence. One reason for the minimal impact of age on political behavior is that other variables are much more powerful. Poor and rich young people are more divided by class than united by some hypothetical generational unity. A young white Southerner and a middle-aged white Southerner find more in common than a young white and a young Black Southerner, or a middle-aged white and a middle-aged Black Southerner. Being the same age as someone else may provide a modest commonality, but those similarities of outlook can quickly be undermined by ethnic, gender, class, and religious differences.

Different **socialization** experiences also help to undermine age unity. People of the same age grow up in wildly different family settings. Under normal conditions, people adopt the values and behavior patterns of the family they were raised in. A person raised in a rural, conservative, Christian fundamentalist household is not going to have much in common with someone raised by Jewish liberals in a Manhattan condominium—even if they *are* both 20 years old and members of "the younger generation."

Is the widespread belief that young people are more "radical" than old people just stereotypical nonsense? Not entirely. The kernel of truth here is that *young people are less set in their ways than older people.* Hence, they are also less predictable and less attached to age-old traditions. That does not mean they will all move automatically to the Left. If the "tradition" in their locale involves voting Left, it is entirely possible that they will break tradition by moving Right. Thus, many young Americans in the 1980s moved toward Reagan (the Right) in reaction to the "failed" (in their eyes) traditional politics of the Left (that is, the Democrats). Similarly, young people strongly voted Democratic in 2006, reacting to the increasingly unpopular Republicans who had been the dominant political force for nearly three decades.

Only one safe generalization concerning the political impact of age appears reasonable. *The older you are, the more stable your political loyalties.* Whatever political tendencies you develop in your first decade or so as a citizen (approx. 18–30), those are the tendencies you are likely to keep all your life. People settle into consistent patterns as they grow older. If you voted for Democrats throughout your 20s, you will probably remain a lifelong Democrat. If you worked actively for Ronald Reagan in your 20s, you will become a lifelong Republican. One develops an outlook on life early and stays with it.

This pattern can help explain the apparent anomaly of quite elderly people voting for strong liberals. The majority of Americans who came of political age during the Depression, those in their 20s during the 1930s, developed into zealous supporters of Franklin Roosevelt and Democrats in general. Those people were entering their seventies and eighties during the Reagan era—yet continued to vote for liberals and Democrats. The hypothetical conservatizing effect of age did not move them from the Left to the Right. It simply kept them anchored (frozen?) in the original voting pattern they had adopted as youths.

In a similar vein, we can expect that young Americans exhilarated by the "Reagan Revolution" of the 1980s will still be voting Republican and conservative in the year 2040! And young people who voted Democratic in

129

2006 may be voting that way in 2066. To understand the way any generational cohort votes, we must carefully examine the conditions that shaped their first decade of voting behavior. Otherwise, the age-creates-conservatism hypothesis is much too simplistic to take us very far.

Other determinants of voting behavior

Class, gender, religion, race, ethnicity, age, place of residence, and region are some of the key factors that determine how citizens will behave in politics. Powerful as they are, these variables do not exhaust the forces that shape political outlooks. One can imagine many others: one's state of health, one's sexual orientation, the experience of military service, and so forth. To predict how any *one* person will vote, we need to know about all those and more.

We must also remember that each variable can either reinforce or undercut the others. **Reinforcement** occurs when we find a *working-class* person who is also a *woman*, who also lives in the middle of a large *city*, who also happens to be a member of a disadvantaged *minority* group—and so on. The overwhelming impact of all these variables, reinforcing the natural tendency of each, is to insure that people with those combined characteristics are *extremely* likely to behave politically in the manner that we would expect. In this case, the woman will surely be voting for a Left-wing party.

Real-world data provides support for that conclusion. In the 1992 election for president, for instance, an astounding 89 percent of African-American women voted for Clinton. That is, nearly all members of this group chose the most Left option of the three available (Bush, Perot, Clinton). That is a rare and striking figure in the often fuzzy world of social behavior, and it shows the clear impact of *reinforcing variables*. Here, race combines with gender and class to produce startling results.

In a contrary manner, those people whose social experiences contradict each other, so to speak, are much less likely than others to exhibit a clear pattern of Left or Right support. If you were born female into a working-class Irish family, for instance, but grew up to become a successful accountant and marry a wealthy businessman, you might be torn between a Leftward orientation induced by your family background and gender, and a Rightward orientation induced by your current upper-middle-class professional position and family wealth. You might vote sometimes Right and sometimes Left. You might occasionally abstain, and even vote for an Independent (Centrist) candidate if one came along (like Ross Perot). On the whole, your voting behavior would be less consistent and less predictable than that of someone in socially reinforcing circumstances.

Political sociologists call this pattern one of **crosscutting cleavages**. It usually leads to moderate, Centrist-oriented political behavior. Often, it causes a withdrawal from politics altogether. That is because it's psychologically taxing to reconcile divergent forces. Should you follow your spouse and vote Left or your work colleagues and vote Right? If you feel it impossible to adjust these contradictory claims, withdrawal from the political fray may appear the best solution. By abstaining, you eliminate the pressure of a difficult decision.

To predict how voters will behave, one needs a final piece of information: the psychological impact of each variable, its *intensity* for each individual. Class identification, for example, is felt strongly by some, hardly at all by others. It will naturally have a greater impact on those who feel it deeply. Workers who see themselves as "working-class" will vote more clearly to the Left than workers who do not—even if they make the same money, do the same job in the same factory, and live in the same neighborhood. Unions play a crucial role in instilling working-class identification. In all countries, unionized workers are more radical (Left-oriented) than workers who belong to no union.

This concept—**psychological self-identification**—is perhaps the most significant factor in voting decisions. If you think of yourself as an X, you'll dress like an X, live in the X neighborhood, and vote like an X. In this regard, political scientists have discovered that of all the predictors of voting, the strongest is one called **party identification**. Simply stated, it means that those who *think of themselves* as Republicans (or Socialists, or Greens) will end up voting, most of the time, for Republicans (or Socialists, or Greens).[35]

That may seem obvious, yet the strength of party identification in any polity has an enormous impact on its pattern of politics. The more implanted party loyalties become in the minds of a nation's citizens, the more stable the system is likely to be. Where stable party identifications occur, each party can count on a basic reservoir of support from election to election. Wild voting swings, which could bring new, destabilizing movements to power almost overnight, become unlikely.

Of course, those dissatisfied with the current state of affairs may chafe at the stability that results from long-lasting party identifications. Reformers may see this as a drag on progressive developments. The system reflects the outmoded party divisions of a prior generation, they will cry. These ingrained party loyalties prevent society from facing its problems with innovation and creativity.

Whatever one thinks of the value or drawback of strong party allegiances, the political analyst must acknowledge their explanatory power. If you want to know how people will vote in any given election, just ask them what party they identify with. Much more often than not, that is the party they'll be voting for.

Conclusion

A small number of variables determine how most people will vote in any given election. Among these are the "objective" factors of class, race, religion, ethnicity, gender, place of residence, region, and age. Each variable has an independent impact on how people vote, but in addition, they all interact with each other in complex ways. They often reinforce each other, as when someone who is wealthy is also a white male who is a member of his country's dominant religion. Not infrequently, however, they work in contradictory fashion, as when a minority woman becomes wealthy or a majority male loses his job.

Most important is what people *make* of these factors in their own minds. One's subjective perspectives, one's self-definitions ("I'm a worker." "I'm a Catholic." "I'm a Republican.") are especially effective in producing decisions about whom to vote for.

Party strategists know all this well. The importance of image-manipulation at election time cannot be overstressed. Winning campaigns find ways to appeal to voters' deeply-held self-images. What's in a voter's head, the result of both her life experiences *and* her understanding of those life experiences, determines the election-day choice.

Questions for discussion

1   Why do you think some people have essentially no interest in politics whatsoever? Can you think of conditions which would encourage more people to get politically involved?
2   Why are unions so weak in the USA? Why is Left-leaning activity, in general, so uncommon in American politics?
3   Using the principles set forth in this chapter, how do you think people in the following groups (not discussed above) would behave in politics? Active or inactive? Left, Center, or Right? Why?

   a   Gays and lesbians
   b   Unemployed people
   c   Islamic immigrants
   d   Frequent Internet users
   e   People in managerial positions in mid-sized companies.

4   The author says rural and suburban people are more conservative than city-dwellers, but is he right to lump those two groups together? Can you think of some likely political differences between suburbanites and people living on farms or in small towns?
5   Based on your own experiences and knowledge, would you expect women to be more Left-leaning than men? Why or why not?
6   Are party allegiances changing in the USA? Getting stronger or weaker? Moving in the direction of Republicans or Democrats? Why or why not?

8

THE BELIEFS OF POLITICAL ACTIVISTS

We have seen that most people are not interested in politics. We have also seen that a large minority of people, **Activists** and **Influentials**, become deeply involved in political life. To comprehend politics, we must learn what these power-seekers and power-wielders are like. How exactly do they differ from average citizens?

Obviously, there are many reasons for sustained political involvement.[1] These include the desire to make friends, the wish to fulfill one's duty as a good citizen, the simple hope for a government job, and more. In Chapter 15, we shall examine the motives and personality traits that lead people into politics, but here, we will focus on values and philosophy: the *ideas* that political participants wish to implement.

Whatever their character and their needs, Activists and Influentials share one characteristic. They hold strong and well-structured political beliefs. They think deeply about what government should (and should not) be doing, and when they attain power, they implement those beliefs—or at least try to. They never stop pressuring office-holders to carry out the policies that flow from their deeply-held values. It is this commitment to a philosophy of governance that sets Activists and Influentials apart from the less participatory members of society.

Their specific beliefs vary, of course—and the content of those beliefs matters. We know by now the power of the subjective. *What we think affects how we act.* When faced with the same situation, a die-hard Catholic will not make the same choices as a true-blue Marxist. To understand political behavior, we must understand **political ideology**. What do participants believe, and how does that lead them to behave?

Many have questioned whether political actors have "real beliefs" at all. Aren't they all just self-serving opportunists who change their ideas with the prevailing climate? To begin countering that argument, let me lay down a basic proposition. *Those deeply interested in a subject develop strong and consistent attitudes toward that subject.* Political activists do exactly that. Like the rest of us, on the subject they know and care about, they have real beliefs that have a real impact on their behavior. Let me illustrate.

133

The power of strong opinions

I will never forget the time in college when I heard some women friends arguing about various schools of dance. The major controversy centered on the pros and cons of Martha Graham's style of choreography versus that of Georges Balanchine. In no time, the debate became heated. Names and terms and schools of dance, none of which I'd heard of, were passionately thrown about. Strong words were exchanged in loud voices full of tension. Faces became red in frustration and anger. I don't remember how it ended, but I do remember thinking: Why are they making such a fuss? Who cares about this stuff, and what difference does it make?

I often think of this incident when I encounter intense arguments on other topics I care little about. I have heard people fight long and hard over:

- Who was the better hockey player: Bobby Orr or Wayne Gretsky?
- What was the greatest car of all time: the Porsche 911 or the Ferrari F40?
- Which rock group was the best: the Grateful Dead or Phish?

I have also heard people debate with passion, the merits of post-modernism (literature), structure-functionalism (sociology), and punctuated equilibrium theory (biology), If you know and care little about these subjects, you will stand bewildered at the passion people bring to these "unimportant" matters.

Yet, we all have topics about which we do care. On those subjects we know a lot and have strong opinions about nuances that others find insignificant. Whether it is the "best" show on television, the "nicest" neighborhood in town, or the "one true" religion, some issues touch us deeply. On those issues, we have firm and cohesive points of view. If we feel strongly about religion, we are not liberal Unitarians one day and orthodox Jews the next. If where we live matters to us, we do not give up a lifelong love of nature to move from Big Sky, Montana, or Southwest Harbor, Maine, to a small apartment on the twentieth floor in downtown Chicago.

On topics that matter to us, we have strong, consistent attitudes that do not change easily. Stability of attitude, cohesiveness of perspective, and intensity of outlook characterize the mind-set of those deeply interested in a given subject. This principle applies everywhere, including politics. Political activists, we should not be surprised to learn, have strong, stable, and cohesive views on political matters.[2]

Average citizens, much less concerned with the ins and outs of politics on a day-to-day basis, are more flexible in their political outlooks. They do not think and argue about politics all the time. Hence, they are under no pressure to develop coherent rationalizations and an interconnected ideological framework to support their arguments. As a result, the perspectives of political activists differ dramatically from those of less involved citizens.

It is possible, for instance, that an average American might favor raising the minimum wage, reducing foreign aid, outlawing abortion, and strengthening affirmative action laws. In the smaller circle of political activists, that combination of attitudes would rarely be found. For ideological and historical reasons, this set of beliefs just don't "go together." Those who spend their lives focusing on politics know that and avoid adopting perspectives that make no sense, either to themselves or to their peers.

More important, political activists, who think, talk, and live politics, know the *logic* that links policy positions to one another. They will rarely adopt positions that are illogical and inconsistent.

The importance of consistency

Most people, of course, strive for consistency. Psychologists who study attitudes stress this drive as a human need.[3] It seems almost innate for us to mistrust those who are inconsistent. We strive to seem consistent even to ourselves, inventing elaborate schemes to rationalize our own apparent inconsistencies.[4] The stability, cohesiveness, and predictability of views among those deeply committed to a line of work is remarkable.

People in politics are no different in this regard from the rest of humanity. Their attitudes about their favorite subject are strong and consistent. What sets them apart from the rest of us is their favorite subject. They follow politics the way many people follow sports or soap operas.

Political participants are just one sub-set of that larger group of humanity (a group that includes most of us) with a deep commitment to some subject of interest. It might be chess, rap music, stamp-collecting, fly-fishing, yodeling—or politics. Why should we be surprised to learn that all of these people, including political junkies, have intense and consistent perspectives on the matters they focus on and think about day in, day out?[5]

Thus, political participants who believe that government has no business regulating wages almost always believe as well that government has no business regulating employment practices. Political activists who feel that sexism is a major social problem, to be addressed by government-sponsored, affirmative-action laws, also feel that homophobia is a major social problem, to be addressed by government-sponsored gay-rights laws.

Furthermore, politicians, like the rest of us on subjects we care about, do not often change their point of view. They are not liberal one year and conservative the next, just as baseball fans aren't Yankees-supporters one year and Tigers-boosters the next. Like most people deeply engaged by a subject, politicians develop consistent and predictable attitudes.

Ted Kennedy was a liberal in 1962 when, not yet 30, he won election to the US Senate. He remains a liberal as I write these words. Bob Dole started political life as a conservative and remained consistently conservative throughout his long political career (1953–1996). Lenin became a teenage radical and stayed radical right to his death. These men represent the norm.

In the world of politics, as in most fields, the Benedict Arnolds are the exception.

Politicians, in short, develop strong and consistent outlooks on social and political issues. That statement may seem obvious, but it contains significant implications. It suggests that politicians aren't as untrustworthy as many citizens believe. They are not liars—at least when discussing issues. They really believe what say. Hence, their beliefs matter, and we had better take them seriously. When we elect a party that promises Q, we are likely to get Q. When we go to the polls, we'd better be sure that we really want Q and understand what the adoption of Q is likely to produce.[6]

One final point may help explain why politicians remain consistently committed to their particular set of stands. Even if they *were* complete opportunists with no firm beliefs of any kind, they would still behave *as if* they were deeply loyal to a clear body of principles. That's because acting in an inconsistent manner is counter-productive. Few of us trust someone who says A and does B. Terms like "flaky," "untrustworthy," and "Judas" are used to describe people who cannot remain true to their stated positions. Naturally, few of us wish to be seen in these terms. If we can possibly do so, we avoid acting in an apparently inconsistent manner.

This point applies especially to politicians. The fortunes of political actors depend heavily on projecting a positive image. Everyone in politics knows that it's not a good career move to become known as someone who "breaks promises," who "can't be trusted," or who "changes positions to suit the prevailing political winds." Sensible politicians work hard to avoid those charges.

We should be surprised, then, to find political actors who engage in obviously inconsistent behavior. In fact, most of us are surprised in the opposite way. We are amazed to learn that politicians are *consistent*, that they try to do in office what they say they believe in.

The reasons for our surprise (and cynicism) are many. For one thing, politics has such a negative connotation for many of us that we imagine the worst about its practitioners. For another, we assume that politicians cannot possibly keep all the promises they make while campaigning. Once elected, they will surely have to break some of them. Also, politicians know that the "flip-flopper" charge can really hurt an opponent, so they themselves use the term freely about each other. John Kerry, for instance, was badly hurt in his 2004 presidential race when supporters of George W. Bush dug up a quote that made Kerry look ridiculously inconsistent: "I actually did vote for the US\$87 billion before I voted against it."

Given how damaging these charges of inconsistency can be, all politicians are tempted to use the tactic in the course of most campaigns. In the end, charges of flip-flopping, even outright lying, are routinely hurled about. Average voters cannot sort out who's really consistent and who isn't. They come to believe that "they're all liars."

There is another reason why we think of politicians as promise-breakers. It derives from a basic rule of life: *we remember the unusual more than the normal*.[7] No matter how many people we know who have never won a cent playing the lottery, we all remember the poor truck-driver from Podunk who won a million dollars playing Power Ball. No matter how many planes take off and land safely every day, we remember the one that goes down.

The same principle applies to politics. Most politicians stick to their beliefs, first because they believe in them, and second, because it is politically unwise to act otherwise. However, we (and the media) pay little attention to this pattern. It is the boring, tedious norm. Let one politician change a stated position, however, and the media goes wild. Pundits talk of little else for days, rivals leap out of the woodwork to criticize this "flip-flop," and nighttime comics pile on. The public, hearing of nothing but this one "betrayal of principle," naturally concludes that the act is typical of all political professionals.

Thus, what we remember about George Bush (senior) is his broken promise to hold the line on taxes. (He once told the country, "Read my lips: no new taxes!" but 2 years later he entered into a compromise with Democrats that resulted in some modest tax hikes.). Bill Clinton is forever seared in our memory as saying that he "never had a sexual relationship with that woman" (Monica Lewinsky). Of course, he was lying. What we do not remember is that nearly everything else these gentlemen did in office was entirely consistent with their campaign promises and previous political actions. In the White House, Bush remained moderately conservative and Clinton moderately liberal, positions they had consistently followed throughout their lives. No one familiar with their pre-presidential records could have been surprised at their behavior in office.

Politicians are consistent

A mass of evidence supports this general argument.[8] Studies show, for instance, that American presidents, once elected, make serious efforts to carry out their campaign promises.[9] Studies from other countries show the same thing. As Elin Naurin says in summarizing studies in a number of countries, "It is more likely that an election promise will be fulfilled than it will be broken."[10] In other words, elect conservatives and you will get conservative policies. Elect Leftists, and Leftist proposals issue forth from the government.[11]

To illustrate this point, let's look at some data compiled over time by a powerful interest group, the Consumer Federation of America (the CFA). This outfit, claiming to represent consumer interests, lobbies Congress on consumer protection, public safety, and health issues. For years, the CFA has been rating members of Congress on their willingness to support pro-consumer legislation. "Consumer-friendly" legislators get scores of 60 or 70 and upwards to 100. Those rated in the 0–30 range are seen by the CFA as unfriendly to consumer interests. Using CFA data, we can see whether legislators do in fact change their voting patterns over time.

To make the test especially exacting, I chose a period of 20 years. That is a great deal of time in the rapidly-changing world of politics. A politician might not change from year to year, but over the course of two decades, he or she might well move from supportive to antagonistic on any given set of issues. If we find even a modest level of consistency over this period, we can feel confident in rejecting the "flip-flop" label for politicians.

For my data, I chose all Senators who had served in Congress for the 2 years following the 1974 election and then *continuously* until the 2 years following the 1994 election. Only 14 Senators met this criterion. For those Senators, I took the average of their CFA ratings for the years 1975 and 1976, then compared them with the average of their CFA ratings for 1995 and 1996.[12] I chose a 2-year period on purpose, to provide perspective. In any one session, quirky things can happen. Ratings may vary from year to year just because someone misses a few key votes due to illness, campaign obligations, family problems, and other one-time factors. A 2-year average will even out the effect of chance or one-shot events, providing a clearer indication of one's support, or lack of support, for a given interest group.

The basic findings on Senatorial consistency relative to CFA interests appear in Table 8.1. (For clarity, Senators are listed in order of most to least consistent.) What can we conclude from this data?

Whatever else, these numbers tell us, they do not give much support for the theory that politicians are inconsistent. After 20 turbulent years of

Table 8.1 Consistency in position-taking: US Senators' roll-call voting behavior on consumer issues, 1975/76–1995/96

Senator	State	Party	CFA rating, 1975/76 (av.)	CFA rating, 1995/96 (av.)	Variation (1995/96 minus 1975/76)
Leahy	Vermont	Democrat	93	93.5	+0.5
Hollings	S. Carolina	Democrat	73	74	+1.0
Domenici	New Mexico	Republican	15.5	17	+1.5
Glenn	Ohio	Democrat	77	83.5	+6.5
Bumpers	Arkansas	Democrat	80.5	87	+6.5
Thurmond	S. Carolina	Republican	0	7	+7.0
Inouye	Hawaii	Democrat	72	80.5	+8.5
Kennedy	Massachusetts	Democrat	96.5	87	−9.5
Helms	N. Carolina	Republican	0	10	+10.0
Ford	Kentucky	Democrat	61	74.5	+13.5
Biden	Delaware	Democrat	88.5	73	−15.5
Roth	Delaware	Republican	41.5	24.5	−17.0
Stevens	Alaska	Republican	33.5	17	−16.5
Byrd	W. Virgina	Democrat	60.5	87	+26.5

political activity, over half of this group of national political leaders deviated little from their original position on matters of interest to American consumers. Senator Leahy, the most consistent, started out as strongly pro-consumer (a rating of 93) and ended up strongly pro-consumer (a rating of 93.5). Senator Helms, the ninth most consistent of the 14, moved marginally from extremely anti-consumer (a rating of 0) to quite anti-consumer (a rating of 10).

Even the five "least consistent" senators are hardly inconsistent. Senator Ford moved from moderately pro-consumer to somewhat more pro-consumer (61 to 74.5). Senator Biden moved marginally in the opposite direction, from strongly pro-consumer to slightly less strongly pro-consumer (88.5 to 73). Even the most "inconsistent" of this group, Senator Byrd, can hardly be called a classic flip-flopper. He started out as moderately pro-consumer in the 1970s (a rating of 60.5) and ended up 20 years later as strongly pro-consumer (at 87). One would be hard-pressed to see a "sell-out of principle" in this development.

This evidence does not support the image people have in mind when they accuse politicians of "inconsistent opportunism." If we saw someone voting 80–90 percent of the time *for* consumer issues this year, but just 10–20 percent of the time next year, we would call that flip-flopping. As it turns out, behavior like that almost never occurs in politics. Most participants remain true over time to their publicly-held positions.

What's surprising is not this conclusion, but the necessity of expending some effort to illustrate it. Anyone familiar with public affairs will know that political participants (that is, Activists and Influentials) remain true to their beliefs—or as true as they can, given the limits imposed by real-world constraints. As Keith Poole concludes after his own extensive research, "members of Congress die in their ideological boots . . . once a liberal or a conservative or a moderate, always a liberal or a conservative or a moderate."[13]

Elite belief systems

Now that we can accept the beliefs of politicians as significant in determining their behavior, we need to see just what those beliefs are. We must start by returning to the Left–Right continuum. Many voters do not realize that they are making a choice along this continuum whenever they cast a vote. Activists and Influentials are much more familiar with ideological concepts. Positions along the Left–Right spectrum are profoundly meaningful to them. We have already been introduced to the ideological continuum, but to understand the mind-set of political movers and shakers, we explore it in greater detail.

Among political elites everywhere, there runs a never-ending argument over the current *distribution of resources* in society. In no society have the bulk of people ever been equal in wealth, status, and power. This *socioeconomic inequality* lies at the heart of political debate. The key political positions taken by most political activists depend largely on how they answer this question: "Who is getting what, why, and is that right?"[14]

In this equation the "what" can involve any number of values (better schools, equal rights, lower interest rates, higher wages). More often than not, it comes down to economic benefits (land, money, and jobs) and the power and status that those benefits confer. No one disputes the *fact* of inequality, and everyone knows exactly which resources are widely desired but unequally distributed. The real debate in politics centers on the *reasons* for inequality. Politicians everywhere divide on this issue. Is the current (and unequal) distribution of resources just or not? If not, how unjust is it, and what (if anything) should government do to reduce the injustice?

Your political ideology determines how you will answer these questions. And your answers will determine your position on the Left–Right continuum.

Leftists, Rightists, Centrists

To put this another way, your political attitudes depend a great deal on how you view the **status quo**. This notion of the status quo is a powerful analytic tool. The status quo describes our culture, and the way things operate in that culture, *right now*. It encompasses society's current economic institutions, its social status system, and its dominant social organizations.

As you read these words, whatever the year, the society in which you live is not **egalitarian**. Some people make more money than others. Some have more land than others. And some have higher social positions than others. In short, some people are doing exceedingly well; others are in terrible shape.

At different times in history the better-off people have been warriors, landowners, priests, scholars, bureaucrats, business people, scientists, sports heroes, entertainment providers, and computer specialists—to name a few. The less-well-off people have always been ill-educated manual workers of one kind or another: slaves, serfs, peasants, farmers, domestic workers, factory workers, and service providers (restaurant workers, sales clerks, and so forth).

In most cultures, an enormous income gap separates the better-off people from the others. Less-well-off people almost everywhere constitute a much larger portion of the population than do wealthy people.[15] The important fact is simply that inequality does exist—in your nation and in all others, at all times and everywhere, in the past[16] and doubtless everywhere into the quite distant future. The particular social structure that exists in a culture at any given time, with its resulting range of socioeconomic inequality, determines the status quo around which political and ideological debates take place.

Politicians can take a range of attitudes toward the status quo. They might, for instance, be content with the way things are. The current structures of society, in their eyes, seem reasonably fair. The way society's resources are distributed makes sense. No major changes are needed one way or the other, and things should continue more or less along current lines. The job of government, in this case, is simply to continue existing programs and provide the law, order, and social security that will insure a continuation of the current, desirable conditions.

A moderate attitude of this sort places one squarely in the center of the spectrum. Appropriately enough, politicians with this outlook are called "centrists" (or moderates). Centrists believe that things are going along pretty well and should be kept that way. Don't rock the boat; all is for the best in the best of all possible worlds.

Leftists disagree strongly with this complacent attitude. They are appalled at the current "maldistribution" of goods and services, believing that "the masses" get too little and "the privileged few" too much. They believe that society's outputs should be distributed equally—or at least in a manner closer to equal than in the current system.

For Leftists, government is the best institution to produce the desired outcome. It represents the only force strong enough to confront the institutions and people who benefit from the current status quo. The more Left a politician, the more unhappy she is with social injustice and the more government action she demands to reduce inequality. Ultimately, those on the *Far-Left* want government to promote a *radical redistribution* of resources that amounts to a change in the entire socioeconomic system.

Rightists take a very different attitude toward equality. They fear and loathe it. To them, some people just *are* better than others: in strength, in intelligence, in morals. Society operates best when it allows its better-qualified members to rise, thrive, and govern. Societies decline when the less talented and the incompetent are allowed to run things. The job of government, for a Rightist, is to insure that a talented elite maintains a high position of power, status, and wealth.

If a favored elite is already dominant in a culture, then government's job (for a Right-of-Center politician) is to do little more than defend the existing social order. If the elite's position is challenged, government may have to use forceful means to "keep the masses in their rightful place." And of course, if the "rightful" elite has been forced from power, than the subsequent government must be overthrown, probably by paramilitary force, and its supporters crushed, so that the elite that "ought" to govern can be re-installed at the head of society's key institutions.

It is apparent that what most distinguishes Left from Right perspectives is the attitude toward equality. *Leftists believe that people should be treated equally and should live in equal (or reasonably equal) circumstances.* Not so, say people on the Right. *Rightists believe that people are inherently unequal.* For a Right-wing ideologue, people with superior talent should be in charge of running society. These "better" people should also reap rewards for their exceptional contributions to the general well-being of all citizens.

This brief overview of political ideologies merely introduces the subject. Let's take a detailed look at what it means to be a Leftist or a Rightist.

Leftist ideologies

An old joke has a Left-leaning political activist boasting about the benefits of communism. "Under capitalism," he says, "you have the exploitation of man by man. But in our wonderful communist system, we have just the opposite!"

Analysts have tried for years to explain differences among the various political ideologies. Unlike our example, most of these attempts have been serious. That's because the ideas that people carry around in their heads have serious consequences. Throughout history, people have lived and died for their beliefs. For that reason, we must take them seriously.

Within both Right and Left circles, attitudes toward equality and justice (and therefore toward the government's proper role in society) vary widely. We will begin by examining variations in the political thinking of Leftists. Remember that the chief aim of Leftists is to achieve greater equality in the distribution of resources. After that common starting point, however, Leftists differ among themselves on four major questions:

1   How severe is society's maldistribution of resources?
2   Who precisely is to blame for this problem?
3   How much and what kind of social equality is desirable?
4   What role should government play to assure the desired equality?

The more radical the answer that politicians give to these questions, the more Left-wing they are considered.

Liberalism

We will begin with the moderate Left. Supporters of this position are known as **liberals** in the USA and **social democrats** in most other nations.[17] *Liberals believe that the gap between rich and poor, while deplorable, can be closed in a relatively easy and peaceful manner, if people of good will work at it. Furthermore, those socioeconomic inequalities that do exist can be blamed chiefly on the impersonal workings of a laissez-faire, free-market economic system, not on the malice or ill will of a vile group of greedy exploiters.* The capitalist system is to blame for inequality, say liberals, but they also accept that it produces many benefits and believe that its deficiencies can be easily corrected with a few reasonable reforms.

The problem, liberals argue, is that a free market puts few restraints on aggressive entrepreneurs. Under capitalism, the strong, the bold, and the tough become rich and powerful. They then exploit the poor and the weak

142

with little fear of reprisal. The Moderate-Left solution to the resultant inequality is simple. Impose a prudent set of government controls over economic activity. These controls would curb some of the destructive activities of the rich, while providing some assistance to those at the bottom. Tinkering with the system is all that's needed. Liberals want no wholesale revision of capitalism, and certainly no overthrow of it.[18]

Liberal controls include an array of familiar programs: a progressive income tax, child labor laws, minimum-wage laws, laws that protect worker organizations (unions), and a variety of laws regulating working conditions (insuring a certain number of bathrooms per worker at work sites, placing limits on the number of hours per week and number of weeks per year that people can work, and so forth). The number of programs that government can undertake, even under this moderate Left-of-Center approach, is large. In recent years, these have included government assistance to schools, colleges, and universities; laws providing assistance to the elderly, the handicapped, and the unemployed; laws regulating stock-market activity; and many more.

As a general rule, moderate Leftists accept the free-market economic system and wish only to correct its major shortcomings. This attitude derives from their answer to question three above: How much equality is right? Liberals and social democrats do not believe it necessary, possible, or even desirable to insure perfect equality. Instead, they distinguish between "equality of opportunity" and "equality of results."

In practice, it becomes difficult to differentiate the two concepts. Still, in theory it means that liberals do not advocate programs to insure that everyone will end up at the same income level. Instead, they stand for programs that (a) allow everyone a *chance* of getting on in life and (b) prevent anyone from falling so low as to reach destitution.

Liberal programs to help the less well off must be funded. The money from those programs, says the liberal, can only come from those who are better off. A system of progressive taxation, therefore, perfectly meets liberal requirements. It provides the moderate redistribution of resources that they advocate. It moves both rich and poor toward the economic mean. Thus, the progressive tax has long stood as one of the hallmarks of the liberal platform.

To an increasing degree in recent decades, liberals also advocate the use of government to regulate behavior. They prohibit certain kinds of action (no discrimination against women or minorities in job hiring) and compel other kinds (people whom you hire must be paid the minimum wage and other benefits). Most of these regulatory restrictions affect the upper strata of society—people with the power to hire, fire, promote, and demote.

Naturally, the programs advocated by liberals (increased taxes on the wealthy, restrictions on the economic freedom of people in business) are stiffly resisted by those with something to lose. In many prosperous nations (the USA being typical), most political disputes revolve around liberal proposals for government aid to the less affluent (proposals supported, naturally, by the less affluent) and conservative opposition to those proposals (opposition supported, naturally, by the affluent). The struggle for political dominance often depends on how the moderate middle-class reacts at any given time to liberal or conservative proposals. Depending on how members of this middle group vote in any given election, liberals or conservatives end up in (temporary) control of the government.

As we know, the liberal or social democratic perspective on social justice generally triumphed in modern nations during the second half of the twentieth century. Liberal programs that roused outrage and disbelief a few decades ago are now accepted by most political participants and are widely popular. Indeed, the key programs of liberalism are so ingrained in our expectations that no legitimate political group dares any more to campaign for their repeal. In a sense, world political developments have pushed the entire political spectrum to the Left. In 1920 in most nations (especially the few democratic ones) governments were small, had relatively few functions, and did little to redistribute resources or assist the lower socioeconomic strata. The situation today is radically different. The triumph of liberalism has given us new terms to describe modern political regimes. Some scholars call them systems of "**welfare-state** liberalism." Others use terms like "corporatism" and "**mixed-economy** capitalism."

In any case, governments everywhere now provide a range of benefit programs that citizens both expect and demand, even though these programs seemed radical to all but extreme Leftists a few decades back. Peruse radical Left proposals from the 1920s, and you will see that what were once pleas for action are now simply descriptions of the status quo. "Extremist" ideas of that time have become Moderate-Left or even Centrist positions today.

Socialism and communism[19]

Despite the ascendancy of the Left-wing outlook, the Far-Left in many places has not been satisfied. Continually outraged at the status quo (no matter that it has been shifting inexorably in their direction), they continue to demand dramatic change in the distribution of resources. For them, the rich are still few in number and powerful; the weak are many and poor. True equality is nowhere near, but must be achieved. How to do this? For radical Leftists (socialists and communists), reforming the free-market system is hardly enough. They seek instead "a radical re-structuring"[20] of social and economic institutions.

Remember the four points on which Leftists disagree?[21] *Socialists* and *communists* part company from liberals on all four counts. On the first matter (the size of the gap between rich and poor), they are appalled at existing power and status disparities. To them, the differences are outrageous and excessive. And unlike liberals, who place the blame for socioeconomic variation on *impersonal* market forces, socialists and communists indict the entire economic system as *unjust*.

For radical Leftists, the problem rests squarely on private ownership of the principal means of production. This central characteristic of the free-market system is deeply flawed. Private economic power, unrestrained by any social institution (like government), allows a few to become obscenely wealthy by exploiting the many. For traditional Leftists, the solution is obvious. Use the agency of the state to remove private economic power from the few and give it to the many.

The attitude of radical Left activists can be understood only by realizing the extreme anger, even rage, they feel toward the institutions of capitalism. They direct this rage especially toward those who run, and thus benefit from, those institutions. The further Left we go, the more anger we find at the status quo and at those deemed responsible for it. The more Left one's position, the more radical are the steps advocated to strip those with money and power of their perquisites.

Thus, radical Leftists wish not merely to take away some part of the wealth of the better-off groups for redistributive purposes. They seek to annihilate the very wealth-producing *structures* that are the central source of private fortune and power. In other words, it's the factories, the industries, and the corporations themselves—the socioeconomic elite's base of power—that are the focal point of Left-wing anger. We must abolish private ownership of these institutions, say members of the Far-Left. Their central aim is a state takeover of economic enterprise. Displace current business leaders, and let the state run things collectively to improve the lives of "the masses."

For these reasons, one of the first acts taken by Left-wing parties on coming to power is to nationalize industries. They oust the current owners and managers of large private enterprises, declare their companies the property of the community, and place state officials in charge of running them.

Left-wing politicians argue that these actions produce three significant benefits. First, the profits of the now-nationalized industries no longer go into the hands of a few (owners, shareholders, top managers) to perpetuate a powerful elite. Instead, money made by the company now flows into state coffers. There it can be plowed back into society through the financing of public programs for the benefit of all.

Second, the state officials who run the enterprises, appointed by and responsible to a Left-wing government, will naturally take the workers' point of view. They will thus operate in a more humane manner than did the previous owners. These new managers could hardly do worse, say Leftists. After all, capitalist owners and managers are vile exploiters of a beleaguered working class. Under Left-wing management, workers will see higher wages, fewer hours of work, and better working conditions than under their previous employers, the "greedy capitalists."

Third, under the new regime workers will have a say in running the enterprises for which they work. They may be allowed to choose their own managers. They will be given every opportunity to convey their point of view to these managers and to the government as a whole. They will have many more rights and privileges than before. Thus, workers will no longer be exploited on the job, they will be happier with their conditions, they will cooperate with each other and with management to produce better goods, and society will become more productive while developing a humanitarian and egalitarian ethos.[22]

The radical Left position stresses the desirability of social equality, especially *equality of outcome*. Given their outrage at status variations, Leftists are willing to take radical steps, including the extensive use of state power, to restrict the wealth of the few and increase the well-being of the many. Naturally, this position leads them to rationalize the need for a strong, powerful, and intrusive government. In their view, however, it's a *just* government, since it is dedicated to enhancing the well-being of most citizens.

Distinguishing socialists from communists

Two major points have over the years, differentiated socialism (the mainstream Left) from communism (the extreme Left). First, socialists have preferred to downplay the degree of force needed to oust owners of those private enterprises they plan to take over. Socialists see themselves as democrats. They want to play by the rules of the democratic game, seeking popular support before taking policy action. They work at coming to power peacefully—through free and fair elections and all the other hallmarks of democracy: speeches, articles, books, rallies, peaceful demonstrations, and legal organizing. They are convinced that if citizens democratically elect them after they have been openly campaigning for socialist policies, then those same citizens would support them when, in power, they democratically put socialist policies into law.

Socialists, in sum, expect to come to power peacefully and put their policies into place through legal means with widespread support.

Communists have traditionally taken a different attitude. Inspired by Marx and Lenin, they have argued that the owners of wealth-producing enterprises ("capitalists") would never peacefully give up power. For communists and other Far-Leftists, elites will use all possible means to maintain their dominant position. Since capitalists currently control the state and all the forces of government (the police, the army, the legal system), they will not be an easy target.

Any attempt to destroy capitalist structures runs headlong into this grasping, vicious oligarchy. It won't meekly abandon its privileged position. Rather, to retain power, it will use the most repressive measures against its enemies. Only violent revolution can wrest control from this "gang of jackals." Holding this hostile view of capitalism, Far-Left leaders do not

146

shrink from revolution. For them, power can be attained only by forcible overthrow of the current, capitalist-controlled state. That will surely necessitate the murder, imprisonment, or banishment of all leading economic, political, and social power-holders.

Marxists see this conclusion as obvious. A ruling class never meekly walks away from power.[23] Only the total destruction of that class will allow the masses—especially the working-class ("the proletariat") and its leaders (the communists)—to come to power and rule in a non-exploitative manner that benefits all.[24] Socialists expect to gain power through the vote. Marxists believe, as Mao Tze-tung put it, that "power comes from the barrel of a gun."

The Far-Left hatred of businesspeople leads to a second distinction between Marxists and other Leftists (both socialists and liberals). Marxists want to abolish the very possibility of private ownership of society's resources. They aren't content with state takeover of the major economic enterprises (the steel mills, the coal mines, the auto plants). They wish to "socialize all labor."

As this works in practice, everyone (barbers, taxi drivers, pharmacists, waiters) would work for the state. No individuals would be allowed to work for themselves. No people could hire others to work for them. Only the state, in an ideal Far-Left world, could determine jobs, wages, and working conditions for all citizens.

Problems with implementing radical Left policies

We now see why violence is necessarily associated with Far-Left positions. As one moves toward the extreme Left, one encounters increasingly radical plans for redistributing personal income and limiting private economic decision-making. To implement these goals, one must use extreme levels of force. People being what they are ("I want, I want, I want . . ."), they do not easily part with their worldly possessions.

This last point needs amending. People do not willingly part with their money and goods, *unless* they get something in return. Many people do squander their funds on seemingly absurd and frivolous matters: lottery tickets, astrologers, "personal" trainers, electric popcorn-poppers. Still, in these cases, people freely choose to waste their own money.

Furthermore, the individuals who make these choices never see them as "absurd and frivolous," any more than some readers of this book think that spending money on opera tickets or good French wine is absurd and frivolous. As long as people can freely choose how to spend their money and dispose of their property, they will not make a fuss about the expenditures.

People become unhappy, however, when government enters the picture. If government provides a fee-for-service charge (for, say, entering a park or driving on a highway), problems are minimal. A freely-chosen exchange of money for service makes sense. (People do not *have* to drive on that highway or go to that park.) But citizen anger grows as governments start to take money through broad-based taxation mechanisms that are quite visible (income taxes), while providing in return benefits that are intangible, or even debatable (an educated citizenry, a "good society"). People want something for their money. Unfortunately, most people have trouble making the connection between specific taxes they must pay and general benefits they receive.

Whether citizens *should* take this attitude is another question. Former Supreme Court Justice Oliver Wendell Holmes argued that "taxes are what we pay for civilized society." The fact remains that few people actually think that way. Edmund Burke, the great conservative philosopher, once said that "to tax and to please, no more than to love and to be wise, is not given to men." Nearly everywhere, taxes are resented. The higher the level of tax and the more visible it is, the more deeply it is resented.

Given the dislike people have for shelling out money to government, all Left-wing parties that come to power face a serious dilemma. How do they take money from the people whom they have targeted for economic "leveling"?

In this regard, liberals have the easiest time of it. The modest increase in tax rates that their programs necessitate would normally not produce severe reactions. Any tax increase will, of course, bring an increase in attempts to evade taxation. It will also generate an increase in anti-government activities by groups whose taxes are being increased. But those groups won't be numerous, and their reactions will be modest in response to these modest tax proposals. Opponents will yell and they will demonstrate, but they won't take up arms to get their way. Opponents of Moderate-Left programs will seek to repeal them by ousting liberals in the next election. Moderate-Leftists, in turn, will urge voters to consider the social value of their programs and play down the "modest" taxes needed to support those programs.

The further Left you go, however, the bigger the political problem becomes. Socialists and especially communists go beyond taking a *modest* percentage of *some* people's goods (an unpleasant enough task). They advocate instead taking much, most, or all (depending on how Far-Left they are) of the worldly goods of the most powerful, most deeply entrenched members of society. They have set themselves an imposing task.

At the extreme Left, one sees the ultimate revolutionary perspective. Advocates there wish to eliminate the independent economic power of most members of society. Is it any wonder that Far-Left policies and principles produce violent reactions? Taking money, goods, or land from people makes them angry. The more you take, the more furious they become. They will resist—often violently. Powerful people are hardly without the means to resist, and neither are the mass of citizens. Extreme Left policies simply cannot move forward without the serious use of institutionalized force. When Far-Leftists are in the opposition, that force consists of guerrilla and paramilitary organizations. When in power, they marshal all the agencies of state control: the bureaucracy, the courts, the police, the militia, and the military.

Those who advocate these extreme Left policies create a ever-intensifying cycle of suspicion, resentment, and hostility. The more Left you are, the more you want to take from the haves and give to the have-nots. The more you want to take from the haves, the more you infuriate them. The more you infuriate them, the more they resist your efforts. The more resistance you encounter, the more you become convinced that these people really *are* evil and deserve whatever happens to them. The more you believe in their venality, the more willing you are to use armed force to impose your policies. The more willing you are to use force, the more your opponents will use force to resist.

As time goes by, this cycle of suspicion escalates. Your opponents start feeling that it is rational to preempt your plots against *them* by moving violently against *you*. If you are not yet in power, they may arrest, banish, or kill you. If you are in power, they will do what they can to overthrow you. Naturally, you will resist these efforts at your own extinction by yourself resorting to severe forms of violence. The actions of an elite to defend itself reinforce Far-Left perceptions that the enemy is truly dangerous and must be suppressed.

The logical consequence of all this is simple. The more Left-of-Center you are, the more opposition you will encounter from entrenched and estab-lished social forces. As a corollary, the more Left-of-Center you are, the more force you are going to need to overcome the rationally-based resist-ance of established forces.

The chances for polyarchy will obviously decline with an increase in the number of Radical-Left activists. Their activity could produce two results, neither of which is friendly to polyarchy. On the one hand, their activities lead to a breakdown of stability and order. The high levels of tension and violence they encourage characterize fragmented cultures.

On the other hand, their activities often bring about an oppressive gov-ernment typical of those in collectivist societies. It is immaterial whether the oppression occurs because the ruling (but frightened) elites take harsh measures to repress Left-wing dissent, or because the Far-Leftists themselves come to power and repress the former rulers. Repression will occur in any case. It is clear that polyarchies will find themselves in serious trouble when faced with a large, well-organized, and deeply-entrenched set of Far-Leftists.

Rightist ideologies

In the mid-nineteenth century, someone coined a famous phrase about snob-bery in Boston. There, it was said, "the Lowells speak only to Cabots, and the Cabots speak only to God." About the same time, a story circulated in New York's high society that Mrs Vanderbilt would not have Mrs Astor over to tea. "Her husband's in trade, you know," pouted Mrs Vanderbilt, disdainfully.

Both the Vanderbilts and the Astors were fabulously wealthy, but there was a difference. Vanderbilt wealth derived from the ownership of land, while the Astor millions derived from activity in the fur trade. At the highest levels of the aristocracy, work is a dirty word—even highly lucrative work in furs.

It turns out that not everyone stresses the value of equality. Even in the USA, a supposedly egalitarian culture, some people are horrified at the thought that others might be seen as their equals. This attitude underpins the thinking of the political Right.

Leftists, as we have seen, relish the notion of equal human relationships. Starting with that value, they advocate a common social status for all—or at least, movement toward equality. As one heads from Left to Right on the political spectrum, the ideological dynamic changes. While Leftists stress *equality* (equal treatment, equal opportunity, equal results), Rightists stress *just rewards*.

Equality makes no sense, say Rightists. Some people *do* deserve more than others. They may make greater contributions to the well-being of society; they may work harder; or they may simply be superior people. For whatever reason, the "better people" in society are entitled to more social benefits than "the masses."

This perspective leads Right-wingers to the idea of justifiable (even necessary) *inequalities*. For political activists on the Right, people are *not* all the same and should not be treated as if they were. Rightists are self-professed elitists, and the further Right you go, the more stress you find on the need for a talented and deserving elite to make things run properly.

Rightists differ among themselves on three basic points:

1   How big is the gap between the elite (this group of "superior" people) and the rest of society? (That is, is the gap easy or impossible to bridge?)
2   What, exactly, makes some people and groups "better" than others? (Is it hard work and perseverance, traits that all of us could adopt if we put our minds to it, or is it some deeper, innate set of qualities that we are, essentially, "born with"?)
3   What must government do to keep the "better" people protected and rewarded, while keeping the rest of society in its "proper" place?

Different ways of answering these questions differentiate Rightists into three major categories: **Conservatives, Reactionaries**, and **Fascists**.

Conservatives

We will start with conservatives.[25] Like all Rightists, they believe that some people contribute disproportionately to society. Heading the list are creative, hardworking entrepreneurs. Conservatives argue that only a small minority creates the wealth from which the rest of us benefit. These talented few contribute to the welfare of all by thinking up, or taking advantage of, new and productive ideas.

For conservatives, people like Edison, Ford, and Gates stand out as models of achievement. They invent new products, use innovative concepts, and adopt cutting-edge technology to provide goods and services that people want. By applying their talents, working hard, and taking risks, they produce valued outputs that would not have existed without their creative labors and managerial skills.

Conservatives do not limit the worthy elite to business people. Many citizens contribute more than average to society. These include superior teachers, brilliant artists, great athletes, and leaders in a range of professions. In all areas of human endeavor, some people contribute more than others to knowledge, technology, and the arts. In essence, these exceptional people create the ideas and products that advance civilization. Given their accomplishments, say conservatives, these ground-breaking leaders should be well rewarded. It is simple justice for brilliant, productive people to receive exceptional rewards: recognition, honors, and wealth.

Having said this, we must note that free-market conservatives do not assume any *innate*, in-born difference between this elite and the rest of society. That distinguishes them from the Vanderbilts, the Cabots, and the Lowells—who did think of people as inherently unequal. These aristocrats were *reactionaries*, whom we shall be discussing shortly.

For conservatives, a gap does separate the most deserving citizens from the rest of society, but it is not unbridgeable. Individuals with grit, drive, and talent can rise to the top. In a free society, says the conservative, anyone who works hard has a serious chance of getting somewhere, of being well rewarded. That is why *character* plays a key role in conservative thought. A good citizen—honest, moral, full of integrity—who meets obligations and puts in a good day's work, will thrive in a just society. That citizen *deserves* to be rewarded for those efforts.

True, the lazy, the less skilled, and the handicapped will always fall toward the bottom, but many of them will deserve to fall. For the truly unfortunate, primarily those who suffer through no fault of their own, conservatives are willing to provide a safety net. Conservatives argue strongly, however, for the importance to society of *differential benefits*. It is crucial for the system to reward productive work and discourage sloth. Otherwise, where is the motive to labor, to be creative? A rational reward structure will encourage *all* citizens to strive to produce more, and all of society will benefit from these collective energies.

Conservative thinking goes as follows. Set up an economic system with incentives (rewards for hard work and achievement, punishments for laziness and failure). Knowing that hard work is well compensated while idleness is penalized, most citizens will apply themselves vigorously in the workplace.

Taking individual responsibility for their fate, they will drive themselves forward toward personal success.

The beauty of this scheme is its overall effect on the nation. Society as a whole will benefit from the myriad accomplishments of all these striving, creative individuals. That's why differential benefits are vital to conservative thinking. The visible wealth of the highest achievers will spur the rest of us to emulate them in the hope of similar results. We end with a society of achievers, all competing for personal betterment and encouraged by the incentive of potential future riches. With all citizens working to better themselves, "an invisible hand" (in the famous phrase of the Enlightenment philosopher, Adam Smith) will insure a thriving economy and a prosperous and powerful nation.

Given this perspective, conservatives see a modest (but crucial) role for government. It should first provide safety for its citizens, protecting their lives and safeguarding their property. You cannot work creatively if you live in fear. You have no incentive to increase your wealth if thieves or corrupt officials may seize your worldly possessions at any moment. Thus, for conservatives insuring social order and sustaining a safe environment is the first duty of a just state.

Second, government should work to guarantee the rule of law. The good society needs a rational legal system run by honest officials whose main job is to enforce the sanctity of contracts. Most social and economic activity should take place on a voluntary basis among willing citizens who enter into mutually-accepted agreements for working productively together. The main job of the state is to insure that untrustworthy individuals do not underhandedly break formal agreements and pauperize partners who entered into them in good faith.

A broken contract, after all, deprives honest, hardworking people of the fruits of their labors. A society in which contracts are not enforced becomes one that discourages effort and hard work. People will grow cynical about the chances of getting ahead, about the possible benefits of working profitably with others. Destroyed are all those incentives to create and invent, since others may with impunity steal your ideas and products. A society not governed by the rule of law produces a stagnant economy operated by alienated, suspicious, and defensive loners or corrupt thugs.

Government has a third role to play for conservatives. It should operate a stable monetary system, one designed to prevent runaway inflation that undermines property values, business interests, and bank holdings. Inflation is the conservative's worst economic nightmare. It eats away at the material achievements of all citizens, thereby discouraging productive efforts on a broad scale. What is the point of working hard and increasing your wealth level by 20 percent, if an inflation rate of 18 percent means that you have made almost no progress? Even worse, an inflation rate of 22 percent means that for all your hard work, you've fallen backwards.

The conservative view of government

Summarizing, we can see that government's job (for a conservative) is to insure that those who have talent and industry are not stripped of their just rewards by crime, corruption, or incompetence. In keeping with this perspective, conservatives demand vigilant police and a strong military establishment. Police are needed to keep crime levels down, thus insuring social peace under which entrepreneurial activity can thrive. (Hence the well-known conservative preference for "law and order.")

A significant military establishment is needed because it is a dangerous world out there. Conservatives (and Rightists in general) think more darkly about human character than do liberals (and Leftists in general). Conservatives (and Rightists as a whole) are ardent nationalists. They see greedy and aggressive outsiders eyeing their own nation's wealth with an envious eye. Only secure borders can protect *our* society's hardworking citizens from being stripped of the fruits of their labor by invasion and destruction from hostile outside forces. Thus, conservatives everywhere push for a strong military—the only sure protection from aggressive external forces.

Finally, conservatives (sometimes grudgingly) accept the need for a modest number of government programs that intervene in the free-market economy. Chief among these are programs of government aid for "infrastructure": highways, ports, railways, canals, airports, space exploration. These projects can be justified on the grounds that they advance economic development in important ways, yet are too expensive or risky for private enterprise. Many conservatives remain deeply skeptical about these programs. Whenever possible, they will fund infrastructure projects through subsidies, contracts ("outsourcing"), and tax incentives to private firms, rather than assign this work to agencies of government.

Conservatives will also accept, again grudgingly, modest programs to aid the disadvantaged. But these programs will be spare, since for conservatives only a few members of society are truly unable to help themselves. Even those few should preferably be assisted by their families or private charity rather than public welfare. If government assistance cannot be avoided, conservatives prefer that it be provided by local and regional, rather than by national, agencies.

With those reservations, conservatives are willing to provide some public funding to assist orphans, extremely handicapped people, and the destitute elderly. Otherwise, they condemn most forms of government assistance to individuals. For them, government "handouts" destroy those incentives to creative work that lie at the heart of a thriving society.

There is a simple reason why conservatives see themselves as stingy in funding government programs. All government funding, they say, is derived from taxation. Taxation is a dirty word on the Right. For conservatives, taxation involves taking money from the productive members of society,

153

those who contribute most to its well-being, and giving it to those who contribute little or nothing. Taxes thus become *disincentives* to work. (Why struggle to better myself, if the government takes most of my additional wealth? Why struggle to better myself, if government programs will support me in a decent manner anyway?)

Thus, a tax (for conservatives) is money taken from hardworking citizens who could use it in creative, socially productive ways. The money then goes to government, famed for its bureaucratic inefficiency, and eventually into the pockets of less productive citizens. Wherever it goes, any tax represents a loss to economic productivity and that is why conservatives oppose "big government." The smaller the government, the lower the tax rate. Under those conditions, citizens can spend their own money in ways that make them better off and advance the economy as a whole.

Reactionaries

As we move from conservatism toward the Far-Right side of the spectrum, we find an intensification of the Rightist belief that some people are better than others. Proponents of the *Far-Right*, however, no longer see human superiority as based solely on productive contributions to society. Reactionaries and fascists see the qualities of the elite as innate (what sociologists call *ascriptive* traits). The qualities that make one "a superior being" are possessed by just a small proportion of humankind and are frequently attained at birth. There is little one can do to acquire the desired traits. One is either born into the "right" family or class, or born possessing the "right" set of genetic traits.

For a **reactionary**, "the right qualities" will vary from one society to the next. Often, a particular family or class is connected with some ancient traditions of a dominant group. One is born into a family of aristocrats, or into a family of large landowners, or into a family that traces its lineage back for generations. Certain genetic traits gained at birth can also set you off as superior. For Rightists, these usually involve whiteness, maleness, and membership in some mythical "superior" ethnic group (e.g., being Tutsi in Rwanda, being Brahmin in India, being "Aryan" in the West).

For the most part, one cannot *choose* to possess the traits that Far-Rightists admire. Most people were not born into the Bourbon, Windsor, or von Stauffenberg families. Most people's parents did not possess a million acres of land or own 30 banks in five countries. Most people are not white German males, or white Serb males, or white Sunni males (all sub-groups that have in the twentieth century made claims to being the "rightful rulers" of their lands).

These attitudes differentiate Far-Rightists from conservatives in significant ways. Conservatives see status differentials as based primarily on behavior. For conservatives, many different members of society can make contributions to its well-being, so the "better-off" or "elite" group can be quite large. In America, conservatives often trumpet the virtues of "the great mass of working and middle-income Americans," a group that would seem to encompass the majority of US citizens.

Furthermore, for conservatives the boundaries between "superior" citizens and the rest are fluid and permeable. With work, creativity, and dedication, most people could make important contributions to society over time. Strong character and hard work allow one to enter the upper echelons of the status system, whatever your background or heritage.

In reverse, one can easily fall from a position of privilege. If those in higher-status groups slack off and abandon the habits that brought them (or their forebears) success, they could soon drop in social standing—and deservedly so, say conservatives. True conservatives have little patience for what they see as "lazy" or "decadent" members of the upper class.

For a reactionary, aristocrats are aristocrats and should never be treated as lazy bums—even when they behave like lazy bums. On the other hand, Jews are vile, depraved sub-humans. No matter how hard they work, no matter how brilliant they might appear, they will always be untrustworthy vultures and the scum of the earth.

Elitism is the word often used to characterize this Far-Right perspective. Reactionaries believe in the right of some small set of people to be "in charge" of things. The favored group may gain its right to rule through its status as a traditional aristocracy. It may have a right to rule because it has mastered contemporary military skills and asserted its dominance by force. It may simply represent the richest or the brightest members of society. For whatever reason, *reactionaries believe in the unquestioned superiority of one set of people*, whose "just" dominance over society derives from some special characteristic that is significant to the Rightist at that particular time and place.

For reactionaries, *the job of government is an oppressive one—and rightly so*. It must enshrine the rights of this superior minority and set up a strong guard against the inferior masses who might try to assert themselves against their betters. At its best, this outlook may view the masses in a paternalistic manner. They *are* needed, after all. Someone has to till the fields, work in the factories, run the errands, cook and serve the food. "Average" people must do the work that ends up benefiting the elites.

Furthermore, as military personnel loyal to their leaders, average citizens provide protection for society's elites against potential aggression from the elites of other nations. In other words, the inferior masses are needed as workers and soldiers. Some reactionaries recognize these necessary roles and even show gratitude toward those who serve them. To the extent that the masses prove *loyal* in their "proper" roles, a reactionary elite may reward them with (patronizing) praise for their efforts, modest incomes, and state protection from outside invasion. Those who prove disloyal, who become disgruntled with their position, who start to make trouble, are ruthlessly suppressed by an authoritarian state.

Naturally, there can be no question of real democracy in a system where a minority is "better" and deserves more rights than the majority. Depending on the particular country where Far-Right activists rule, they may (or may not) allow sham elections. They will sometimes set up rigged elections (often called plebiscites) to create a pretense of mass involvement, to drum up support for the state, and to provide a cover of legitimacy for themselves. Sometimes not even the pretense of an election occurs. (In Saudi Arabia the Royal Family rules and that's it.)

Fascists

As one moves even farther Right, one finds ever stronger the conviction that one set of people is superior. Phrases like "master race" start being used to characterize the chosen few. In *fascism* (of which German **Nazism** was a variant), a mystical notion prevails that one people on earth stands above all others. Its mission is to assert its dominance, purge all "inferior" elements, and lead the world to glory and greatness.

In more recent times, Serbs invented the term "ethnic cleansing" to describe this attitude. It urges the elimination of all "inferior" peoples from the master group's domain. This attitude leads necessarily to an extreme and aggressive militarism. Ultimately, it produces **genocide**, the mass killing of entire ("inferior") nationalities.

Force and power are central elements in the fascist perspective. War is desirable. It is a baptism of fire that purges the weak and steels the strong. The chosen few must use ruthless force to keep the rest of society in its place. They must also use force to suppress and conquer enemies beyond their borders.

Fascists thus expect and advocate an authoritarian police state ruled by and for the idealized elite. They also promote a strong military to subdue the "lesser peoples" and the "decadent nations" in their region. At the extreme, fascists see themselves as the rightful dominators of the world. Hitler, after all, claimed to be ushering in "a thousand-year Reich." This attitude naturally brings them into armed conflict with a host of other states whose inhabitants don't necessarily agree that submission to a self-proclaimed "super-race" is either logical or necessary.

The consequences of extremism

With Far-Right doctrine, we come full circle to an element it shares with the Far-Left outlook. *Both ideologies create their own enemies.* The Left sees its mission as destroying all the forces that benefit from modern capitalism. Naturally, those forces do not care to be destroyed and will take counter-measures to insure their security. The Right sees itself as rightful

156

ruler of the nation and perhaps the world. Naturally, people in the rest of the nation and in the larger world disagree with that assessment. They too will take measures to resist succumbing to Rightist daydreams. In the end, both Right and Left create intense, often violent, reactions from those groups whom they have targeted for destruction.

When they are small in number, activists on either the Far-Right or the Far-Left seem like harmless crackpots. They will declaim their wild ideas on public soapboxes before lone hecklers. (These days they may run blogs perused by a few dozen adherents.) But when the number of people with these perspectives becomes numerous, social tensions are going to rise. Their ideas practically cry out for stiff, tough responses. Groups that would suffer terribly under a regime of the Far-Left or the Far-Right will take vigorous measures to prevent their coming to power.

These observations lead to some obvious conclusions. First, tensions in any society will rise in proportion to the number of political activists at the extremes. Levels of violence, too, will increase. Ultimately, this process can undermine the operations of a functioning democracy. Weimar Germany, to take the most famous example, moved toward collapse in the 1930s when large numbers of Nazis and Communists started fighting each other on public streets, while weak police and military forces sat on their hands.

Given the eagerness of both Far-Right and Far-Left activists to control society and impose their own ideas on everyone else, a second conclusion clearly follows. Under both Far-Left and Far-Right rule, government will be large, intrusive, and oppressive. Both Far-Left and Far-Right supporters see "enemies" everywhere. In power, they feel justified in using state authority for extreme measures. First, they will put the state police to work at eliminating those perceived enemies. Then, once in total control, they will use harsh state powers to consolidate their hold on society.

One of the central efforts of ideological extremists is "re-education." They wish to mold the very minds of the people under their control. That way, they can insure the triumph of their ideas, while at the same time preventing even the possibility of enemies springing up to challenge the truth and majesty of their regime. Far Leftists and Far-Rightists are passionately committed to their beliefs. If they ever gain power, they make sure that no ideological alternatives are allowed to challenge their own perspective. This approach has often been labeled **totalitarian**. The term beautifully captures the mania to control all aspects of social life, including private behavior and beliefs.[26]

Changing the way people think requires a high level of coercion. Making sure that all written and spoken communication does little more than parrot a party line requires a huge degree of supervision. It also requires a massive police presence to find and punish offenders. For these and many other reasons, life under the totalitarian control of Far-Right and Far-Left regimes is singularly unpleasant.[27]

Table 8.2 Chart of political positions.

ISSUES	LEFT → Communists	Socialists	Liberals/Social Democrats	Moderates	Conservatives	Reactionaries	← RIGHT Fascists/Nazis
View of the current status quo	It's rule of an exploitative capitalist power elite! Must overthrow it, give power to workers.	It's rule of the big banks and corporations! Must nationalize all large enterprises.	It's business-oriented! Let's put in more regs, and provide more safety-net programs.	It's fine, except for small problems here/there; let's work on them.	Too much big govt.! Must roll back welfare handouts and regs. on business.	It's rule of the mob. Must return to rule of "the best."	It's rule of the weak! Must overthrow it by force.
View of equality	All should be equal in economic and social results.	Govt. must work to move society toward economic equality.	Govt. must do more to insure real equality of rights and opportunity.	Strong support for legal equality and for equality of opportunity.	Some achieve more, some less; reward achievers, not the lazy or ineffectual.	It's an illusion. Aristocrats/those from best families should rule.	Nonsense! The strong must rule. That's us!
View of need for violence, revolution	A violent revolution needed to overthrow the capitalist system.	Violence needed if far Right acts up, but a Socialist revolution should be peaceful.	Never use violence; revolution not needed, but civil disobedience is a good tactic.	Violence/revolution is unjustified; solve problems by discussion, negotiation.	Violence is OK against fanatics; Revolutions are bad, undermine traditions.	Violence may be needed in a counter-revolution if the Left goes too far.	Yes! Need to destroy our enemies, overthrow the state.

The role of government when we're in charge	Nationalize industries and farms; appoint all managers; set wage scales; create regs. for all jobs; create police force to make sure it all happens.	Nationalize major industries; more regulation of business; increase wages; cut work hours; expand welfare programs.	Expand programs for healthcare, education, environment, aid to poor; decrease business subsidies; increase business regs.	Continue the programs now in place, but find ways to make them work efficiently.	Provide subsidies for business; promote religion; stop abortion, drugs, pornography, illegal immigration.	Wipe out the welfare state; deport those of impure ancestry; restrict voting.
View of justice or the just society	"From each according to his ability; to each according to his need" (Marx). Government insures that all are close to economic equality.	Govt. runs the major enterprises, insures good wages and working conditions in both public and private businesses. Free healthcare, education for all.	Capitalism is restricted by regulations, progressive taxes, and programs to aid the unfortunate. Govt. helps provide widespread access to healthcare, education.	A system of free-market capitalism prevails, tempered by a range of humane govt. programs to aid the unfortunate.	Free-market economics prevails; rewards go to achievers; moral and religious values widely supported; old traditions are revered.	Those in the aristocracy or the proper families rule; ordinary people do their jobs docilely.

Smash domestic enemies! Build up the military; invade neighbors.

Strong men of our race rule; lesser races are slaves or exterminated; women are mothers.

Conclusion

The chances for polyarchy diminish as Far-Left or Far-Right activists increase. Trust and tolerance are vital to the health of polyarchal systems. People must feel secure enough to allow those who disagree with them to speak out, organize, even gain power. But that's a hard attitude to develop toward people who are significantly different from ourselves. If other activists are reasonably close to us on the ideological continuum, we can accept (if grudgingly) their right to activity and even power. But for those at a major distance from us, levels of tolerance fade into fear and prejudice.

The history of modern polyarchies suggests that activists ranging from conservatives to socialists can live together in peaceful competition. That is, their many points of disagreement will express themselves in non-violent forms. A strong polyarchal system can even survive the activity of small numbers of Far-Left and Far-Right extremists. But once the number of extreme ideologues reaches a critical mass (say, twenty percent of all activists), polyarchal stability is endangered.[28]

As extremists grow in number, the very nature of a polyarchal regime will change. It could degenerate into violent anarchy, taking on the characteristics of a fragmented culture; or one group of extremists could take power and impose its will on society, producing a collectivist system. In either case, the outlook for polyarchy is bleak when ideological extremism is strong.

Questions for discussion

1   Does the argument that politicians are consistent make sense to you? Can you think of examples that run counter to this statement? How about examples that support it?

2   Can you take 5 or 10 world figures and place them in one of the positions along the Left–Right continuum (see Table 8.2)? (Do not limit yourself to people in your own country or era.) Then do the same for 5 or 10 current politicians in your own state or country.

3   What arguments do you think extreme Left-wingers give for motivating people to work, if "everything is owned in common" and "the state provides for everyone?"

4   What arguments do you think extreme Right-wingers give for inducing loyalty among the masses, most of whom these Right-wingers define as "below average" or even "sub-human?"

5   How do you think moderates should behave in a political system veering toward the extreme Left or extreme Right? Should they adopt oppressive counter-measures or maintain the traditional democratic tolerance for diversity?

9

POLITICAL IDEOLOGIES AND POST-INDUSTRIAL VALUES

Our analysis of ideology and politics has plowed some traditional ground. The Left believes in equality, and the further Left you go, the more government is needed to ensure equality. The Right believes that inequality is not only inevitable, but preferable. The further Right you go, the more government is needed to insure the rightful dominance of the few who deserve power, wealth, and status. Centrists are generally content with the status quo, which varies from era to era but can be characterized in our time as welfare-state liberalism. Centrists (or Moderates) advocate little more than a fine-tuning of current policy, based on close attention to popular demands.

How does one become a Leftist, a Centrist, or a Rightist? As we know, people generally adopt political beliefs that best serve their interests. Thus, we can hardly be surprised to learn that political participants who represent business interests are found on the Right, while activists supported by workers and union members adopt a Left-leaning political perspective. Business leaders, after all, prefer little government intervention in their affairs, while workers see government attempts to redistribute income from rich to poor as likely to benefit them.

Despite this usual alignment of interest and belief, we must be wary of pure cynicism about political motives. The politicians who hold one or another position along the ideological spectrum really do believe in the ideas they express. Because they believe those ideas, they act to implement them whenever they can. That is why we must understand those beliefs. They are not phony. They cannot easily be exchanged for others, even when advantage is to be gained. These ideas are deeply held, and they have real consequences. *If you know the ideology of the government's leading politicians, you can predict what policies their government will enact.* Elect conservatives, and you will get conservative policies. Elect socialists, and you will get socialism.[1]

The Left–Right spectrum cannot, of course, explain everything about politics, but it remains a useful explanatory tool. Knowing the basic attitudes held by people in the Right, Center, and Left allows us to predict quite a bit about individual political behavior in a vast number of countries. For instance, people in any country who argue that "we need a stronger

161

defense" are usually Rightists. Understandably, when Rightists come to power, they increase spending on the military and take a hard line in international affairs. On the other hand, it is almost always Leftists who argue that working people are badly treated; they deserve higher wages, better working conditions, and subsidized housing. When Leftists come to power, they use government to enact pro-worker policies.

New political issues

Despite the analytic utility of these Left/Right divisions, their explanatory value has in recent decades declined. A host of new issues have arisen that do not seem relevant to the old arguments. Where, for instance, does abortion fit into the continuum? What exactly does it have to do with attitudes toward equality and the distribution of resources?

Similarly, it is not intuitively obvious how Left and Right activists would think about environmental protection. Is there some reason why socialists would be more concerned about dioxins in our drinking water than reactionaries? And what about the issues of gay rights, feminism, pornography, assisted suicide, water fluoridation, school vouchers, illegal immigration, drugs, terrorism, and crime? None of these issues (and many others that have inflamed passions in recent decades) seem immediately related to the classic debates over wealth, ownership, and economic equality that once defined a political party's place on the Left–Right spectrum.

Clearly, it is possible, if you work at it, to shoehorn attitudes on all these issues onto a Left–Right continuum. Since these issues did not enter the political scene all at once but appeared only gradually over time, lifelong political participants have managed to incorporate them into the traditional framework. Activists *know* that a "pro-life" stand is conservative, while support for gay rights is liberal. Still, the logic placing those attitudes on the Left–Right scale is not always clear.

Remember the original meanings of Left and Right. These terms categorized how people felt about the current distribution of socioeconomic resources. Conservatives want to reward economically contributing members of society and keep government intervention in the economy to a minimum. What does a belief that "abortion is murder" have to do with this traditional perspective?

In like vein, liberals hope to use government programs to tax the wealthier members of society so that funds become available for programs that benefit less well-to-do citizens. In what sense does a show of support for gay and lesbian members of society fit these traditional liberal concerns? After all, there are plenty of wealthy gay people, along with many poor homophobes.

Nothing in pure logic links a desire to help the poor with support of gay rights, just as there is no logical connection between supporting business

162

interests and opposing abortion. So why should liberals support workers' rights *and* gay rights? Why do conservatives back *both* business interests and pro-life interests? It turns out that ideologically-inclined elites are good at developing explanations. Both liberal and conservative activists have found ways to justify these separate and seemingly unrelated positions. To most politicians and political activists, the issues seem inextricably connected.

Making those connections clear to the general public, however, is not easy. It becomes increasingly difficult as new issues accumulate that have, on the surface, nothing to do with the original Left–Right rationale. The perfect example may be water fluoridation. Nothing more clearly differentiates Right from Left activists than their stands on this issue. Just why that should be the case is nearly impossible to explain through the customary Left–Right continuum.

A host of new issues ("clear-cutting," "free trade," bi-lingual education," "getting tough on crime") have come to the fore in all modern nations. The effect has been a decrease in the explanatory value of traditional ideologies. Those positions seem especially unable to sum up the outlook of many citizens. How can the traditional ideologies explain why a pro-life stand on abortion always goes together with a tough-punishment stance on crime? Why does support for "socialized" medicine go hand in hand with a will-ingness to tolerate pornography? Even political activists have trouble explain-ing the connections between the traditional (socioeconomic) issues and the newer subjects of the post-industrial era.

Until recently, activists and analysts alike have dealt with the emerging topics by forcing them into the traditional framework. A more effective approach might be to expand and develop that framework. Many of the new issues can be seen as related to each other along an entirely different dimension, one quite removed from the traditional debates over equality and the distribution of economic rewards.

Various scholars have been calling our attention to this new set of issues and have suggested a new ideological dimension to explain them. The most well-known theory comes from Ronald Inglehart in work he has been producing since the early 1970s.[2]

Essentially, Inglehart argues that we now live in an age of **post-industrial values**. (At least, those of us who live in the wealthier nations do, and the rest of the world is trending in the same direction.[3]) During the industrial period, politics *did* center on the conflict between the economic haves and have-nots. Political debate focused on the proper distribution of society's wealth. Political struggles were shaped by worker-employer conflicts, and political attitudes on these matters could be neatly summarized by the Left–Right spectrum.

Soon after the Second World War, according to Inglehart, things began to change. The enormous increase in wealth that occurred, first in a few leading-edge places, then in the majority of the world's countries, meant that economic confrontations over a small pie did not necessarily take center stage. Social differentiation, furthermore, became increasingly complex. The factory, with its clear division between workers and bosses, is no longer the central site for work. Professional, white collar, and service jobs have multiplied.[4]

What's the result of these trends? The old social divisions have given way to a large, amorphous, and reasonably content middle class. The computer and the Internet are changing work patterns and social structures in ways we cannot yet comprehend. The political divisions and arguments appropriate to an industrial age, while still relevant in many circumstances, no longer encapsulate all of the social issues that average citizens care about.

Once people have enough money to live comfortably—even to buy luxuries like CD players and power lawnmowers—debate over the distribution of wealth becomes less ferocious. Other issues arise concerning the *quality of life* in a society of affluent, educated people. These issues involve such questions as how much government support of the arts should occur, how much government activity should occur to insure high air and water quality, and how much government intervention should occur to protect individual rights like free speech, reproductive freedom, and lifestyle choice.

Inglehart (and others) label as "post-industrial values" an entire array of positions on issues that arose (or gained special prominence) in the last quarter of the twentieth century: feminism, environmentalism, gay rights, reproductive freedom, freedom of speech, freedom of the press, and attitudes toward drugs, sexuality, and family structure. Other analysts have called these "social" or "cultural" issues.[5] All have noted that, as with the cluster of attitudes that define groups on the traditional Left–Right continuum, politically aware citizens tend to adopt a coherent set of positions on this entire array of issues.

For instance, one rarely finds a political participant who believes that abortion is murder *and* who also believes that the legalization of marijuana makes a lot of sense. Similarly, one must look hard to find a politician who demands that we get tough on criminals, but who also supports gay marriage. Nothing in logic makes the simultaneous holding of these particular views impossible—as opposed, say, to the illogicality of being a pacifist and supporting a given war. In the real world, however, people who are pro-life are almost always opposed to the recreational use of marijuana, just as those who say we should be "tough on crime" also condemn "deviant" sexual behavior.

What holds these various attitudes together? According to Inglehart and others, we must accept the notion of another defining perspective on the political process, a perspective growing out of the new, post-industrial society into which we are all moving (those in economically advanced countries most clearly of all). We might label this perspective the **cultural dimension of politics**. It stresses lifestyle issues rather than pure economics. An entire complex set of attitudes exists along this cultural continuum. People at one end of it hold a set of beliefs that cohere and that differentiate them from people at the other.

The social/cultural continuum

Social analysts have focused on this cultural dimension of politics for much less time than they have on economic divisions. For that reason, it is not easy to pinpoint and describe a number of precise positions along it, as we have done for the Left–Right continuum. The best we can do, at present, is describe the polar attitudes found at the opposite ends of this cultural continuum. Political participants gravitate toward those extremes, while most voters range all over the spectrum but clump largely around the middle.

Toward the extreme that some would characterize as the "liberal" or "radical" side, one finds the people labeled by Inglehart as **post-industrialists**. These are strong supporters of feminism and environmentalism, backers of the pro-choice side on the abortion issue, proponents of the rights of every kind of minority (gays, blacks, ethnic groups, and immigrants). They are usually non-religious and secular. Indeed, they are often opponents of organized religion, and they are especially critical of any state intervention to promote religious values. They oppose capital punishment, support international cooperation and worldwide peace initiatives, and oppose strong defense postures. They are strong civil libertarians and proponents of total freedom on "lifestyle" matters. For instance, they believe that whether to take drugs or not should be a "personal choice," not the dictate of any government. One should also be free to view pornography, to write scathing critiques of "the system," or to request medical help in dying.

On the opposite side of the spectrum, we find the **traditionalists**. These people are deeply religious and *welcome* state support of religious activity. They are appalled at the "dilution" of society's traditional "core citizens" by the increasing number of "inferior outsiders." They oppose immigration and bemoan increasing birth rates among minority groups. At the extreme, they favor sending members of these groups "back to where they came from."

Traditionalists are outraged at the practice of abortion and believe it should be criminalized. (Some even advocate the death penalty for doctors who do abortions.) To deal with "society's increasing crime rates," they urge upping the severity of punishments, including state-sponsored execution for the worst offenses. (Traditionalists worry about crime a great deal, and in their eyes it is always increasing.) Everywhere, they see the decline of character, the decline of traditional moral values. The "old ways" are being replaced by a decadent, mad pursuit of pure pleasure ("sex & drugs & rock 'n' roll").

No one, say traditionalists, takes personal responsibility for their actions any more. No one's willing to work hard the way people did "in the old days." People just want to sit back and take government handouts.[6] Traditionalists yearn for strong state intervention in many areas of social life to change this state of affairs. Let's use government powers to "reaffirm traditional values," restore things to "the way they used to be," put God back in public life, punish the foreigners who've taken our jobs, and get tough with the lazy decadents who take our welfare dollars. We've got to make the nation great again through a strong defense and a patriotic, hard-working, racially pure populace.

Naturally, there is something of a caricature in these presentations. Few traditionalists hold *every* "standard" position outlined here, nor do most post-industrialists. Like fascists and communists at the extreme ends of the traditional Left–Right spectrum, extreme proponents of the post-industrial and the traditional positions do exist. However, the "pure" attitudes depicted here represent the ends of the scale, not what most participants in modern polyarchies believe.

While many activists tend towards one of these ends or the other, many others fall closer toward the Center, and that is certainly where most citizens cluster.[7] As in any polyarchy, moderate attitudes will dominate on this array of potentially divisive issues. Still, the positions outlined above set the scene for battles on this cultural dimension. When people argue about these issues, they tend to assume that their opponents stand at the far edges of this particular continuum.

Figure 9.1 provides a visual representation to illustrate this new dimension of political conflict.

A new way to classify political positions

We now find ourselves with two entirely separate ways of plotting political tendencies. Each dimension (the economic and the cultural) helps us understand what political participants believe and what they are likely to do in office. By combining these two dimensions, we can achieve deeper insight into the divisions that split political activists in modern nations. We will also understand why average citizens have come to feel a disconnection between their perspectives and the policies enacted by the people they elect to office.

Note what happens when, as in Figure 9.2, we combine the two dimensions of political ideology. We end up with four quadrants, each representing a legitimate, conceivable set of political orientations—**Libertarians, Traditional Conservatives, Traditional Liberals** and **Welfare-state Traditionalists**.

To understand this, consider that *these four perspectives reflect views of government's proper role in both the cultural and the economic spheres*. Government's role may be (a) significant in both arenas, (b) weak in both arenas, (c) strong in

166

economic but weak in cultural matters, or (d) weak in economic but strong in cultural affairs. We end up with four distinct orientations toward political life.

In the lower right quadrant, we find people who dislike government altogether. Individual freedom is their highest value. Usually labeled **libertarians**, people in this group denounce any restriction on personal liberty.

Libertarians agree with traditional conservatives that "big government" should stay out of the free-market economy. They hate the welfare state's "unwarranted restraints" on freedom of economic choice. But they dislike most other forms of government activity as well. *Any* government action, say libertarians, is a restriction of freedom.

Staying perfectly consistent with their abhorrence of any and all government controls, libertarians believe that government should place few restrictions on personal liberties. Here libertarians part company with social conservatives. They advocate keeping government out of our bedrooms, out of a woman's right to choose an abortion, out of anyone's right to choose to die, and out of our right to buy drugs if we wish. With these positions, they end up shocking many of their conservative economic allies. Naturally, these anti-government cultural attitudes delight many liberals, although those same liberals castigate libertarians on economic policy.

Conservatives

In the upper right quadrant, we find an outlook that could be called **traditional conservatism**. It is neatly congruent, in the USA, with the core values of the contemporary Republican Party. On the one hand, this group prefers few government restrictions on a citizen's right to act as he or she wishes in the economic realm. In contrast, when it comes to personal life

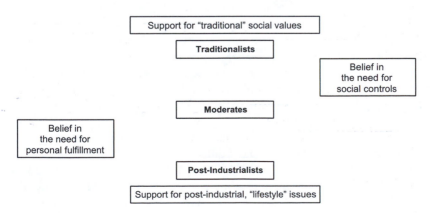

Figure 9.1 A model of possible positions on issues relating to social and cultural concerns.

choices (that is, issues connected to cultural matters), advocates of this perspective use government to impose a wide array of restrictions on behavior.

We have already reviewed the limits on personal freedom that cultural conservatives support. They are eager to use the powers of government to curtail sexual activity, stop abortions, end drug use, and impose prayer in school. An extended illustration may be useful to outline the sharp differences between cultural conservatives and libertarians, because their strong agreement on the need for a small government in economic matters makes them seem superficially indistinguishable. Let us look closely at their respective attitudes toward the use of drugs.

Cultural conservatives find drug use particularly offensive. It symbolizes a degradation of *character*, and character is a central value in the conservative belief system. Drugs represent a search for irresponsible pleasure. They thus undermine core conservative values: the principles of seriousness, hard work, and personal responsibility. Drug use destroys families, the backbone of any good society. Finally, drug use leads to crime, thus weakening the entrenched system of law and order and threatening the very fabric of society itself.

For conservatives, this social scourge must be eliminated, even if it takes an entire panoply of governmental resources. A "war on drugs" run by "a government drug czar" is not only reasonable, but necessary. Spare no effort or expense to eliminate this affliction.

Libertarians, in contrast, are maddeningly blasé about drugs. Freedom being their ultimate value, they let people make their own decisions about practically everything. If someone wants to buy and use a product, why not?

What harm, asks the libertarian, do drugs actually do? If people ruin their lives, so be it. They made their choice freely and must live with the consequences. They would probably have found some way to destroy themselves in any case. Drug addicts may even serve as negative examples for the rest of us. Seeing their fate will lead us to avoid that path of self-destruction.

If government steps in to curb drug use, say libertarians, it will cause more harm than the original problem (if problem it is). The result: an increase in the number of government bureaucrats, higher taxes, more controls over our lives (thus, less liberty), and more unlawful attempts to avoid those ineffectual controls (remember the problems of Prohibition). Most of the harm that drugs cause, libertarians say, comes not from *use* of the drug, but from *criminalizing* that use. If all drugs were legal, then hundreds of thousands of people who are currently considered criminals would no longer be so considered. Many real criminals (drug dealers) would be put out of business—or simply become legitimate business people selling a legal product. Crime would by definition decline. If drugs were bought and sold in any regular store like corn flakes, we would all live in a safer society. We would also live in a freer society that enshrined the notion of individual choice so dear to the hearts of libertarians.

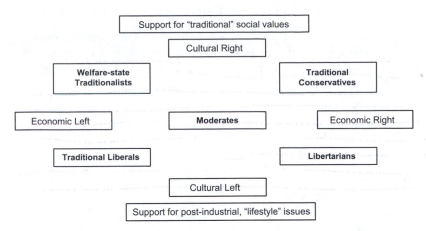

Figure 9.2 A model for classifying political activists along two dimensions: The interplay of economic and cultural outlooks.

What you think of these two (obviously polar) positions is your opinion. Whatever you believe, it is important to note that the traditional conservative view of drugs does lead to advocacy of a much bigger government, many more state expenditures, and increased taxes.

Consider, for instance, what it would take to have a *real* "war on drugs." I often point out to my students that we cannot even eliminate drugs from American *prisons*. If in those tightly controlled environments, drug use can flourish, then how could we eliminate its use in society at large? We could do so only through a huge increase in governmental powers. We would need many more drug agents, law-enforcement officers, prosecutors, courts, judges, and prisons than we now have. We would also have to pay more in taxes to cover the cost of these operations.

One could run through the numerous other conservative positions on cultural issues to show that most of these policy desires would likewise produce greatly increased government spending. Imagine how much more government we would need, for instance, to criminalize abortion, to force teachers to lead students in prayer in public schools, or to stop illegal immigration. Traditional conservatives may want no governmental interference in the economy, but their social and cultural objectives will produce lots of it.

Libertarians are more consistent. They want no government, period. Of course, even libertarians have to allow for some government—for police, courts, the military, road-building activities, and so forth. But compared with other groups, they see government as a bare-bones entity that should beg for every penny it gets.

Liberals

Conservatives are not the only group whose policy aims appear contradict-ory. The **traditional liberal position** (lower left side of the quadrant in Figure 9.2) contains a crucial inconsistency. Liberals want serious govern-ment interference in economic matters, but next to none in the area of social and cultural affairs. That is, they advocate the use of government agencies to limit (by regulation) the free operation of business owners and upper-level managers. They applaud governmental activity to collect moneys from better-off segments of society in order to create programs that benefit less affluent people. But in the area of speech, press, and personal behavior, liberals are adamant that government has little role to play. Adults should be able to say what they want, print what they want, read what they want, watch the movies and plays they want, engage in the sexual activities they want, buy the drugs they want, die when they want, and so forth.

In the interest of fairness, we should make it clear that most liberals and libertarians do not particularly condone drug use or promiscuity. They believe that freedom and privacy are so essential, however, that it is more important to allow people to act as they wish, even though some may indulge in reprehensible behavior, than to authorize governments to expand their police powers to the point where they can rein in and punish those activities. As long as your behavior harms no others and is done on your own or with other consenting adults, government should stay clear.

One must also note that neither liberals nor conservatives would accept the conclusion that their political outlooks contain inconsistencies. As we already know, people dedicated to a line of work are good at developing coherent explanations for what they do. Thus, conservatives say that gov-ernment intervention in some areas is necessary to insure *order*, a key requirement for economic prosperity. Governmental controls, they argue, can help to prevent social breakdown, the symptoms of which are crime, drugs, abortion, illicit sex, family break-ups, and so on. Only in a low-crime, strong-family society, say conservatives, can individuals work freely for their own *economic* advancement and count on enjoying the fruits of their labor. Government intervention in cultural matters, then, can be justified as insur-ing the social stability needed to encourage entrepreneurial creativity.

Liberals too can justify their seemingly contradictory plea for less gov-ernment on cultural matters but more in economic affairs. Their main aim, liberals claim, is the advancement of *human happiness*. Government interven-tion in the economy adds to the sum of that happiness. Government taxes and regulatory policies help improve economic circumstances for most citi-zens. Even those who are hurt by those policies, say liberals, are already so much better-off than most of us that their marginal losses still leave them wealthy and powerful. Thus, little harm is done to them and great good to everyone else.

On the other hand, government intervention in cultural affairs *undercuts* the sum of human happiness for most citizens. Liberals claim that governmental controls (over what people can say and write, whom they can marry, and what they can do with their bodies) limit the free choices that average citizens can make. It thus limits "the pursuit of happiness" so dear to liberal hearts. In short, government regulation of the economy increases mass happiness, so it is good. Government regulation of culture decreases mass happiness; therefore it is bad.

Whatever contortions liberals and conservatives must go through to explain the ambiguities in their various policy positions, outsiders may be forgiven for seeing these explanations as illustrative of the human ability to justify what we want to believe. Thus, liberal denunciations of government as "Big Brother" when it comes to censorship of books or movies ring a bit hollow when those same liberals ask for government to regulate, say, nursing homes in minute detail. Similarly, conservative tirades against "the nanny state" for regulating us into "despotism" sound hypocritical when those same conservatives plead for more government to stop abortions or punish people who won't speak English.

In the end, both liberals and conservatives want "more government"— but only when government does the things they like. They both want "less government" when they detest what government is doing. Like all humans, they want what they want—and will find ways to explain why their wants are not just reasonable and logical, but also morally right. So it goes.

Traditionalists

The fourth quadrant is occupied by people who accept a role for government in *both* the economic and the cultural-social spheres. They believe, like liberals, that government should rein in some of the worst excesses of free-market capitalism. They favor progressive taxation that takes money from the more affluent to help those with less. They especially support social welfare programs. In the USA, these include Social Security, Medicare and Medicaid, unemployment compensation, veterans benefits, aid to education, and environmental protection.

In other words, people in this group support broad-based programs designed to help "average citizens" in times of difficulty and need—they support the panoply of New Deal and Great Society legislation, programs that have come to form the backbone of the modern social-welfare state. Try abolishing any of these programs, and you will hear quite a ruckus from people in this group (and also from those in the traditional liberal group, of course).

People in this fourth quadrant are not full-fledged liberals, however. They are strong traditionalists when it comes to core values. They bemoan "the breakdown of authority in our times," decry "the unwillingness of kids to

171

work hard any more," and fulminate against "the growing immorality of our society." They worry that immigrants and minorities (that is, people unlike themselves) are undermining "the traditional fabric of our culture." For them work, order, discipline, authority, respect for religion, and support for "traditional ways" are central and compelling values.

These values are so pivotal that, to secure them, people in this quadrant are happy to accept significant governmental controls on private behavior. Abortion should be outlawed and punished, as should euthanasia, drug use, and pornography. Governments must promote religious values, by mandatory prayer in public schools at a minimum and, ideally, by *Bible* study in school. Of course, these citizens are strong in their support of police and the military establishment. "Outsiders" are to be feared and defended against. Immigration must be curbed. Illegal immigrants must be rounded up and deported. Trade barriers must be erected to prevent "unfair competition" from workers abroad. On the entire range of cultural issues, people in this quadrant take the traditionalist perspective that would, if implemented, lead to a great deal of government activity. Their goals thus produce "big government" in both economic *and* cultural affairs.

Describing the people in this group is easier than naming them. Handy labels exist for the other three segments of the population. No single term for this fourth group has yet found universal acceptance. Decades ago, the influential sociologist, Seymour Martin Lipset, coined the term "working-class authoritarian" for people with this perspective.[8] That phrase today seems patronizing. It is also unclear (what does "authoritarian" mean?) and not accurate (not all in this group are "working-class").

During the Reagan presidency, journalists used the phrase "Reagan Democrat" for this group. It signaled that their normal Democratic inclinations (as supporters of the welfare state) had been trumped for a time by Reagan's appeal to their traditional cultural values. That term too has its shortcomings. For one thing, it falsely suggests a specific time and place: the USA in the 1980s. This same perspective has been held by voters in many countries and long after the Reagan era.

Still, each label suggests something important. These citizens tend to spring from lower-middle and barely-middle-income ranks. They (or their families or people they know) have benefited from many broad-based programs of government assistance, and they are only a few paychecks away from needing government aid themselves. They would not want those programs abolished—or even scaled back. Yet they are inherently conservative in their support for traditional social patterns.

So, they support welfare-state programs but hold to traditional cultural perspectives. I propose the term **welfare-state traditionalist** as a reasonable way to describe this set of people. While indicating their support for broad-based programs of state aid, the phrase also suggests their willingness to use state powers to uphold traditional social values.[9]

Politics under new rules

We now find ourselves with a four-fold breakdown of the politically interested citizenry. Obviously, political life is still more complicated than this categorization suggests, but at least the model provides greater complexity than does the one-variable Left–Right continuum. A brief discussion will illustrate this point.

For well over a century after the Civil War, American politics was fairly simple. Most voters held clear allegiances to either the Democratic or Republican parties. Democrats tended to come from the middle to lower ends of the socioeconomic ladder, and Republicans from the middle to upper ends. Modest variations from that pattern occurred as a result of long-standing regional loyalties that became solidified after the Civil War. From the 1860s onward, for instance, even wealthier Southerners voted Democratic, because they identified Republicans as the party of Lincoln, Grant, and northern invasion. In the same way, poor northerners, especially in the traditional rural areas (New England, the Midwest) voted Republican, because that was the party of Lincoln, Grant, and victory in the Civil War. Otherwise, generally speaking, the parties divided along class lines.

However (and this is a big however), class divisions between the two parties were small because Americans have always had a large middle class. It was large to begin with, given American wealth, and became even larger because both wealthy and poor Americans often *identified* themselves in the middle. Thus, psychologically (if not actually), the majority of voters were "middle class." Both parties were always assured of a strong base of core supporters (workers for Democrats, upper-middle-class professionals for Republicans). The real game of winning elections then centered on appealing to that large set of less committed, middle-class centrists. Whichever party provided the strongest appeal to those voters in the middle usually won.

Those appeals almost always focused on the centrist voters' pocketbooks. Republicans were advantaged in the first several decades after the Civil War. In an expanding economy, middle-class voters identified upward and rewarded the party that pushed economic development. After the Depression, middle-class voters began to fear downward mobility and rewarded Democrats, the party that supplied safety-nets and security to those in trouble.

Obviously, Democrats did not lose every election during the era of Republican ascendancy, nor did Republicans lose all the time after Democrats became dominant. Both parties had strong bases in the electorate, and during their period in the minority could win elections in those exceptional years when the majority party faltered. That could occur for any number of reasons: a short-term economic slowdown, a particularly weak candidate, or an episode of scandal and corruption. Besides, each party had strong local and regional bases where they could always be sure of winning the majority of elections.

Growing voter disaffection

Since the 1960s and especially the 1980s, political life in modern democracies has grown more complex. We will focus here on developments in the USA, but similar patterns can be found in many developed polyarchies. To start, *voters are becoming disaffected from political parties—and from politics in general*. Many Americans now have no allegiance to either party. Citizens who claim to be "unaffiliated" with any party, or who have weak rather than strong attachments to one of the existing parties, have grown increasingly numerous in most democracies. "Partisan dealignment" is the term political scientists use to describe this general movement away from all parties.[10]

This detachment, even alienation, from politics keeps many citizens from showing up at the polls. Since the number of uncommitted voters is now large, parties must expend much effort appealing to this set of "undecideds." But since it is large, it is also diverse. Thus, a simple appeal to uncommitted centrists is not the obvious strategy any more. The group of non-party-attached voters is not necessarily homogeneous. It is not even necessarily centrist.

Furthermore, the game of winning elections often hinges on who shows up at the polls. When only 35–40 percent of eligible citizens vote in American mid-term elections and only 50–60 percent of the electorate votes for president, outcomes could be entirely different if one set of people instead of another make up that 40 (or 50 or 60) percent of the population. Getting your people to the polls, while discouraging the other crowd's supporters, has always been a significant strategy in democratic politics. It now lies at the core of determining who wins and who loses elections in America, because a large number of people may or may not vote on election day.[11]

Political effects of the new cultural divisions

An even more significant political development has occurred in modern democratic society. We have already encountered this trend: *It is the rise of post-industrial values, and the subsequent backlash to those values represented by the traditionalist position.* What has been its political effect?

We can start by assuming that most political activists take either the "traditional liberal" or "traditional conservative" set of positions outlined above. In this group, a liberal on economic issues is a post-industrialist on cultural issues. Similarly, a conservative on the economy is a cultural traditionalist.

Many voters, however, are not as easy to categorize as political activists. Some of them are out-and-out libertarians. The less government of any kind, the better. Some people with these views go so far as to move to parts of the country where government is less intrusive. The states of New Hampshire, Wyoming, Idaho, and Alaska have particular appeal.

Just a small segment of the American population can be called libertarian.

In most elections, their candidates do well to get one or two percent of the vote. Because of their resources and intensity, however, libertarians carry much more weight than their actual numbers might suggest. They are constantly placing their opinions before the world—on talk radio, over the Internet, and in letters to newspapers and political leaders. They operate major "think tanks," such as the Cato Institute, and the Reason Foundation, from which they publish books and articles in line with their ideology.

Libertarians are also willing to put money and time into promoting their ideas. For that reason, they make up a bigger percentage of political contributors and campaign workers than of voters. Their articulateness, their intensity, and their commitment insure an influence on public affairs well beyond their numbers. That is partly because libertarian ideals fall on fertile soil in the American context. The "small government" theme has long been a core American value. Thomas Jefferson expressed it well when he reputedly said that "that government is best which governs least." Although in practice Americans like government to do many things, in theory they do not. So people denouncing "big government" often gain a hearing—and sometimes adherents.

For instance, people with the libertarian outlook played a major role in helping defeat President Clinton's 1993 healthcare plan ("Too much government bureaucracy!"). They also helped keep defeat Republican-sponsored efforts to restrict the Internet ("Hands off the Internet!"). In both cases— the first favored by traditional liberals and the second by traditional conservatives—they helped defeat plans that would have led to increased governmental powers.

For all their skill in policy debates, however, libertarians are given short shrift by the parties at election time. Their numbers are not yet sufficient to make them a group worth courting. After all, *elections are won or lost by appealing to (a) large voting blocs that (b) are not locked into a permanent, partisan commitment.* Libertarians satisfy part (b) of this axiom (they are not automatically supporters of either major party), but there just aren't enough of them to center a campaign on.[12]

Other groups satisfy part (a) but not part (b) of this proposition. They form large numbers, but parties often just take them for granted because they are deeply committed politically and unlikely to be swayed one way or another in a campaign. African-Americans, for instance, vote in overwhelming numbers for Democrats. Christian evangelicals do likewise for Republicans. It usually makes no sense to pitch an entire campaign around an appeal to either group. Their members are already with you or against you, no matter what. No short-term campaign strategy can change these voting patterns.[13]

When it comes to core support groups, parties focus on **reinforcement** and **activation**. Give key supporters the traditional message (reinforcement) and make sure that they get to the polls on election day (activation).

It is the welfare-state traditionalists, voters in the upper-left quadrant of our diagram, who have become the key to many a recent election. That's because they satisfy both elements in our axiom about how to win elections. To start, they compose a significant element in the population. Perhaps one-third of Americans are people with this mind-set. That is more than enough to sway any election one way or the other. Then remember that these people are torn between the key perspectives of each major party. They could vote for Democrats if economic problems are the issue or for Republicans if "values" or national defense are the issues. It is both a large and a fickle group. No wonder party strategists have to think carefully at each election about how to win these voters' favor.

So the game of American politics has become one in which the two parties, led by people with the traditional liberal (Democratic) or traditional conservative (Republican) perspectives, vie for support from the welfare-state traditionalists. Party leaders face a tough task. They must stir their core supporters into enthusiastic action, but they must do so while at the same time campaigning on messages not central to those party loyalists, messages that might excite loyalty from people in the welfare-state traditionalist group. (And it is crucial to appeal to this group because there just are not enough voters in either the traditional liberal or the traditional conservative segments of the population to win elections. According to all polls of the past decade, Liberals make up about 20% of the American citizenry and conservatives 35%.) We will now see how this game works in practice.

The Democrats' strategy

Democrats can appeal to welfare-state traditionalists in one of two ways. First, they can try to make the core campaign issues economic. This group, after all, looks to the state as the economic safety-net of last resort. When they get sick, old, or laid off, they want to be sure that a state program is there to provide assistance. The more insecure their own economic position, the more likely they are to support the party that promotes state intervention in the economy to help the disadvantaged. Thus, as the economy declines, Democrats become the party that members of this group turn to.

Obviously, this assertion will not apply in those cases where Democrats have been in power during an economic downturn. Then they get defined as the party of hard times and face major problems. Jimmy Carter found that out the hard way in 1980. But the strategy works beautifully when Democrats are perceived as the "out" party during hard times—as in 1992.[14]

The strategy of playing on economic fears has the advantage for Democrats that their message for welfare-state traditionalists is then identical to their message for core supporters. Government is needed to solve the economy's problems. The party can thus stay "on message" and remain unified. A disadvantage stems from the fact that economic downturns occur only sporadically. Besides, half the time those downturns occur when the Democratic Party itself is in power and getting blamed for the problem. Since elections occur constantly (every year, in one state or another), this economic-woes ploy falls short as a long-term strategy. Democrats must find other ways to appeal to welfare-state traditionalists. Clearly, that means moving in their direction on cultural issues.

However, as soon as Democratic leaders start making those moves, staunch supporters from their core base start yelling, "Traitors!" That is, Democratic leaders who try to appease conservative traditionalists on cultural matters end up infuriating their most loyal, long-time supporters. On the other hand, there is trouble if Democratic leaders stay squarely within their ideological quadrant. If they do, they find themselves extremely popular among rank-and-file followers, and they may make a splash at party gatherings of the faithful, but they end up losing elections. Stressing the post-industrial-values side of their ideology alienates welfare-state traditionalists.

Bill Clinton and Jesse Jackson have typified two different Democratic approaches to leading the nation. Jackson, more than perhaps any other figure of the late twentieth century, represented the core values of the traditional liberal Democratic activist base. The party faithful loved him. He could rouse core Democratic constituencies to shouts and tears at any time. Unfortunately, his appeal never went beyond that single lower-left quadrant, because he horrified traditionalists of every stripe. They saw him as standing for radical social change, for a decreased commitment to the military and to "law and order," for abortion, and for "special rights" for minorities and women. To put it succinctly, Jackson was unelectable at the national level because he could not expand his appeal beyond the core base of Democratic supporters.[15]

Clinton, on the other hand, learned to expand the Democrats' appeal. In doing so, he irritated many traditional liberals. Still, he deliberately set out, early in his career, to find ways of appealing to those with traditionalist perspectives, knowing that without their aid, neither he nor most Democrats could hope to win elections and govern. He called for the death penalty, vowed to produce better schools, denounced violent and sexually suggestive lyrics in popular music, and claimed *not* to be a "big-government" Democrat. These and other stands that Clinton took, first in Arkansas and later in the nation, sent a message of empathy to traditionalists.

Of course, they didn't all buy it! Clinton hardly helped his cause by the famous incidents in his personal life suggesting that, while preaching traditionalism, he pursued a lifestyle defined by the 1960s "hippies," a lifestyle loathed by traditionalists. Still, Democrats who pursue this strategy do not expect to win all the traditionalists—they don't need to. If they can hive off a significant fraction, then they have an excellent shot at winning any given election.

Democrats who adopt this strategy do have to walk a fine line. They must broaden the party's appeal without alienating the faithful. Clinton did, in fact, irritate many core party loyalists as he worked his tortuous way from being a moderate governor of a conservative state (Arkansas) to leading the more liberal of America's two parties to victory in a conservative era.

The Republicans' strategy

If winning elections under these conditions is a stretch for Democrats, it is not particularly easy for Republicans either. Republicans at their core are traditional conservatives. They want the state to stay out of the economy, but they encourage it to intervene in cultural life to keep society peaceful, orderly, and traditional.

Like Democrats, Republicans do not have enough core supporters to get elected to office by running solely on this particular set of values. They too must branch out. Like Democrats, they won't make many overtures to libertarians. That group is small in number and utterly rejects many Republican proposals to restrict individual freedom. Plans to outlaw abortion rights, criminalize drug use, censor the Internet, and force religion into public schools enrage libertarians. Movement toward the lower-right quadrant seems to most Republican strategists (correctly) as an ineffectual way to go.

Like Democrats, Republicans have to go where the votes are. It is among welfare-state traditionalists that Republicans can find a large group of potentially supportive voters. In exactly the reverse fashion from Democrats, Republican appeals to these citizens must stress the degree to which they empathize with their economic fears and concerns. These voters already agree with Republicans on the "traditional values" matters. But they worry that Republicans want to dismantle those welfare-state programs of assistance, security, and support on which they have always depended.

Republicans can calm these fears in two ways. They can modify their traditional denunciation of these programs, or they can govern in such a way that the economy spurts forward, winning admiration from welfare-state traditionalists for their sound and responsible economic management. Traditionalists will support any party seen as producing economic growth. That growth will increase their take-home pay, fatten their pension plans, and generally reduce their near-constant sense of economic insecurity.

Tensions within the Republican Party derive from the efforts of party leaders reaching out to assuage the economic worries of welfare-state traditionalists. Remember that core Republican loyalists hate state intervention in the economy. Take one of the unquestioned tenets of faith among Republican activists: minimum-wage laws. Conservative activists see these as an abomination, representing all that is wrong with state intervention in the economy. Minimum-wage laws derive from a presumption that all-knowing government officials can set wages better than the most efficient system ever devised for that purpose: a free market economy based on supply and demand.

All minimum-wage laws do, say conservatives, is distort the economic system, making it less efficient while giving power to unelected bureaucrats.

Contrast that vehemence toward minimum-wage laws with the view taken by welfare-state traditionalists. In this group, it is an article of faith that minimum-wage laws are not only beneficial, but should be raised quite a bit higher than they now are. Anyone running on the blatant promise to abolish the minimum wage would meet first astonishment, then horror from these voters.

This example indicates the difficulties that face Republican leaders as they develop ways to appeal to welfare-state traditionalists. As they stress hot-button issues like the minimum wage that activate their core supporters, they alienate this second group of voters that they must also attract. But when they try appeals to *that* group, they get denounced by party zealots for "lack of principle" and "selling out."

President George H.W. Bush faced this problem when he ran for re-election in 1992. Having made the concessions necessary to attract welfare-state traditionalists, he was denounced by purist Pat Buchanan for his "betrayal" of party ideals. In 1990, Bush had been forced to renege on his "no new taxes" pledge of 1988 in order to get Congress to pass a federal budget. Bush did get a major concession; Democrats agreed on important spending limitations. In the end, everyone got something, no one was satisfied, and government did not break down. It was a typical democratic compromise in a complex polyarchy, but the party faithful on both sides were horrified. The moderate Bush suffered the most. Buchanan, a dedicated conservative, ran a tough race against him in the Republican primaries. That weakened Bush enough to make victory in the general election impossible.

President Bush's son, George W. Bush, faced this same kind of problem when he tackled social security reform. Republican and conservative activists have long believed in "privatizing" social security. (Indeed, this view is another article of faith in conservative circles.) Privatization gets government out of the pension business, conservatives argue, allowing full play to powerful and benign market forces that will help people lead satisfying lives beyond their working years. Let people invest their own money in the market instead of having it taken from them for the social security system. They will end up much better off in their retirement years, and we'll have a lot less government bureaucracy. This argument sounds quite reasonable when conservative economists put it forward.

There is a big problem with it, however. Politically it's a loser.[16] Social security (a system of old-age pensions that all modern nations have adopted in one form or another) is one of the most popular of government programs, especially among welfare-state traditionalists. Thus, Republicans who push "privatization" reinforce their base (people who hold an almost fanatical belief in this concept) but lose the large group of uncommitted voters to whom they must appeal if they wish to win elections. The standard pattern for Republican leaders has been to toss the "red meat" of privatization out to true believers at party meetings, while ignoring the issue altogether during campaigns and while in office.

George W. Bush followed this pattern very nicely; he never campaigned on privatization. He did, however, try an end-run on the subject. He waited until *after* the 2004 campaign (his last campaign, just coincidentally) and his re-election to the presidency before making a serious proposal to privatize Social Security. The results were just what one would expect. Party loyalists were delighted, but no others.

Liberals seized on the issue to enhance their standing with the electorate. By playing it up as "the end of Social Security," they managed to attract support not just from their own base but most important, from welfare-state traditionalists who turned in fright from the Bush initiative. By pushing an idea abhorrent to this large swing group, Bush and Republicans lost credibility and support from many of them. Of course, Bush also failed to achieve his reformist aims.

This entire episode bears an eerie resemblance to Bill Clinton's failed healthcare initiative. There, conservatives managed to persuade welfare-state traditionalists that their traditional "freedom of choice" (of their own doctors), as well as their current level of healthcare benefits, would be undermined by the proposal. In both cases, major reform plans that delighted the strongest followers in each party (liberals in one case, conservatives in the other) failed because the true-believers were unable to convince the large group of undecideds among welfare-state traditionalists that the plan carried more benefits than drawbacks.

Conclusion

This extended discussion of contemporary American politics is specific to a time and place, but it illustrates some broad principles of political life. Parties and political tacticians in most democratic settings confront the same strategic problems that face leaders of the Democratic and Republican parties in the early twenty-first century. The lessons to be learned are these:

- Active members of any party hold reasonably cohesive ideological perspectives
- In democracies, multiple parties exist, thus insuring multiple ideological perspectives
- No single one of these ideological perspectives ever dominates the mind-set of the majority of citizens, most of whom are relatively apolitical and hold seemingly inconsistent political attitudes
- Therefore, no one party will ever be able to base its long-term strategy for gaining power on simply promoting its own ideological perspective
- All parties in any democracy will find that to gain enough support to

180

govern, they must first shore up and galvanize their base supporters, but then must branch out to appeal to other groups of voters who do not hold all the core values of the party faithful

- In undertaking to broaden their appeal, parties will aim to attract those groups closest to them and choose those elements of their ideology most likely to please these nearby groups, while playing down party ideas distasteful to that nearby group
- Tensions will always exist as parties veer between the twin needs of placating devoted followers and of branching out to potential allies
- The parties best able to accomplish this task of enlarging their appeal will be those that:

   a   are already large and need but little new support to gain power

   b   are relatively moderate, so that they can move in a variety of directions in their efforts to gain new supporters without alienating loyalists

   c   have ideologically flexible supporters, so that movement toward other perspectives will not create dramatic intra-party schisms.

Tension is inherent in the political process. One particular tension will always exist: that between the true believers, those who constitute any party's base of dedicated workers, and the much less committed members of the general public, who must be vigorously courted if the party wishes to gain power. The strain of this relationship constitutes a central plot on the high stage of power politics.

Questions for discussion

1   Take some current issues like affirmative action, gun control, gay rights, free trade, global warming, and support for a strong military. Which of these fit into the old Left–Right continuum, which into the new "traditional-postindustrial" continuum, and which (if any) seem to stand by themselves as uncategorizable along either spectrum?

2   Which of the four ideological groups outlined above is likely to grow in coming years? Which is likely to decline? Why?

3   Does decriminalization of drugs, as libertarians want, make any sense? Or should we be cracking down even harder than we do now on illegal drug use?

4   We know that people do not like to live with inconsistencies. How do you suppose liberals justify more state intervention in economic life but less in social life? How do conservatives justify the opposite approach: small government economically, but big government socially?

5   Which party seems best situated now to take advantage of the complex mix of attitudes illustrated by Table 9.2, and build a majority coalition?

Part III

INSTITUTIONS AND
SYSTEMS IN POLITICS

10

INSTITUTIONS AND BEHAVIOR

The impact of voting systems

Just as personality, values, and beliefs shape our behavior, so do institutions. We get up at 6 in the morning not because we want to, but because we work at some institution (an office, a factory, a school) where "the rules" dictate our presence in an alert state by 8 a.m. We go to church on Sunday (or Saturday, or Friday) because that's the day our religious institution sets aside for spiritual observance.

Within institutions our behavior is also structured—often highly so. We do not scream and eat hotdogs in church. We do not bow our heads in prayer at football games. We do not drink beer and schmooze with our buddies on the assembly line.

Institutions structure our behavior in countless ways. That is especially true in the highly structured world of politics. Everyone used to bow to the king in the 1600s. Today, everyone is quiet as the tomb during Supreme Court hearings, and everyone yells wildly during political conventions. In structured, institutional settings, we don't behave "just as we want to." We don't "express our individuality." Rather, we "go with the flow," and act as we are "supposed to."

We will now examine how political institutions shape behavior—and thereby affect the overall political process.

Institutional effects of the electoral college

One of the strangest elections in American history occurred in 1824. The presidential campaign that year was the first hard-fought race since 1800, when John Adams and Thomas Jefferson engaged in a bitter contest for power. Following Jefferson's narrow victory, the nation saw three stable, 8-year presidencies—first under Jefferson, then under two of the leading statesmen of the day, James Madison and James Monroe.

None of the elections after 1800 was particularly competitive. Monroe was re-elected in 1820 almost by acclamation. His widespread approval symbolized voter contentment in a time of peace, prosperity, and expansion. The attitude of the day was encapsulated in a simple phrase: "the era of good feeling." This term is always used to describe the period from roughly the end of the War of 1812 to the mid-1820s.

By 1824, new class and sectional hostilities had emerged to heat up the political scene. With the original "Founders" of the Republic dead or ailing, there existed no obvious successor to President Monroe. Four leading figures entered the race, each representing a faction bitterly opposed to the others. The primary struggle pitted the quintessential "Establishment" figure, John Quincy Adams, a conservative Boston aristocrat (and son of the second President, John Adams), against military hero, General Andrew Jackson, symbol of the rising forces of the West, the frontier, and the "average American."

Also in the running that year was the formidable Henry Clay, who had already served a dozen years, on and off, as Speaker of the US House of Representatives. Rounding out the list of candidates was William H. Crawford, Secretary of the Treasury and favorite of the American south. Party played no role in this race, as only one major party existed: the Democratic-Republican Party of Jefferson, Madison, and Monroe. All four candidates were nominally members of this organization.

Issues in the campaign swirled around sectional rivalries. Each of the men stood for the interests of his region. Thus, Adams was strong in the northeast, Crawford in the south, and Clay in the west. Jackson too appealed to westerners, but his fame and heroic image gave him a broader appeal beyond sectionalism. This situation advantaged the charismatic Jackson, a military hero renowned for his victory over the British at the Battle of New Orleans (1815) and for his triumphs in various skirmishes with Native Americans.

Still, with three strong opponents, Jackson was unable to win a clear-cut majority. Once counted, the popular vote totals were as shown in Table 10.1. Quite a difference between Monroe's unopposed re-election of 1820 and these murky results!

Before we proceed, let us stop and ask: What *should* happen after an election with this outcome? Our first response might be: Why naturally, Jackson should be declared President! After all, he got the most votes.

One could, however, make a plausible case for the election of John Quincy Adams. Jackson at the time was seen by everyone, supporters and opponents alike, as the "outsider" candidate. Each of the other three men

Table 10.1 Popular vote totals, US Presidential election, 1824.

Candidate	Vote total	Votes (%)
Andrew Jackson	151,271	41.34
John Quincy Adams	113,122	30.92
Henry Clay	47,531	12.99
William H. Crawford	40,876	11.17

represented various factions of the "traditional order," the "Establishment" of that day. One could argue that nearly three-fifths of the electorate in 1824 had rejected the "upstart" Jackson; voters showed a clear preference for someone representing the established traditions. Because there happened to be *three* traditional candidates, the conservative electorate split its vote, allowing Jackson to emerge on top. Still, the voters' message in 1824 cannot be disputed: Give us a leader from the "Establishment" for president.

If we accept this interpretation of the election results, then surely Adams must be the man to occupy the White House after the 1824 balloting. After all, of the three traditional candidates, he was by far the most popular. The elevation of Adams to the presidency may well have represented what a majority of voters in 1824 "really" wanted.

This discussion illustrates the difficulty of interpreting ambiguous elections. How can we tell what voters are thinking when they send mixed messages like these? In elections with unclear results, there are essentially no good outcomes. Whoever becomes President will face a strong majority of people who voted against him.

Institutions for dealing with ambiguous election results

Nations have evolved three major ways (that is, institutions) for dealing with these situations.

Coalition governments

First, many countries use a parliamentary form of government with a voting system called **proportional representation (PR)**. These systems are explained later in this chapter. Here we need simply note their main effect. They produce a nearly-identical correlation between the percentage of votes that a party receives in an election and the percentage of seats that it wins in the legislature. Thus, a party winning 17.2 percent of the vote will win somewhere between 16 percent and 18.5 percent of the legislative seats. The ultimate result of the PR system is a legislature composed of several parties, none with a majority. Two or more need to reach agreement in order to form a **coalition government**.

For instance, in Sweden a result such as the one obtained in this 1824 election would mean that about 40 percent of national legislators would be "Jacksonians," about one-third would be "Adamsites," and so on. Legislators would then have to wheel and deal among themselves to produce a majority coalition that could agree on a **Prime Minister** and a **Cabinet** to govern the country.

Most likely, a conservative coalition of Adams, Clay, and Crawford supporters would emerge. It would put together a government in which Adams, as head of the largest coalition party, would become Prime Minister.

At the same time, Clay and Crawford would each receive top cabinet posts, and the key supporters of each man would be named to other high government positions. If this coalition were successful, it would govern until the next election. If not, it might break up and a new coalition government formed—after, e.g., 1–2 years. The Crawford forces might defect from Adams and align with Jackson, producing a Jackson-coalition majority and making Jackson the national leader.

Mechanisms of the electoral system

A second way of dealing with this situation occurs through **the electoral system**. A number of countries have set up election systems that anticipate unclear election results and provide a solution. In France, for instance, if no presidential candidate wins a majority in the balloting, a second national election is held two weeks later in which *only the top two* candidates are allowed to participate. That way, the ultimate winner must by definition win a majority of the votes. He or she thereby holds a legitimate claim to represent the nation at large. ("More than half of our great people put me in office.") No danger exists of someone being called a "minority president."

In Ireland, voters in most elections are allowed to list second-place, third place (and so on) preferences. That way election observers and analysts don't have to speculate (as we did above) about whom voters "really" would have preferred if their own candidate makes a poor showing. If Americans had used this system in 1824, ballots cast for Clay and Crawford, who were clearly out of the running, would have been re-examined to see whom those voters liked after their preferred candidate. Once the second-place, third-place, and fourth-place votes of Clay and Crawford are added to the totals already achieved by Adams and Jackson, one of those two gentlemen would clearly gain a majority. There would no longer be a question about whom the voters "really" wanted.

Plurality voting

As we all know, the USA follows neither of these two patterns for dealing with mixed voter signals. We have neither a parliamentary system nor a tradition of coalition government. Nor do we use voting methods that automatically produce a clear majority. In most elections, Americans use a system of **plurality voting** for choosing the winner, not **majority voting**. That is, the winner is simply "the candidate with the most votes."[1] We follow this rule even when the winner's vote total comes nowhere near a majority of the ballots cast.

This system has produced some strange results. Two interesting examples occurred in the 1990s, when independent Governors were elected in Maine and Minnesota. Angus King, became Governor of Maine in 1994 with just

35 percent of the votes. It wasn't much, but it did beat the other candidates. Likewise, Jesse Ventura won his race for Governor of Minnesota in 1998 with a mere 37 percent of the vote. In both cases, nearly two-thirds of state voters ended up with a leader they had opposed.

Americans generally accept results like these because they occur rarely. Given our traditional two-party system, the vast majority of campaigns present a simple face-off between two candidates. One of them, by definition, wins a majority, leaving little room for debate and interpretation.

Even when one candidate fails to win a majority because of other contenders, those "third-party" candidates usually win such a small number of votes that, psychologically, the result is the same. Voters see the race as between a Democrat and a Republican. Whoever wins more votes (even if somewhat less than a majority) is seen as the clear winner. Thus, if a Republican wins 48 percent of the vote for, say, Attorney General of Montana, and a Democrat wins 44 percent, with an independent candidate taking 8 percent, citizens do not hesitate a moment before accepting the Republican as Attorney General.

The electoral college: a unique exception

Despite this rule of "plurality wins" for nearly all elections, Americans have an entirely different set of rules for deciding the outcome of *presidential* elections. In world perspective, these rules are unique. No one else chooses a national leader this way, nor do Americans themselves choose any other official this way. The system is a true oddity.

We actually use two devices for selecting Presidents, but the central institution is called the **Electoral College**. Its importance derives from a simple fact. According to the US Constitution, only those who win a *majority* in the Electoral College can attain the American Presidency. Because of the peculiar way this "College" works, it is entirely possible to win a majority of **Electors** while winning nothing like a majority of actual voters. For instance, Abraham Lincoln won *under* 40 percent of the electorate in 1860, yet he easily won a majority in the Electoral College (59.4 percent of Electors). Bill Clinton won just 43 percent of the vote in 1992, yet won 68.8 percent of the votes cast in the Electoral College.

This kind of result is common. Thirteen times in American history (out of 55 elections through 2004), the candidate who won the presidency gained less than 50 percent of the popular vote. Fortunately for political stability, when the Electoral College system converts popular votes into electoral votes, it almost always does so by giving a majority to the candidate with the most popular votes. It does so even when no candidate has won a majority of those popular votes. Nearly all the time the Electoral College repeats the common American pattern: It produces a victory for the candidate who comes in first in the popular vote count. In its unusual way, this peculiar institution ends up giving the country an uncontested and legitimately-accepted national leader.

That's the general rule. However, you may have noticed a key phrase in the conclusion above: "nearly all the time." After three American elections (1876, 1888, and 2000), the Electoral College named as president the candidate who came in *second* in the popular balloting. Those decisions, however, were not as outrageous as they might at first appear. In 1876 and 1888, it would be better to say that the candidate who *apparently* came in second was named president. Both elections were extremely close, and in that particular era corruption was common. With all the stuffed ballot boxes and "graveyard voters" on both sides, we will never know for sure who did end up with the greatest number of votes in those elections.

Something similar happened in 2000. Votes of all kinds were in dispute in several states, especially in the state that determined the outcome: Florida. It took a Supreme Court ruling to decide which votes would and would not be counted. People will argue forever over the merits of the final count, but in the end, Florida officially went for George W. Bush by the narrowest of margins. The resulting Electoral College numbers gave him a slim national victory, despite the fact that he received half a million fewer popular votes than his opponent, Al Gore.[2]

The lack of clarity in all three of these elections gave the Electoral College a little leeway in its own decision-making. Essentially, these races were toss-ups, so the Electoral College as an institution closed its eyes (so to speak) and picked one of the candidates. It could as well have picked the other. Luckily, the nation was strong enough to live with the results and move on. It left many disgruntled citizens in each case, but no guerilla activists. As in any strong polyarchy, people got back to their lives, and the most disgruntled plotted to change these results at the next opportunity (i.e., the next election).

In two other American elections, the Electoral College failed entirely at its job. Instead of giving the country a minority president, it gave the country *no* president. That is, it gave no candidate a majority of its votes. Thus, the Electoral College was unable to tell the nation what person to install in the White House.

The first of these cases, the election of 1800, need not detain us, as the system in place at the time was changed soon after that election. Since 1800, the new method of choosing American Presidents through the Electoral College has never failed to produce a clear winner, *except for* the election that we started this chapter with—that of 1824. Most unusually, as it happens, the Electoral College that year split in much the same way as the American electorate did. Instead of giving us a clear winner, as it almost always does, it produced the results shown in Table 10.2.

As in the electorate at large, Jackson still led all candidates. Adams came in a strong second, but no one met the constitutional requirement for presidential selection.

Table 10.2 Electoral college vote totals, U.S. Presidential election, 1824.

Candidate	Vote total	Votes (%)
Andrew Jackson	99	37.93
John Quincy Adams	84	32.18
William H. Crawford	41	15.71
Henry Clay	37	14.18

Remember that key *institutional* rule: it takes a *majority of Electors* to win the presidency. What happens when, as in this case, no one wins a majority?

The USA has a back-up system (so to speak), in case the Electoral College fails to do its job. If the College does not produce a president, the back-up system calls for the House of Representatives to choose the President. That sounds simple, but the Constitution provides some added complexities.

The first feature kicks in as we contemplate what the House might have done in 1824 if it could have chosen from among the four candidates listed above. Remember that in 1824 Henry Clay was Speaker of the House and had held that position for years. Wouldn't House members have voted for Clay if they'd had the chance?[3]

It turns out they never had the chance. According to that document's Twelfth Amendment, the House of Representatives chooses the President when no one has a majority of the Electoral College, *but* the House cannot choose just anyone. After this divisive campaign with ambiguous results, the House might have been tempted toward a radical move: ignore the bitterly-divided official candidates and select a prestigious outsider who could heal and unify the country. Or it might have chosen one of its own members, some political insider with little mass appeal. These options were never possible, however. The Twelfth Amendment says that the House must choose from among the top *three* candidates only. In other words, it cannot run amok and choose someone who hadn't even run for President that year.

So the House in 1824 had to pick one of the top *three* vote-getters. Fine, you might say. Why did they not choose Clay, since he, the leader of this very body, had run third in the election? Well, he had, and he hadn't. He did come in third in the popular vote, just ahead of Crawford. Unfortunately for the ambitious Clay, he came in *fourth* in the Electoral College vote, just *behind* Crawford! He was out of the running, with no chance for the presidency that year. The rules, as laid down in the aforementioned Twelfth Amendment, say that the House must pick a president from among the top three candidates *in the Electoral College voting* (not in the popular vote). That rule limited the choice of House members to Jackson, Adams, and Crawford (Table 10.2.).[4]

A second little-known twist to the presidential selection process derives from the way the House actually votes for president. It is not individual

House members who vote, but states. Thus, House members meet in little caucuses, state by state, and decide as a group whom to support. Each state then casts one vote, and one vote only, for president.

A problem with this method could occur in cases where state delegations are evenly split. A state with four House members might have two Democrats and two Republicans. These legislators would presumably split their votes and cancel each other out. One might expect at least a few states to produce a split result in any election requiring the House to choose the President.

This kind of split result would seem unimportant except for the third little-known twist provided by the Constitution relevant to the choice of President. When the House decides the matter, the winner *must* receive a majority of votes cast. Since votes are cast by states, the winner must therefore receive a majority of state delegations. In our time, that would mean winning 26 of the 50 state delegations in the US House of Representatives. Now what if an election thrown into the House produced something like the following?

- Republican candidate: 22 States
- Democratic candidate: 19 States
- Split delegations: 9 States

What happens is simple. We have a national (or world) crisis. That is, there would be no American president!

Actually, of course, someone *would* be president. It just wouldn't be any of the people who ran for that office in the previous election. We all know that when there is no president, the vice-president takes over. Now the question becomes: who is vice-president if the House cannot decide on a president? Normally, of course, the vice-president is the winning candidate's running mate, but in this case there *is* no winning candidate.

What happens in these circumstances derives from two final twists of the rules. First, that same Twelfth Amendment gives to the *Senate* the task of choosing the vice-president. Second (and fortunately), there is a provision in the document that ensures governmental stability. Senators are allowed to choose the vice-president from among the top *two* candidates only. Some vice-presidential candidate is bound to have a majority, and therefore the nation will always have a vice-president. Thus, it will always have someone available to fill a presidential vacancy.[5]

Still, if this scenario ever occurred, we can imagine that the country would feel itself in something of a crisis. After all, the Senate might be dominated by the party whose presidential and vice-presidential candidates came in *second* (or even third) in the national balloting. It would thus, under this scenario, be entirely possible for the nation to end up with a *president* who had been, just a few weeks earlier, the *vice-presidential candidate on a losing ticket.*

Of course, these are unlikely events. Not since 1824 has the US House had to decide the presidency, so we needn't lose sleep worrying about it. The basic rule is that *the Electoral College properly sorts out who should be President in almost all cases.* Even in the few cases when it "messes up" and chooses the "wrong" winner (that is, the candidate with fewer popular votes), American citizens accept the outcome as an unfortunate aberration in a tightly-contested election. They seem to view it as the case of an umpire making an erroneous decision on a very close play. Fans yell and scream, but they don't mob the field and disrupt the game. Eventually, they subside, and play goes on. (At least that's how things work in a stable polyarchy, which since the Civil War, the USA has proven to be.)

A close corollary of this rule is that, in the very unlikely event that the Electoral College fails to produce a president, the House will take on, and successfully carry out, that task. (It has succeeded at the job twice in its two opportunities.) In 55 presidential elections from 1788 through 2004, covering the first 216 years of the Republic, this system has worked. The odds are small for that wild scenario—the possibility that the system would not produce a president from among the legitimate candidates for that office.[6] Even in that case, we end up with a president—after the Senate chooses a vice-president.

What happened in 1824?

Let us return to the actual results of the 1824 election. Clay, seeing himself out of the race, threw his support to Adams, and the combined strength of these two established statesmen carried the day. Adams squeaked through to victory, winning the bare minimum of state delegations needed. A total of 13 of the 24 states supported him. Jackson won seven, and Crawford four. Adams thereby became president—barely.

Oddly enough, the ethically-upright Adams went on at that point to seal his fate. He named Clay Secretary of State. That move allowed Jackson and his supporters to spend the next 4 years plausibly denouncing an apparent deal between these two. They popularized the catch-phrase, "bargain and corruption," to suggest an unholy alliance designed to keep "the people's will" from happening.

It is hard to say how much injustice was done to Jackson, given the unclear election results. Still, if an injustice did occur, it was repaired 4 years later, when a repeat of the Adams-Jackson competition gave Jackson an easy victory.[7] He went on to serve a full 8 years as president, the maximum allowed (by convention) at that time. His place in history is secure, despite his questionable loss in 1824.

The impact of institutions on behavior

Why spend so long on this obscure and distant event? The point is that politics cannot be explained simply by looking at individual personalities. The actions of political participants are everywhere channeled through institutions. Formal structures with their own organization and rules shape what people do and what outcomes will result from those doings. Different institutions produce different effects, and we cannot understand the politics of a time and place without grasping how the institutions of that time and place operate.

In the short run, the Electoral College produces one president instead of another. A slightly different set of election rules could have made Andrew Jackson or Henry Clay president in 1824, not John Quincy Adams. The long-term impact of this institution is even more significant.

We can see from our 1824 example that the electoral-college system practically imposes a majority-seeking strategy on American politicians. Only a large party with support across classes and regions can succeed at winning enough popular votes to gain that crucial, necessary majority in the Electoral College. Any individual with ambition, and any organized set of politicians trying to gain power, will develop election strategies with that aim in mind.

This institutional requirement has influenced the entire course of American politics. It produces groups and individuals who work at creating broad national coalitions. Parties and candidates with a narrow focus or a regional appeal have little hope of winning anything. They will either fade away or broaden their message. Only very large, nationally-oriented, and usually centrist organizations can hope to rally enough voters to compete for that decisive majority. All other groups will lose every presidential election.

In other words, "The South Shall Rise Again Party" or the "United Teachers Party" will never get anywhere. A party that can appeal to just 5 percent or 10 percent of the electorate, or even 20 percent, is always condemned to loser status in American politics. Ross Perot discovered this when he scored a remarkable 19 percent of the vote in 1992 after running for president as an independent candidate. That got him exactly nothing in terms of power and influence within the system.

Most politicians know these facts and draw clear lessons from them. To have even a shot at power in the USA, they have two choices. On their own, they can develop broad, large, and almost necessarily bland organizations (American parties are often called "centrist" or "catch-all" outfits because they must appeal to many segments of society). Or they can join one of the already-existing broad and large parties (currently, either the Democrats or the Republicans). Naturally, it is easier to do the latter than the former, so most political activists head toward one of those two organizations.

American politicians know that if they take neither course, they are doomed to powerlessness on the sidelines—like Perot. Most shun that option.

They modify their purism and get into one of the parties with a chance at winning an Electoral College majority.[8]

There are, of course, just two parties that fit the bill. For that reason, both Democrats and Republicans are always crammed with every kind of personality and outlook. They are always struggling to contain restless factions and ambitious mavericks. The party best able to develop unity in the short run usually wins the presidency. Given the conflictual nature of politics, however, no successful party stays unified long, and the in-party's schisms give the out-party a chance to get back in power.

The majoritarian impulse given to American politics by our method of choosing Presidents goes a long way toward explaining why a large, diverse nation like the USA has evolved a political system characterized by just two parties. After all, we could easily have a dozen or more parties: a Southern Party, a Pro-Life Party, a Gay Rights Party, a Feminist Party, a Flat Tax Party, and so on. Groups that might be tempted to form third parties soon realize, however, that in isolated clumps of true believers, they have little hope of gaining power. Their followers either become discouraged and fade away, or decide that they can work for their goals more effectively within one of the two large parties.

Partly for this reason, the two-party system has been around in one form or another for most of American history.

The impact of voting systems on political behavior

Methods of voting, as we have seen, can seriously affect political outcomes. The Electoral College is just one of the many ways people have devised to distinguish winners from losers in ballot contests. *How* voters choose their leaders varies a good deal.

This process is not trivial. If Germany and the UK were to swap electoral systems, politics in both countries would change dramatically. The UK, which almost never operates with coalition governments, would immediately have to learn how. Germany, which almost never has one-party-majority government, would now find that condition normal. The simple act of changing an electoral system can have significant effects of this sort.[9]

Most Americans have no idea that we *have* "an electoral system." When an election occurs, we vote for one of the candidates, and the person with the most votes wins. What more can one say?

We have already seen with the Electoral College that there is indeed a lot more to say. It turns out that the particular method we think obvious ("vote for one of the candidates, and the person with the most votes wins") is just one of hundreds of ways of voting. Luckily, the large number of possible systems derives from tiny variations on just two primary methods. We will focus on the central features of each and then sketch a few of the many possible variations.[10]

Plurality or proportional voting systems?

We begin with the system most readers know best. If Americans are choosing an individual leader (a Mayor, a District Attorney, a Governor), we simply vote for one of the various candidates in the race. The votes cast for each candidate are added up, and the person with the greatest number of votes wins. A majority is not needed; in most cases, a simple plurality will do. That is true even if candidate A wins just 30–32 percent. As long as no other candidate gets as much as A, then A is the winner.[11]

If we are choosing an entire group (a city council, a state legislature, the House of Representatives), the rules become slightly more complicated. Under these conditions, the geographic area holding the election (the city, the state, the nation) divides itself into a number of sub-divisions. These are usually called **districts** or constituencies. The lines of these districts are drawn so that each contains approximately the same number of people. The actual number of districts will vary widely. The state of Maine uses 151 districts for its 151-member House of Representatives, while the much larger California uses just 80 districts for an 80-member House. The number of members in any political body reflects evolving choices made over the years. It is based on chance events, local history, political calculations, and cultural norms.

Once district lines are drawn, voters in each constituency cast ballots for one of several competing candidates. Votes are then added up, and the person with the greatest number gets to represent that district in the body being elected. This method of choosing leaders has various names. I prefer the descriptively accurate **single-member-district-plurality system**, henceforth referred to as **SMDP**.[12] It is often called a **first past the post system** (especially in the UK) and abbreviated as **FPTP**. Both terms indicate that you do not need a majority to win, just more votes than any other candidate. (Remember that "winning a plurality" means getting more votes than anyone else; "winning a majority" means getting at least 50 percent plus one of the votes).

SMDP has long been used in elections for most public offices in the USA, Canada, UK, and India and at one time or another (and is still being used) in dozens of other places. While this system of voting may seem obvious, it is in fact *not* the electoral system of most of the world's long-term democracies. The clearest alternative to SMDP, and perhaps the most popular voting system in the world, is **proportional representation** (always abbreviated as **PR**). Nations that use some form of PR include Germany, Israel, Belgium, Japan, Sweden, and many others.

In the simplest version of PR, voters' preferences at the polls are reproduced exactly in the distribution of seats for the body being elected. Thus, if 31.2 percent of voters in New Freedonia mark their ballots for the Progressive Party, then that party will win 31.2 percent of the seats in parliament.

Since the underlying aim of PR advocates is "true democracy," they hold that the distribution of power in the elected body should be a perfect reflection of the voters' will.

Both SMDP and PR have advantages and drawbacks that scholars, journalists, and activists have debated for decades. Over the years, many variations on each form have been tried in the real world, and we are no closer to a consensus on what is the "right" or the "ideal" electoral system. Each has its strengths and its weaknesses. Each benefits some groups and hurts others. To understand the claims and counter-claims, we'll take a closer look at each system.

Voting systems compared

We will start with the simplest example of SMDP. If an election is held in country A, and one party gets 55 percent while a second gains 45 percent, we would expect the legislature to be divided more or less 55 percent for A and 45 percent for B. That is what usually happens in the USA.

Note, however, the dramatic distortion of the voters' will that *could* happen if the distribution of party strength were nearly even across the country. In every district, party A would get about 55 percent of the vote (say, between 52 percent and 58 percent), while party B would get somewhere between 42 percent and 48 percent. As a result, party A would win every seat, and party B would win none. In not a single district would B get above 50 percent, so it would win no seats. The legislature would be staffed only with members of party A, leaving 45 percent of citizens with no voice to represent them.

In practice, distortions like this are rare in two-party systems. Both parties have their geographic bases of strength. In its stronghold districts, the minority party will manage to get candidates elected, even while losing a majority of seats nationwide. Still, SMDP almost always advantages the larger party.[13] James Campbell has shown that from 1954 to 1992, the Democratic Party gained, on average, 25 more seats in the US House of Representatives than it would have achieved under a purely proportional system.[14] (Democrats averaged 54 percent of the votes in each House election, but gained 60 percent of the seats.) And those extra seats, Campbell argues, had a real impact on policy outcomes. Thanks to SMDP, Democrats won more legislative victories than they were "entitled to."

This modest advantage of the larger party becomes pronounced when that party is dominant. If a party gets 52 percent of the vote nationally under SMDP, and a second party gets 48 percent, the bigger party will win about 56 percent of the seats. But if the vote ratio were 62 percent to 38 percent, the large party would now win 81.2 percent of the vote to the smaller party's 18.8 percent.[15] This effect is logically easy to understand. A party averaging 62 percent across, say, 100 districts will probably win between 50 percent and 75 percent in nearly every one of them. In only a few

197

districts will it win fewer than 50 percent. Thus, it will win nearly every race in these 100 individual districts. Yes, it will deserve a large majority of seats, but is it healthy for them to have over 80 percent of those seats while facing a greatly-reduced minority party that it can largely ignore?

Distortions in an SMDP system become especially dramatic when *three* or more parties compete. Say a new party enters a formerly two-party system. It appeals to a broad range of citizens and conducts a serious campaign, ending up with *20 percent* of the ballots cast. Given its uniform appeal, its votes are not concentrated in any particular area or region. Under these circumstances, the party might win *no seats at all*. More likely, it will win here and there but end up gaining just 1 or 2 percent of the legislature's members. How can this be? How can a party get so little payoff when 20 percent of the nation adores it?

Simple. If the party's support is fairly evenly divided across the country, then it will presumably average between 15 and 25 percent of the votes in most districts. In some places, it may go as high as 30 percent, in others as low as 10 percent. But in a three-party race, even 30 percent does not give you a victory. You will normally need 35–40 percent of the vote in a three-party race to have a chance at winning. A party that averages 20 percent *evenly* across the country will certainly not get as high as 40 percent in most districts. Hence, few (if any) of Party C's candidates are elected.

Contrast this outcome with the results for Party D, which, e.g., enters the same system a few years later. D is a regional party, representing the voice of citizens in just one part of the country. It runs candidates in just 10 of the 100 districts and wins just 4 percent of the vote nationally. But its vote is concentrated entirely in these ten districts, and it ends up winning *all* of them. Thus, Party D could end up with 4 percent of the vote and *10* percent of the seats in the same election that gives Party C its usual 20 percent of the vote and *2* percent of the seats!

These are not fanciful statistics. Highly distorted results of this sort occur frequently in SMDP elections. In 1978, for instance, an election for the provincial assembly of Saskatchewan produced the outcome shown in Table 10.3.

After this election, the New Democrats ruled the province unobstructed for several years. They rode roughshod over a puny opposition of Progressive Conservatives (and no Liberals). Thus, NDP policies became law, *despite the fact* that a majority of voters had rejected this party at the polls.

Other distortions of the SMDP system can be seen in the British general election of February, 1974. These extraordinary results are worth studying in detail (see Table 10.4).

We note first that no party won close to a majority of the electorate, yet the two largest parties ended up with nearly all the seats. The Liberals won one-fifth of the electorate and more than half of the votes of each of the two big parties, yet they finished with under a *twentieth* of the seats obtained by

Table 10.3 The distorting effect of SMDP: Example 1, results of the 1978 election for provincial assembly, Saskatchewan.

Party	Votes (%)	No. of seats	Seats (%)
New Democratic Party	47.5	44	72.1
Progressive Conservative Party	37.6	17	27.9
Liberal Party	14.9	0	0.0

Table 10.4 The distorting effect of SMDP: Example 2, results of the February, 1974, UK general election.

Party	Votes (%)	No. of seats	Seats (%)
Labour Party	37.2	301	47.4
Conservative Party	37.9	297	46.8
Liberal Party	19.3	14	2.2
SNP (Scottish Nationalists)	2.0	7	1.1
Plaid Cymru (Welsh Nationalists)	0.6	2	0.3
United Ulster Unionist Coalition	1.3	11	1.7
Social Democratic & Labour Party	0.5	1	0.1

Conservatives and Labour. They provide a textbook example of what happens to a third party with support that is not concentrated in any specific region. Liberals were widely popular, but captured a mere fourteen seats in the 633-seat House of Commons.

In contrast, the Scottish Nationalists, a party concentrated in one section of the nation, won a *tenth* as many votes as the Liberals, yet took half as many seats (7 to the Liberals' 14). The Unionist coalition did even better. Winning just 6 percent of the votes obtained by Liberals, they won almost as many seats (11 to the Liberals' 14). In an SMDP system, it is not the number of people who vote for you that matters, but where those votes are cast. The Unionist votes all came in a small number of districts: the Protestant sections of Northern Ireland.

Of course, the most dramatic result of this election was the "triumph" of the less popular party. The Conservatives won 225,000 more *votes* that Labour, but Labour ended up with four more *seats* and the right to form a government.[16] One academic wag wrote these brilliant words: "The general election of February 1974 might almost have been designed by the Electoral Reform Society to display the anomalies of the plurality system."[17]

One can multiply these examples, but the point is clear. The more parties in a SMDP system, the greater (and the more outrageous) are the distortions in the votes-to-seats ratio.

A final problem in SMDP systems is the "wasted vote." The desires of many voters are not reflected in the legislature. It is a winner-take-all system, so in every district votes for the losers have no impact. If you are a conservative in a district where liberals won 51 percent of the vote, you and the 49 percent of your follow conservatives get no representation.

But in PR systems, every vote counts. Your vote will be added to all the other votes for your party across the nation, and all the people in your camp will gain the representation you deserve. Thus, your vote counts at the national level, even if you live in a town where your party is insignificant. The very structure of this system, say PR advocates, encourages turnout and participation. No one can claim that their vote is wasted just because they are a Red living in a Blue district.

Under SMDP, say its critics, there's little point in voting, or even getting active in politics, if you live in a non-competitive district. If you're in the minority party, why bother? But that's also true if you are in the majority. Your party is sure to win, so you personally do not need to waste the time and effort of getting involved.[18]

Under PR, it always makes sense to become active and to vote. Your effort will count in the larger picture, even if the local scene is bleak. To illustrate, take the state of Massachusetts in 2004, entitled at that time to 10 members of the US House of Representatives. Operating under the SMDP system, it divided itself into 10 equal geographic districts and proceeded to elect a Democrat in each district. This clean sweep occurred on the same day that 37 percent of Massachusetts voters opted to support Republican George W. Bush for president.

Presumably, about that same percentage would have wanted Republican representation in Congress. But under SMDP, this three-eighths of the electorate was cut entirely off from any connection to power in the House. If Massachusetts had used a 10-member-district system with PR, it would have ended up with at least three and probably four Republican House members instead of none.

With any election using the PR system, Massachusetts Republicans would have a huge incentive to get to the polls and to work hard at getting others to the polls. They would know that they have statewide support in the 35–40 percent range. Every extra vote gained over the 35 percent level could bring them closer to another seat. Acting passively, however, might drop them below 35 percent and down to a total of just three seats. The payoff possibilities are clear. The system propels the rational actor to expend resources: time, energy, money.

As it was, however, Republicans lost miserably in all 10 districts. They may have controlled 37 percent of support state-wide, but 37 percent (plus or minus a bit, depending on district) never wins anything in a two-person race. And it was worse than that. Four of the House seats were not even contested. In those districts, the Republican party could not even find candidates. Knowing they were certain to lose, potential challengers figured they had better things to do.

In a PR system, a major party will contest every seat in a multi-member district and almost always win some. Not only did Republicans fail to compete in four districts, but even in the six contested races, challengers did a poor job. They averaged just 28 percent of the vote. None attained the 37 percent level of Bush, the national leader.

In a PR system with multi-member districts, several members of the minority party can expect to win seats, so nominees will be of a higher caliber and do a better job of campaigning than occurred here in Massachusetts. As we have seen, the entrenched nature of the dominant party in an SMDP system discourages talent and leads to under-performance by the minority party. Voters are cheated of the varied options provided by competitive politics. They may become cynical as entrenched incumbents start taking them for granted.

One benefit of SMDP often touted by its backers is its ability to produce a stable, majority government. Since it almost always enhances the power of the leading party, SMDP often pushes that party over the vital 50 percent mark from a vote percentage in the 40s. In the UK, this occurrence is common. In many elections, the largest party has received 40–49 percent of the votes, but a majority of the seats. That is good for, say SMDP supporters, as it eliminates the need for coalition government and its instabilities. SMDP opponents, of course, decry this result. Why, they ask, give a party with less than majority backing several years of unchecked power to make policy? And what is wrong with forcing leading political factions to compromise and work together in a coalition?

To summarize, what SMDP does in the short run, is to (a) increase the power of a country's largest party and (b) decrease the power of most other parties, especially non-concentrated third parties, but (c) increase the power of geographically-concentrated third parties. The broader impact of SMDP is to enhance the likelihood of stable, one-party governments, while poorly reflecting national opinion in the seats of power. The system as a whole is also likely to depress participation rates, because votes (and political activities in general) are wasted in non-competitive districts.[19]

Reforming SMDP

Many proposals have been made—and adopted—to remedy the perceived ills of SMDP. One variation is to keep single-member districts but go to *majority* voting. This is sometimes done through a runoff election. At some date after the first balloting (1 week to 1 month later), a second election is held with only the top *two* contenders allowed to compete. Someone then *has* to gain a majority, so the problem of minority winners is eliminated. This system is called single-member-district voting with a run-off, or sometimes single-member-district-majority voting.

France has used this system for decades. In votes for parliament (the

National Assembly), the country is divided in 577 districts, and in districts where no candidate wins a majority (that is, most of them), a run-off occurs 1 week later. At that time, only candidates who have won votes in the first round equal to 15 percent of the *registered voters* of the district are allowed to compete.

The effect is to limit candidacies in the second round to two or three (very rarely, four). The winner more often than not breaks through the 50 percent level. Regardless, no third round of voting is held, and a simple plurality at this point wins the seat. In elections for the presidency, the second round of voting is held *2* weeks after the first, and *only* the top two candidates are allowed to compete. This system insures that the President of France can always claim to represent a majority of the electorate.

Another device to improve SMDP is the Australian method of *preferential voting*, sometimes called the **instant-runoff voting system**. Here, you vote for every candidate running for each office. You do this by indicating your first, second, third (and so forth) preference next to each name on the ballot. Thus, if Jones, Brown, Smith, Hill, and Dale are all running for Mayor, you might mark your ballot with a 3 after Jones, a 2 after Brown, a 5 after Smith, a 1 after Hill, and a 4 after Dale—revealing your level of support for each candidate.

When ballots are tallied, all first-place votes are noted, and anyone with 50 percent is declared the victor. If no one gains a majority, the candidate with the fewest first-place votes is eliminated. That person's *second*-place votes are then counted as first-place votes for the remaining four candidates and added into the totals. Thus, if your favorite, Hill, is eliminated after the first count, then another first-place vote is given to Brown, your second choice. If no one has a majority after elimination of the weakest candidate, the next candidate with the fewest first-place votes is eliminated, his or her votes are redistributed, and the process continues until someone finally surpasses the 50 percent marker.

Both the instant-runoff and the second-round systems insure that a majority of voters in each district is highly or at least fairly satisfied with the winner. If that person was not your first choice, then it was your second (or possibly third) of several candidates. This way, your vote is less likely to be wasted. Even if your most desired candidate gets nowhere, your second or third choice may end up in office. You've still helped elect your representative and feel some connection to her.

While these modest alterations of SMDP have their supporters, both can produce a legislature even less representative of the popular will than the original system. They usually eliminate extremist parties, those that generate intense support but also intense opposition. These parties usually exist at the margins of the political spectrum (Fascists, Communists), but they could also be parties representing a particular religion, nationality, or region. In many districts they may have enough appeal to get 30 percent or 40 percent of the vote. In a multi-party system with SMDP, they could win a number of seats and make life in parliament difficult for the mainstream parties

Legislative representation for a party like this will be greatly reduced under a *majority* voting system (either through run-offs or preferential voting). Given the intense nature of its appeal, you either love or hate such a party. If you love it, you'll vote for it in the first round (in a run-off system) or give it your first-place vote (in a preferential system). But *no one else will ever vote for it* in a second round or give it second-place or third-place votes. Thus, in both systems extremist parties never get more than their original 30 percent or 40 percent, while second-place votes go to one of the more moderate candidates who came in second or third to the extremist party in the original voting. The extremist party ends up with a lot fewer seats than it might seem entitled to, while moderate parties get more.

A good example of this phenomenon can be seen in the 2002 French presidential election. There the extreme Right-wing candidate, Jean Le Pen squeaked into second place in the first round of voting with 16.9 percent of the vote. That number represented, essentially, his peak among French voters. In the run-off, 2 weeks later, Le Pen won exactly 17.8 percent of the vote. The contrast with his winning opponent could hardly be greater. Jacques Chirac, a moderate conservative, got only 19.9 percent of voters to choose him in the first round, but 82.2 percent in the second round.

In other words, the candidate who's less divisive, who's acceptable as a second or third choice to people who can't get their favorite into office, is advantaged in the SMD run-off system. That is also true for parties. Le Pen's National Front party gained 11.3 percent of the vote in the 2002 parliamentary election, but gained no seats at all. They just could not pick up many additional votes in the second round. In similar manner, the French Communist Party (during its rigid, far-Left phase) gained 21.3 percent of the parliamentary vote in 1962, but ended up, after the second-round of voting, with just 8.8 percent of National Assembly seats.

Some people see these results as a *strength* of the single-member-district-majority method. France, in fact, adopted this run-off system precisely to eliminate or weaken extremist parties. As we have seen, the system works exactly as intended. It produces a tiny number of far-Right and far-Left officials in France (and elsewhere). Thus, extremists who might undermine a polyarchal system are kept from the levers of power.

Supporters of this system play up these results. Whatever your own views, it is clear that institutions are never neutral. By a "simple" change in the electoral law, France changed the composition of its National Assembly and the entire tenor of national politics. Where once it was raucous and rowdy, French parliamentary politics has become calm and stable with the near-elimination of its most extreme elements.

Proportional voting systems

The most common alternative to SMDP is the PR system. That is most likely to be adopted when a country has many parties. The primary argument for PR is that it provides an accurate reflection of the popular will. Thus, if 42 percent of Israeli voters want Labor, then 42 percent of the Knesset is Labor. Not 57 percent, not 31 percent, but 42 percent. The party's strength in the electorate is honestly reflected in parliament.

This system insures representation for many points of view. Any group that bothers to organize and field candidates for office has some hope of winning seats. True, even under PR, some parties get so few votes that they gain no seats, but these will be parties with extremely low levels of voter support. In most PR systems, any group that can entice five percent of the nation to vote for it will win parliamentary representation. In many places with PR, parties well under that level can win legislative seats.

The major result of PR is that many parties win some seats, but *almost never* does one party win a majority. Hence, a PR system almost always necessitates **coalition government**. Some tout this effect as positive. It forces disparate parties to work together. It forces social, economic, and cultural compromises, and it makes parties less likely to treat each other with inflexible hostility. They all know that they might have to work together in some future government.

Coalitions can also be seen as negative. PR opponents claim that they are unwieldy and unstable. Further, they produce incoherent policies and weak governments that are constantly falling. These criticisms apply especially to countries with many political parties. It is difficult to build stable governing coalitions when those coalitions contain three, four, and even five parties of wide diversity.

How PR works

To understand the PR system and its effects, we must learn exactly how that all-important legislative proportionality comes about. How do we create a legislature that matches the voters' will? It is not as simple as it sounds.

To achieve legislative proportionality, the most common method relies on a system of **multi-member districts**. After all, if Party Q wins 20 percent of the vote in an area, it cannot win 20 percent of the seats if that area consists of a *single*-member district. A single member cannot be divided into less than one. If Party Q is to get its 20 percent, then the district must have *five* members. Then Party Q can get one of them (20 percent of five). The simple math of PR makes multi-member districts seemingly necessary.[20]

So PR generally works by dividing the country into *multi*-member districts. And the PR system will be closer to accurate when those districts are *large*. If all the districts have five members, then Party T with 8 percent of the vote still gets nothing (8 percent of five is four-tenths, not enough to win even one representative). But if the district contains *ten* members, a party with 8 percent of the vote gets one legislator (eight-tenths of 10 equals 0.8, usually rounded up to one). So proponents of a very accurate PR result always want larger districts. The whole point of PR is to insure an accurate reflection of the popular will, so there is always a push in PR systems for large districts.

In Israel, to take the extreme case, there is just *one* district: the entire country! The result is that even very small parties get national representation. In the Israeli election of 2003, for example, the United Arab List party won 2.08 percent of the national vote and two of the 120 seats in parliament (the Knesset). In the 1984 election, the extreme-Right Kach party gained a mere 26,000 votes (1.2 percent of the total) but still managed to elect a Knesset member.[21]

Problems with PR

Critics find two main drawbacks to PR. First, voters are now far away from those they have elected. A multi-member district must be geographically large, and it is possible that none of those elected will live anywhere near a good number of the voters. If we wanted a district of five members of the US House in northern New England, for instance, we would have to combine the states of Maine, New Hampshire, and Vermont. By the quirks of the election process, it is possible that all five elected legislators from this district would come from Maine and New Hampshire, leaving Vermonters feeling unrepresented.

In any case, if you are represented in Congress by five people, it becomes hard to identify with any of them—or identify them at all. Most Americans cannot name their current member of Congress. They would be hopelessly muddled about who represented them if they lived in districts with five members. The problem gets much worse when, as in many countries, districts become even larger. For instance, voters in the German *Land* of Baden-Württemberg (equivalent to a state or province) have *30* people representing them in the Bundestag (the lower house of parliament). When voters there say, "I'm going to complain to my representative," to whom precisely are they going to complain?

Recognizing this problem, supporters of PR have tried a variety of remedies. Typically, these involve dividing the country into single-member districts to elect part of the legislature (usually half or more), then adding additional members to the legislature to make sure that the distribution of seats is proportional to the distribution of national votes.

In a simple demonstration of this method, let's say that the result of single-member-district voting across the country gives Party H 14 percent of the national vote, but just 1 percent of the seats. Party H will be now allowed to add enough additional members of its party to the legislature to bring its total in that body up to the 14 percent level. In the USA from 1954 to 1994, that would have meant that Republicans could have named, on average after each election, an additional 25 members of the House of Representatives in Washington.[22]

This apparently clever solution carries with it another problem. Just who gets to name those additional legislators? In most systems, it is the party apparatus. That is, party leaders get to choose, and they will obviously choose *themselves* and their loyal party associates. This again could produce a legislature not closely tied to voters in the districts.

One drawback of PR should now be clear. No matter how one achieves a legislature that's roughly proportional to the voters' wishes, it is impossible to produce a legislature *all* of whose members have popular support among the voters *and* close local connections to them. You can have close constituent connections through SMD and proportionality through PR, but you cannot have both.

The Japanese have a marvelous term to illustrate this problem. **Zombie Dietmen** are members of parliament (the Diet) who lost in their district races, but were later named to seats gained by their party via proportionality. In other words, these representatives were "killed" in their districts, but still live to hold seats in the Diet. They are like the walking dead—hence, zombie Dietmen.

A second, and much more telling, argument against PR is its effect on political stability. PR gives much more power to smaller parties than they would have under SMD systems, while at the same time decreasing the power of the larger parties. Parties that get 5, 10, or 18 percent of the vote would be eliminated under SMDP, but under PR they receive representation in parliament proportional to their vote totals. The effect is a legislature with many parties, several of them rigid or extreme, complicating the task of coalition-building for effective government.

Reforming PR

Recognizing the problems of constructing coalitions based on numerous parties, several countries have tried to limit the number of parties that gain parliamentary seats. Many believe that Germany has best succeeded at this task. It has devised a way of melding the SMDP and the PR systems. The result is an entirely new set of structures that political scientists call a **mixed electoral system**.[23]

In Germany, it works this way. Half of all national legislators are chosen by the traditional SMDP method. Thus, every citizen lives in a relatively small district and elects a locally-based representative chosen by plurality vote. Nationally, however, the distortions of SMDP are avoided by a device that ensures a PR result for the entire legislature. The other half of parliament is chosen through a multi-member-district, PR-list system.

206

There are 16 of these districts. They correspond to the 16 *länder* (a *land* is a regional area equivalent to an American state or a Canadian province). The number of legislators to be chosen from each *land* ranges from three (Bremen) to 72 (North-Rhine-Westphalia). On the same ballot where voters mark their choice for district legislator, they also make a second choice, indicating which **party list** they prefer. The percentage of votes that each party receives in a given *land* represents the percentage of seats they will be given in parliament (the Bundestag) from that *land*. Thus, if the Social Democrats win 38.4 percent of the votes in Hesse where 42 seats are in play, they would be entitled to 16 seats from that *land* (38.4 percent of 42 is 16.13).

Now remember that half the *land's* seats are determined by district plurality voting. Let's say that of the 21 seats determined by that method, the Social Democrats had won 10 of them. Since they are entitled to 16 seats altogether, they clearly have another six coming. Those six parliamentarians are determined by the party list previously referred to. The first six names on that list are added to the 10 district-elected legislators to give Social Democrats their 16 members of the Bundestag from Hesse.

This system produces the supposed benefits of PR (a fair representation of the popular will, the chance for smaller parties to gain office), while adding an advantage of SMDP (voters are all represented by one geographically-close legislator).

In addition, a German twist on this system undermines another major criticism of the PR system. No party can gain representation in the Bundestag unless it passes a crucial popularity test. It must win *5 percent* of the vote nationally or win *three* single-member districts outright. This is such a rigorous test that since the early 1950s, only five parties have met it, greatly easing the chances for stable coalition governments.[24]

The German system has often been regarded as a good model. Over the years, it has produced a legislature that is a close mirror to national opinion, while keeping out narrow and extremist groupings, and allowing all citizens to feel close ties to at least one national legislator from their area. Perhaps for that reason, a number of other countries have adopted the German system or some variation of it.

Unfortunately, most nations adopting mixed electoral systems have been newly-democratizing, and often unstable, countries. Many have dropped this system as unworkable after just a few years of experience with it. It remains, for now, unclear as to whether that happened because unstable nations frequently change the basic rules of the game, or because there is something inherently weak in the mixed system itself. The leading students of this system conclude that "the jury is still out on whether or not mixed systems combine the best of the majoritarian and proportional worlds."[25]

Conclusion

Election systems are not neutral. They each produce certain effects, and those effects will be seen as either positive or negative by various members of the political class. No election system will ever be universally viewed as perfect. In the long run, citizens must decide which effects they can live with and which they abhor, then construct the electoral system that best comports with their values and interests.

In the short run, however, all members of a polity, especially its political activists, must accept the electoral system as a given. It is simply there, part of the understood political environment. They must work it into all their calculations as they go about their daily activities.

Electoral systems are deeply ingrained in the working apparatus of any stable democracy, and they won't be changed until the majority of participants agree that their interests would be better served by some other system. It is not easy to change deeply-ingrained institutions, because political participants are well aware of the **law of unintended consequences**. No one knows exactly what will follow after major institutional change. In contrast, *everyone* knows what to expect from the current system. Like Hamlet, we usually prefer to "bear those ills we have / Than fly to others that we know not of." Once set in place, electoral systems (like other institutions) have long lives. They become an accepted part of the environment, structuring the strategies, choices, and actions of all political participants.

Questions for discussion

1   Can you think of three ways in which your own political actions are constrained by the institutions of your society?
2   Why has no nation but the USA adopted the Electoral College system to choose its leader?
3   If the leaders of a new country asked your advice on the electoral system they should adopt, what would you tell them? Why?
4   If the USA were to change its method of choosing a President, should it adopt a popular-vote method with a plurality winner, a majority winner, or some other system? What might be the political repercussions of each possibility?
5   What might happen in Congress if the USA were to adopt a PR form of electing legislators?

11

INSTITUTIONS AND LEADERSHIP

A comparison of parliamentary and presidential systems

Americans are at a disadvantage in trying to understand democratic politics elsewhere, because their system differs from the others. Unlike Americans, most people in stable polyarchies live under **parliamentary government**. Knowing how their own system works, they can readily grasp the general nature of politics in similar countries.

Americans, however, are different. They live in what's variously referred to as a separation-of-powers, checks-and-balances, or (simply) **presidential system**. *No other stable, long-term polyarchy operates this way.* Scholars have long debated why. Some believe that structural factors make parliamentarism more compatible with democracy than presidentialism.[1] Others see the correlation between polyarchy and parliamentarism as an historical accident. Parliamentary systems, they say, just happened to be introduced in cultures whose values were compatible with democracy.[2]

We cannot resolve that debate here. Since both systems exist in at least one strong polyarchy, it is clear that nothing inherent in either system makes it incompatible with democracy. We will now focus on differences in the two systems as they operate within stable polyarchies. What, if any, political effects do these different systems produce?

How do these systems differ?

The quickest way to illustrate the difference between **presidentialism** and parliamentarism is to ask this question. When will the next election for national leader occur in the USA? When will it occur in the UK, Italy, Norway, and Holland? In answering, you must be precise. Name the exact day on which each election will occur.

This is an easy question for Americans, but impossible for citizens in *any* parliamentary system. I can name the very day when Americans will vote for President in 2172. Assuming that there is still a USA and that the Constitution and the election laws have not changed, then that date will be Tuesday, November 3. In 2284 Americans will be voting on November 4, and in 2416 it'll be November 8.

How do I know this? Simple. The Constitution says that the President will be elected every 4 years (starting in 1788), and federal law says that the election for president will take place on the first Tuesday after the first Monday in November. Once you know those two facts, it is a simple matter of heading to a universal calendar and checking for that particular Tuesday in 2008, 2012, 2016, and so forth.

Ask the same question for any nation with a parliamentary system, and *it can't be answered*. The reason lies at the heart of the way this system works. Once we understand that system, we will see why election dates are rarely firm until a few months (or even a few weeks) before any election.

The parliamentary system explained

We will start with the strangest fact (for Americans). There is *no* election to fill the country's top post. National elections occur for the legislature only. That body then goes on to choose the national leader, always one of its own. In parliamentary systems, executives *must* be members of the legislature. In the USA the president *cannot* hold a seat in either house of Congress. It is constitutionally forbidden.

Thus, executives in parliamentary systems are not independent of the legislature. They run for a legislative seat like all other candidates for parliament. To become the national leader (usually termed Prime Minister), you must be chosen to head your political party, and you must then run and win a parliamentary seat at election time. Once in parliament, you must get a majority of legislators to back you. This will occur automatically if your party has a majority of seats. You are its leader, after all, and you helped it gain that majority in the recent campaign. Even if your party fails to win a majority of seats, you can still become Prime Minister if you and your party form coalition alliances sufficient to produce a majority.

In any case, the road to executive leadership always runs through the legislature.

That difference between systems is just the beginning. Let's return to our original way of showing the central difference between parliamentarism and presidentialism. Remember that no one can pinpoint the date of the next election in a parliamentary system. True, elections must be held every 4 or 5 years, depending on the country (as we explain below).[3] Otherwise, there is no "term of office" for a Prime Minister, and there's great uncertainty about how long any leader will last.

You become Prime Minister because your party or the coalition you head represents a majority of legislators. You remain Prime Minister as long as you can keep that majority support. Lose the majority, and you're out. At that point a new election could take place, whether it's 6 months or 5 years since the last one. In addition, Prime Ministers can call for new elections pretty much whenever they want. Because we can't know in advance when

Prime Ministers will (a) lose their majority or (b) decide to call an election, we can never know exactly when the next election will be.

That's the short version of parliamentary politics. Now we will look at the operation in detail.

In most parliamentary systems, ultimate power rests in one institution: the popularly-elected house of the legislature.[4] There are no "checks and balances"—at least, not as Americans conceive them. In the USA, relatively equal independent political units are chosen in different ways, endowed with different legal and political powers, and given a variety of ways to check each other's actions. In most parliamentary systems, "the buck stops" in the more powerful house of the legislature. When a majority there decides on a policy, that policy *will* take effect.

This is a key point, and one quite unfamiliar to Americans. If the US House of Representatives passes a bill, the Senate can stop the bill dead in its tracks by refusing to vote for it. If both House and Senate pass a bill, the President can veto it (and vetoes are very hard to override). If House and Senate pass a bill, and the President signs it, the Supreme Court could declare it unconstitutional in a later court case. On it goes. Each of the four most powerful institutions of American politics must be in accord for a policy to go forward.

It is quite different in most parliamentary systems. Once a bill is passed in the most powerful body of the legislature, no other political entity can stop it. The second house, if there is one, is much weaker and can, at best, slow down ratification of the bill. The Prime Minister cannot veto the bill. Remember that Prime Ministers are members of the legislature and have just one vote like all other members. And in most parliamentary systems, courts cannot overturn laws passed by the legislature. Either by law or by convention (sometimes both), they just do not have that power, which Americans call **judicial review**.[5]

Only parliament itself can amend or abolish its original policy. That usually happens after the voters have spoken in a new election and chosen a different set of leaders. In any case, power in parliamentary systems is *concentrated*. It is tied to one key institution rather than dispersed among several, as Americans expect it to be.[6]

Elections in a parliamentary system center on the choice of members of the "popular" house of parliament (the one elected by the people). It is this house that chooses the Prime Minister. Its members are directly elected, something that is usually not true of the second and weaker house.[7] We concentrate here on operations in the dominant legislative body.

The name of this entity varies widely. It is the House of Commons in English-speaking countries (Britain, Canada, Australia, New Zealand, even India), the National Assembly in France and other French-speaking countries (including Canada's province of Québec), the Bundestag in Germany, the Folketing in Denmark, the Diet in Japan, and the Knesset in Israel. We will refer to this body from now on simply as "parliament."

All democratic parliaments share some key characteristics. First, members are chosen in a widely-publicized vote via free and fair elections. Second, the election struggle involves multi–party competition. More than one party (almost always several) strive to get candidates elected. Finally, once elected, members of parliament (specifically, members of the majority party or majority coalition) get to name the **Prime Minister**.[8]

Let's start with the day after an election, to illustrate just how parliament uses its power to name the country's top official. Parliament has been chosen and is now composed of members of various parties. There are two main possibilities, as described below.

Majority government

In the first scenario, one party wins a majority of seats. That party on its own can now name the Prime Minister. This person will be no stranger to the nation. Each party's leader is well known long before the campaign, and voters know that a vote for party X is a vote for the leader of party X.

Party X's leader, now Prime Minister, goes on to name the entire Cabinet. Again, no surprises. Most cabinet members (known as **ministers**) are leading members of the majority party. They themselves have just been elected (or re-elected) to parliament after promoting the party's fortunes in the just-concluded campaign. The Prime Minister and the other ministers now govern the country in their executive capacity, but they all remain members of parliament. They attend its sessions, report to it on a regular basis, propose the major pieces of legislation that have any chance of passage, and are subject to lengthy and hostile interrogation about the course of their developing policy decisions. At the same time, each of these ministers runs a government department: defense, education, social services, and so on.

Here we see a major difference between parliamentarism and the presidential/checks–and–balances system. In the USA, it is unconstitutional to be a member of both the legislative and executive branches. A Senator who's appointed to the Cabinet must resign the Senate seat. A Secretary of Agriculture who runs for and wins a Senate seat must resign from the Cabinet. These two branches are truly separate from each other.

It is the opposite in a parliamentary system, where they are intertwined. The leaders of the executive branch (the prime minister and the cabinet) are *also* the leaders of the legislature. They do not stand apart from parliament, but are chosen by it, answerable to it, and deposable by it. They also remain members of it until the next election. If they are "deposed" by the legislature (that is, defeated in a vote and forced to resign—about which, more later), they do not go away, they simply change where they sit.

Coalition government

In a second (and common) scenario after any parliamentary election, there may be *no* majority party. Several parties win seats, but none attain that crucial fifty-percent-plus-one threshold. At this point, a coalition of parties comprising a majority of legislators will form, and the leader of the largest of these parties is usually named Prime Minister.[9]

It is standard practice in parliamentary systems for the Prime Minister to name members of the cabinet. That is always a delicate operation, but is even more complex under coalition circumstances. First, each party's numerical strength must be considered. Party A provides, e.g., one-fifth of the coalition members, so it would expect a fifth of the cabinet seats.

Beyond numerical considerations is the fact that cabinet positions vary in power. The Defense Ministry is a plum. The Ministry for Sports is a consolation prize. Cabinet positions also vary in their significance to each party. The Green Party, for instance, would place great value on the Environment post, while the pro-business party would maneuver instead for a Finance or Commerce ministry.

The composition of each coalition will depend on party numbers in parliament, historical relations among the parties, and numerous other factors. The most stable coalition outcome is usually an alignment of two parties that are ideologically close. Typical of this situation was the alliance between two Left parties in Germany, the Social Democrats and the Greens, between 1998 and 2005. In the same vein, two Right parties in France, the Gaullists and the UDF,[10] have frequently found themselves in parliamentary coalitions. On the other hand, coalitions of three or more parties are often unstable, especially if they comprise parties of diverse tendencies.

The life and death of governments in a parliamentary system

Once named, whether representing a majority or a coalition, the Prime Minister and the Cabinet proceed to govern until they lose power. Note this phrase: "until they lose power." Unlike the USA, the phrase is not "until the next election" or "until the end of their term." In a parliamentary system, there *is* no term for the Prime Minister and his or her government. They can remain in power for years and years . . . or for just a few days. They remain in control of government until, to repeat, "they lose power." How does that happen? In just one way: when the Prime Minister loses control of their majority.

As long as Prime Ministers retain support from a majority of legislators, they can remain in office indefinitely.[11] But once a parliamentary majority loses confidence in the government and refuses to support it, the Prime Minister, with the entire Cabinet, must resign. Journalists usually refer to this development

213

as "the fall of the government" after "losing parliament's confidence." When is a **no-confidence vote** likely to occur?

If a government was formed as a coalition of parties, its chances for long-term survival are slim. To govern, a coalition must retain all (or nearly all) of its members for votes on all major issues, but what are the chances that members of two or three parties (sometimes more) will all agree on all the major policy matters that governments must deal with? It is hard enough to get all members of just one party to stick together!

So coalition governments are inherently shaky. They usually last less than 2 years. For a while, the parties may be able to cobble together compromise agreements on some key matters, and they may find ways to put off dealing with policies on which they could never see eye to eye. Eventually, however, some tough issue will arise which they cannot finesse and cannot resolve. The Prime Minister will have to propose a policy, and one of the coalition partners will be unable to support it. That party will pull out of the coalition and vote against the government, ensuring a parliamentary expression of no-confidence and forcing the government's downfall.[12]

A second and less common end to a government occurs when one party has *majority* status in parliament. Normally, the party will remain united and give the Prime Minister a string of victories until the next election. A particular Prime Minister may, however, prove so unpopular that the party decides to make a change. This is a delicate operation, usually achieved by forcing a Prime Ministerial resignation, followed by the immediate selection of a successor from the same party.

Britain in 1940 provides a clear example. The majority of Conservatives forced the resignation of their discredited leader, Prime Minister Neville Chamberlain, replacing him with another Conservative, Winston Churchill.[13] Conservatives followed this same pattern in 1990, replacing an unpopular Margaret Thatcher with another of their members, John Major. In the summer of 2007, the majority Labour Party replaced its long-serving Prime Minister, Tony Blair, with a top party official, Gordon Brown. None of these cases of national leadership change derived from a popular election.

The most common end to a parliamentary government comes after a national vote. In democracies, the parties that control government are bound to lose elections on a regular basis. Let's say that Party A holds 57 percent of the seats in parliament before a general election (and has thus served as governing party for several years). Its policies were not terribly popular, however, and after the next election it finds itself with just 41 percent of the seats. No longer controlling a majority, the Prime Minister (and the entire Cabinet—that is, the government) must resign immediately. The new majority party (or coalition) takes over, forms a new government, and the game continues.

To summarize, *governments in parliamentary systems last as long as they retain the ongoing support of a majority of legislators, but must resign when they no longer have that support.* This lack of support most commonly reflects a government's unpopular policies. The government then falls after being punished by legislators through no-confidence motions (most likely to occur during periods of coalition government) or after being punished by voters at the polls.

When do elections occur in parliamentary systems?

We now arrive at a central question, and the one Americans find most curious about parliamentary systems. When do these elections, the primary event that can cause a change in government, take place?

As we already know, there is no set election date in parliamentary systems. Concerning these dates, there are two basic rules. First, Prime Ministers may call an election whenever they want. Second, there is a major exception to that rule; elections cannot be put off indefinitely. Parliaments everywhere are elected for a set number of years. The number varies, but is usually four or five.[14] In other words, Prime Ministers have wide leeway in determining the date of an election, but they cannot postpone it forever. In keeping with democratic principles, voters must be allowed to state, on a regular basis, how they feel about the job their rulers are doing.

Let's look more closely at this process. Say an election occurs in North Ruratania on March 7, 2028, and the parliamentary term under Ruratanian law is 5 years. Now let's consider the most likely outcomes of the election. First, a stable government majority exists. Either one party has gained a majority, or a stable coalition forms between two closely-allied parties. In this case, the Prime Minister can usually count on retaining that majority for the entire term of the legislature, and an election need not be called for several years.

Note, however, that the Prime Minister is unlikely to wait until the final days of the 5-year term before calling that election. She or he is more likely to call the election after 3.5–4.5 years in office. That's because prime ministers wish to call an election at the most advantageous time. They wish, naturally, to bolster their chances of being returned to office with a continuing majority. If they wait until the last minute, they will have lost all their options.

Like all good politicians, prime ministers know that the public is fickle. It may love you today, but despise you tomorrow. Everyone knows that "a week is a long time in politics." George W. Bush's popularity soared (2001) after his strong response to the 9/11 tragedy. Similarly, his poll numbers plummeted in the wake of Hurricane Katrina (2005) and the mishandling of that crisis. All politicians have ridden the popularity roller coaster, both up and down. Prime ministers know that waiting until the last minute is a gamble. Better call an election when you're high in the polls.

Under this reasoning, one might ask why Prime Ministers don't remain in power forever. Wouldn't savvy leaders call for a national vote every year or two, just as soon as pollsters assure them that they are bound to win?

To ask this question is to see the likely answer. Citizens don't particularly *enjoy* political campaigns and the folderol connected with an election. They would resent being called to the polls every year or two, especially for no reason. A popular Prime Minister with a solid majority has no plausible justification for calling an **early election**. Doing so might backfire, as opponents take advantage of the public's annoyance. ("He's called an unnecessary election to satisfy his excessive ambition," and so forth.)

Thus, calling an election "too soon" could prove unpopular and therefore dangerous. Remember that fickle public. But waiting "too long" could leave you with no options and might also be dangerous. What to do: find some middle course.

Around the 3-year mark of a 5-year term, government leaders start thinking seriously about the next election. If the signs are favorable, they might call an election at the 3.5-year point. More likely, they would wait until 4 years have passed. That's far enough from the last election that voters won't be annoyed. (The government can claim a need to "renew our mandate," "let the people speak," and so forth.). It is also far enough from a term's end that leaders won't be boxed into a specific date by the force of circumstance.

Only when a government has been unpopular for a long period of time, will it wait until the last minute to call an election. If the governing party is likely to lose an election called after 3, 3.5 or even 4 years, it will continue to hold onto power to the bitter end, hoping for an eventual turn in public sentiment. John Major did this in Britain in the 1995–1997 period, hanging on to power as long as possible in unpopular circumstances. It did him no good. His party was trounced when he was finally forced by law to call the election.

Americans sometimes claim it's "unfair" that Prime Ministers can "call their own balls and strikes" by shopping around for the best election date. Oddly, this seeming advantage makes no difference at all in leadership longevity. If we compare the UK with the USA, for the 110-year period from 1896 to 2006, we find that 20 Britons and 19 Americans held their country's top post. These men spent an almost identical number of years of in office: an average of 5.5 (UK) and 5.8 (USA).

In other parliamentary systems, leaders with the supposed advantage of being able to name the date of the next election fare generally worse than in the UK, as Table 11.1 shows. During these same 110 years, New Zealand had 23 national leaders, Holland 26, and Denmark 31. The timeframe for other countries varies a good deal because of varying historical experiences, but it is clear that parliamentary leaders in polyarchies do not often have the longevity of American presidents in a fixed-term system. Only Canada, of the major parliamentary systems had fewer leaders than the USA during the

Table 11.1 Time in office of executives in polyarchal systems: A comparison of selected countries.*

Country	Period	Number of national political leaders (presidents/prime ministers)†	Average time in office (mean no. of years)
Germany	1949–2006	8	7.1
Canada	1896–2006	16	6.9
USA	1896–2006	19	5.8
UK	1896–2006	20	5.5
New Zealand	1896–2006	23	4.8
Norway (post-WWII)	1945–2006	13	4.7
Holland	1896–2006	26	4.2
Australia	1901–2006	25	4.2
Denmark	1896–2006	31	3.5
France (5th Republic)	1959–2006	17	2.8
Italy	1946–2006	24	2.5
Japan	1956–2006	20	2.5
Norway (pre-WWII)	1905–1940	15	2.3
France (3rd Republic)	1878–1938	44	1.4

* The timeframes were selected to reflect lengthy periods during which each country experienced polyarchal governance.
† This number includes "repeats." For example, Giulio Andreotti is counted just once, even though he held the premiership of Italy in three different time periods. If the number of different *governments* were counted instead of just individual leaders, then all countries except post-Second-World-War Germany would fall behind the USA, including Canada (22 governments, but only 16 leaders, since 1896).

110-year period of time, and it had only three fewer, at 16. Germany has clearly been quite stable since the Second World War, but for decades before that it alternated between rigid authoritarianism and unstable democracy.

In any case, the evidence is clear. The ability to choose your election date *doesn't* necessarily produce longer stays in office than the fixed-term system.

Of the many possible reasons why leaders cannot "game the system" to get themselves re-elected, perhaps the most obvious is that day-to-day politics is complex and unpredictable. Reading the public's mind is still an art form, subject to much slippage. Many a Prime Minister has chuckled happily at having chosen an advantageous polling date, only to awake sorely disillusioned on the day after the election.

Perhaps the most dramatic example of an unexpected polling result occurred in July 1945. After leading his country to victory over Hitler, thereby (in his own mind) "saving the world," Winston Churchill called an election expecting to win handily. Instead, voters unceremoniously booted him from office in favor of the Labour Party and his uncharismatic rival, Clement Attlee. The reasons they did so are many, but two stand out. First, Churchill's Conservatives had been in power for over a decade, and people were ready for a change. Second, they were especially eager for change after

217

having suffered years of severe economic deprivation. True, one might "objectively" trace their troubles to wartime conditions that would have obtained no matter who was in power, but people living in "hard times" look for someone to blame, and there's no better scapegoat than a long-time governing party.

Parliaments with unstable coalitions

So far, we have been discussing parliaments with stable majorities (one party or a cohesive coalition). Let's now see how parliamentary politics work when an unstable coalition forms the government.

Quite frequently after an election, several parties with differing programs get together to form a majority-supported cabinet. Sometimes, it is just two parties, but they don't share many common aims. Reasons vary for the unlikely combinations that form a government. They range from agreement on at least one major issue of the day to friendships among the particular leaders, pure opportunism, or stark necessity (the country's in crisis and some government *has* to be formed).

Whatever the reason, governments formed in these conditions usually fail soon. Long before the official end of the parliamentary term—in a few months, 2 years at the most—prime ministers lose a vote of confidence. They then find themselves with two options. They could dissolve the legislature and call for new elections. Or they could forego elections and simply resign. That's the path most frequently taken. Someone else then puts together a majority coalition, a new government takes power, and the game continues.

There are several reasons why leaders of unstable, short-lived governments will not call elections. Remember, first, that voters do not like elections that follow too soon after the last one. They might well punish the Prime Minister and the party that's identified with the early-election decision.

In addition, *legislators* like elections even less than voters. Every election creates job insecurity. Everyone is vulnerable, no matter how safe a district appears to be, so every election produces anxiety and the possibility of a career-ending defeat for every politician. In any case, even if you're sure of winning your own seat, every election disrupts normal life. Instead of living nicely in the capital and debating grand policy matters, you must now enter the whirlwind of campaign activity. You have got to make pleading calls for money, give speeches, travel far and wide, knock on doors, and beg for support from all and sundry. It is a necessary part of political life, but few people want to do it every year or two.

So legislators will resent anyone calling an election that seems "unnecessary." The person who does so will not be popular with the political class. The Prime Minister who heads a fragile coalition in a fragmented government and calls for a new election after just 18 months will definitely be unpopular. Legislators will see this person not just as someone who put them to a lot of trouble and endangered their careers, but also as someone who acted quite foolishly.

After all, why would anyone call an election after losing the confidence of the legislature? The only purpose would be to *win* the election, to be returned by the people with a decisive victory. But what are the odds that *any* Prime Minister would win majority support in a fractionated political system with numerous parties? Very slim. Remember, for starters, that the Prime Minister's party never did have a majority. That's why it needed the help of other parties to form the government. After 18 months, it is not likely to be *more* popular than it was at the last election. Popular leaders do not lose votes of confidence. Beyond that, many voters will be unhappy with the Prime Minister just for calling that early election, if for no other reason.

So what could you, as a Prime Minister losing a vote of confidence, be thinking in calling an election? You are already unpopular (as illustrated in that no-confidence vote). Then you irritate the public further by calling a snap election just 18 months after the last one. Not a good strategy. The Prime Minister who does this could emerge from that election worse off than before.

There's more. Remember that we are in a multi-party system, so the Prime Minister's party probably won between 20 percent and 35 percent of the votes in the last election. In these already shaky circumstances (the government has fallen, its leader calls an early election), the odds are practically nil that the leader's party will be returned with a resounding show of public support. Much more likely is that this party will lose votes and find itself with a reduced number of seats. No matter what happens, the party won't have anything approaching a majority.

Knowing all this, most Prime Ministers will *not* call a new election. They are rational beings, after all. Following a no-confidence vote, they will ask themselves, "What is now best for me and my party?" They will realize that dissolving parliament won't help them and could insure their long-time absence from the seats of power. They won't win enough seats to form the next government, and the other legislators will be so mad at them for having called the election that they won't be invited to take part in the next coalition government. The discredited Prime Minister's own party will probably choose a new leader, and when that party eventually gets back into government, the disgraced former Prime Minister may well be overlooked when top cabinet posts are handed out.

No, the sensible thing to do, after losing a confidence vote in a multi-party system, is to resign and wait for a new government to form. It is possible that your party will be invited to participate in that government (this time as a junior partner, but at least you are still a key player). By taking the easy path (of resignation), you keep possibilities open for the future. You are, after all, still the leader of an important party. It is entirely possible that you'll be named to a top cabinet post in the next government (Minister of

Foreign Affairs, say, or Defense). And if not now, then surely in a later government (and governments come and go, after all, in this unstable system.)

Since most leaders think this way in fragmented parliaments, the "rules of the game" dictate the current government resigning and a new government forming, rather than the current government dissolving parliament and calling a new election. Eventually, an election *will* have to be called, but only after several governments have come and gone, and the date nears for the mandatory end of parliament's term. When 4 years have passed and the fifth government of that parliament loses a vote of confidence, then no one would be surprised to see that particular Prime Minister call for new elections. All will agree that there is no working majority to be found in this particular parliament, its term is almost up anyway, and it's about time for the people to be given another chance to express their wishes.

We now see why it is impossible to predict the precise date of an election in a parliamentary system. True, if an election occurs on April 17, 2026, we know that the next election must occur by April 17, 2031 (in a system with a 5-year term for parliament). But we also know it's unlikely that an election will take place on that *particular* date. Few Prime Ministers will wait until the last possible minute to place their fate in the voters' hands. Elections could occur in less than a year if the situation within parliament is particularly volatile. (Britain had *two* elections in 1974, one in February, one in October.) Elections might occur in a year and a half to two if an unexpected vote of no-confidence occurs (Canada held an election in June, 2004, and another in January, 2006).

What is most likely in a parliamentary system is that elections will occur after 70–85 percent of the term has been completed. It all depends on circumstance. The day after any election, we simply cannot know what circumstances of the next few years will be. Therefore, we can never know exactly when that next election will occur.

Effects of the parliamentary system and its election uncertainty

The seemingly arcane fact that the timing of elections in a parliamentary system is always unknown has an enormous impact on how politicians operate. We know that environment is a central variable for understanding behavior, and uncertainty about the time of the next election is a key element in the environment of any politician. American Senators (with a fixed term of 6 years) can act like "statesmen" for the first 2 or 3 years after their election. They can "take the long view," consider broad theoretical matters, and avoid automatic responses to constituent demands. Representatives, who run every 2 years, pay continuing attention to mundane constituent wants. (Many are called "errand-boys" for good reason.) We would expect politicians in parliamentary systems, people who might have to run for re-election *at any minute* (so to speak), to behave differently from those operating in a fixed-term system. Just how differently is worth exploring.

Among stable, long-term democracies, only the USA has a fixed-term system for all national officials. Presidents serve 4 years before having to face another election. House members serve 2 years, Senators six, and federal judges serve for life (specifically, "during good behavior"). Once in office practically nothing can force someone out until the next election—or until death, in the case of judges. (Yes, impeachments and ousters are technically possible, but almost never happen.)

The impact of these fixed terms is dramatic. They reinforce (even make possible) the desire of the writers of the Constitution for a separation-of-powers, checks-and-balances system. How? They keep the members of each center of power independent of each other. Think, after all: short of violence, what is the most important hold you can have over someone? It is the threat to dislodge them from their cherished job. High political office is valued, and those who can give it, or take it away, have great power.

In the USA, Presidents simply cannot give someone the job of senator, nor can they fire any senator. Supreme Court justices cannot make anyone a member of the House of Representatives. Senators cannot appoint presidents, and House members cannot name Supreme Court justices. It is true that the President *and* the Senate *combined* can put someone on the Court, but once there they cannot remove that person. (No justice has *ever* been forced from office.)

Of course, presidents and senators, representatives and justices, all have ways of influencing each other. They all have varied power resources to wield in the ongoing political struggle. But the fixed-term system shelters members of each unit from total control by members of another. It gives them all some leeway for independent action. In the end, it creates a system with multiple points of access to the powerful, while limiting the power of any one leader.

American politicians think like this about members of another branch: Since I did not get my job because of you (at least, not directly because of you), and since in any case you cannot fire me from my job, you cannot order me around. Yes, you have various resources and tactics you can bring to bear against me, including persuasion, but so do I against you, meaning you have to pay some attention to my interests, just as I do to yours. Neither you nor I are forced slavishly to follow each other's desires.

Relationships under these conditions center on bargaining and negotiation rather than on command and obedience. In the end, each political unit has power, and each can block the wishes of the other units. Sometimes Congress wants something that the President opposes. In that case, he can veto their legislation. Sometimes Congress and the President want something that the Supreme Court does not like, in which case the court can thwart both institutions by declaring a law unconstitutional. On it goes. No person or institution is "supreme" in the American system.

The lack of a single center of power in the USA is hard for non-Americans to absorb. In most countries (democracy or otherwise), there is one clear power point. In parliamentary systems, it is the popularly-elected house of parliament. There's no "separation of powers." Indeed, the core principle is *concentration of power*. Power is centered on the legislative majority. Whoever controls that controls politics in that system.

Now let's return to our crucial point. None of the legislators in a parliamentary system have fixed terms, including the leaders they have chosen (prime minister and cabinet, usually referred to as "the government"). The political fortunes of legislators and executive officials are interdependent to a much greater degree than they are in the presidential, fixed-terms system. Let's see why that should be the case.

As we have seen, there are two main patterns in parliamentary governance: (1) either the Prime Minister safely controls a stable majority or (2) the Prime Minister heads a complex and shaky coalition of diverse parties. Each of these options illustrates the interdependence of parliamentary systems and the effect of the no-fixed-term situation on internal politics.

Prime ministerial control

In the first case, the prime minister dominates parliament. His supporters know that voting against this leader on any key matter could lead to the downfall of the government and a new election. We know the logic here: if the prime minister heads a government controlled by a dominant party or two strong, closely-aligned parties, the odds are good that she would call an election after losing a vote of no-confidence. Members of the legislative majority know this and shrink from ever voting against their leader on key issues.

If John McCain opposes President Bush on social security reform, what happens to John McCain? He might make some members of his party unhappy, but so what? He is still senator, and after all, you cannot please everyone all the time. And what happens to President Bush? He may lose on this issue, but you can't win 'em all—and he's still president.

Now what happens if Jerzy Blatzflyk votes against Prime Minister Schlossnik in East Ruratania? If Blatzflyk's action helps defeat Schlossnik on a key vote, Schlossnik might decide to call new elections. Remember that politicians do not relish elections. In addition to all the uncertainties and personal hardships they bring, things are even worse for the Blatzflyks of the political world. All faithful members of the majority will detest Jerzy for having caused this turn of events. Furthermore, the most powerful members of his party (the Prime Minister and cabinet) will be furious at him. Those hostile feelings will multiply if the election goes badly. Then, everyone in the previous majority will look at Blatzflyk and his associates as the people responsible for causing the downfall of "the rightful rulers of the nation."

In politics, people don't just get mad; they get even. The future of the Blatzflyk faction will be bleak. Members will never get top posts within the party; when the party regains power, they will get no appointments to high office; and it is entirely possible that they will be booted from the party altogether. After all, these "traitors" took us from a position of controlling the government to a position of helpless opposition. Their fates will not be pretty.

Given these facts, what would *you* do if you were a legislator inside the majority in a strongly-supported government? You'd obviously support every major government initiative. Few people like to commit professional suicide.

Besides, it is easy to rationalize this behavior. Even if you oppose a major government policy, and even if you are willing to sacrifice your own career, you know that you support *most* of this government's policies and like *almost none* of the opposition's. Why jeopardize everything the government stands for over just one issue? If you (and others) cause the government's downfall by forcing an election that the party loses, you go from getting 90 percent, say, of what you want to getting perhaps twenty percent (under the new government).

The result of this interdependence of government and legislature is to ensure straight-line party voting on all important matters. That in turn leads to straight-line party voting on almost everything. First, legislators get in the habit of voting with their leadership, and second, it is hard to tell which votes are "important" and which are not. If governments lose a string of votes on "minor" issues, it starts to look as if they are weak, don't have the country behind them, can't control their own supporters, and so forth. Each new "minor" vote starts to look "major"; it is part of an ongoing set of indicators of government support. In the end, it's simpler and becomes the pattern just to vote with the government *all* the time, rather than be seen as someone who's helped to weaken your party's control over the levers of power.

Parliamentary control

There is a second major pattern in parliamentary governance. It occurs when parties are many, coalitions are shaky, and governments are weak. Now the tables are turned. When governments are weak, legislators know that any threat of dissolving parliament is an empty one.

As we have already seen, prime ministers who head a relatively small party and are riding herd on a fractious governing coalition simply cannot call for new elections. They would lose those elections and destroy their own career in the bargain. Since everyone knows these facts, *the Prime Minister in this situation is the captive of the legislature.* His term is now entirely dependent on his ability to please the members of his coalition on all important issues.

Remember that crucial parliamentary norm: governments must resign or call new elections if they lose parliament's confidence, and the loss of a key vote is one definition of losing parliament's confidence. Again, we see the effect of the no-fixed-term aspect of this system. Americans too have known weak presidents or presidents with little popular support. Harry Truman, Jerry Ford, and Jimmy Carter come to mind, as do certain periods in the presidencies of the first President Bush and Bill Clinton. Still, no matter how weak presidents might become, they never become Congress's spokesperson. They always retain a good deal of independent authority and power. In the end, they retain much freedom of action because, very simply, Congress can't fire them. In a parliamentary system, legislators do have that power, and they're much more likely to exercise it in an unstable coalition situation.

We know that legislators hesitate to overturn a prime minister whose party might win the next election. But when prime ministers are unlikely to come out of a new election in good shape, they are much more likely to resign than dissolve parliament. That's just fine with the legislators who are thinking of defecting from the governing coalition.

The reasons why legislators might vote against a government they currently support are many. These range from personal ambition to fury over a government policy. All legislators everywhere want, at one time or another, to vote against a given government policy. In a checks-and-balances, fixed-term system, many will do that and suffer few consequences. In a parliamentary system with a strong majority-supported government, few (to none) will do that for fear of dooming both the government and their own careers. But in a parliamentary system with a multi-party, shaky coalition, many will consider this option. Defection is always part of the system and can be used as a lever in the bargaining game. Since it is always possible, it is bound to occur from time to time, making clear to everyone that this outcome is not just plausible, but even likely.

The result is that the legislature now controls its leadership. Prime ministers of weak governments will pay extremely close attention to legislators' desires—or demands. Leaders know that legislators control their jobs. Lose a key vote, and they must resign. Hence, they'll pay close attention to what members of parliament want.

We now see clearly the three patterns of polyarchal governance.

1   Under the fixed-term system, *independent bargaining* occurs among relatively equal actors who don't control each other's immediate fates.

2   Under the parliamentary system with a strong majority, *executive dominance* is the rule.

3   And under the parliamentary system with a weak majority, one finds *legislative dominance*.

It is clear that in a parliamentary system, the lack of a fixed term, along with the need of governments to win all key votes, concentrates power. Whether it concentrates that power in legislators or in executives depends on the strength of the dominant party in government. If that party can hope for majority support at the polls in any future election, the executive leadership will dominate politics. If not, legislators will dominate the system. In either case, there is no question of individuals with independent bases of power confronting each other with varying degrees of potential influence. Power is either quite clearly in the hands of one set of actors or another.

As an aside, it's worth stating that whether the legislature or the executive controls power in parliament, we're not talking about dictatorial power. Prime ministers, even strong ones, can retain their majority only by a continual process of consultation and persuasion. In any case, the next election is never far away. Voters will ultimately pass judgment on the substance and style of any government.

Effect of the parliamentary system on party loyalty

It is now clear that this external, structural, environmental variable (presidential or parliamentary system) seriously affects behavior. Most dramatically, parliamentary systems produce much greater party loyalty than occurs under presidentialism. Remember that in a parliamentary system no one knows the date of the next election. Everyone does know, however, that the odds of an election rise when Prime Ministers lose a key vote. Even if the Prime Minister does not call for new elections after a no-confidence vote, he or she will have to resign, the party will lose its power to govern, and many members of the party will lose a variety of perks.

No one wants any of this. It is simpler just to vote with the party at all times. For that reason, party-line votes become the absolute rule in parliamentary systems.

Americans are often startled at this strict party-voting norm. They wonder why foreign legislators cannot "think for themselves," the way American lawmakers supposedly do. Note, however, that people in the same party, in whatever nation, usually share the same values and policy preferences. Consequently, they will vote the same way on most bills that come before them. Even in the American Congress, party is the most significant predictor of voting behavior. No other variable (state, region, age, income, gender) comes close to this one in predicting how a member of Congress will vote on any given bill.

So politicians everywhere vote with their party—hardly a surprise. Party-line voting is stronger in parliamentary than in presidential systems, however, because the consequences for disloyalty differ significantly. In a parliamentary system, deviations from party loyalty can lead to disastrous consequences for one's party—and for one's own career. In a presidential system, deviations might make some people temporarily unhappy, but they do not destroy your party's hold on power, and they do not necessarily hurt your own career chances either.

So far, we have explained only why politicians in the *governing* party (or coalition) vote together loyally. The same logic drives those in the minority. What is the best chance for minority party members to become the majority (and thereby gain access to control of policy, status, and favors)? Naturally, it's to defeat the government in a key vote, thereby forcing the government's resignation. After that, there'd either be a new government, perhaps with your party now in charge, or a new election, which your party might win. In all events, your future hopes depend entirely on defeating the current government. Thus, you will vote in a bloc against them at every opportunity.

Conclusion

The parliamentary environment goes a long way toward explaining the high degree of party discipline in most polyarchies outside the USA. The English and the French and the Italians are not more conformist than Americans. Far from it! They just happen to operate in an environment that demands party loyalty. If Americans adopted a parliamentary system, our legislators would soon be acting the same way. They'd be voting with their party 99.9 percent of the time—once they saw the disastrous consequences of *disloyalty* to their career chances and to their party's hold on power.

People often ask: which of these systems is "better?" There is, of course, no right or wrong when it comes to political structures. It is just a question of which behavior each structure encourages and which behavior one prefers. In any case, once a pattern becomes common in a society, it becomes the "expected" one, and anything else seems odd and deviant.

Americans are used to a system with many independent bases of power and no one dominant. Compromises and clashes among political actors are all worked out in a very public way. It is confusing, even infuriating, to the mass of citizens. They are especially unhappy at never knowing who to blame (or less frequently, reward) for a given policy. Is it the Democrats (who control some power centers) or the Republicans (who control others)? Still, American culture would almost certainly rebel at a system that concentrated power in one institution (and almost surely in one person—a Prime Minister with majority control of the legislature).

On the other hand, parliaments seem entirely rational for the rest of the polyarchal world. When voters speak, is it not reasonable that they should get their way? Should there really be some other power centers blocking their will? No, say backers of parliamentarism. With all power concentrated in the dominant house of the legislature, whoever emerges with a majority there *should* get to rule for the next few years. Let them carry on without obstruction. At least, we will know who is responsible for national policies. If we do not like the results, we will kick them out at the next election.

So, depending on whether you like power fractured, complex and murky, or concentrated and responsible, you will prefer either a presidential or a parliamentary system. Of course, most people never have to choose one or the other. We are simply used to "our" system and imagine that any other way of operating makes no sense. Government structures become part of our cultural expectations. Embedded in the consciousness of a nation's citizens, they develop a lengthy and deeply-entrenched life of their own.

Questions for discussion

1   What if the USA adopted a parliamentary system? How would that change the American political process? Would there be any support for this change in the American public?
2   Do you think American politicians would be able to make coalition governments work?
3   Within parliamentary systems, the time that leaders stay in office varies a good deal—7 years in Germany and Canada, 2.5 years in Italy and Japan (Table 11.1.) What do you think accounts for these variations? Since they all use the same system, why don't leaders stay in power for about the same length of time?
4   Can you think of any situation in which a prime minister who heads a diverse, multi-party coalition could exercise strong leadership?
5   The author argues that the ties of party loyalty are strong everywhere. In your experience, does that generalization apply to American politics?

INSTITUTIONS AND THE BALANCE OF POWER

"Men make their own history," Karl Marx once wrote, "but they do not make it as they please; they do not make it under self-selected circumstances, but under circumstances existing already, given and transmitted from the past. The tradition of all dead generations weighs like a nightmare on the brains of the living."[1]

We don't have to accept everything in Marx to recognize the broader truth here. None of us acts in a world that was created yesterday. We are born, live, and die in a long-established web of relationships. The social structures of our time, our **institutions**, affect both what we do and what we think.

What Marx said about history applies equally to institutions. We do not choose them. We inherit them from the past, and we learn to live with them. Of course, some of us try to "make our own history," as Marx says. Some try to change the norms and mores of society, including its institutions. But that is no easy task because they do weigh heavily upon us.

We have already seen the impact of some institutions: voting systems and the structures that define legislative-executive relations. In this chapter, we shall examine three more institutions central to political life: federalism, courts, and interest groups. While different on the surface, these social structures have at least one thing in common. They exert enormous power over the lives and behavior of political participants.

Federal or unitary system?

People live, by definition, within a particular geographic space. That space is subject to the rules of a variety of political entities. Most of us live in a town or city that is governed by a town or city council. The town or city we inhabit is usually part of a broader geographic area called a county (borough, department, shire, district, or autonomous region, depending on the country). These larger political units also have governing bodies, and they in turn are often part of still larger units called, variously, states (USA, Australia), provinces (Canada, Spain), *länder* (Germany), republics (Russia), regions (Finland,

France), and so forth. Beyond all these levels is a national government. Still further, all countries belong to international bodies (e.g., the UN) or alliances (e.g., NATO) that themselves have governing organizations.

All of these entities can make rules with the force of law to govern the behavior of people in their jurisdiction. Only two of these units, however, come close to exercising real **sovereignty** over those within their boundaries: the national government and the sub-national unit of government usually known as the state or the province.

"Sovereignty" refers to the level of government with "final say" on any legal or political matter within its geographic space. For instance, in the USA if a town council voted to deny some group the right to vote, that would hardly be the end of the dispute. Members of the affected group could appeal the decision through the courts, starting locally, moving on to state courts (if necessary), and ending at the US Supreme Court. If they lost in this locale, they could try to get Congress to change voting-rights laws, and they could try to enlist the President in the effort.

They would not, however, go to NATO or the UN to remedy the situation. Those entities do not have sovereignty on this matter. That is, no one believes that these organizations have the right to rule definitively on voting matters within the USA, and no one would pay attention to, or try to enforce, any rules laid down by those organizations about voting in the USA. Similarly, groups denied the right to vote by a locality would normally not stop their struggle to overturn the decision at the county or state level. It has long been recognized that voting is so important in democracies that decisions about who can and who can't vote are made at (or can be appealed to) the national level.

Let's turn to another issue. Let's say you live in the USA, and your town decides to increase property taxes by 5 percent for the coming year. Outraged, you get in touch with your town councilors, but they brush you off. You organize a group of fellow property owners, form a statewide organization, and urge state legislators to pass a law forbidding tax increases of more than two percent in any given year. This fails, as does an effort to get state courts to overturn the tax increase. At this point, you've exhausted your immediate options.

You can, of course, keep working for change at both the state and local levels, but you cannot go any further. You cannot go to Congress, say, and certainly not to NATO. It is widely recognized (legally and politically) that American states have sovereign power to set and regulate property taxes. They can, and often do, delegate some of those powers to municipalities, but the ultimate power of decision rests with the states—not the localities, not the central government.

Note that in France, both of these matters—voting rights *and* property taxes—would be settled, as a last resort, at the national level. Every political issue in France could, theoretically, end up being determined in Paris, whereas many issues can be decided only at the regional level (state, province) in, e.g., the USA or Canada. This difference stems from the different way countries organize their political-geographic space. The USA and Canada operate as **federal systems** (with two levels of sovereignty). So do several other countries, including India and Germany. In contrast, France and countries like Holland, Japan, and Israel, have **unitary systems** (just one level of sovereignty).

In federal systems, state powers are divided between two levels of government. By agreement (both legal and consensual), one level of government has the right to carry out definitive decisions in a variety of areas, while the other level is given that same right in other areas. In unitary systems, all political decisions could ultimately be made at the national level.

In practice, life is more complicated than this simple dichotomy suggests. In unitary systems, many powers are delegated to lower authorities, and over time expectations become deeply ingrained that those authorities *should* have the final say on these matters. Thus, if a local school board in Cornwall, England (unitary system) decides to start the school day at 8 a.m. instead of 8:30 a.m., it would not occur to most parents to appeal this decision to the Prime Minister, the Secretary of State for Education, or the British Parliament —although theoretically (and legally) those actors have the ability to overturn the decision.

Matters are not neat in a federal system, either. A struggle is always occurring over just which issues are "really" in the hands of the central government, as opposed to being legitimate subjects for regional units.

For instance, who decides on curriculum matters in the American states? Theoretically, education is a matter almost entirely within the realm of state sovereignty. Each state can decide what it wishes to teach and how it wishes to evaluate the results of its teaching. Yet, the federal government supplies such a large amount of money to education in each state that state authorities pay close attention to the federal government's wishes. If they fail to teach the "right" subjects and cannot show evidence that students are actually learning those subjects, education departments in the states can be deprived of large sums of money. No state takes that route. By default, therefore, the federal government does have a say in education matters, despite the supposed sovereignty of states in this area.

The distinction between federal and unitary political systems remains important, despite fuzziness in the way both systems actually operate. Here is one key difference: politics is more complex in federal systems. For one thing, there are more power points, and therefore more actors whose wishes and interests impact others in the political struggle. For another (and following from the first), the entire process becomes murkier because it's never clear which decisions will get made where.

It is easy enough to say that, in theory, one level of government has the right to make decisions in X, Y, and Z policy areas, while the other level has authority in A, B, C, and D areas. It is another thing to know precisely where one policy area begins and the other ends. Decisions by one level of government on a subject within its policy jurisdiction often affect policy in areas reserved for the other level of government. Resolving these jurisdictional disputes becomes central to political life in federal systems.

For instance, in the USA a decision by a local school board to exclude blacks from the list of people eligible to attend schools would obviously be overturned by the federal government—not because the federal government has jurisdiction over education matters, but because it *does* have jurisdiction over civil rights matters. Of course, that power itself was unsettled in the 1950s and 1960s, when many southern states claimed that *they* could rule on racial matters. They claimed jurisdiction based on a **states' rights theory** of the Constitution.

The states had reason to believe their own claims. Decades before, the matter had been settled in their favor. Numerous laws and court decisions starting in the late nineteenth century gave states the right to discriminate against minorities. The most notorious of these acts was a Supreme Court decision in 1896 holding that a man who was one-eighth "black" could legally be ejected from the "white" passenger car of a railroad and forced to travel in the "colored" section. This decision, known as Plessy v. Ferguson, held that states could pass laws segregating blacks from whites, as long as blacks were provided "separate but equal" public facilities.

Things are different today. In 1954 the Supreme Court overturned its Plessy decision by ruling that "separate is never equal." That is, separating a group of people from the rest of society simply on the basis of race represents an unconstitutional violation of the "due process" clause of Amendment 14 of the Constitution and could not be tolerated, either by the state or the federal governments. That decision started a momentous change in American society. It also brought major change to the power distribution within American federalism. Civil rights matters, as well as many other issues once deemed state concerns, are now resolvable at the level of the federal government.

On the other hand, no power distribution ever remains set in stone. In recent years, courts have moved to allow some powers previously "federalized" to flow back to the states. Under federalism, deciding which matters belong to which level of government produces a never-ending set of debates.

The complexity of federalism

Life in a federal system is complex precisely because issues of jurisdiction are murky. Everything one level of government does can be seen as affecting policy at the other level. Both levels will be constantly vying for supremacy in numerous policy areas. Citizen activists will constantly be turning to one level or the other to insure that their desires are met. Except for a few constitutional theorists, no one *really* cares which level of government does what. We all just want to win our case, and we'll go to whatever jurisdiction will provide a victory. We can always rationalize a constitutional theory to justify our move—or find a lawyer to do it for us. Thus, under federalism those who lose at the state level will often turn to the federal government, and vice versa.

This situation could rarely be better seen than in the 2000 dispute over the outcome of the election in Florida. In the race between George W. Bush and Al Gore, election results in the rest of the country were so close that whoever won the Florida vote would become president. In turn, the vote in Florida was so close that its outcome hung on ways to count (or not count) a range of disputed ballots. Democrats, who usually prefer settling legal disputes at the federal level (where they have more frequently triumphed) in this case argued that the matter should be resolved at the state level. By coincidence, the Florida Supreme Court was controlled by Democrats. Republicans, who usually argue for states' rights, suddenly felt that this matter should be resolved by the US Supreme Court (where it just happened that Republicans were dominant).

That court, as we all know, overruled the Florida Supreme Court in Bush v. Gore, effectively stopping the vote count at a point where Bush held a miniscule lead. That gave him the state's electoral vote and national victory. In this case, as in all others, no one cared about the "principle" covering which unit of government is "supposed" to decide on an issue like this one. People want their interests supported and will turn to whatever unit of government will give them a victory. Later, they will create an intellectual justification for the right of that unit to make that decision. Since their opponents are doing the same, only in the opposite direction, life is never dull in a federal system.

Politics in unitary systems

Things are simpler in unitary systems. There, *all power is centered in the national government.* All lower units of government, all local and regional bodies, and all government officials are subordinate to those at the national level. Local and regional officials must carry out the laws and policies set in the capital. They can foot-drag on policies they dislike, and they can provide information aimed at changing those policies, but ultimately they must obey and implement them. Laws and rules decided by the national government supersede those of lower government agencies.

The best way to illustrate the difference between federal and unitary government is to pursue this idea of sovereignty. Sovereignty is a slippery term. No entity is ever wholly sovereign, if to be sovereign means to be "supreme and independent within one's geographic sphere"—a common way to define this term. Even the greatest empires have failed to achieve this state. All countries have been subject to the military, cultural, and economic influence of other nations. Most have also been subject to the rules of international treaties they have signed or international organizations they have joined. The USA today, powerful though it is, does not control many aspects of the world economy. As a result, numerous global trends affect Americans *within our borders* in many ways that neither the federal government nor any state government can control.

Still, governments that are called sovereign can, within their sphere, create and enforce most of the laws that govern their citizens. Most of the time they need not worry about some other authority overruling them. When the federal government of the USA decides to fund the Defense Department or to reform Medicare, it does not wonder that some higher level of government will override or negate its policies. That is not the case when a school board, a town council, or a county commission makes decisions. Every single decision of these groups can be modified or even negated by the action of some higher level of government.

How does one know if a given level of government is sovereign? Try the simple self-preservation test. Can a higher level of government actually abolish your level of government? If yes, you aren't sovereign. If no, you are. As it turns out, in the American system of federalism, only the states and the national government meet the sovereignty test.

We shall spend little time arguing the national government's sovereignty. Obviously, no entity can legally add to, subtract from, or obliterate the powers of the US government without that government's formal acquiescence.[2] The government could decide to add territory to the country (e.g., create a new state). It could agree to cede some powers to the states. It could even agree to give up certain powers altogether. But none of these changes could happen without the government expressly taking legal action to bring them about.[3]

Consider now a *town* or a *city* within any given state. We often think of the place where we were born and grew up as eternal, but in fact most American towns and cities have had their boundaries changed, added to, subtracted from, or even created in the not-too-distant past. *All* governmental units *within* each state are the creations of that state. The state can change their boundaries, change their powers, abolish them, create new ones—as it chooses.

Portland, Maine, where I live, was once part of a neighboring town, Falmouth. Deering, currently just a neighborhood of Portland, was once an independent town. Likewise, what we call New York City has existed only since 1898, when the five independent cities of Manhattan, Queens, Brooklyn, the Bronx, and Staten Island saw their individual city councils abolished. These five municipalities each became mere boroughs, part of a larger city with one governing body, the New York City Council. The Indianapolis of today did not exist 40 years ago. In 1970, the Indiana legislature voted to meld the relatively small area then known as Indianapolis with a number of surrounding suburbs to create a new and larger city. It obliterated a number of towns and drastically changed the reach and power of the state's largest city.

These examples show that no town, city, or county in the USA has sovereignty. All were created by, and exist at the pleasure of, a higher governing authority: the state. Whenever they choose, state legislatures can re-draw the boundaries of towns, cities, counties, school districts, and even legislative districts. True, they do not choose to do this often. There are always political costs to these actions, so there must be weighty arguments for taking them. The fact remains that states can legally make these decisions if they deem them necessary.

The federal government has nothing like this power over the states. It cannot add to or subtract from the territory of any state, even if it desperately wished to do so. It certainly cannot abolish a state (by, say, combining it with another). Much as tiny Rhode Island seems like an anomaly "in this day and age," the federal government cannot simply roll it in with Connecticut to make a new state of, say, Narragansset. Likewise, the federal government cannot combine the two Dakotas into one state (Prairieland), nor split California into two states (e.g., North and South Pacifica).

The federal government cannot legally take these actions, because the Constitution gives sovereign rights to the states over a number of matters. First and foremost is their right to existence. The constitution says quite plainly that "no new States shall be formed or erected within the jurisdiction of any other State; nor any State be formed by the Junction of two or more States, or parts of States, without the Consent of the Legislatures of the States concerned."[4]

So the states are sovereign in that they can't be changed or destroyed *without their consent.* They have also been given a number of powers by the Constitution, including all the powers that have not been given specifically to the federal government[5] or directly to the people.

The same situation applies in most other federal systems. While variations exist in the precise legal status of regional governments, their essential sovereignty holds good in nations like Canada, Australia, Germany, and India.

The contrast with unitary systems is startling. In France, the national government in Paris has absolute power to dictate policy to sub-national units of government. It can create and abolish those units at will, and it can re-draw their boundaries at any time. Just in the past few decades France has created ten new *départements* (counties) for one reason or another.[6] It also created, out of the blue, a system of twenty-two regions to take account of demands for the de-centralization of government. Naturally, the power of these regions is limited. They were created by the national government and can be changed, diminished, or destroyed by it any time.

Political consequences of federal and unitary systems

All citizens in democratic nations live in either federal or unitary political systems. In both cases, these systems provide national, regional, sub-regional, and local units of government. In both systems, citizens have the right to elect officials at every level and are free to influence their policy decisions. Federal systems and unitary systems differ mainly in their degree of centralization. A federal system gives major power to regional units of government. A unitary system concentrates power at the national level. The practical results of this difference are many.

Policy differences

In federal systems, policy will be more varied from place to place than in unitary systems. To put this in reverse, policy in unitary systems will be more consistent and uniform. Take a federal system like the USA. Welfare benefits vary a good deal from state to state, as does the age when people can marry, the requirements for getting a driver's license, and the punishments for violating similar laws. In Canada, another federal state, French is the official language of Québec, but not Alberta. And in the German federal system, schools in some *länder* (states) forbid Muslim teachers from wearing headscarves, while schools in other *länder* do not.

The contrast with unitary systems is striking. Jean Zay, a French Minister of Education in the 1930s, used to look at his watch and boast that at that moment every tenth-grader in the country was reading the exact same passage of a particular Latin text. Local and regional units of French government have no leeway to vary the strict school curriculum decided upon in Paris. Imagine how upset Americans would be if the Secretary of Education announced that every tenth-grader in the country would be reading *Macbeth*, dissecting frogs, and studying the Civil War during the first 2 weeks of November. As usual, what seems normal in one system is outrageous in another.

When central authorities make all the important decisions, there is little room for local variation. Whether this is a good or a bad thing is beyond the scope of this text. There are pluses and minuses to each method. The point is simply that the **environment** shapes political outcomes, and we need to know that environment to understand the politics within it.

Federal systems ensure room for variation and experimentation, but may create policy confusion, unfairness, and excessive diversity leading to strong regional conflict. Unitary systems produce clearer lines of policy and clear lines of responsibility. Whatever happens, it is always the central government's "fault"—or "genius"—so everyone knows whom to blame—or reward. The results, however, could produce a stifling conformity, a tendency to ignore new ideas coming from below, and excessive power in the hands of a few national officials.

Power points

More power points exist in a federal system than in a unitary one. To illustrate, although France is almost twice as populous as Canada, it has exactly one Cabinet toward which ambitious politicians can aim their sights, whereas Canada (with its 10 provinces) has 11.[7] Thus, compared with France, Canada provides a far greater number of desirable positions for each aspiring political leader.

Since sub-national units of government are weak in unitary systems, officials of those units are politically insignificant. All their major decisions are subject to review by national officials, so they have little independence or autonomy. Since all political actors know this, local and regional officials are widely dismissed as unimportant. If you wish real power in a unitary system, you must gravitate toward the national level as soon as possible. In unitary systems, therefore, all serious political struggles and all real policy decisions occur in the nation's capital.

This institutional arrangement has the effect of intensifying the political struggle. Compared with federal set-ups, far fewer positions of power exist in unitary systems. Thus, the effort to gain a top post is highly competitive and can produce sharp, bitter contests.

Even more significant, the struggle to set policy can produce widespread social antagonisms. In a federal system, your party may not control policy at the national level, but it surely does in a number of regional entities. You can act there to offset and undermine national policies you dislike. Thus, in federal systems politics is not a winner-take-all game that can sometimes lead losers to desperate measures. Groups may feel less alienation and hatred toward policies that hurt them, if there are places in the country with countervailing policies that favor them.

The numerous power points of a federal system make national politics less intense in another way. With many more offices available for ambitious politicians, there are fewer out-of-office malcontents seeking that small number of high offices in the nation's capital. Those eager to rise have various ways of channeling their ambition. Many of them actually will attain office and be tested by the responsibility of running some part of government. In this experience, they may learn to develop good leadership skills. Conversely, they may falter and be rejected by voters at the next election, thus undermining their chances for a future at the national level. In any case, the system will work to improve the quality of national office-holders and diminish the number of desperate challengers for national power.

Complexity

Politics in a federal system will always be more complex than politics in a unitary system. Policy arguments will be endlessly played and re-played at different levels and in different locations. A group that wins a national victory will see its gains reversed in regional units. A group that persuades one regional unit to go its way will see opponents try to prevent similar victories in other regional units. Groups that win in several regional units will see enemies try to convince the federal government to override the policy. On it will go, in a never-ending struggle to set policy and gain power in many different locales.

In unitary systems, you either win or you lose. That is, you either gain control of the national government, or you don't. If you do, you enact your policies. If you don't, you keep trying to gain control of the national government so that you *can* enact your policies. You don't focus on gaining control of lesser units of government to enact your policies, because your opponents in control of the national government would either declare those policies illegal or refuse to fund them, thereby preventing them from going into effect.

All policy struggles in unitary systems are nationwide struggles. In federal systems, they take place regionally as well as nationally. The possibility of winning in some places (if not others) mutes the intensity of the debate and softens the struggle itself.

Judicial politics: the effect of courts on behavior[8]

The well-known nineteenth-century military historian, Clausewitz, famously said that "war is merely the continuation of politics by other means." Much legal activity is also "the continuation of politics" by other means. Beyond using the ballot, the soapbox, and the parliamentary maneuver to gain their ends, people also hire lawyers and turn to courts. Political activists resort to the judicial process because they have lost battles in other arenas. Courts provide one more institution for airing social conflict. Here, groups continue to pursue their interests, hoping that the different setting with its different norms and rules will work to their advantage. The judicial system provides another arena for addressing group conflicts and assigning (temporary) winners and losers in the never-ending struggle for power and for control of policy decisions.[9]

Not all institutions are created equal. Like every social structure, courts will have more power in one era than another, on some issues than on others, in some countries than in others. Still, they are always political entities, and their actions must be understood as forming part of the political process. As James Eisenstein has put it, echoing the widely-accepted opinion of judicial scholars: "The legal process is an integral part of the political system."[10]

The most casual observer can discern the political nature of the American judicial system. If you drove anywhere in the South during the 1960s, you would inevitably pass signs demanding that Congress "Impeach Earl Warren." Here was a clear political claim that would have been unthinkable

237

in any other country at the time.[11] Warren, the Chief Justice of the USA, symbolized to many white southerners the desegregationist policies they abhorred. Decades later, conservatives were railing against "activist judges" (that is, liberal judges) who allowed gay marriage and abortion, while forbidding prayer in public school.

On the other side of the ledger, the liberal Abraham Lincoln urged the country simply to ignore a major Supreme Court decision that legitimated slavery (Dred Scott v. Sandford, 1857). Berating the justices, Lincoln issued this radical statement: "If the policy of the government, upon vital questions, affecting the whole people, is to be irrevocably fixed by decisions of the Supreme Court . . . the people will have ceased to be their own rulers."[12]

In like vein, economic liberals in the 1930s, incensed at rulings of the Supreme Court that struck down some of Franklin Roosevelt's New Deal reforms, denounced these decisions as reflecting the political whims of "nine old men." They called the most conservative justices "the Four Horsemen of the Apocalypse." Liberals demanded that justices reverse their rulings. If not, the court should be expanded to appoint a majority of liberals.

A Roosevelt plan to do just that, often known as his "court-packing scheme," went nowhere. Finally, at the height of the conflict in 1937 one justice changed his position, producing a 5:4 pro-New-Deal court. Some wag promptly dubbed this "the switch in time that saved nine." Soon thereafter, conservative justices began to retire or die, allowing Roosevelt to appoint liberals. The crisis was deflated and quickly passed into history. It is clear that American courts have been deeply involved in politics. Sometimes their actions please liberals, sometimes conservatives. When courts make decisions, they step into the midst of ongoing social controversies. By that very act, they enter the world of politics.

Political conflicts become judicial conflicts

Alexis de Tocqueville made many memorable statements about American life,[13] but among his most famous is the assertion that "there is hardly a political question in the United States which does not sooner or later turn into a judicial one."[14] Generations of scholars have noted this tendency. Nearly all the contentious issues in American life eventually reach the Supreme Court.

Think of the most dramatic conflicts in American history: tariffs, trade issues, taxes, regulation of business, slavery, civil rights, abortion. Tocqueville was right. It *is* hard to think of a serious political matter that has not found its way into the American legal process.[15]

Americans take this pattern for granted. If we do not like something, we'll "take it to court." Only when we examine political life in other countries does **American exceptionalism** again become obvious.[16] Until recently, nowhere else did courts play much of a role in dealing with high-conflict issues. It was rare to find nations where people commonly resorted to *legal* action to gain the satisfactory resolution of a *political* dispute.[17]

The reasons for this pattern are many, but it will not surprise readers of this book to learn that culture is high on the list of explanations.[18] The key American values of individualism, liberty, and egalitarianism play a central role. Americans from earliest times saw themselves as individuals equal under the law, a law that allowed and indeed encouraged them to pursue their own interests with vigor.[19]

Americans continue to view law as a means of protecting their "rights" and their interests. In other countries, if a law said X, X happened. If the legislature approved Y policy, Y policy was implemented. In the USA, it was never that simple. Even after legislatures passed laws, executives signed them, and bureaucracies began to carry them out, citizens who disagreed with the laws continued to dispute them through the judicial process.

Courts became especially powerful in the USA for other reasons. One derives from deep-seated American values, especially the norms stressing egalitarianism and support for democracy. These norms have led Americans to set up elections for practically all public offices, including *most* judgeships. Under these circumstances, officials lose any aura of "majesty" they might have in other systems. For Americans, elected politicians are "one of us," "chosen by us," "our servants," and any time they get "too big for their britches," we can "cut them down to size" at the next election.

This norm led Americans to have little reverence for their "leaders." Ignoring the rulings of those leaders, or appealing their decisions to whatever arena is available (including the courts) seems entirely reasonable.

The Constitution, of course, institutionalized this attitude. It appeared to make the Supreme Court a co-equal branch of government, along with Congress and the President. What the Constitution-writers actually meant has been much debated, but two centuries of practice have made the threefold **separation of powers** idea a reality.

Judicial review

The impetus for the court's strong political role in American life began in 1803. In the landmark case of **Marbury v. Madison**, the strong Chief Justice of the time, John Marshall, claimed a power for the court that we have come to call **judicial review**. With his claim, Marshall created something new in history. He asserted a doctrine that had little effect at the time, but which has come to have enormous impact in the USA *and* around the world.

Marshall argued that courts have the power to nullify the actions of legitimately-chosen legislators and executives. This assertion would have stunned power-holders in all other countries at all other times. Yet Marshall's statement became the basis for court powers for two hundred years. How did he justify this crucial decision? More interestingly, how did he get away with it?

Three elements allowed Marshall to make his decision and make it stick. We have already alluded to two of these: one cultural and one institutional. On the cultural side, we know that respect for courts, belief in **the rule of law**, was always a strong American value. When courts took positions, even back in the eighteenth century, they could count on popular support—not always for the decision, but for their right to decide. That support for the *legitimacy* of court power remains strong today.[20]

At least as important as general respect for courts was the institutional situation that allowed Marshall to make his decision stick. The USA was the first nation to give itself a written Constitution. But what did having a Constitution mean? Marshall, asking that question, asserted that the Constitution must serve, in essence, as a "super-law." It must stand supreme. All other laws would have to conform to its basic principles and specific directives.

With this reasoning, Marshall went on to make an obvious point. If a given law violates some element in the Constitution, then that law must be invalid. It has to be declared null and void. The reasoning is sound, but Marshall then asked a tough question. "Who shall declare the law null and void?"

At this point, he took a significant political step and gave that power of nullification to the courts. In words that have become famous, Marshall wrote that "it is emphatically the province and duty of the judicial department to say what the law is."[21] His extended argument need not detain us here. What's crucial is that his decision came to be accepted. Few at the time argued his point; no one challenged it. Why?

To start, courts already had much prestige in American society. In addition, many people believed that judicial review was strongly implied in the Constitution itself (though not specifically mentioned). It was also implied in the very notion of a *written* Constitution. If there's a "super-document" governing the nation's laws, it stands to reason that "ordinary" laws must be subordinate to it. And who better than a court to determine a point of law?

The culture of his day and the logic of the situation both favored Marshall's argument. But perhaps the most important reason why Marshall's power grab was never challenged derived from practical politics. The decision Marshall was justifying had the effect of comforting the dominant powers of that time.

Marbury v. Madison gave a victory to Thomas Jefferson, James Madison, and their rapidly-rising party of Democratic Republicans. It did disturb the Federalists, but they were a declining party. Furthermore, just one person was actually hurt by the decision: a would-be justice of the peace named Marbury, who was prevented from gaining his commission. Marbury clearly had a legitimate grievance here, but no one else was hurt badly enough to make a fuss.

This decision was, in effect a brilliant political move by Marshall. He asserted a major power for the court, yet did so on such a minor issue that no opposition arose. It helped that the decision overturning a law passed by Congress required no action by anyone. If the Marshall court had ordered Jefferson actually to do something, a major constitutional crisis could have ensued. The Marbury decision instead told the executive branch *not* to do something they didn't want to do anyway. (Do not deliver a commission to Marbury, a Federalist whom we detest.) So they didn't do it. End of story. As a result, the principle of judicial review was never challenged.[22] It could be (and has been) used by future courts on issues of much greater import.

The assertion of court powers

Over the course of American history, courts have acted on many crucial issues. "Acted on" does not mean prevailed. Like every institution in a complex polyarchy, courts don't always get their way. Even when they do temporarily, matters are rarely settled definitively. Actors who lose in the courts explore other avenues to promote their cause. One way or another court decisions have often been reversed, or at least diluted. Still, courts remain vital political actors. Their power can be seen in a brief review of some key issues they have dealt with over the years.

Federal powers

Courts have frequently intervened to delineate the relative powers of federal and state governments. In McCulloch v. Maryland (1819) the Supreme Court enunciated a "federal supremacy" doctrine that favored the actions of Washington over those of state governments. But other high courts over the years have seen the complex federal-state relationship in various ways. They have more than once veered back to favor the states in confrontations between the two levels of American government. That has been a clear trend of the past two decades, according to most judicial observers.[23]

Civil rights to minorities

In the nineteenth century, the Supreme Court became deeply involved in the politics of race, coming down firmly on the side that opposed human rights. Dred Scott v. Sandford (1857) not only accepted the legality of slavery but even denied the authority of the federal government to regulate slavery's spread to states outside the south and to the new Western territories. In effect, the Civil War (1861–1865) nullified this decision, but a later Court took a comparable stand in Plessy v. Ferguson (1896). Here, the Court announced a "separate but equal" doctrine that justified *unequal* treatment to African-Americans via segregation.

241

In the mid-twentieth century, courts began to side with disadvantaged minority groups, especially black Americans, in their efforts to gain equal treatment in schools, at the polling booth, in public facilities, and elsewhere. The dramatic moment signaling this turn of events was the famous decision outlawing segregated schools in Brown v. Board of Education of Topeka, Kansas (1954).

Free speech

Courts over the last few decades have been increasingly favorable toward individuals who confront government efforts to restrict their freedom to say and write what they please. Landmark decisions in this area allow written and spoken statements highly critical of government officials (New York Times Company v. Sullivan, 1964) and governmental activities (Brandenburg v. Ohio, 1969), even in time of war (New York Times Company v. United States, 1971, often known as "the Pentagon Papers case"). These and other Court decisions have produced a situation where today anyone can say or write almost anything about politicians or the government without fear of legal retribution.

Criminal law

Courts have granted greater rights to people accused of crimes. The symbolic decision on this topic came in Miranda v. Arizona (1966). The entire world is familiar with the effect of this case, which requires that police inform criminal suspects of their rights, including the right to remain silent.

Abortion

The well-known case of Roe v. Wade (1973) opened up the possibility of abortion for millions of women. It scarcely resolved, however, the bitter political struggle between proponents of "a woman's right to choose" and supporters of the "pro-life" position. Recent Supreme Court decisions have been chipping away at the "absolute right to an abortion" that supporters of Roe would prefer. Of course, from the pro-life point of view, the Court has yet to take the "right" step and overturn Roe.

Government regulation of business

The Court has taken many different stands in this complex area. Over a century ago, it slapped down child labor laws and attempts to impose a national income tax. In early New Deal days, it declared invalid some key laws designed to regulate industry. Eventually, it came to accept many forms of government regulation in the workplace (minimum wage laws, safety requirements, support for unionization). In recent years, it has veered back toward greater sympathy with business interests.

One could go on at length, enumerating court activities on many other sensitive political topics.[24] The point should be clear. Any political matter of significance in American life comes up before a court somewhere and often before the nation's top court.

Are courts democratic?

The power of courts in a democratic system raises interesting questions. Is "rule of the people" compatible with court power? If people are supposed to be self-governing through elected representatives, why do they allow a few non-elected and non-accountable judges to overturn laws enacted by politicians chosen by the people to do the people's bidding?

Supporters of court powers find four answers to this question. First, neither the American system nor any polyarchy is meant to be a direct democracy. Indeed, many features of the system set up in 1787 were meant to *restrain* democracy. Courts were one of these devices.

People often refer to the American system as one of **checks and balances**, not direct democracy. It is a system with many relatively independent points of power, each with means of checking the other, thus necessitating discourse and trade-offs among the players. Even majorities can be checked in many ways. In such a system, especially a system in which norms like the rule of law run deep, it is not surprising that jurists would be among the key political actors.

A second argument sees courts and the judicial system as relatively democratic anyway. The vast majority of judges in the USA are directly elected to office. Most of the others, including all federal judges, are political appointees. They are chosen by directly-elected executives and approved by directly-elected legislators, putting them just a step away from direct democratic selection. True, once appointed, they can rarely be removed, but a lifetime of absorbing the norms of a democratic culture means that few of them will act in ways isolated from the tides of public opinion.

A third argument reinforces this point. It is best summarized in the words of the celebrated American humorist, Finley Peter Dunne: "The Supreme Court follows the election returns."[25] Or in scholarly language, "justices rarely act, for a long period, in a way that the general public repudiates,"[26] "the federal judiciary has not often bucked the political branches of the federal government,"[27] and "the policy views dominant on the Court are never for long out of line with the policy views dominant among the lawmaking majorities of the United States."[28]

Scholars have long debated the exact degree to which American courts, and the Supreme Court in particular, can withstand widely-held citizen desires. As these quotes suggest, most analysts agree that courts rarely hold out for long against a determined President and Congress backed by a strong majority of the American public.

Of course, what gives courts their power is that few circumstances like that ever arise. Politics usually takes place in a murky atmosphere where various groups take one stand or another, public opinion is split, ambiguous, or passive, and Congress and the President provide no clear leadership. In these (more ordinary) circumstances, courts can wield major power by taking decisive stands on the matters brought before them.[29]

Many observers use a fourth argument for the democratic nature of courts. They point to the jury system that radically reinforces the notion of popular input into the legal process. Something like one-quarter of adult Americans have served on a jury.[30] It's clear that public involvement in the judicial system is widespread.

That's especially so given the famous American trait of **litigiousness**. Americans show little hesitation about using courts to pursue their interests. (After all, "I know my rights!") Given Americans' easy familiarity with, and frequent involvement in, the system of justice, the notion that it's an undemocratic feature of American life is hard to maintain.

The "rights revolution" and the globalization of judicial review

We have seen clearly that *judicial actors play a significant role in American politics.* Beyond that, American courts in general, and the Supreme Court in particular, have become powerful influences on the *international* scene. Some go so far as to suggest that the American model has sparked an international **rights revolution**.[31] Citizens in many lands are turning to courts to promote their interests, and courts in many places are asserting their right to rule on political matters previously thought beyond their reach.[32]

Several nations, most prominently Germany and Japan, have directly borrowed from the USA the institution of a higher court that could rule on constitutional matters. In other countries, the influence of the American example has encouraged a growth in the powers of existing courts. The noted judicial expert, Donald P. Kommers, has called these developments **the globalization of judicial review**.[33]

Courts are now seen as a central element in the "democratic revolution" sweeping the globe. Even in once-totalitarian bastions of repression like China, people have been turning to courts for redress of grievance.[34] Courts far and wide have come to play a role in politics they had avoided in decades past. This development, not seen by all scholars as positive, has been called the "judicialization of public life,"[35] "the politicization of the judiciary,"[36] or even "juristocracy."[37] In all events, it signals the growing power of courts and their willingness to intrude their opinions into public policy areas.

The courts, a new player

We are thus witnessing the entry into world political life of an additional player. As in any game, a new player and new rules change the nature of the action. Courts have their own rules for behavior, their own strengths and weaknesses.

A key feature of struggles within a courtroom is the high level of intellectual argument. Jurists, judges, attorneys: all are educated people. All have been shaped by a profession that stresses rational argument and logical thought. Those whose positions rest on simplistic, irrational, or emotional thinking will be disadvantaged in a courtroom. James Eisenstein, speaking for many observers, goes so far as to say that courts are *status-quo enforcement agencies*, where "the civil process is structured to protect and enforce middle-class values."[38]

This statement may apply even more strongly in settings outside the USA, where judges are never chosen "by the people"—or even by the people's representatives. Instead, they are "middle-class professionals," specialists in legal affairs who spend years studying to be judges and then work their way up in the hierarchical bureaucracy of their court system. Furthermore, in most countries that have adopted judicial review, it's not an ordinary court that rules on a law's constitutionality. It's usually a specialized body, far removed from "the people," set up solely for this single purpose.

In short, the degree to which court systems are "democratic" will inevitably vary. Of course, all systems reflect their own cultures. In places where judges, along with most citizens, have been taught deference to authority, courts will be less likely than in a freewheeling culture like that of the USA to act aggressively against political authority figures.

Whatever the precise pattern of political struggle, in most places these days it includes courts as key actors. Citizens pursuing their interests intersect eventually with the political process, and many citizens in many nations are finding that their pursuit of interest takes them into the courtroom. Successful political players must therefore become adept at legal matters. In the USA, for example, all serious participants must understand, at a minimum, cases like Roe v. Wade and Brown v. Board of Education. In other countries where courts are growing in power, politicians and social analysts alike are now forced to pay attention to the impact of this institution on political outcomes.

Interest groups and political behavior

The American Sugar Alliance is, by any standard, a successful interest group. It spent a "mere" US$7 million on lobbying activities between 2004 and 2006, but it got a good return on its investment. Government support to the sugar industry has come to more than US$1 *billion* dollars a year for some time.[39] As a result, the American consumer spends two or three *times* the amount that sugar costs on the world market, but a few thousand people in the sugar business make a lot of money.

Another, quite different group is the Alliance for Marriage. It has successfully promoted a number of "anti-gay-marriage" proposals. In more than a dozen states from 2004 to 2006, voters have supported bans, backed by this group, that prohibit marriage between people of the same sex. The Alliance has been less successful at its main goal: an amendment to the US Constitution prohibiting gay marriage. That effort has gone nowhere.

A third group of a still different sort is the National Council of La Raza. It is a support group for Americans of Hispanic origin. It sponsors legislation favorable to immigrant interests, seeking subsidies for schools and organizations that serve immigrants from Spanish-speaking countries. Conservatives usually oppose this group as "radical" and "favoring illegal immigration." As a result, it usually loses funding for its desired programs when Republicans hold office.

These three groups represent a tiny fraction of the colorful kaleidoscope of political life known as "interest group politics."

In a free society, people can associate with each other almost any way they please. In polyarchal cultures, where active citizens abound and few barriers to political involvement exist, we will always find huge numbers of every conceivable kind of group. Active in the USA, for instance, just to name a few at random, are the Citizens Flag Alliance, the Friends of Tobacco, the Farm Animal Reform Movement, the American Council for Capital Formation, the National Association of Letter Carriers, and the Beer Institute.

American culture is particularly prone to group activity. From Madison and Tocqueville to the present, social observers have noted the large number of American organizations. The "joiner mentality" propels Americans into groups of all kinds. As Tocqueville famously put it, "Americans of all ages, all stations in life, and all types of disposition are forever forming associations."[40]

Of course, most groups have little connection to politics. Groups will unite people with a common hobby (the American Society of Genealogists), people in a given neighborhood (the West End Neighborhood Association of Portland, Maine), or people with similar social interests (the Elks, the Women's Literary Guild). Most of the time, most groups do not affect politics. Political interest groups are a small subset of all the groups that people can and do form.

What distinguishes these groups is their focus. In a clear and concise definition, a leading student of groups, Theodore Lowi, and his colleagues define an **interest group** as "*an organized group of people that makes policy-related appeals to government.*"[41] In other words, if your group tries to influence what government does, it's an interest group.[42]

246

The number of these groups is large, and they vary in many ways, adding to the complexity of political life. In our first exposure to the subject of interests, many of us take the American Sugar Alliance as typical. We see it as a small group of privileged people whose narrow aims undercut the "public good." "Special interests" are the bugaboo of reformers everywhere. Books with titles like *The Best Congress Money Can Buy*[43] and *Elites, Special Interests, and the Betrayal of the Public Trust*[44] suggest the dominant political influence of small groups with big money.

In fact, groups vary enormously in aims, size, and impact. Not all are focused on material benefits for a few. "Cause groups" abound, like the Alliance for Marriage. They attract people with ideological aims, and they work for broad policy changes that may not provide members with any material benefits. Then there are "solidarity groups" like the National Council of La Raza. They work to provide disadvantaged minorities with a variety of benefits and opportunities. Other types exist, such as MoveOn.org (a "new technology group"), Common Cause (a "public interest group"), the National Rifle Association (a "single-interest group"), and the American Enterprise Institute (a "think tank").

Generalizing about interest groups is not easy. Table 12.1 shows one way (among many) to categorize them. Overall, many groups exist, they take a variety of forms, they represent an array of interests, they range from small to huge, poor to rich, and they vary dramatically in power. To make it still more complex, the power of any one group—not to mention its size, its wealth, and its tactics—may vary from year to year. It depends on political circumstances, changing public moods, chance events, and many other factors.

Elitism

Among scholars, there's no particular consensus about the role groups play in democratic life. Many analysts play up the narrow, self-interested aims of interest groups. In this view groups use government to serve themselves and undermine the **public interest**.[45] Of course, a major problem is that no one can ever define "the public interest"—or rather that all of us define it in a way that serves our own needs. Since every group can rationalize its own desires as publicly beneficial, it's hard to say that any given group hurts or helps the democratic process.

A more serious criticism of interest groups holds that the majority of groups represent higher-status people. Those with education, wealth, and social power know how to organize to promote their interests. They are much more likely than lower-status individuals to belong to effective groups. The resulting system creates a **mobilization of bias**: away from lower-income and minority groups, toward upper-income and higher-status people.[46]

Analysts who make these points go on to claim that the people most

Table 12.1 Classifying interest groups in the USA.

Type of group	Examples
Socioeconomic	
Producer	American Trucking Association, Petroleum Energy Group, Manufactured Housing Institute (or any business like General Motors or United States Steel when it tries to influence government)
Worker	United Auto Workers, Teamsters, Communications Workers of America
Umbrella	AFL-CIO, Chamber of Commerce, National Association of Manufacturers, National Federation of Independent Business
Cause	
Conservative	Christian Coalition, National Right to Life Committee, Family Research Council, Concerned Women for America
Liberal	Sierra Club, National Organization for Women, Americans for Democratic Action, People for the American Way
Solidarity	
Racial	National Association for the Advancement of Colored People
Ethnic	National Council of La Raza, National Italian American Foundation
Specialized	American Israel Public Affairs Committee, American-Arab Anti-Discrimination Committee
Single-interest or special focus	National Rifle Association, American Automobile Association, American Association of Retired Persons
Public Interest	
General	League of Women Voters, Common Cause, The Interfaith Alliance
Rights-oriented	American Civil Liberties Union, Amnesty International, Child Welfare League of America
New technology	MoveOn.org, MeetUp.com, DemocracyAction, Project Vote Smart
Think tanks	Cato Institute, Heritage Foundation, American Enterprise Institute, Brooking Institution, Twentieth Century Fund

advantaged by interest group activity are those who belong to small, well-organized outfits that provide clear material benefits to members.[47] Typical of such groups are those organized around business interests (like the American Sugar Alliance) or labor unions. Large groups of people with diffuse interests (like consumers, people without health insurance, or opponents to a given war) will find it difficult to create effective groups. They'll be hampered by a phenomenon called **the free-rider problem**. The marginal benefit that people might gain from group activism (lower prices, lower healthcare insurance, an end to the war) does not compensate for the expenditure of resources (time, energy, money) they have to put forth in establishing the group, mobilizing members, pressuring government, and fending off rivals and opponents.

Scholars who take this bleak view of interest groups see them as undermining the democratic process in various ways. Interest groups serve the few who are already well-placed in the social structure. We are living under a system of **elitism**, these scholars claim. Things are run by and for the better-off. One proponent of this approach calls the current American system "democracy for the few."[48]

In a variant of this approach, Lowi has suggested that we are governed by *multiple elites*.[49] In his view, specific powerful interests in society "capture" the very government agencies that are supposed to regulate them, then go on to develop a cozy connection to the congressional committees that fund and oversee these agencies. The result is a set of **iron triangles**, in which wealthy, powerful groups fund the campaigns of legislators, who in turn pressure the executive-branch agencies to develop policies favorable to these groups. No one group controls everything, but the pressuring groups in each specific issue area get much of what they want. And these groups represent the better-off elements of society, who gain still additional benefits from this system while the rest of us get little.

Pluralism

A second approach, and perhaps the dominant one in political science, takes issue with this perspective.[50] It sees groups as beneficial for democracy. They allow citizens to come together to promote common interests. They encourage input into politics by a wide variety of people. Proponents of this perspective are optimistic that citizens of all classes will find ways to break into the system and force policy-makers to pay attention to their wants. In a classic statement, one leading scholar asserted that in the normal course of American politics, "there is a high probability that an active and legitimate group in the population can make itself heard effectively at some crucial stage in the process of decision."[51]

In this view, the widespread activism of citizen groups may even disrupt the supposedly iron triangles, those cozy connections of established power. It argues that groups representing a broad cross-section of society will enter the political arena. As a result, the iron triangles will break down. So many different groups will be pressuring legislators and agencies that no one will be able to gain their favor all the time and win all the battles. Instead, looser connections develop, known as **policy networks**. These networks cluster all the contentious groups interested in a given issue area and conjoin them with the institutionally-designated policy-makers (legislators, bureaucrats). Resulting policy decisions take into account a broader range of views than under the iron-triangle system, thus insuring input from groups further down the social ladder.[52]

Beyond allowing people a voice in government, groups encourage feelings of **social trust** as people learn to work together. Many scholars emphasize that group interactions help build **social capital** that encourages cooperative behavior in many areas of social life and a positive acceptance of public policy decisions.[53] They also encourage support for the belief that government is responsive, since active and organized citizens find that they *can* influence policy outcomes.

The approach we have been discussing has been labeled **pluralism**—or in its more recent incarnation, **neopluralism**.[54] It stresses the multiplicity of organizations that get involved in political life, especially the many citizen groups that have been active in recent decades. These represent not just small, wealthy minorities, as elitist theory would have it, but large blocs of voters, many from modest situations.

Groups like the NAACP on the liberal side of the spectrum and the Christian Coalition on the conservative side have long been active in American life, have involved millions of people in political activity, and have won significant victories well beyond the narrow interests of a few wealthy people. Consider the broad-based organizations that spearheaded the civil rights movement, led opposition to the wars in Vietnam, the Persian Gulf, and Iraq, promoted environmentalism and feminism, and fought for equal rights for non-heterosexuals, as well as the many organizations of the resurgent Christian and conservative right. It is hard to think of these groups as representing some kind of upper-class elite gaining victory after victory for the powers that be.

Groups in perspective

Groups come with a bewilderingly array of titles and causes. True, many of the traditional groups based on narrow economic interests tend to promote the goals of better-off segments of society. But even among these groups, unions are well represented, and they hardly speak for the upper classes.

Beyond that, one finds an array of broadly-based citizens groups, many in what has been called the "New Politics" tradition of radical activism. Other groups represent the millions of middle or lower-income Americans who see themselves as conservative Christians or evangelicals. And while it may be true that certain segments of society (the unemployed, the uninsured, the poor) are not well served by political groups, the potential is always there for people to organize and push those agendas.

Americans are conflicted about the organization of interests. They fear the power of groups that they oppose, but they all expect the right to form and join the groups they favor. Given those attitudes and the legal protections that any mature polyarchy provides for group activity, we can be sure that the staggering number of groups and the complex political process they create will remain a central feature of democratic life.

Conclusion

As Marx suggested in the quote that began this chapter, none of us creates the world we inhabit. As we move from childhood to adolescence to adulthood, we find ourselves enmeshed in a fully formed and deeply structured society that we simply take for granted.

By adulthood, we see our particular institutions as "obvious," almost God-given. Americans have a two-party system. If you want power, influence, or office, you join one of those parties and work within it to gain your ends.

It is different elsewhere. If you had been an ambitious Russian in 1960, you would have joined the Communist Party. And if you had been an ambitious Frenchman in 1700, you might well have considered a career in the Catholic Church.

Institutions are never static. They change with time and circumstance. Today, ambitious French people and striving Russians do not join the Catholic Church or the Communist Party. At least most don't, as they now have other (and more effective) options. But at any given moment, institutions seem solid, almost eternal. They define our circumstances, and we tailor our behavior accordingly.

Our individual personalities, of course, come into play. They affect how we operate *within* the structures of our time and place. Still, whatever our personal quirks and traits, we must behave in certain specific ways because the rules and expectations of our environment demand it. In the USA during the latter part of the twentieth century, if you wanted to become President you had to spend lots of time in New Hampshire. Those who failed to understand these institutional requirements and instead spent lots of time in Idaho may have enjoyed some beautiful scenery, but they never came close to winning the White House.

Our freedom to behave "just as we please" is illusory. It's subject to a thousand institutional constraints. To believe otherwise is to ignore reality and misunderstand the complexities of social life.

Questions for discussion

1 Why do you think some countries adopt federalism and others don't?
2 Would major issues like global warming or welfare policy be handled differently in federal versus unitary systems?
3 If you were an ambitious young politician, how would your career calculations differ in a federal, as opposed to a unitary, system?
4 Do courts have too much power? What should be the role of courts in a democratic society?
5 Do courts necessarily expand rights? Can you think of examples when they have restricted them?

6   If you headed an interest group pushing for a higher minimum wage, would you operate differently in a federal versus a unitary system? How about if you were heading a group to curb immigration?

7   The author does not say much about money in politics. Do you think that interest group outcomes depend primarily on the amounts of cash that each group has at its disposal?

13

THE IMPACT OF PARTIES ON POLITICAL BEHAVIOR

A central institution of modern life is the political party. Those who wish to gain power must work through parties and know how parties work. We shall now see how this key variable affects political action.

How many parties?

A major influence on voters and activists alike is the *number* of parties. Here again, as in many things, the USA stands out. No other stable polyarchy operates with just two parties. Everywhere else, several parties compete for power, win elections at all levels, and regularly form part of the national governing coalition.

A multi-party system is the norm in free societies. This pattern is so common that political scientists always find it necessary to explain the American exception. Many standard textbooks ruminate on "why the United States has just two political parties."[1]

We will return to that question ourselves.[2] First, let's examine the consequences of different party systems. Do people behave differently in nations with one party, two parties, or seven? It turns out that parties matter, and the number of parties does affect behavior.

The one-party option

We can deal quickly with the one-party system. If there is just one party, we are not in a polyarchal culture. Democracy rests on free and open competition. People are contentious beings; if given freedom, they will quickly form opposing and competing groups. No government can satisfy everyone, so once a party has taken over government and ruled for a time, many people will be dissatisfied. Some will organize to change policy or take over the government, if they are free to do so. An open polyarchal culture will always produce at least two competing parties.

A **one-party system** is the hallmark of a non-democratic nation. If that party is rigid, authoritarian, and in tight control of society, the culture is probably a collectivist one. If the party is factionalized and only temporarily ruling a chaotic land with ineffectiveness and thuggery, it is probably operating in a fragmented culture. In no case can a culture be polyarchal with just one party.

How does a one-party system affect political behavior? Obviously, anyone with political inclinations must join that single organization. Furthermore, with no competition, it is almost always run in an authoritarian manner. Those at the top give orders and those below carry them out. To rise politically, join the party, parrot the ideas of the higher-ups, and ape their behavior.

A second option is to embark on the dangerous (and usually short) life of the dissident. For people with drive and ambition, the choice is easy. The one-party system imposes conformity and obedience on the lives of all citizens, especially on those with political inclinations.

Competitive parties

Democratic systems offer a range of choice for political activists. One is the choice of parties; closely related are the choices within each party. Although party loyalty in democratic systems is strong, and members always feel pressure to conform to the party line, the strength of party leaders in competitive systems pales in comparison with their authority in one-party nations. And that's precisely *because* several parties exist. In a system with more than one party, political activists can always leave their party and join another. They can even start one of their own. Or they can simply leave, period, dropping out of political life with no personal consequences. These facts govern the internal life of parties in competitive systems.

Knowing that party members have various options beyond simple obedience, party leaders cannot be ruthless dictators. If leaders behave too harshly towards followers, they may find themselves with no followers. Followers will either support another leader within the party or defect altogether.

To keep members loyal in a polyarchy, party leaders must use a mix of threats, promises, favors, persuasion, popular policy proposals, and openness to ideas from below. This democratic style of leadership gives party members a degree of autonomy. Without fearing for their lives, they can provide input to leaders, discuss policy proposals, bargain for favors, and make a range of demands in return for their loyalty.

Nearly all parties in a competitive system share this trait of democratic openness in internal party matters.[5] Polyarchal systems vary, however, in the *number of parties*, and that number affects the behavior of citizens and activists alike. The precise number of parties can range from two to a great many. In any free system, anyone can start a "political party." Technically, the number of parties in every polyarchy is large. Most of them, however, are unimportant. The USA, for instance, has a Marijuana Party, a Christian Falangist

Party, a Multicapitalist Party, and a Pansexual Peace Party. The impact of these and similar parties on American politics is nil.

What matters to political scientists is the number of **effective parties**, those that have some chance of winning elections and influencing policy. There's no absolute definition of "effective." Three or four characteristics, taken together, can suggest a party's significance within a given political system.

We start by asking how a party does in national elections *compared with other parties?* Notice those qualifying words. The Libertarian Party in the USA is insignificant. It gets on average, 1 percent of the vote in national elections, while the two major parties get 40–60 *times* as many. Compare that result with the Israeli parliamentary election of 2006. There, 31 parties were running, the largest got just 22 percent of the vote, the next one 15 percent, and no other party broke into two digits. Under those circumstances, the party with just 1 percent does not look so puny. Indeed, more than once parties with that level of support have won seats in parliament.

Another important criterion for determining an effective party: whether its members get elected to the national legislature. In the USA, even "serious" third parties like the Greens and the Libertarians have trouble winning the occasional School Board race, let alone seats in Congress. In Israel, with an electoral system that rewards even very small parties, the 1-percent, 2-percent or 3-percent party cannot only win parliamentary seats, but end up providing crucial backing to the majority coalition. Israeli governments have fallen, after tiny parties have withdrawn their support. Even in opposition, small parties in a parliamentary system have a daily platform from which to trumpet their ideas. So winning seats in parliament is an "effective-party" criterion.

To determine the number of parties in a system, start with the parties that have held seats in the national legislature (or in regional legislatures, if the country has a federal system) for a number of years. There is no exact science here, but if a party has held at least five seats in parliament for, say, 10 of the last 15 years, it would seem to have established itself in the system.[4]

Another indicator of a party's strength is the *number of party members* and the ability of party leaders to mobilize those members to political action. This action can range from simple attendance at meetings to public demonstrations on issues of the day. A party can be strong and significant, yet still have few members elected to legislative positions.

In France, mainstream political leaders have long structured the electoral system in a way that diminishes the number of legislators from extremist parties.[5] Election laws have especially hurt the Communist Party (extreme Left) and the National Front (extreme Right). Both parties have many members. They are active and organized, they can arrange mass demonstrations with tens of thousands of people, yet they each have few members of the National Assembly and little impact there. In trying to determine the number of effective parties, one must consider organizational prowess and the parties' existence "on the ground," as well as their number of votes and elected representatives.

All things considered, polyarchal nations produce three patterns of party competition—if by "party competition" we mean competition among *effective parties*.

1   In a small number of countries two parties dominate. They alternate forming governments and setting national policy.
2   In a large number of countries, just a few parties (three to six) are significant, in that they can win elections, influence policy decisions, and even participate in the formation of governments.
3   And in another large set of nations, many parties exist, none dominate, and politics involves an ever-shifting set of alliances and coalitions among numerous relatively small parties for the right to participate in a weak, multi-party government.

Using hypothetical data for illustration purposes, Table 13.1 shows how each system's legislature might line up after a recent election.

Two-party-dominant systems

Some nations, mostly those that have evolved from a British tradition, have what we might call a two-party-plus or **two-party-dominant system**. We see the result in Pattern A. Two major parties win most of the seats, and one of them has enough to form a majority government. Occasionally one of the large parties must form an alliance with a small party in order to govern. Even more occasionally, a minority government is formed (usually for just a short time), or the two large parties form a governing coalition.[6]

By far the common pattern in a two-party system is for one of the two big parties to win a majority of parliamentary seats and govern for several years until the next election. Essentially, the country chooses one party over the other, the members of that party vote cohesively in support of their leaders, and policy is determined inside the Cabinet, which is usually dominated by the Prime Minister. The prototype of this system has been Great Britain, where majority governments have been headed by either Conservative or Labour leaders since 1935 (with a 10-month exception in 1974, when a Labour government had slightly fewer seats than a majority).

Multi-party system, stable

A second system (and perhaps the most typical among democratic nations) is seen in Pattern B, a **stable multi-party system**. In this situation, a

Table 13.1 Patterns of parliamentary government: Hypothetical distribution of legislative seats after a typical election.

Type of Party	Number of legislative seats
Pattern A: a two-plus party system (examples: UK, Canada, Australia, New Zealand)*	
Conservative party	52
Social democratic party	37
Liberal party	8
Regionalist party	3
Pattern B: stable multi-party system (examples: Sweden, Switzerland, Norway, France, Germany and the former West Germany†)	
Communist party	6
Green party	14
Social democratic party	39
Liberal party	12
Conservative party	27
Reactionary party	2
Pattern C: unstable multi-party system (Italy, Croatia, Argentina, French 3rd and 4th Republics, 1870–1940 and 1946–1958, and Weimar Germany, 1918–1933)	
Trotskyite party	3
Communist party	14
Green party	8
Social democratic party	21
Liberal party	7
Moderate party	4
Conservative party	18
Catholic party	16
Anti-immigrant party	3
Separatist party	2
Libertarian party	4

* The USA is not included here because our focus is on the kind of governments likely to emerge after parliamentary elections, and the USA operates under a presidential, not a parliamentary, system. The USA certainly falls into this category of "two-plus party system." Indeed, it almost merits a separate category as a pure two-party system. Although many small parties exist, nearly all officials chosen in partisan races are members of either the Democratic or Republican parties.

† Germany is hard to classify. It falls between the two-party-dominant system and the multi-party system. It has two large parties that together win most of the votes and seats. On the other hand, it also has two or three smaller parties that do get into parliament and regional legislatures, and one of them is *always* part of a governing coalition somewhere. On the whole, it seems a better fit for the stable multi-party category than in the two-party-plus slot.

relatively small number of parties (three to six) gain seats in parliament, and none is big enough to form a majority government.

In these circumstances, the seats are never divided equally. Two parties are often much larger than the others (in the 30–45 percent range). One of them usually holds close to a majority of seats. That party can usually find a smaller party to ally with, producing a coalition with enough seats to form the government. Sometimes it takes three parties to achieve a majority. Sometimes the party with the most seats will fail at constructing a majority coalition. In that case, the next biggest party will find a way. Occasionally, the two largest parties will form a coalition, but this is rare as they are usually the most direct competitors in the system and have a long history of antagonism.[7]

Party coalitions are sometimes formed before an election; two or more parties close to each other on key policies may find it expedient to campaign together. They may already be serving together in the current government. Just as often, coalitions are formed *after* an election. Until the voters have spoken, after all, no one knows the exact distribution of seats. That distribution forms the political context in which each party can weigh the benefits of a coalition with one or more other parties.

In stable, multi-party systems, some jostling and bargaining occurs after the election in order to produce a government, but the job is not impossible. In our example from Table 13.1, the Social Democrats would be asked to produce a majority coalition. The largest party is given first shot at forming the government—that's an unwritten norm in parliamentary systems.[8] The Social Democrats' first decision must be whether to move Left or Right. They could ally with the Greens, producing a majority of 53 percent. They could just as well join with the Liberals to get a 51 percent majority.

Their decision will reflect a host of factors. Traditional alliances come into play. Greens and Social Democrats are usually allies. Recent history must be factored in. Perhaps the Greens and the Social Democrats have been feuding lately. And electoral developments play a role. If the Greens lost seats in this election while the Liberals shot up, the Social Democrats may decide to move right and ally with the Liberals to reflect changing public opinion.[9]

Once set up, the alliance is likely to be stable, since both parties realize that their fortunes depend on sticking together—at least until the next election. The same logic of party loyalty that pertains to two-party systems applies here. If you vote against the coalition government, it might fall. That's what you'll do all the time if you're *not* in the coalition, because you *want* it to fall. But if you're *in* the coalition, you'll vote constantly *for* the government because you want it to stay in place.

Politics in these systems isn't quite as stable as in the two-party arrangement, where only one party controls everything, but it is not much different. The alliance set up after the election is based on hammering out a number of common positions and on agreements to share Cabinet positions in a manner that both parties deem fair. Once the hard bargaining over these matters is sorted out, the alliance can usually hold together for the three or four years needed before the next election. Members of both parties have a lot to lose if the government falls, so they usually stick together.

Multi-party system, unstable

The third pattern, an **unstable multi-party system**, is the most volatile. Many parties (seven or more) gain seats in parliament, and none is close to a majority. Forming a government is difficult, as coalition possibilities are many. Immediately after the election, each party will start maneuvering to get into a majority alliance under the best possible terms. Given the typical seat totals (as illustrated in Table 13.1, Pattern C), it will take at least three parties (possibly four or five) to form a parliamentary majority. It will take energy, cleverness, and luck to put a governing coalition together. The bargaining and the deal-making will be intense. Everything could fall through if one party's leader does not like the cabinet post he's offered, or if a policy agreement acceptable to four parties is anathema to the fifth.

Once a government *is* formed, things don't get easier. The odds are great that this multi-party alignment will soon fall apart. Any coalition in this system will bind together rival parties with separate ideologies and interests. The leaders of each party, presumably strong personalities, will have to work together on a daily basis, and on each issue all must agree on a common policy stand.

Americans can get a sense of the difficulties by trying to imagine how long a coalition government of Democrats and Republicans would last. How long could both parties' top leaders, meeting in cabinet *daily*, agree *all the time* in policy areas like defense, the budget, and the environment, let alone on emotional issues like abortion, prayer in schools, stem cell research, and the right to die? Remember that failure to agree on *any one* of these policies means the loss of your majority and the downfall of your government. How stable would American politics be under these circumstances?

It would be no more stable than in countries that actually face these circumstances. What usually happens is that the toughest questions (abortion, say) are put off as long as possible. The government starts by implementing the few policies on which all can agree. Eventually, disagreements within the coalition can no longer be ignored or papered over. An issue will arise that forces coalition partners to confront their differences. Ultimately, one of the parties will find that its core values would be compromised by accepting the government's stand. An event of this sort can occur in just a few months. It almost always happens within a year of two of the coalition's formation. Then one party will withdraw from the coalition, and the government will fall.

At that point, a new election is unlikely. We have already explained why.[10] The outgoing Prime Minister will find few benefits in going back to the country. Rather, he or she will simply resign and let a new coalition form. It is quite likely that this same Prime Minister will be back in the cabinet soon—as Minister of Finance, Defense, or Foreign Affairs. An

259

adept politician could even return as Prime Minister after the fall of another government or two. Giulio Andreotti served as Prime Minister of Italy on seven different occasions.[11]

In some cases, an outgoing Prime Minister might be asked to form the very next government. This scenario happened recently in Italy. After the 2006 election, a coalition put together by Socialist Romano Prodi barely eked out a few more seats than its rival, the coalition of conservative Silvio Berlusconi. But Prodi's coalition contained *10* parties, ranging from the center to the far Left. Everyone knew it had a shaky future. Sure enough, just 10 months later, Prodi lost a key Senate vote and resigned. The President of Italy then urged him to put together a new government, even though no one expected that one to last long either.

In an unstable multi-party system, once the original government falls, a lengthy period (sometimes weeks) will go by without a new government, as bickering and bargaining among possible new coalition partners take place. Finally, a new coalition will form, but (for reasons we already know) won't last long either. After the nation stumbles through three (or four or five) of these weak, shifting coalition governments, the time will come at last for a new election. As the end of parliament's term approaches, some Prime Minister will at last dissolve the legislature and let the people again choose from among the dozen or more parties pleading for support. Given the number of competing parties, many will win some seats, but none will come close to a majority, and the dance begins again.

Italy stands as the model for this system. After each election, it finds itself with many parties in parliament, complex and shaky coalitions, and frequent government turnovers. Between 1946 and 2006 Italy had *60* different governments—that is, about one a year. It ends up with weak national leadership and a political system lacking the legitimacy to address pressing policy problems.

Many observers believe that such a system is inherently unstable. A popular explosion of discontent must eventually occur, producing either social chaos (a decline into fragmented politics) or a turn to strong-man rule (collectivist control). However, years of history in Italy and in other nations, notably France, belie that expectation. In fact, nations can muddle along for decades under these circumstances. Inglehart and Welzel argue that "low levels of confidence in public institutions can and do go together with strong preferences for democracy over autocracy."[12]

It turns out Italians vote in much greater numbers than do Americans. Over 90 percent of them agree that "the democratic system is good" and "better than all other governments." Furthermore, nearly 90 percent are "proud" or "very proud" to be Italians.[13] One of the great experts on Italian politics, Joseph LaPalombara, argues that Italy may well be seen as a "mature democracy."[14] It may look unstable on the surface, he argues, but that's just a show. At the core of the culture lies a people content with the progressive policies of the political system, policies supported by all the major parties despite their raucous differences in public.

LaPalombara concludes his provocative study of Italy with these remarks:

> The real miracle of Italian democracy is this: whereas Italy represents a plural, divided society with a high potential for exaggerated conflict, those same individuals and institutions that might be expected to promote or exacerbate conflict have worked to dampen it . . . at the level of making and implementing policies, where it really counts.[15]

The voters, activists, and leaders in other systems of this sort also learn to operate effectively within their environment. To outsiders, the pattern may seem incomprehensible, even bizarre. Not to those within the culture. We must remember that an unstable-multi-party-system *is* a system, not just a set of circumstances in transition to something "better" or "worse."

The impact of party structure on behavior

We now know that people will behave differently depending on which party system they live under. Just as clearly, party structure and organization can affect political behavior. A fascinating example from the American past will serve to illustrate.

Citizens often say (wrongly, in most cases) that "there's no difference between the candidates these days." No one was saying that in 1896. The American electorate that year was given a dramatic choice between two distinct presidential contenders.

William Jennings Bryan, the Democrat, was the quintessential charismatic figure. Known as the boy orator, he was just 36 when he awed the Democratic Convention with his famous "Cross of Gold" speech. Addressing the 1896 delegates at a dramatic moment in the debate, Bryan delivered a stunning and powerful denunciation of the gold standard. The conventioneers were so moved by his performance that they not only adopted his radical, populist ideas, but went on to make him their presidential candidate. During the campaign Bryan stumped across the nation, delivering rousing speeches to adoring audiences wherever he went.[16]

In contrast, his opponent, the quiet, conservative William McKinley, never even *attended* the Republican Convention. After winning the nomination anyway, he waited *several weeks* before accepting it. Then he did not exactly "run" for office. Throughout the campaign, he stayed put in his little home town of Canton, Ohio. He spent the entire fall of 1896 sitting sedately on his front porch.

Actually, that is not entirely accurate. McKinley did rise frequently from his easy chair on that porch to greet the throngs who came to see him. He

gave a number of speeches from the steps of that porch to the many supporters who visited Canton every day of the campaign period. He also
shook thousands upon thousands of hands, as people from across the land
trooped up his steps to greet "the next President of the United States."

So history gives us this election of contrasting candidates. We see Bryan,
the "prairie radical," eloquent orator, tireless crusader, traveling about at a
furious clip greeted everywhere by shouts and applause. Then we note the
calm, sedentary McKinley, representative of business interests, unwilling to
venture even a few miles from home to solicit the electorate's support.
Imagine an election like that today. It is hard to imagine someone as unwilling to campaign as McKinley winning his party's nomination, let alone the
presidency.

Yet that's exactly what happened. McKinley, despite his quiet campaign,
beat Bryan and became a popular President, and beat the still-crusading
Bryan even better 4 years later. How could this be? We must start with an
important fact about that era. *Political parties were powerful organizations* and
shaped the behavior of all political players.

In contrast, the power of personality, so significant today, was modest
then. The media, a key institution of our time that magnifies the influence
of personality, hardly mattered in 1896. McKinley won, very simply, because
he had the backing of the majority party of his day. The Republican Party,
as an institution, gave McKinley its nomination and secured him the victory.

Bryan lost because he represented the minority party of the day. It did not
help, of course, that the party he represented had just been in power during a
recession and was blamed for the resulting "bad times." No single variable is
ever enough to explain a complex phenomenon. Still, the power of the
Republican Party is central to understanding McKinley's victory in 1896.

It is hard for Americans today to grasp the meaning of the phrase, "a
powerful political party." Although we have all heard of political parties, and
many of us assume that they play a major role in politics, they are essentially
invisible to most citizens. As one study put it, "party organizations have
almost no detectable presence in Americans' everyday lives."[17]

The point is valid. Most Americans could not name the location of their
local party headquarters. Yet if an institution is important, we know where it
is. We can direct strangers to a nearby mall, to a bank, a church, a gas station,
a Cineplex, or a hospital. Why don't we know the site of our political party?

The answer is complicated, but to simplify: parties in our era are organizations mostly on paper. These days, of course, they are also electronic organizations. In the past, however, they had real locations that were centrally
located and clearly marked. People knew where party officials could be
found, because they *needed* those party officials—for information, for jobs,
for help. The party, for its part, needed to be located in the midst of the
population. Party members had to be able to locate supporters and potential
supporters, keep them happy between elections, keep their party loyalties

alive, get them aroused during campaigns, and get them to the polls on election day.

Parties, in short, were once a major force in American society. A century ago, they were significant institutions. A large percentage of the electorate worked in one way or another for the party—or depended on people who did. That work ranged from providing a little help on election day to full-time party organizing. Most people knew the location of their party's headquarters and could name at least one local party leader. Almost none of this is true any longer.

Parties still exist, of course. They have organization charts, they have set up Internet sites, and political activists all belong to a party. Indeed, most *voters* are nominal party members (they are "registered" Democrats or Republicans). Party stalwarts come out of the woodwork at election time, set up temporary headquarters here and there, make phone calls, distribute posters. But try to find any evidence of political parties 2 weeks after an election. They have disappeared like ghosts, to show up again perhaps 20 months later, just in time for the next campaign.

In other words, if parties play any role at all in the lives of average people, it is a modest one for 2–4 months every couple of years. What other social institution behaves like this? Not one that matters.

Political parties still exist in form, and they do exist in reality for political elites. But they do not play any role in the lives of most citizens. They cannot be seen. There are no manifestations of them in wood, concrete, or steel, in the places where people live, work, and play

Things were different in the 1890s. How did McKinley get nominated and elected without putting in the vigorous campaign work that today seems essential? It's because parties in his time had real clout and real personnel. McKinley did not have to do it all himself. In fact, like other leaders of that age, he had a very specialized role. His job was to behave in a statesmanlike and presidential manner. His supporters—that is, the hundreds of thousands of loyal and active Republican Party members—did the bulk of the work.

It was the Republican workers who staffed party headquarters in village, town, and city throughout the nation. It was they who went door to door, neighborhood after neighborhood, bringing the good word about McKinley (and other Republicans) to friends and neighbors, party backers, potential party voters, and undecideds. It was they who helped organize trainload after trainload of loyalists and possible loyalists for the trip to Canton to meet the great man on that fabled front porch. It was they who channeled the enthusiasm of those who returned from Ohio, eager and excited, into local public relations activity, telling all and sundry about McKinley's godlike qualities.

Party workers, in short, did the grunt work at the local level, the work of firing up voters for the party cause. No wonder McKinley did not have to run madly all over the country. All he had to do was impress the zealous party workers coming through Canton, and those marvelously organized activists did the rest.

Of course, it is also important that top party loyalists raised large sums of money to fuel McKinley's campaign. That money helped bring those party workers to Canton in the first place. McKinley's campaign manager, Mark Hanna, became famous for the money he raised on McKinley's behalf.[18] But if Hanna hadn't done it, others would have. The party was organized for such activity. Today, candidates must be their own fund-raisers. If they don't do it, nobody will. In the past, they could leave that onerous task to party officials.

Decline of the patronage party

Why, you may be wondering, aren't parties structured like this today? As we know, *institutions reflect their time and culture*. As societies change, so too will their institutions. The political party of the high industrial age could not be the political party of the information age. That's because a knowledge-based culture stressing *competence and merit* could not possibly support a spoils-based institution stressing *favoritism and patronage*.

The traditional political party that got McKinley elected without excessive activity on his part was an organization based on the exchange of favors. At the core of the system were ties that connected party leaders, party activists, and potential party supporters. Roughly, it worked this way. Party activists helped elect party leaders to political office. Party leaders then used the perks of office to supply jobs, favors, contracts, and money to party activists. The party activists could then turn around and use their privileged position to supply minor favors to party supporters and potential supporters. Those citizens would then vote the party back into power at the next election, giving the leaders control of jobs and perks again, and the entire cycle continued.

It was the rank and file party workers who did the leg work in this system. They walked the district, chatting to local citizens, discovering who needed help, learning who was in trouble, finding out what city services were most desired. (They were identified by the slang term, **ward heeler**—a most appropriate phrase.) By doing petty favors for all and sundry, the party activists could count on the voters' gratitude at election time. They insured party victory at the polls through this continuous cultivation of the voters.

As long as they kept winning elections, party leaders kept everyone happy and the organization strong. They used their control of public office to channel jobs and money back to the party workers. Everyone benefited—at least everyone in the majority party. Leaders got power and money; rank and file workers got jobs; and voters got personal assistance in time of need.

Of course, those in the minority party suffered. Their leaders won no offices, their followers could count on no jobs, their voters were given no favors. In fact, people who lived in sections of town that voted "wrong" were often punished. Streets were not cleaned, garbage was not picked up, and so on. Those who helped the winners, gained much; those who didn't, lost a lot. But in any case, no one in the 1890s would ever say that parties were "unimportant," and few would ever say that they "had no idea" where the local parties were located.

This traditional party system has, of course, fallen hopelessly apart. Its decline illustrates a basic principle: If the causes of a phenomenon change, the phenomenon itself will change. The party as patronage-dispenser and favor-doer existed because citizens desperately needed the menial jobs and small favors that parties could provide, and because once a party gained control of government, it could provide those benefits. Neither situation holds today. Most people are no longer desperate for the petty favors that parties used to provide, and parties can no longer, in any case, provide those jobs and favors.

Today, most people can find jobs and get ahead on their own. Those who truly need help turn to non-party-controlled agencies of government for assistance. The old system has had its underpinnings gutted. Parties today have little to offer most people, so they have slowly atrophied.

To understand how this happened, we need to remember the exact nature of the benefits that party leaders provided. The important favors consisted of jobs, especially jobs working in government. Before 1900, nearly every job in government at every level (federal, state, and local) was subject to party leaders' approval. Today, fewer than 10 percent of government jobs at every level meet that criterion. In other words, whereas once party leaders could actually place people in government jobs, today they essentially cannot.

You can grasp this point immediately if you know how to answer the following question. What is the single best thing you can do to get a job in government today? If you answered, "Hang around party headquarters, offer to work hard for the local party bigwigs, and curry favor with them in every way possible," then you remain far behind the times. The real answer is to study hard, get as much education as possible, and do as well as you can on a government civil service exam. In other words, the **merit system** has replaced **patronage** (or the **spoils system**) as our current means of staffing government offices.

The reforms that led to our modern civil service system cut deeply into the power of the old party "bosses." Another set of reforms further weakened the power of party leaders. They once had the ability to nominate people for office. To be specific, they used to determine which names would be placed on election ballots as officially representing the party for each contested office. Gaining a party's nomination is huge. You cannot win elected office in the USA unless your name is on a ballot with either a Republican or a Democratic label.[19] Whoever controls that access-point has major power.

All serious office-seekers must know who controls nominations and learn to please those people. Since one party typically dominates in any given geographic area, nomination alone within the dominant party of a particular area is often enough to insure victory. Most elections occur in one-party-dominant areas. Whoever gets the Democratic Party nomination in Chicago for *any* office wins election to that office. In like manner, a nomination by Republicans in Idaho is tantamount to giving someone that office.

It is clear that a key rule for ambitious office-seekers in the strong-party days would have to be: Do not displease party leaders. In fact, find ways to please them, because the route to office runs directly through them. Only they can give you the nomination you need to get elected. A story went around Chicago in the 1950s about a leading Democrat who asked Mayor Daley, the party boss, for a judgeship. Daley is reputed to have said, "Sorry, it takes brains and talent to be a judge. I'm going to send you instead to Congress!"

If party leaders lose the effective right to put people in office, they lose a lot of power. That is precisely what happened. A new method for nominating party members to office sprang up in the Progressive Era (early twentieth century). It slowly grew in popularity and has now become the almost universal way to determine which names get placed on official ballots and which do not. We are speaking of that crucial institution known as the **party primary**.

Winning your party's nomination

Nominations for most offices in the USA now go to those people who can win party primaries, not to those people who can please leading members of the party organization. As it happens, to win a primary you need a vastly different set of skills than those required to impress party professionals. These new skills include the ability to raise money, the ability to conduct a full-scale public relations campaign, and the ability to create a positive image of yourself before a mass electorate.

The successful candidate these days must be a money-raiser, a spin-doctor, and an image-manager. Those skills imply the ability to perform well on the electronic media, particularly television. That's quite different from what party leaders were seeking in pre-primary days: loyalty, hard work, teamwork, cooperation, seriousness, and the avoidance of grandstanding and maverick activities.

In a system that distributes power through primaries, those who wish to be elected will ignore party honchos and set out to find ways of making a name for themselves before the public. They may even find that declaring *independence* from party "bosses" and their "puppets" is a clever strategy. It makes them look like lone individualists, thus appealing to a deeply-held value within American culture.

266

Change institutions, in short, and you change behavior—not to mention outcomes. If institution A is the means for self-advancement, competent young people will gravitate to that institution and follow its norms and rules. If the power of institution A fades and that of B rises, young people will move from A to B. A will atrophy and disappear. B will grow strong and robust. And the skills that it takes to succeed in institution B will produce a different kind of people and politics than those produced by institution A.

That is the story (in brief) of what has happened to American political parties. They have atrophied, while media power has grown. *The key institution of our time for political recruitment and socialization is no longer the political party, but the media, especially the electronic media.* In the past century, we have moved from a politics of party to a politics of media (discussed in Chapter 14).

Other sources of party decline

Of course, it is more complicated than this. Several other factors account for the party's demise. Many of the favors that party leaders once did make little sense now. Leaders once helped constituents who were out of work by giving them small handouts and finding them modest jobs. They did this either directly ("You can sweep out the basement of City Hall") or indirectly ("My cousin Vinnie down at the dock has some freight he needs moved; go tell him I sent you").

Today, if you lose your job, you do not go to the party boss. You go to a government office, where objective criteria determine whether you are eligible to receive modest weekly sums of money ("unemployment compensation") and where you can receive a variety of help in looking for your next job.

If you are really down and out, there are other formal government programs designed to assist you: AFDC, food stamps, and so on. In essence, the welfare state has taken over the favor-doing functions of the old party system, doing it on a broader scale and in a less biased fashion. You do not have to "know somebody" to get unemployment benefits, Medicaid, or housing support. The growth of these modern state services has cut deeply into the pool of rewards that party leaders can offer. They thereby cut deeply into the pool of possible party workers and grateful voters.

Modern conditions of life have also undermined the party's former function as supplier of knowledge and entertainment. It used to be that parties were prime sources of information. They had their own newspapers, and they also spread news through informal social networks, starting with "those in the know," spreading to the party rank and file at political clubhouses, and moving out into party-friendly neighborhoods through general conversation and gossip. Parties contributed to leisure-time activities, putting on social events, picnics, parades, and circuses. They also provided neighborhood meeting-places where people could hang out, shoot pool, play darts, and drink beer.[20]

Today, information is supplied from a thousand media outlets. Sources of entertainment are numerous beyond imagination. No one needs to rely on a party newspaper to discover what is going on in the world. No one needs to wait eagerly for the party's Fourth of July parade and fireworks to have a little fun. And no one looks forward to the end of the work day so that he can go quaff a few brews at party headquarters. Parties, as organizations on the ground, embedded in the lives of average people, have gone the way of the dodo bird.

The decline of the American political party followed inexorably from the rise of a large, wealthy, and self-confident middle class that embraced individualist values. That group slowly came to dominance in American society during the course of the twentieth century, imposing its orientations as it grew in power. Norms of the group stressed the attainment of success through merit and personal effort. Its members despised the idea of parties organized around petty favor-doing. They were appalled at the thought of a government run by patronage and corruption rather than by objective ability.

Self-interest must always be considered in explaining someone's politics. Members of this emerging middle class were often frustrated at finding their own potential control of government blocked by men of another class and ethnic status. Party leaders in 1900 often came from second-generation immigrant families. Party followers, even lower in status, were usually working-class and first-generation immigrants. In contrast, the middle-class reformers were of "old Yankee stock" (the proverbial WASPs, white Anglo-Saxon Protestants).

In the institutions of the welfare state, the party primary, and the civil service, these wealthy white Protestants who opposed the old party system found a way to undermine it. They doubtless believed that the changes they proposed were objectively "good." Who, after all, could be against a "merit system," "party democracy," and the other "reforms?" Still, these changes surely worked to their benefit, by making control of government harder for working-class ethnics and easier for people like themselves.

The rapidly growing wealth of American society helped leaders of this expanding middle class destroy the old party structures. Inexorably, most citizens began to rise on their own. The petty favors of party bosses became unnecessary and even laughable. As time went by and as impartial access to a wide array of government services became the rule, even less fortunate citizens turned away from party and toward formal agencies of the state for assistance.

Political parties still exist in the USA, but not in the day-to-day lives of most citizens. Parties have adapted to changed circumstances, but in doing so have become for most people little more than "virtual parties." They exist mainly as ideas in our heads. Most Americans do not go to party meetings, pay party dues, or know the location of party offices, but they do *think of themselves* as either Democrats or Republicans. These psychological identifications influence their occasional political action. That happens primarily at election time, when most Democratic identifiers vote for Democrats and most Republican identifiers choose Republicans.

Otherwise, party plays next to no role in the lives of most people. Listen to the conversations of your family and friends for a week. Note the number of times that someone spontaneously starts talking about "the Democratic Party" or "the Republican Party," and good luck!

In contrast, parties do remain significant for political activists. As repositories of major belief systems, they help structure the struggle among political elites. Party has always been and remains today the single best indicator of how members of Congress will vote on any given issue. Party also serves as the organizing tool for both houses of Congress, every state legislature (but Nebraska, where non-partisan elections prevail), many city councils, and other government bodies. At the elite level, party is central to American political life. At the mass level, political parties in the USA are mighty thin on the ground.

Conclusion

What have we learned about political institutions? Most important, people cannot operate without them. Human beings find anarchy disagreeable. We like security, order, and predictability. To those ends, we organize our lives and relationships, encourage systematic patterns of behavior, and create formal rules for action. These norms and rules then guide us when we make decisions.

For example, if you wish to gain political power in the USA, run in a party primary. If no one has a majority in the Electoral College, turn to the House of Representatives. By providing clear guidance for decision-making, institutions save society from having to start from scratch in deciding how to operate as each new day dawns.

Ultimately, an institution is little more than some widely-agreed-upon conventions about how people should behave under one circumstance or another. No one can see an institution. In some cases we can see built structures that supposedly *house* institutions (the Capitol building in Washington, St Peter's Cathedral in Rome), but institutions themselves are just ritualized patterns of behavior that people simply accept.

When people stop agreeing about the behavior, question whether it produces any benefits, or ask whether the behavior should occur at all, institutions change, decline, or disappear. Slavery, for instance, was an institution that existed throughout most of human history. It is now nearly extinct, after much questioning of the institution and violent arguments over it.

We must never forget that institutions *matter*. As forces that structure our environment, they affect our behavior (just as do internal forces like ideology and ego strength). American politics, past and present, would look quite different if we had never had an Electoral College. Likewise, American politics operates quite differently today from the way it did in 1900 because we live in an era of weak, rather than strong, political parties.

Questions for discussion

1   Do you know where your local party headquarters is? When was the last time you went to a party meeting or were contacted by a party official? What do you conclude from your answers?
2   What would American politics look like with seven or eight parties, none with more than 30 percent of the vote?
3   Are there other ways you can imagine for choosing party leaders besides a system of primaries? (Remember that no country but the USA uses this method for choosing leaders.)
4   Do you think the Internet will undermine or enhance the power of political parties?
5   Why do you think that some countries have just a few parties, while others have a dozen or more?

14

HOW THE MEDIA STRUCTURE
POLITICS

In 1940, the USA was emerging from the Depression; the Second World
War loomed dead ahead. A popular Democrat, Franklin Roosevelt, was pre-
paring to run for an unprecedented third term as president. In the spring of
that year, a well-known international businessman, Wendell Wilkie, decided
to seek the presidency as a Republican. It is not surprising that Wilkie, eager
to gain maximum publicity for the start of his campaign, invited reporters
from around the country to a press conference where he announced his
candidacy. What is surprising—to us, early in the twenty-first century—is
that Wilkie held this press conference at the New York City penthouse
apartment of his mistress.

Was this a disaster for the presidential hopeful? If Clinton was impeached
in 1999 for having a mistress, wouldn't Wilkie have been laughed out of the
race in the much more prudish year of 1940? Not at all. But that is not
because Americans then were more open-minded. They just never learned
about this side of Wilkie's life. Not a single journalist reported that titillating
bit of information.
Wilkie's extramarital activities, though well known to insiders, remained
a secret to the American public. So they didn't hurt him at all in his creditable run for the White House. Wilkie's posthumous reputation is solid and
positive. He's seen as a key architect of the post-Second-World-War world,
one whose ideas helped lead the USA out of isolationism and into its role of
democratic world leadership.[1]

It is safe to say that today, in the post-Clinton era of politics, no major
candidate for office in the USA could follow Wilkie's example. No politician in our era can expect much of a private existence. Political participants
and members of the public alike assume that every incident in a public
figure's life—no matter how modestly titillating, no matter how far in the
past—could tomorrow become the subject of national attention, debate, and
ridicule.

Change in the media environment

Nowhere has change been more dramatic than in the world of the mass media. Transformations in the way we communicate with each other have become so profound that many have labeled ours "the information age." It is an era of instantaneous transmission of knowledge (and ignorance!) from any part of the globe to any other part.

The benefits of this new system cannot be denied. We're all empowered by easy access to every kind of information.[2] The new pattern undermines the age-old monopoly on knowledge once held by a small, privileged elite. Knowledge really *is* power, and those with access to it are always going to be more powerful than others. If only a few people are allowed to gain information, primarily through a traditional system of education, then those few will become the rulers of society. They start to lose their dominant position when their stranglehold on knowledge is broken.

When masses of people gain access to information, when they have been given a decent education, when they can read about, hear about, view, and comprehend the main political developments of their day, then they can no longer be controlled by a small, literate elite. Mass forms of education and communication lie at the heart of democratization. When most citizens have access to multiple forms of non-government-controlled information, authoritarian government is impossible. *An open, complex, pluralistic media system is congruent with and reinforces a democratic political culture.*

It is no coincidence that dictators always clamp down on the media. Few tyrants can survive looking into a television camera and answering hostile questions about their oppressive actions. Here again we see the interplay of personality and institutions. Authoritarian personalities do not get far in a political environment structured by free and multiple channels of communications. Conversely, when authoritarians do come to power, the first thing they do is seize control of the media.

We now see why the explosion of communication channels in the last 50 years goes hand in hand with world democratization trends. The modern media are helping to transform politics in formerly non-democratic nations. In those places, activists whose values, beliefs, and personalities are not congruent with patterns of obedience and control are using the various media channels to spread their anti-authoritarian messages to a formerly submissive population.

These messages have an impact. Citizens used to a stream of competing ideas rarely support a dictatorship aimed at suppressing the free flow of ideas. The increasing pluralism of the world's media supports the increasing world trend toward democratization.[3]

Beyond affecting countries with formerly closed media systems, the all-pervasive nature of the modern media has also brought significant change to the politics of stable polyarchies. One result is that popular figures are no longer allowed a zone of privacy for their personal behavior. Journalists no longer shelter the congressman who drinks, the governor who fools around. That's produced, among other things, a dramatic decline in respect for authority figures.

A healthy skepticism about leaders is surely necessary for a thriving democracy, but deep cynicism about the political process can discourage the citizen involvement that's also necessary for democracy. Whether one applauds or censures the impact of the media on politics, one can't argue about the key role they play in modern political systems. We must therefore examine this institution in depth to learn the causes and consequences of its rise to political power.

The modern mass media system

We will start with a basic insight about human behavior. *People don't speak up when things are going well.* In good times, we rarely acknowledge the benefits we receive. Often we do not even recognize how we got those benefits or who provided them. We don't think deeply about the positive things that happen to us. We accept them as normal, natural, even our just due. There is an old saying to illustrate this complacency of the satisfied: "He was born on third base and thinks he hit a triple!"

But when things go wrong—watch out! People will hear no end of our criticism and bellyaching. Anyone in a position of authority can quickly confirm these conclusions. As a teacher, I often heard from students unhappy about their low grades, but never from students who thought I had given them "too high" a grade.

The media understand this phenomenon. Basically, "good news is no news." It is bad news that gets our attention.

Like the rest of us, the media are mostly silent about the good things of life. Like students with poor grades, they speak up loudly and critically when something goes wrong. And of course, in the world at large things go wrong a lot. The media can always find negative stories to report, and so the public hears mostly about scandals, disasters, and tragedy. With the media feeding people a steady diet of catastrophe, it is no surprise that people become cynical. Who wouldn't develop contempt for our institutions, given what we constantly hear about them?[4]

Let's focus on media coverage of political news. To begin, there is much *more* political news than there ever used to be. Just two to four decades ago, news was a scarce commodity. The Internet did not exist. There were no 24-hour radio or television news channels. There were no radio talk shows, no viewer call-in programs on television. Legislative sessions were not recorded or televised. Most people had access to just two, three, or four television channels, on which only a few minutes a day were set aside for local, national, and world news. It is true that newspapers were more plentiful a few decades ago, but the quality of their political reporting left much to be desired. In any case, then as now most people used newspapers less to catch up on political news than to glean information about local happenings and store sales, to follow sporting events, and to read the obituaries, the comics, the bridge column, and the movie schedule.

The situation today differs drastically. News can be found everywhere and at all times. Citizens in modern states can see, hear, and read political news literally 24 hours a day. There is now more political news being reported and consumed than ever before in history.

This situation produces a huge **news hole** that needs to be plugged. It puts pressure on news providers to keep the public always updated on "late-breaking developments." ("This just in from Samarkand . . .") It means hordes of journalists searching minute by minute for new stories to break. ("We're standing by for the Senator's press conference, due to start any time now . . . but first this statement from the White House . . .") New media institutions and new media mores have created a new media culture with enormous consequences for the political process.

Under these conditions, what will be the character of the stream of news that we see, read, and hear? First, it will be overwhelmingly negative. Remember, people speak out when things aren't going well, when they have something to complain about. Thus, journalists hear from unhappy people, people with grudges, gripes, and grievances. To the extent that journalists report what they are exposed to, they will be reporting on the world as seen by perennial grousers.

Furthermore, journalists, like the rest of us, find little of interest in things that work well. It is boring to report the positive, so the positive rarely gets reported. Both reporters and consumers of news just take for granted facts that would be amazing in any other time. Simply being able to *report* criticism of government officials without being arrested is an astounding development of recent historical vintage. The fact that average life expectancy in many nations has increased twenty to thirty *years* in just a century is also an amazingly positive social development. So is the incredible increase in average wealth and education levels for most nations of the world over the past half century. And let's not forget the remarkable spread of democracy, combined with the near-disappearance of militaristic regimes that could threaten democracy's very existence.

"Good" trends like these are the dominant developments of our age, but rarely appear in any news channel. "Bad" events instead dominate news coverage. Bad news does sell. The public pays attention to the negative, so "if it bleeds, it leads." We are all fascinated by stories of corruption, incompetence, conflict, and tragedy, and there is no shortage of evil or disaster to report. Given the nature of human beings and the hazards of life, journalists will never run out of sensational material to amuse, shock, or titillate. "Ingrained cynicism," writes media expert Thomas Patterson, "is the media's real bias."[5] Scholars routinely refer now to the media's **bad–news–bias**.[6]

Let's put these trends together. *The media accentuate the negative, there's a huge news hole to fill, and there's intense competition among journalists to uncover new stories.* What do we get? A situation in which *modern citizens are bombarded 24 hours a day by a multiplicity of disastrous images, an incessant drumbeat of stories about conflict, scandal, and violence, and a never-ending array of doom-laden messages.*

Effects of the modern media system

The average citizen is likely to draw two conclusions from this pattern. First, "times are bad." That is, problems exist everywhere; disasters abound. Second, "those in charge" may have caused the problems through their own incompetence, greed, and lust for power. At the least, relevant authorities seem incapable of solving the problems or coping with the disasters. In fact, their meddling may just make things worse.

These are the dominant messages provided every day (every hour) by the democratic mass media. No wonder citizens develop contempt for the central institutions of their society.

Two additional reasons explain the political cynicism produced by the mass media. An eighteenth-century wit once said, "No man is a hero to his valet." The closer we get to people, the more human they appear, and the harder it becomes to idolize them. We notice the warts and the wrinkles that we missed from afar. We see the odd, annoying habits that distant observers never discern. We learn about Wendell Wilkie's mistress—and Bill Clinton's philandering.

All great leaders have had their critics. Winston Churchill was a crotchety, difficult man. Thomas Jefferson and George Washington owned slaves. Charles de Gaulle was cold and imperious. Abraham Lincoln was a manic-depressive. Yet all were great men. Character flaws go with being human. The question is: Do we focus on the flaws or on the character?

No human is without flaws, but that does not mean that all humans are nothing *but* flaws. For a judicious perspective, we must evaluate all aspects of someone's character, pluses and minuses. The media's focus on the immediate and on the negative keeps us from seeing the broader picture.

Any middle-aged person who reaches a position of political power will have many strengths, many admirable traits, but flaws and weaknesses as well. The worst faults used to be known only by a few people: friends and close associates. Even when their faults became known to a larger circle, they were not considered fit for broad public dissemination. Thus, Lincoln's depression, Franklin Roosevelt's physical handicaps, and John F. Kennedy's affairs, though widely known to insiders of the day, were never publicized during their lifetimes.

This past secrecy shocks us today when the ethos of the media is to focus on the personal, the negative, and the sensational. Given the large news hole to fill and the competition to be first in breaking a dramatic story, modern journalists find that they can fill both needs through exposé stories on the shortcomings of people in power. When Senator Smith throws a punch at a heckler or Governor White spends a night in a brothel, they fulfill both of these journalistic needs. They fill the news hole, and they fill it with a dramatic, sensational, "bad-news" story. By showing the worst side of public figures, the media contribute to our current mood of cynicism.

These traits of the modern media almost certainly produced a Democratic takeover of House and Senate after the 2006 congressional elections. Their incessant coverage of the corruption scandal associated with lobbyist Jack Abramoff and his Republican "friends" put Republicans on the defensive for much of the campaign. Then weeks before the election a major uproar occurred when a Republican congressman, Mark Foley, was discovered having made inappropriate advances to underage male congressional pages. The final blow to Republican hopes of holding onto power came when Senator George Allen uttered a racial slur against his opponent's dark-skinned aide. During election season, it often seemed that the American media were giving these three stories as much attention as if a second Pearl Harbor had occurred.

This media focus on the dark side of personality derives largely from the rise of television as prime provider of political news. Television is first and foremost a medium for entertainment. It has gained world appeal by producing a never-ending set of riveting images. The effects are powerful and can convey significant meaning, but they have their limitations. To understand complex subjects, images alone will never do. There is simply no substitute for reading. To become knowledgeable on any topic, one must read deeply. One must also talk with experts, and in addition, one needs to attain practical experience in the area under consideration.

Television is practically useless in furthering any of these standard methods for mastering a subject. It cannot give you practical experience. It cannot help you read. It can, by all means, let you listen to experts, but few turn to television for this purpose. In a medium characterized by rapidly changing images, stationary talking heads seem dull and colorless. It's especially boring to watch experts talk at length on specialized topics.

Television trains us to expect rapid movement, exciting drama. In a standard news program, announcers do not just sit and read the news at us. No sooner have they started telling us the lead story than the camera cuts to tanks rolling across a distant plain, to winds whipping up surf on a deserted beach, or to crowds of screaming people at a political rally in Washington, Wichita, or Walla-Walla.

Television is a visual medium. It is superb at providing entertainment, but as enlightener and explicator, as teacher and mentor, it leaves much to be desired. Images alone cannot explain how a country's budget process works, how agricultural subsidies operate, or how multilateral trade policy functions. These subjects could certainly be explored on television. Programs *could* spend hours showing informed reporters conversing in depth on complex subjects with experts in the field. Specialists could even use charts or give power-point presentations. But few television programs do this. The reason is simple: No one would watch them. At least not enough people to make them commercially viable. C-SPAN offers programs of this sort, but only a small minority of citizens watch its channels, and it is not a commercial venture.

Even politically interested viewers avoid most television attempts to "educate." They turn instead to those shouting-match "debate" programs, where partisans yell at each other and the camera jumps back and forth to show faces contorted in anger. Another option for political junkies is the "investigative" news program, where reporters, purporting to uncover scandal or incompetence, catch on camera the faces of sweaty, sputtering miscreants.

Thus, the political news that television does cover, especially for a broad audience, veers toward the sensational, the negative, and the scandalous. Otherwise, few people would watch political news. The message received by the public from this programming is alienating. Citizens come to believe the worst about public figures. They decide that politics is a dirty business, so there is no point in trying to grasp it or influence it. They end up failing to understand the nuances and technical details of complex public issues. Consequently, they distance themselves from politics, seeing it as a cesspool of self-interested activity rather than the arena where free citizens work openly on ways to govern themselves.

A simple phrase, **the fallacy of the dramatic example**, helps explain the power of media negativity.[7] *We remember the unusual more than the typical, and then go on to assume that the unusual **is** the typical.* Dramatic events stand out in our minds and make an impression. Most of us are not trained to put events into context. We follow some dramatic story in the media and assume it's common or usual. In fact, we are often in error. The story probably illustrates some quite unusual development.

After all, news is by definition "new." It's out of the ordinary, uncommon, *not* typical. The old saw goes that "dog bites man" is not a news story, but "man bites dog" is.

Journalists look for *exceptional* events to report. One student of the media refers offhandedly to "the journalist's habit of ignoring the average, the typical, and the routine."[8] We should practically assume that most of the stories we hear about politics reveal *the exact opposite* of how politics works, since the stories are (by definition) exceptional. They are not the dull, ordinary, and boring norm.

Thus, a headline that screams:

"SENATOR JONES CAUGHT TAKING A BRIBE!"

should alert us to the fact that this behavior is *unusual*. If most Senators took bribes every day, then the *real* news story (being new, not typical) would look like this:

"SENATOR SMITH TOOK NO BRIBE TODAY!"

Since we do not see stories like that, we are surely right to conclude that "he took a bribe" describes unusual, not ordinary, behavior.

Cynics who would claim that bribery is common, just rarely caught, do not understand the intrusive power of the modern mass media. We know entirely too much about current political figures, up to and including their preference in underwear. With such knowledge and with so many journalists desperate to make their careers by uncovering sensational stories of corruption, the fact that bribery still constitutes news suggests that it is indeed unusual.

Since the dramatic (but atypical) political events provided by the media are almost entirely negative (politicians caught in bribery scandals, discovered in improper sexual dalliances, taped saying something stupid), we conclude (wrongly) that this behavior is standard for political leaders. Hence, our negativity toward them increases.

Is there a media conspiracy?

It is difficult to accept that *much of what we get on the news is NOT typical*, and we can all think of opposing arguments. Most of these won't hold up to serious scrutiny, but one in particular is worth examining. We could call it a "conspiracy theory," if we dislike it, or an "establishment-dominance" theory, if it appeals to us. In essence, the theory argues that a **power elite** rules society in its own interest, suppressing news that is critical of elite members.[9]

According to this perspective, close ties interconnect those at the upper echelons of society's main institutions. Cozy relationships bind together a country's top politicians, leading business figures, influential publishers, star reporters, high-ranking military officials, top officials in church hierarchies, and similar bigwigs. When scandal threatens to engulf any element of this cabal, they close ranks to keep the dark doings secret—or at least, to minimize exposure.

The media are an integral element in this web of connection (goes the argument). Thus, journalists are loathe to report critical news that might cause their sources among the powerful to dry up or alienate their media bosses, who themselves are part of the elite. In any case, publishers will refuse to print critical stories about their peers in "the Establishment" that might slip through the tight reporter–politician network. These activities are often referred to as **gatekeeping**.

From this perspective, we do not get *enough* bad news. The really bad news is ruthlessly suppressed: that a small elite runs society for its own benefit and to the detriment of the rest of us.[10]

One finds many variants of this power-elite thesis. However, the line of reasoning—that a small, unified group runs the country—seems inadequate to explain power distributions in complex, modern societies. A more sophisticated view that we've already encountered, **pluralism**, provides a more nuanced perspective.[11]

Pluralists do not deny that power is always unequally distributed and always falls into the hands of the better-off, better-educated members of society. Pluralism admits, as well, that these well-off, educated people who hold political power are usually situated at or near the top of other social institutions. However, pluralists argue that clear restraints prevent these people, or any single group, from getting all they want in an open society.

For one thing, huge cleavages exist within any group alleged to monopolize power. These divisions keep the group from attaining long-term unity. That allows mass influence to impinge on elite decision-making. Some segments of the divided elite will find that they can bolster their own position through alliance with groups lower in the social pecking order. Other elements of the elite follow suit to remain competitive, and before long voices from across the social spectrum are being heard and heeded in the halls of power.

Power-elite theory seems especially weak in explaining how the modern mass media work. For those who study politics on a day-to-day basis, the idea that there is any unity among people with power is ludicrous. In any democratic system, politicians, along with their supporters, onlookers, analysts, and general busybodies of all kinds, are constantly heard in loud disagreement with each other. These disputes make good copy. They get widely reported. Covering up a major story is hard to do—and rare. Every reporter knows that one of the best stories is some powerful person's attempt to cover up a story.

The general rule can be stated this way: *If there is conflict at high levels in an open society, it will be reported—and the more intense the conflict and the more colorful the characters, the more widely the conflict will be covered.* The media in most places are highly competitive, not in collusion with each other. Owners and reporters alike want to beat their rivals into print (or onto the airwaves) with dramatic new stories. The idea that a conspiracy exists among the major distributors of news, let alone among them *and* the other top institutions of complex, open societies, runs against all the evidence.

Of course, norms and habits of news reporting do develop that can bias reporting in certain directions and away from others. But that is hardly the same thing as saying that a power elite (a) directs all news reporting and (b) directs it away from negative news about the elite itself. No elite in any polyarchy is that strong. Even if the major news institutions leave stories with dramatic potential uncovered, there will always be forces at the margins with a keen interest in reporting them. Once a story is reported anywhere, if it has mass appeal and even a modicum of credibility, the major news institutions are forced to pick it up. Reporting is just too competitive to keep any exciting story bottled up. *Suppression of major negative news stories may occur, but it is rare in open, pluralistic societies.*

The lessons of Watergate

Nothing better illustrates the development of the modern mass media than the story of Robert Woodward and Carl Bernstein. These journalists entered into legend with the notorious Watergate scandal (1972–74). Their exposé of criminal executive branch activities led to Richard Nixon's resignation from the American presidency. That was a towering symbolic event. From 1788 (election of George Washington) to 2008, only *one* President was forced to leave office before the end of his term: Nixon.[12] In the mythology of the Watergate episode, Woodward and Bernstein get primary credit for Nixon's downfall. As the fable has it, two fearless, unknown investigators, searching only for truth, brought down the most powerful man in the world.

As with any legend, the perspective is simplistic and overblown. The story of Nixon's ruin goes far beyond these two young men. It involved dozens of actors and all the top institutions of American political life. Yet myths grab our imagination and hold fast. The Woodward-Bernstein tale offers a dramatic role model to aspiring journalists and aggressive publishers alike. In many ways, it has changed the shape of the modern media—and in so doing, changed the way politics works in modern societies.[13] To see why, we must take a closer look at this story.

In early June, 1972, Bob Woodward and Carl Bernstein were utterly unknown. They were third-string journalists covering local crime at a second-tier newspaper. That's a blunt way to put it, but fair. These two, both in their late 20s, worked on local stories at the city desk of the *Washington Post*, still not the powerhouse publication in stature and influence that it aspired to be (and soon became). When a break-in and bungled robbery occurred at Democratic Party National Headquarters in the Watergate Hotel, Woodward and Bernstein got the assignment to cover the story because it had all the markings of a petty, botched local crime. (Ron Ziegler, Nixon's press aide, famously called it "a third-rate burglary.")

Other, more senior reporters didn't want the story. Most saw no future in it. Some feared that it could harm their careers, making powerful officials furious at them. (That indeed happened with Woodward and Bernstein, but with fewer connections to the high and mighty, they had less to lose.) Many top reporters were already covering the story from more prestigious positions, inside the White House or at Capitol Hill, but in those places they could do little more than report on official reaction to events, not uncover events themselves.

So Woodward and Bernstein were initially lucky to be on the ground floor of a story with the potential for making national and international news. Of course, they *were* talented journalists. Their reporting skills did play a significant role in the ongoing investigation that led to the end of the Nixon presidency. But the story of what they reported is not the focus here. We will now concentrate on some *results* of their reporting and on the way legions of later journalists have interpreted those results.

As one result of their investigations, these two men became the best known and most lauded journalists in the world. In June, 1972, they were poorly paid and unknown. In June, 1974, after publication of their book, *All the President's Men*,[14] a work that quickly became an international best-seller, world-famous movie star Robert Redford was *pleading* with producers to make this a movie and let him play the part of Woodward.

At the same time as Woodward and Bernstein were enjoying the fruits of their new-found fame, their newspaper, the *Washington Post*, experienced a parallel and related rise in stature and prestige. By the end of the Watergate era, the *Post* had risen from its former status as one of a number of decent second-tier newspapers in the USA to a position that it has maintained ever since: the nation's most serious journalistic rival to *The New York Times*.

Media people draw a simple conclusion about this entire episode. Woodward and Bernstein, backed and supported by the institution of a powerful newspaper (personified by a determined editor, Ben Bradlee, and a supportive publisher, Katherine Graham), uncovered the secrets that brought down a powerful but arrogant, corrupt, and out-of-touch presidency. In acting as they did, everyone involved became wealthy, powerful, and celebrated.

The mythology of these events has become ingrained in the minds of journalists, editors, and publishers everywhere. They study Watergate and come away with the following guidelines for professional action:

- *Journalists*: Be unrelenting in your efforts to uncover scandal on the most powerful people in the land. With a little luck, you may strike gold and cover yourself with glory.
- *Editors*: Encourage your entire staff to discover scandalous, corrupt behavior in high places. Success could solidify your place in history as a righteous, crusading journalist who looked power in the eye and never flinched.
- *Media owners*: Encourage investigations by your staff into high-level shenanigans wherever possible. Back them as they strive to uncover corruption, and your media outlet too may enjoy a boost in prestige, along with increasing commercial success. (Katherine Graham's prestige rose

precipitously after the Watergate episode, and she is now universally praised as a far-seeing, sensitive manager of the *Post* organization.)

Watergate and the Woodward–Bernstein story did not create muckraking and the negative bias in modern news reporting, but they did much to further and solidify trends in that direction.

This story suggests the absurdity of a conspiracy-theory perspective on journalism. The modern mass media are hardly eager to cover up the misdeeds of some supposedly unified political elite. The modern mass media themselves are not unified, but instead are intensely competitive. They contain thousands of prying journalists, all eager to become the next Woodwards or Bernsteins. They are backed by editors and publishers who hope to emulate Ben Bradlee and Katherine Graham. They all hope to gain fame and fortune by uncovering abuse of power at the highest levels.

Watergate, as it is known in shorthand, ushered in our current media era. Powerful journalists (and those wishing to be powerful) now search constantly for scandals to report. Since 1974, not a year has gone by without a major media "feeding frenzy" reminiscent of Watergate.[15] Among the more prominent of these have been "Koreagate" (1977–80), the Iran-Contra affair (1986), the Whitewater investigation (1993), the Monica Lewinsky scandal (1998), the Abu Ghraib prison tortures (2004), the Mike Foley matter (2006), the case of the fired federal prosecutors (2007), and many, many more.

This trend has been exacerbated, if that is possible, by the rise of Internet journalism. Now anyone with a website and some energy can set up as an independent "reporter" and commentator. This development has multiplied the number of media people eager to make their mark, and Internet journalists are mostly unbeholden to established institutions. They do what they can to gain attention and an audience, thus adding to that chorus of media voices putting out negative messages and (supposedly) discovering scandal.

Journalistic competition is intense because the rewards are great. The Woodward–Bernstein story never loses its appeal. Since most journalists are intelligent and trained professionals, we would be naive to think that the entire lot of them—working independently to uncover "wrongdoing" in an open competitive system where politicians, eager to bring about the downfall of their rivals, leak gossip to media contacts on a regular basis—contrive somehow to miss significant improper actions on the part of high government officials.

In fact, journalists do their job of exposing "evil" rather too well. It was once said of a veteran reporter, William Safire of the *New York Times*, that he had uncovered seventeen of the last five scandals in Washington! Negative news is constantly reported. It does not necessarily reflect reality, but most of us *think* it does.

What's the result of this steady diet of news negativity? For the average citizen, one who's not terribly interested in politics but who pays sporadic attention to the news, the current media environment produces a sense of "one damned thing after another." Most of the news—in newspapers and newsmagazines, on radio, on television, and now over the Internet—focuses bleakly on scandal, corruption, disaster, and tragedy.

And this news never stops. With the 24-hour news day, news changes hourly in response to the journalist's norm that "yesterday's news is stale news." Change that to "last hour's news is stale news."

Most stories do not stay around long enough for citizens to get a handle on them. At breakfast, you see a headline in the paper about a crisis in the Middle East. At noon, you hear a radio report about a terrible car accident in Tulsa. In the evening on television, you see damage caused by an earthquake in Bolivia. The next day things start all over again with the story of a political assassination in Germany.

Who can get perspective on these rapidly-passing events? What does any of it mean? The average citizen cannot make sense of it, except to draw a couple of general conclusions. First, it is a dangerous, dirty world out there. Dark, painful things happen all the time, for no obvious reason, and much of what happens is the result of venal or incompetent politicians screwing up or screwing around. Second, the world beyond my own community or expertise is so complex as to be incomprehensible. Journalists report all these events, but rarely explain them. Why did Aragonians invade Translandia yesterday? Why did the government of Mazamba fall this morning? What were those bloody student demonstrations in Hok Pang all about?

None of these continuing disasters are ever made comprehensible. The media portray an endless array of misery, but never explain it—and almost never show anything good happening. In this environment, it is amazing that anyone following the news still shows an interest in civic engagement. Of course, many do not. Mass alienation and apathy are, many scholars argue, a key by-product of these current media processes.[16]

Other effects of the mass media

Does the name *Jamie Whitten* ring a bell?

I didn't think so. Yet for decades in the latter part of the twentieth century, he was one of the most powerful men in American politics. His power derived from a simple fact. He headed the Appropriations Committee of the US House of Representatives. Every cent spent by the American government had to be approved by Whitten's committee. In those days, the word was: You want some money for your pet project? Better go see Jamie—and make sure you're on good terms with him.

This is a nice position if you want power and influence. Yet Whitten was unknown to most Americans. He was even unknown to many interested observers of American politics.

Why did we never hear of this man? Simple. He never gave interviews! He never talked to journalists. He was the perfect congressional insider. He kept his mouth shut in public, while cajoling, persuading, dealing, and twisting arms in private. How could the media cover a man with such infuriatingly anti-media habits?

Besides, Jamie Whitten made poor copy for any media types who did try to cover him. His bland, colorless style made him useless to journalists. What could one say to catch the attention of people used to the high drama of the Watergate hearings, the civil rights debates, and the anti-Vietnam demonstrations? ("Now let's learn about Jamie Whitten, whose favorite color is brown.")

Whitten served nearly 53 years in the House, longer than anyone else in history. He attained great power, yet was virtually unknown. It is unlikely one could duplicate his pattern in the media age. Today, it is hard to gain power outside the media system.

The media today, as a whole, have become a major social institution. Like all institutions, they influence behavior and outcomes. One media effect concerns the kind of politicians likely to thrive in an age of electronic journalism. Different kinds of people get drawn into politics. Some of those participants will benefit from the modern media system, while others will be disadvantaged. It would appear that media professionals, pursuing their own ends, doing their jobs as they have come to understand them, unintentionally promote the career patterns of some politicians and not others.

We will begin with a simple query: "What do journalists want?" That's an easy question for social scientists. Study after study has made it clear.[17] *Journalists seek stories that are new, sensational, full of drama, able to provide "good visuals," and preferably about familiar, powerful people confronting each other in tense contests for money, status, and power.*

I wrote the previous paragraph years ago for a class handout. After re-reading it years later in September, 2005, I took a break and watched the news on television. The five leading stories of the day involved (in this order):

- high government officials bickering over blame for a bungled rescue effort after a major hurricane in New Orleans
- a high-ranking congressman being indicted for corruption
- sad stories (with much live footage) of people whose lives had been ruined by the destructive hurricane
- a story about military men who had sent gory photos of dead and mutilated Iraqi citizens to a web site in exchange for free Internet access to pornographic pictures
- and a story on the continuing levels of violence in Iraq.

All five stories conform perfectly to media requirements for news, and all five encourage pessimism and alienation in anyone watching.

Given these media patterns, we can be sure that stories about abstract, impersonal forces or complex, social trends are buried in the back pages of "quality" newspapers, if reported at all. Sober, substantive, in-depth news stories appear almost never in electronic news reports—the places where most citizens get their news. When was the last time you heard this startling announcement? "And now, stand by for an in-depth, 2-hour investigation of land reform in developing countries!"

How do journalistic habits dovetail with the interests of political participants? Successful politicians need favorable media attention. The best way to get that attention is to know what journalists need. *Successful politicians will help journalists meet their criteria for a good story, while insuring that the story focuses on them positively and on opponents negatively.*

Toward these ends, successful politicians will develop several strategies. First, they will work to provide journalists with *new* quotes, information, and story lines. (Remember, yesterday's news is stale.) They will cultivate journalists, developing good connections so that media people will automatically turn to them for stories and reactions to "breaking" developments. Have you ever noticed how the same 10 members of Congress (and the same ten "political experts") are always the ones commenting on national news stories? It is not a coincidence. These people work hard to be in that position, to be a "go-to person" for the media.

Good politicians develop a knack for doing or saying something *dramatic*. That produces strong reactions from other players in the system. The "best" of them make strong, heated responses of their own. Journalists get the story they prefer, with drama and conflict, while the most colorful politicians get media coverage and public attention.

Successful politicians also learn to provide the media with *colorful photo opportunities*. It helps to be photogenic or charismatic in the first place, but these are qualities that can be enhanced, even created, with the help of consultants, public relations people, "image counselors," and clever staging techniques. The best politicians become such familiar names, even celebrities, that the public *expects* media coverage of them on a regular basis, and the media are almost required to comply.

To insure coverage, even without celebrity status and charisma, it helps to achieve some *significant power position*. Media convention dictates that *official sources*, people in institutional positions, should be given respect and therefore coverage. The most important of these positions include the chairs of major legislative committees,[18] top presidential aides, Governors, Senators, Cabinet members, and of course the President. Journalists always turn to those in institutional power spots when they need information to flesh out a breaking story or when they seek reactions to a new political development. As a result of this media norm, ambitious politicians are always scrambling for an official title or position.

Political success in the media age also depends on exhibiting skill in strategic political discourse. That is, politicians must be adept at discussing politics from a game perspective. That is the journalists' favorite angle. Study after study show that the media focus much more on the "horserace" aspect of politics, who's winning and who's losing, than on the content of public issues. Being able to "talk politics" is a sure way to get attention from reporters.

Here's where the mastery of **spin** is crucial. Good politicians will make their own actions (and those of their faction or party) appear as great victories. If that's not possible (after, say, an election defeat or a thwarted policy initiative), their efforts will be touted as glorious attempts to help "the people" that were callously blocked by "pig-headed, self-centered enemies." The successful political leader will be, in short, an excellent **spin master**.

Media journalists, of course, won't fall for these rationalizations. They will simply pit two opposing spin masters against each other. This technique provides color, conflict, and drama, while leaving the public dazed and confused. It also elevates the power of media personalities. They come across (or try to come across) as the jaundiced, knowing, above-it-all referees of shallow, petulant politicians' immature feuds.

The confrontation device puts reporters above the fray. They can pass themselves off as detached observers, sardonically pointing out the self-interested arguments of the opposing sides. Journalists rarely confront the substance of a politician's argument. Rather, they point to the *political* reason it is being made and then ask a second politician with opposing views to knock it down.

The entire exercise seems likely to fuel public cynicism about politics. It also promotes a false view that all arguments are equally balanced. "Senator Jones has argued that the earth is round. For an opposing view, we now turn to Raven Lunee, president of the Flat Earth Society."

As a result, the public gets a false impression of the true state of expert opinion on many subjects. From media reports, one might think that there are just as many scientists who doubt the theory of evolution as those who support it, just as many experts who doubt global warming theory as accept it. In fact, of course, the overwhelming majority of scientific experts back both theories.

In addition, since "spokespeople" chosen by the media to represent any given side of any controversy are always the most outspoken, the public gets the impression that most political figures are wildly confrontational. Of course, that starts to become the case. With the media favoring provocative characters, people with combative personalities get the attention they need to become public figures. They then have good shots at winning elections and gaining high office. After a while, the seats of power are filled with argumentative types who are not particularly good at the give-and-take of day-to-day politics and who also do not have the expertise to solve complex problems in specialized areas.

We now see the tightly-connected links between media professionals and political activists. What conclusions can we draw from this web of connection? Whatever else it produces, *the norms of modern journalism inevitably advance the career prospects of loudly opinionated and strongly assertive politicians. In like vein, these norms undermine the chances for success of quieter, policy-focused participants.*

Journalists want stories with flair, conflict, drama, and color. *Conflict-provoking politicians are much more likely to meet journalists' needs and thereby gain media attention* than politicians whose behavior tends toward the reduction of conflict. Confrontations give journalists the compelling story they seek. Tales of cooperative behavior, or of technical work on complex issues, just don't sell.

For instance, the media paid little attention to George H.W. Bush's "thousand points of light" program. That was an attempt to publicize charitable work in the private sector. It practically ignored Al Gore's work at "re-inventing government," (an effort to make public bureaucracies more efficient). To the media, both projects were simply boring.

When Bush vomited in public on the Japanese prime minister, however, and when Gore supposedly claimed that he'd "invented the Internet" (he actually said, "I took the initiative in creating the Internet"), both absurdly minor matters got major media attention. By making Bush senior and Gore look foolish with these stories, the media undermined the power of these less than charismatic politicians.

Voltaire supposedly said, "Let me cite five lines from any author, and I will have him hanged." He understood that we've all done or said things that we're not necessarily proud of. The question is, are the actions reported by the media typical of someone or an unusual deviation? In the case of less-than-colorful political actors, the media look for exceptional and unusual stories to report. Their ordinary activities would hardly attract an audience.

In most cases, the media will just ignore hardworking, moderate, consensus-builders. They love a politician who says of another, "He's a lying phony!" They shun politicians who express disagreement without being disagreeable. Would-be leaders will never make the national news with this line: "I'm sure that my learned colleague has honorable reasons for taking the position that he does, although I cannot entirely agree with him on this point; let me explain."

Effects of the media–politics link

Media professionals love politicians who talk in colorful **sound bites** and who generate controversy. Woodward-Bernstein wannabees cover cranky individualists, not quiet, informed team players. They thereby confer power on one set of politicians and not on another.

How does media coverage confer power? The answer may seem obvious today, but the very question would have been incomprehensible to politicians of a previous age. Just a few decades ago, media coverage meant little for a politician's career. Remember Jamie Whitten? He avoided the limelight, and it didn't hurt him. Why is it nearly impossible for power-seeking politicians to behave that way today?

To answer this question, we must ask another. What did a political actor do in earlier times to get elected and gain power? The answer was simple—and still is in many countries. To work your way up in politics, join a political party and prove yourself a party loyalist. The media had little effect on your career. In fact, too much media coverage could hurt you. Party leaders might see you as a "grandstander," a "show horse" rather than the "work horse" they preferred.

Party, not the media, used to determine your career path. You had to work within the party structure for party goals, you had to gain the trust of party leaders, and you had to build up a following of your own within the party. *If* the leaders liked you, *if* you showed yourself adept at turning out voters on election day, *if* you proved yourself responsible and a team player, *if* you showed some ability to speak well in public *for the party*, then *eventually* you might hope to win a party nomination for a lower-level office. If you succeeded at that level, you might slowly work your way up to higher offices, always through pleasing important party officials, by working for party goals, and by helping fellow members of the party. Providing jobs to party followers and favors to party supporters whenever you could was a significant determinant for being well seen by other party officials.

Party loyalty, in short, used to be crucial for political success. Today, party loyalists are denounced by ambitious outsiders as "bosses" or as "pawns of the party machine." If you tried to rise through the party today, you would be tagged with these epithets by your rivals, derided by the media, and find yourself sinking from public favor in a hurry.

In any case, parties as on-the-ground organizations hardly exist any more in the USA, so rising in politics via the traditional party structure simply makes no sense.[19] No one does it that way in our time, least of all the most ambitious politicians.

Today, politicians must create their own personal organizations to get ahead. They must attract a following on their own, and an important way to do this is to become a media celebrity. In our democratic age, with political parties on the decline, the way to political power is through the ballot box. Those who can capture the public's imagination, who know how to get media attention, who can make a regional or national name for themselves—those politicians have a strong leg up in the process of getting elected to high positions of power. The newly-empowered institution of the modern media help people with public-relations and rhetorical skills move upward.

Politicians with these traits benefit from another element of current political life. If they wish to attain office, the people they must especially please are the most ideologically committed citizens. To rise in any party these days, you must convince the "party faithful" to support you—in primary campaigns and party meetings, at caucuses and conventions. Most of the people who vote in party primaries or go to party meetings are "true believers,"[20] deeply committed to the party's ideological doctrines. In the USA, they will be activists holding the "traditional liberal" or "traditional conservative" attitudes.[21] These people do not want moderates representing them. Nor will they be happy with a political style of tolerance and judicious incrementalism.

Being ideological purists, activists today are looking for candidates who "preach the good word." Politicians who *look* like purist ideologues and use a take-no-prisoners approach will win their favor. In modern times the strategy of "pleasing the base" and winning media attention reinforce each other. Nominations, elections, and media attention have started going to loud, harsh, play-for-keeps combatants, drastically changing the nature of the political process.

Conclusion

The institution of the modern mass media has helped to advance the career prospects of conflict-exacerbating political types. This pattern helps produce an alienated, cynical, and apathetic public. Many citizens believe that politicians are phony manipulators more interested in promoting their own careers than in furthering the public's interests. To the extent that the media helps public-relations-oriented opportunists rise to prominent positions, there is some justification for this belief.

Among the many consequences of these developments are:

- declining rates of involvement in elections
- widespread public support for "plague-on-all-your-houses" measures that would punish *all* public officials—such as term-limit laws
- a decline in support for government programs in general; and, more dramatically
- a decline in support for the very idea of government as a positive institution that can solve social problems and achieve socially-desirable ends.

These are trends only. The world is not coming to an end with this growth of mass media power. Already, counter-forces are emerging that may undermine these trends. Increasing levels of education, combined with the informative power of the Internet, may combine to counteract the glitzy superficiality of television images. Still, if every age has its positive and negative tendencies, the growth of an intertwined connection between media power and conflict-exacerbating politicians is one of the more troubling of our time.

Questions for discussion

1 Could a democratic political system co-exist with a government-controlled media system? Conversely, could an authoritarian regime co-exist with a free media system? Is there a clear connection between the political system and the way the media within that system operate?

2 We take "transparency in government" for granted these days, but were there any advantages to the media system of several decades past when little of what went on inside government or in the lives of political leaders was revealed to the public?

3 Do you agree with the author's implication that the more we know of people, the less we respect them? Doesn't it depend on what exactly we know and on whether, as individuals, they are worthy of our respect?

4 The author argues that power has passed from the traditional parties to the modern media? Do you agree? If so, what are the pluses and minuses of this development?

5 Does the existence of the Internet and the "blogosphere" change the rules of the media game, as outlined in this chapter—or strengthen them?

15

THE PERSONALITY OF
POLITICAL LEADERS

"Suppose you were an idiot," Mark Twain once said. "And suppose you were a congressman. But I repeat myself." Twain also remarked that "there is no distinctly American criminal class except Congress." With his cynical humor about "politicians," Twain spoke for many citizens everywhere.

Yet the political analyst must get beyond these negative (and shallow) stereotypes. The personality of political leaders, those assertive top-level operators who gain and wield power, will clearly affect the institutions they head and mold. We earlier referred to career political activists as Influentials.[1] They staff and run the major institutions of society. Since their power far outstrips their small numbers, we must learn who they are and what they are like. Could they really be the stupid, immoral crooks imagined by Twain and the rest of us?

If we think for a minute, we will realize that blanket generalizations about all members of any group must surely be wrong. People are diverse and complex. Just within our own circle of friends and family, each of us knows many different individuals, and they're not "all alike." Why do we unhesitatingly accept assertions about the nature of "all politicians?"

The answer can be found in a basic human tendency. *The weaker our knowledge about a phenomenon or group, the broader and shallower our generalizations about it.* After an American embassy is blown up abroad, one hears that "Africans are just violent people," or "What do you expect from fundamentalist Muslims?" But when Timothy McVeigh blew up a federal building in Oklahoma City, few Americans went around saying, "Hey! What do you expect? Americans are just violent people," or "It's not that surprising. After all, he was a white Protestant." Americans could recognize that McVeigh was a deviant case, not the norm, because they knew the culture within which he was operating.

Essentially, the better our knowledge about a set of people, the less willing we are to tolerate simple-minded generalizations about them. We can apply this principle to politicians. Just how many do you actually know? I don't mean the five or ten about whom you have some hazy second-hand knowledge through the mass media. I mean people you've actually observed in person, physically met, and engaged several times in conversation. If you are like most people, the answer is close to zero. Why is it, then, that you are willing to make sweeping statements about a group of people of whom you know next to nothing?

Politicians—like used-car dealers and mothers-in-law—make amusing scapegoats for stand-up comedians. We must, however, get past superficialities for a serious understanding of political personality. If we give even brief consideration to what we already do know about politics, we can readily think of many political leaders who have been radically different from each other. Abraham Lincoln was often gloomy; some scholars see him as a depressive personality. Theodore Roosevelt, in contrast, was wildly outgoing, optimistic, and exuberant. Winston Churchill and Charles de Gaulle were self-confident to the point of arrogance, while their contemporaries, Clement Attlee and Edouard Daladier, were modest, insecure men. Nevertheless, the latter two rose to the same position of power in Britain and France (Prime Minister) as did Churchill and de Gaulle.

We can multiply these examples forever. The cruel psychopath, Josif Stalin, was a politician. So was the sunny and affable (if ineffectual) American president, Warren Harding. The point is, we cannot settle for unsophisticated generalizations about the similarity of "all politicians." Stalin and Harding were both politicians, yet shared few personality traits. The universe of politicians is simply not homogeneous.

In just the small group of men who have been American presidents, one finds the gregarious Teddy Roosevelt and the retiring Franklin Pierce; the heroic George Washington and the inept Ulysses S. Grant; and Abraham Lincoln, "Honest Abe," versus Richard Nixon, a dishonest man who had to give up the presidency to escape impeachment. Take the last five American presidents: Jimmy Carter, Ronald Reagan, George H. W. Bush, Bill Clinton, and George W. Bush. I see five remarkably different personalities there. Even Bush father and son seem quite different from each other. We find diversity just looking at occupants of the same job in the same culture in the same era.

It is not just in the USA but everywhere that politicians differ from each other in temperament and style. In the late twentieth century, the British were ruled by the caustic Margaret Thatcher, the genial Harold Macmillan, and the aloof Alec Douglas-Home—and they were all Conservatives. Russians have lived under the paranoid Stalin and the frank, open Gorbachev. The Japanese have been led by the rabid fanatic, General Togo, and more recently by a dreary succession of political bureaucrats. And the Philippines went from a brutal autocrat like Ferdinand Marcos to the open and nurturing figure of Cory Aquino.

You can easily discover for yourself that politicians differ. Start attending political meetings in your area. Watch how the politicians behave. Go up and talk to five or ten of them. See if you still think that "all politicians are alike."

I have spent decades in activity of this sort. I've tracked down and interviewed politicians in a variety of settings. In these respondents, I saw clear personality differences. Even political activists who held the same position and shared objective characteristics spoke and acted in radically different ways.

Comparing politicians

We will now look at two "average" state legislators. They are both women: Betty Gardner and Joan Moore. On the surface, they are remarkably similar. Both are middle-aged, middle-class Republicans. Both were state legislators, members of the Maine House of Representatives, when I interviewed them in the summer of 1984. Both lived in small towns, had spent years of activity in local government, and planned no career beyond the Maine legislature. Despite these outward similarities, one needs only a few minutes with these women to know that they are not at all alike.

Betty Gardner is nervous and timid. She cannot quite understand what she is doing in the state legislature. It is way beyond her. She was "amazed" when her party's town committee asked her to run for a vacant seat.[2] When she actually won the election and reached Augusta, she felt "all alone." Her first day on the floor of the House appalled her. She thought, "I'll never understand what they are saying. What have I gotten myself into?" Self-confidence is not Gardner's strong suit. In fact, this fearful woman needs constant reassurance to bolster her flagging self-esteem. Towards that end, she works at being friendly to everyone. A sense that others like her is crucial to her well-being. When people accept her and welcome her into their social circle, it alleviates, even if temporarily, her deep-seated fear of rejection.

This desire for social acceptance leads her to see the people in her environment as congenial and pleasant—even if they aren't. She needs to perceive other legislators as warm, welcoming people, or her chance of being surrounded by a comforting cocoon of friendship would vanish. Thus, she describes political peers in an extremely positive light.

> The other [legislators] are really great. I knew only one other person in the legislature [before the session began]. But everyone came up and shook my hand; they were all friendly and nice. They're a great bunch.

Not all activists think of other politicians in this optimistic a manner. Gardner's need for support from others leads her to see them all as "great," whatever their actual traits. She cannot be objective, because being liked by all these "great" people is her central goal. She even finds Governor Brennan, leader of the opposing party, a warm, congenial figure. That is an especially odd assessment, since most observers of the day found him cool and restrained, if not downright distant.

This tactic of seeing the best in others has a payoff. By focusing on their positive traits, Gardner does make people like her. Her own friendliness ensures that they will view her amicably. Thus, she avoids the criticism her weak ego dreads. Her eagerness to please shields her from hostility.

At the same time, her need for acceptance keeps her from ever being a leader or having an impact on issues of the day. Any clear stand on an important policy matter would bring opposition from somebody. So would any attempt to seek higher position. (She'd have to compete against others to achieve it.) Striving never to give offense, Gardner avoids assertive behavior. Her need to please others produces a follower mentality and a passive behavior pattern. She was recruited for the legislature, much to her *dismay*. Some typical politician! She will surely not go beyond this level of government.

In vivid contrast to Gardner stands Joan Moore, another Republican legislator. Moore, a woman of boundless enthusiasm, exudes self-confidence as she heartily describes her numerous political activities. "I tend to be a doer," she says. "I like to get involved and get things done."

Moore leaves little doubt about the accuracy of this statement as she describes issues she has pursued in city government. Bird sanctuaries, sewer problems, the spending of HUD money, historical landmarks, housing starts—these are just some of the policies she's eager to talk about in our conversation.

As a state legislator, Moore is proudest of her work to reform the state's education system. Problems and solutions form the focus of her attention. She shows no interest in anything but policy matters. By way of contrast, the insecure Betty Gardner hardly spoke of policies at all, her focus being on personal relations with others and on whether or not people liked her.

As opposed to Gardner's hesitant speech pattern, Moore talks rapidly and with vigor. Her dynamism is impressive; her passion contagious. As for politics: "I love it. I get up every morning, and I can hardly wait to look at the newspaper." She claims to be "a very organized person," who is "never floored by anything." No one who has met this ebullient woman could doubt the truth of that last statement.

The self-confident Joan Moore stands in sharp contrast to the diffident Betty Gardner. The two women differ also in their willingness to take strong stands on controversial issues and in their inclination to wield power. Moore does not hesitate to say what she thinks about current policy matters. Gardner prefers to avoid thinking about them. Moore chairs a legislative committee. Gardner could not imagine holding a leadership post. No one would ever mistake one of these women for the other.

Personality differences hardly confine themselves to women. Contrasts between male politicians are equally striking. Compare Maine State Representatives Roland Giguere and Will Maddox. Their *objective* similarities are not quite as obvious as those linking Betty Gardner and Joan Moore. At 60, Giguere is 25 years older than Maddox. And Maddox represents a rural area, Giguere an urban one. Still, both are male state legislators, Democrats, and lifelong residents of a small, sparsely-populated, homogeneous state. If "all politicians are alike," these two should turn out to be pretty similar in character.

In fact, they are anything but similar. Giguere is a dogmatic moralizer, while Maddox is an ambitious riser out to make a name for himself.

Giguere seems almost a Lancelot figure. He focuses on doing the right thing, promoting his principles. "I try real hard," he says, "not so much to please everybody, but to do what is right." As is often the case, "doing what is right" means taking strong stands that anger others. The thick-skinned Giguere does not mind in the least. "I do take a stand," he declares, and goes on:

> I've taken some very strong stands on law and order and on . . . moral issues. I am an opponent of the E.R.A. [Equal Rights Amendment] because I believe that the E.R.A. will work *totally* against the good of the woman.

Giguere proceeds to criticize welfare cheats, castigate liberal judges, and denounce the moral decline of modern society. This strong-minded man sees the world in black-white terms. He and his supporters are "clean-living, hard-working, and pure." Those who oppose him are "weak characters," have "shady backgrounds," and "lead immoral lives."

Being an outspoken conservative in a liberal party bothers Giguere not a whit. He simply must express his indignation at the creeping rot he sees everywhere. No wonder he always finds himself in the midst of political turmoil. His uncompromising support of controversial positions makes him a likely target of abuse. His personality almost naturally creates enemies. Giguere stands light years away from Betty Gardner, whose personality automatically produces friends. What's more, he surely destroys one political stereotype. Those who think that politicians are all mealy-mouthed and wishy-washy have never spoken with Roland Giguere.

Will Maddox is another sort altogether. This guarded young man works hard to hide his true sentiments on anything. After listening to him talk for an hour, I had trouble defining exactly where he stood. Was he a liberal or a conservative? Or even a moderate? I still don't know. I did learn something about him, however. Maddox is eager to go far in the world of politics. His career is the one topic of abiding interest to him.

Even though he won't talk about current issues enough to indicate where he stands, Maddox can recount in some detail his early campaigns for the legislature. He does not hesitate to express his desire for a committee chairmanship post in the next session. He also makes clear that he won't be content to accumulate power gradually in the Maine House of Representatives. His real aim is rapid national recognition.

> If [serving as committee chair] is a successful time, I see some possibilities for advancement. I mean a *real* advancement. I don't see myself as . . . Assistant Majority Leader, Majority Leader . . . I guess the only dream or the only goal that may be possible, it would be down the road, ten years down the road. It would be to run for Congress.

Maddox is self-absorbed: a careerist, pure and simple.

This focus on moving up quickly, on personal success, leads him to be deeply suspicious of others. Their ambitions could get in the way of his own. Therefore, he trusts no one, thinks well of no one. In politics, he says, "you meet with a lot of people that have large egos." His caustic cynicism surfaces time and again. "You can't trust very many people in the legislature," he claims. "Politicians are pretty much out for themselves." It is hard not to see these statements as projections. Maddox himself has a large ego and *is* pretty much out for himself. He doubtless finds it easier to accept those traits in himself, by coming to believe that they characterize everyone else as well.

Ultimately, Maddox is a tense, worried loner. Wrapped up in his struggle for a place in the sun, he loses sight of political reality. Issues, moral questions, the positive qualities of fellow legislators: he just cannot focus on these matters. His own drive for glory takes all his attention and energy. Maddox is as different from the moralistic Giguere as "lean and hungry" Cassius was from the "honorable" Brutus.

A fifth member of the Maine state legislature exhibits a still different set of personality traits. Ray Roberts loves politics for the sheer sport of it. He revels in the competition, taking almost childish delight in explaining how he developed a winning door-to-door campaign strategy. Here is how he presented himself at the home of a potential voter:

> I did not invite a debate or make it easy for a person to discuss issues. My purpose was to get a vote, not to debate or argue. I made it a point to *observe*, before I went into a house. If I'd see a beagle, I would ring the doorbell, and let's say the man answered, I'd say, "Oh, I see you've a beagle out there. How's the rabbit hunting?" Not even bring up politics immediately.

Roberts tunes in to the needs of others, but not like Betty Gardner so that they will like him. He wants to know people so that he can manipulate them into helping him win a political contest.

The manipulation, however, is low-key and not vindictive. Roberts wants to maintain allies, the better to win future victories. His happy, optimistic air is well suited toward that end. He's a naturally likable fellow. You cannot help but enjoy his company and his stories, especially his rules for playing the political game successfully. He's a calculator, but one who operates on the rule of "enlightened self-interest." A good calculator by that rule will not use people too obviously or hurt them needlessly, because you never know when you may need them again. Treat everyone well today, and you will have allies tomorrow: that seems to be his motto.

Roberts expresses this idea of moderation in political life when he stresses that "the art of legislating is to work out compromises." He may be a clever player of the political game, but he is also a team player. Ray Roberts plays to win, but in doing so he won't make waves and he won't make enemies.

The study of personality types

One could expand these examples, but surely the point is made. If you take personality at its fundamental level, politicians are hardly all alike. This diversity of character should also be reflected in a diversity of action. That is because *politics is a world of choice.* Political roles are not clearly defined, as they are in an office typing pool or an Army basic-training camp. In these circumstances, it does not matter what you are like as a person. When the boss gives you a memo to type, you type it. When the sergeant tells you to run the obstacle course, you run it. The external conditions determine most of your behavior.

But what do you do once you have been elected to the legislature? Do you go around making friends with everyone? Do you give press conferences every day and try to make the television news reports? Do you spend your time behind the scenes promoting a key policy reform, or get up on the floor every day and give a firm opinion about every issue? There are no clear answers. Legislators will settle each question in their own manner, and we can well imagine that Betty Gardner, Joan Moore, Roland Giguere, Will Maddox, and Ray Roberts will answer these questions differently. In the process, they'll carve out quite different roles for themselves.

Personality matters, then, because in a world of options, people will choose to behave in ways that suit their individual needs. No one will expect the insecure Betty Gardner to run for Speaker of the House. Equally, no one would anticipate that the combative Roland Giguere will be found masterminding delicate compromises on controversial legislation.

We need to know about the personality of politicians because they will behave one way or another, depending on their motives, drives, needs, and desires. *Knowing the character of political participants will help us understand and even predict their actions.* Harold Lasswell started making this point in the late 1920s. Lasswell, a giant in several fields of social science, proposed the existence of three political personalities in his landmark study, *Psychopathology and Politics:*[3]

- the **agitator**, a "rabble-rouser" who sought to rally the public behind dramatic social changes
- the **administrator**, who focused on the details of organizing day-to-day bureaucratic tasks
- and the **theorist**, who worked almost in isolation on the perfection of broad ideas to describe political realities.

Lasswell theorized that the different drives and motives of these types could account for their different patterns of political behavior.

A number of scholars have carried out work in this same vein. The most famous was James David Barber, a student of Lasswell's at Yale. Barber extended and deepened Lasswell's work on political personality types.[4] In his work on Connecticut state legislators and later on American presidents, Barber concluded that four different kinds of people are likely to enter politics.

- The **lawmaker** (or active-positive) type enters politics out of a love for problem-solving
- The **spectator** (or passive-positive) type enters politics out of a need for belonging
- The **reluctant** (or passive-negative) type enters politics out of a sense of obligation
- and the **advertiser** (or active-negative) type enters politics out of a need for glory and recognition.

Barber's work is widely known to students of the presidency, but neither Barber nor his followers did much to apply this typology to elites in other political positions or cultures. Other scholars *have* pursued that goal, hoping to identify common personality patterns among elites in a wide array of settings.[5] Although no single schema has attracted widespread acceptance, an examination of studies in the area of **political psychology** suggests that many analysts have observed similar character types.

My own research falls into this area. I and my colleague, James L. Payne, along with several collaborators, have extensively described different personalities that we've observed in politics.[6] We use the term **incentive types** to delineate different political actors based on their primary motive or drive ("incentive") for politics. Table 15.1 presents a snapshot of our findings. The chart lists seven incentive types and briefly sets out their leading traits.[7] Since the people listed here are the ones who will wield power in most political systems, it will pay to take a close look at them. We need to know what they are like, how they are going to behave, how they will influence the institutions they are part of, and how the institutions they are part of will in turn advance or impede their career chances.

The conviviality type

We will begin with an extremely typical figure. **Conviviality type participants** *enter politics to make friends and gain reassurance.* Like Maine state legislator Betty Gardner, they are insecure people with a desperate need for acceptance. Their weak ego needs constant massaging. In warm, harmonious relations with others they find emotional reinforcement. They need support, approval, and friendship. What especially reassures them of their own worth is the warm endorsement of prestigious leaders. Their thinking goes something like this: "If these important people know my name and allow me into their circle, then I must be all a worthy person, after all."

Essentially, conviviality participants cry out to be liked. They enter politics because the shallow camaraderie of much political life gives them that feeling of close connection to others that they crave. They themselves develop the superficial heartiness of the small-town booster, a mentality from which they often spring. On the surface, conviviality politicians are friendly, but their need to be liked comes across as weakness. They are, in fact, likable enough, but they seem spineless, lack leadership qualities, and can be easily manipulated.

These eager-to-please people will be strongly molded by the character of their environment. In a corrupt setting, they will be the boss's lackeys, the "good ol' boys" who serve the machine well. In a moralistic culture, such as that associated with various northern American states (e.g., Maine, Vermont, Iowa, Oregon) they will absorb the good-government, hard-work ethic of their society, carrying out with honesty and earnestness the basic tasks expected of government officials. In short, they will blend in with the local culture, doing what those in their environment expect them to do.

The essential behavior trait of the conviviality politician is favor-doing. They will always be looking for ways to "help people" and thereby make themselves liked. If "helping" (in their culture) means hand-holding and listening, they will do that and be very good at it. But if, in their setting, "helping" means getting jobs for supporters and bribing judges, they will also do that. Conviviality types don't initiate corrupt systems, but they have no trouble working within them. The need to please takes precedence over other values.

Conviviality types rarely rise high in politics. They shun leadership roles, where they would necessarily find themselves the target of criticism. When they sometimes find a leadership role accidentally thrust upon them, they fail miserably at it. Trying to please everyone all of the time, they end up pleasing no one most of the time.

The obligation type

A second kind of politician differs dramatically from the conviviality type. **Obligation-type-oriented politicians** *are moralists, obsessed by a need to*

Table 15.1 An introduction to political personality: The incentive types classified and described.

Political type	Image of politics	Focus of attention	Words that describe
Mission	War	Enemy; truth; doctrine	Militant; extremist; ideologue; fighter
Obligation	Moral crusade; duty	Moral precepts; proper ethical behavior	Opinionated; rigid dogmatic
Program	Hobby; puzzle	Problems; solutions; details; facts; results	Problem-solver; businesslike
Game	Fun; a game; a complex structured interaction	Strategy; tactics; techniques for winning	Robust; flexible; wily; a game-player
Status	Jungle	Personal success; prestige; recognition; fame	Loner; aloof; arrogant; opportunistic; cut-throat
Conviviality	Club; family	Getting along; friendship with others; personal relationships, in general	Good old boy; goodtime Charlie; Miss Congeniality; follower; spectator
Adulation	Theatrical stage	Being at the center of a throng of admiring followers	Ham; life of the party; self-dramatizer

follow their conscience, to do what is right. Like Roland Giguere, they are drawn to politics out of a sense of responsibility. They exhibit a deep-seated need to "do the right thing," and they want to see others do the right thing as well. The "right thing" means, to begin with, "getting involved." Good citizens are supposed to serve their community and their country. Obligation types try to do that, but they go further. Once in politics, they see their job as "cleaning up the unholy mess" that corrupt or incompetent others have made.

Like most moralizers, obligation types are opinionated and preachy. They are purists appalled at the lack of principle, or the wrongheaded principles, of all others in the political world. Despite their good intentions—their desire to "set things straight" by bringing morality to government—they often come across as loud, dogmatic, and rigid. Their inability to understand other viewpoints prevents them from making the compromises necessary for a smooth, working relationship with others. Their open hostility toward those with whom they disagree generates more heat than light.

It is clear that a preponderance of obligation types in any political setting would create sharp, difficult-to-resolve divisions and raise the temperature of the political waters. These observations produce a simple conclusion: *The more obligation types active in politics, the more severe the level of conflict in that setting.*[8]

The program type

Not all politicians raise the level of conflict. One political type contributes to the rational discussion of policy issues, working via compromise to achieve reasonable solutions to society's problems. Politicians with a **program orientation** enjoy collecting information, analyzing consequences, drafting measures, and bringing about desired changes. Like Joan Moore, they know how to work with others, and they focus on details of the job to be done. They operate in a businesslike manner, avoiding the counterproductive tactics of self-promotion and angry rhetoric. They prefer to work behind closed doors until widely-agreed-upon settlements can be produced.

Many of us fail to realize the key roles that hard work and compromise play in the democratic process. These mundane activities produce little attention and bring little glory. Yet that marvelous guide to American government, the Constitution, came about only after much serious labor had occurred, along with a number of significant compromises. Obligation types would have called these "deals." Americans hate to think of their sacred "Founding Fathers" doing deals, but they did. If purists had dominated the 1787 Constitutional Convention, they might have stopped the process in its tracks by objecting to the various compromises that had to be struck.

The excessive purism of rigid moralists can lead to a self-defeating rigidity. Obligation types take an all-or-nothing approach that frequently nets them nothing. Program politicians understand that compromise is necessary to gain at least some of their desired policy goals. *An ability to see the perspective of others* is also essential to achieve common ground and promote cooperation. Program types have it; obligation types do not.

The game type

A fourth personality type resembles the program types in displaying high levels of flexibility and an appreciation for tactical common sense. What distinguishes them from program types is their central focus. It's not on issues, but on strategy. **Game participants** *don't enter politics to shape policy, but rather because they love competition.* Like Ray Roberts, they are turned on by the manipulative side of politics. Organizing elections, winning nominations, "spinning" the press, winning votes in the legislature: these are the activities that fascinate and preoccupy them. Game politicians enjoy maneuvering and manipulating, and they do it with zest and finesse—simply because it's fun. For them, politics really is a game.

Competitive as they are, game types do not see politics in cutthroat terms. It's not a jungle. Jungles aren't fun; games are. Jungles have no structure, are unpredictable, and can lead to harm, even death. Games have a clear structure, are predictable, and are safe. That's what attracts these personalities to political activity. They seek competition within an ordered environment, governed by a stable set of rules. Only under these circumstances can their strategic genius be allowed free play and be appreciated by others. Since game types like structured interaction, they keep to the rules of civil engagement. They are courteous, and they generally treat others well. You never know when you will need an ally, even one far removed from you on the political spectrum. Humiliate or infuriate someone today, and they won't be available for you to put into play tomorrow.

In addition, one of the key rules for game types is group loyalty. They are team players who respect other participants. They especially respect skilled professionals, like themselves, even if those skilled players happen to be on the other side of a given political struggle. They are good at the skills needed to move a variety of individual temperaments toward complex policy goals. In elaborate games of coalition-building, they use intricate combinations of persuasion, negotiation, bargaining, and even threats to achieve their goals. And those goals are simple: winning battles and gaining respect for their skills in the never-ending game of attaining and displaying power.

These superb politicians provide grease, or flexibility, to the political process, helping to keep levels of conflict low. They know that going for the jugular would only gain them a reputation for viciousness, not skill, and vicious players may not be chosen to play next time. Hence, game participants tone down their most aggressive traits, often under a veneer of hearty cordiality.

These game-focused activists rarely become policy experts, as program types do. Learning the ins and outs of some specialized subject does not fit their free-wheeling style. They specialize first and foremost in *politics*— bargaining, trading, negotiating, promising, strategizing. They work cooperatively with others, they keep their word (once they give it), and they rarely castigate opponents in public. Thus, they help insure that issues are dealt with fairly, compromises are struck and kept, and the system flows smoothly with a minimum of violence. These are no small achievements in the rough-and-tumble world of political conflict.

The status type

Another type of political activist combines some of the negative traits of both the game and the obligation participants. **Status types**, like game politicians, have no particular interest in policy, yet they tend, like obligation types, to be rigid, loud, and uncompromising. In some ways they resemble that stereotypical politician we all carry around in our heads. *Status-type* *politicians seek personal fame and glory. They want to be somebody, and they want to be seen as somebody.* As with Will Maddox, the desire for social recognition lies at the core of their need structure.

Given their aspirations, status participants become preoccupied with rising quickly to positions of prestige. They move ahead fast—or at least try to. Staying in one place is for them the equivalent of failure. Given their drive to move upward, they will normally comprise the majority of the younger members of any socially prestigious group. Whether it's legislators, novelists, executives, or university presidents, whenever someone is described as "the youngest person ever" to achieve some plateau or distinction, it's a safe bet that the person in question has that fixation on rapid upward mobility typical of the status participant.

Projecting their own climbing orientation onto others, status types are scoffers and cynics. They see the worst in everyone. Their disaffected attitude makes them particularly uncooperative in groups. They are weak in those social interactions that require delicacy, understanding of others, and compromise. They are uninterested in the details of policy. They are happy to latch onto popular proposals that could enhance their careers, but their actual discussion of issues is superficial. It involves, for the most part, mouthing a series of simplistic clichés.

Status types are not always easy to identify, because they work hard at image-management. They wear the best clothes, find expensive hair stylists, and take speech lessons. From a distance, they look and sound good. It is only when you get close that their cool self-absorption stands out.

These personalities are extremely sensitive to status gradations. They will patronize people below them, compete fiercely with peers, and suck up to anyone above who can help them. They are also quick to criticize those who hold positions they crave. Distant and aloof to underlings, hypercritical of rivals and opponents, they are fawningly eager to impress anyone who can do them favors or provide publicity.

The average status-oriented politician is a self-promoting climber who works poorly with allies and makes enemies easily. Status types, as a whole, produce major problems for any political system. Their hostile public tirades raise levels of conflict, while their demagogic pandering to the public raises false expectations of easy solutions to difficult problems. These hopes, sure to be dashed, can only lead to public cynicism and alienation when the proposed "solution" proves a failure.

The mission type

Two other kinds of politician have been identified, although they appear infrequently in American settings. Politicians with a **mission drive** need "to be committed to a transcendental cause that gives meaning and purpose to life."[9] They attach themselves with religious zeal to some political movement. Eric Hoffer nicely characterized people with this orientation as "true believers."[10]

Dedicated movement supporters, mission types become preoccupied with matters of doctrine and ideology. The slightest deviation from the party line is heresy. Life, for them, is an all-consuming struggle to promote the movement and its truths. Conversely, they must also work to destroy the enemies of their faith. They view other participants in a dichotomous light: they are *either* comrades-in-arms *or* evildoers who must be obliterated.

This all-or-nothing attitude makes them dangerous opponents and difficult allies. You must be an unquestioning follower of their movement, or they will view you with suspicion. People like these are found toward the extreme end of the ideological spectrums: communists, fascists, religious zealots. When their numbers rise in a political system, we can be sure that levels of social conflict will also increase. People with this orientation don't hesitate to impose their views—with violence, if need be.

The adulation type

In this category, are politicians with a **need for adulation.** First and foremost, they seek "praise and affection."[11] They want "to be loved; . . . to experience the outpouring of popular gratitude."[12] Adulation types need admiring followers around them at all times. They relish the cheers of well-wishing throngs, the lavish praise of fawning supporters, the thanks from grateful recipients for various and sundry favors. Being extolled for their magnanimous actions is what adulation types crave.

These participants are forceful personalities, almost outrageously self-confident. And they never shirk from conflict. They are constantly pushing themselves onto center stage, elbowing others off. If they perceive themselves being robbed of their desired acclaim, they will fight back with unmitigated antagonism. If there are many adulation types in a given setting, the political in-fighting can become intense, even violent.

How personality interacts with the institution of the modern media

We already know that institutions affect political outcomes. We also know that our current media system represents a powerful institution of our time. In one of their important effects, the media play a major role in **political recruitment**. Those who wish to succeed in politics must know how to get media attention. If, as we know, the modern media promote sensationalism and a "bad-news bias," then politicians who can play to those angles will get coverage. Essentially, the media will cover people whose personalities exacerbate conflict.

Given what we now know about political personality, we can see that some types will appeal more to the media than others. Which will they be?

Surely, status participants will catch the media's eye. Focused on making a name for themselves, these politicians will work at cultivating journalists. Seeking news coverage, they will learn what reporters want and find ways to supply it.

Status types work hard at burnishing their image. Since journalists want to cover attractive and charismatic people, status types often fill the bill. They dress well, hire "image consultants," and develop rhetorical skills. They invent "major policy proposals" and tout them with the clever sound-bites that journalists love. They go for the jugular in criticizing political rivals, knowing that personal attacks will get them attention (and will undermine those rivals).

Consider the following stories:

- "Jones accuses Smith of Mafia connection"
- "Jones urges Smith to re-examine deregulation of the pharmaceutical industry"

Which will become a leading news story? Status types know and proceed accordingly.

What especially aids status politicians is their temperament, their personality. It is perfectly suited to the age of electronic media. They seek the spotlight in an era that glorifies celebrity. They know how to create pleasing impressions of purpose and dynamism. They have been perfecting the technique since running for president of their freshman class in high school. As adults, they find themselves operating in a system that rewards glib, colorful acts of self-presentation. Seeking the limelight, they work at "making good copy." Since they provide "good visuals" and create "great sound bites," they encourage journalists to find and cover their stories.

In the end, journalists get the stories they require, and status-type politicians get the publicity they need. The symbiotic relationship between media professionals and status politicians could not be clearer.

Conflict-reducing types and the media

What about the other political personalities? Under modern media conditions, we would not expect game, conviviality, or program politicians, on average, to get much media attention. **Conviviality types** do not *want* to draw attention to themselves. They practically work to avoid it. Preferring to blend into a crowd rather than lead one, they will rarely draw a journalist's attention. If reporters see them at all, they are noted as bland and colorless— "nice people," perhaps, but not interesting for a news story.

Program types, too, will be unpopular with most journalists. True, their character is quite different from that of the self-effacing conviviality types. Strong, self-confident, and knowledgeable, program participants know where they stand on issues of the day and can speak intelligently on policy matters. The trouble is (from the journalist's standpoint), they speak on these subjects *too much*.

Most of us have made the mistake of casually asking some simple question of an expert. We find ourselves, an hour later, bitterly regretting that decision. As the expert drones on about "throw-weights" (defense specialist) or "Vaernamo issue items with Obermüller certificates" (stamp collector) or "DC rotary type solenoids" (auto mechanic), our eyes have long since glazed over, and our one thought is how to get out of this immensely boring conversation.

Journalists feel the same way when they try to get stories from a program politician. Remember, journalists are looking for a neat sound bite or two, ideally one that makes another politician react furiously. They, like the rest of us, are bored to tears by in-depth discourse on subjects they know little about. They assume (correctly) that the public feels likewise.

Providing extensive coverage to the words and actions of program types would quickly lead journalists to the unemployment line. Program types love to discuss the ins and outs of their favorite issues. They get into details, analyze the subtle ramifications of this or that complex reform idea, suggest options for improvement, and outline the intricate pros and cons of each option. For them, the policy world is not simple or shallow, and it is also fascinating. They go on at length about soybean subsidies, molten metal technology legislation, and government aid to urban mass transit systems. All these subjects are doubtless important, and we should be grateful to have people with expertise in these areas. But for those with no expertise or interest (most of us), the standard reaction to a lecture on these topics is, "Spare me, please!"

Like accountants and bureaucrats, program types do needed work. No one can deny their valuable contributions to society, yet no one particularly wants to know a lot about those contributions. (We may enjoy the benefits of flying, but who wants to know how an aircraft engine works?) Journalists find that covering people who talk in depth about complex subjects makes no professional or financial sense. Woodward and Bernstein did not become Woodward and Bernstein by covering Latin American trade policy.

Program types will probably get more journalistic attention than conviviality participants, simply because their expertise does occasionally prove useful or necessary. Once in a while—say, after a major hurricane—journalists do need to spotlight someone with detailed knowledge of the Mississippi delta flood reclamation issues. And program types are not handicapped by the lack of self-confidence that keeps conviviality participants from rising. So they will be found at all levels of the political ladder, even if their personality pattern makes them second-rate political campaigners compared to status types.

Game types will normally occupy an intermediate rung on the ladder of media attention: higher than program participants but lower than those with a status incentive. While unlikely to denounce rivals in public (a status type's surefire method of getting attention), game participants do what it takes to stay at the center of the action. Appearing on television is one indicator these days of political clout. Thus, they may cultivate journalists, just as they cultivate anyone with power.

But the strength of game participants lies in their behind-the-scenes work. Their power derives from reinforcing potential allies, stroking friends, suggesting arguments that might result in defections from rival camps, or whispering veiled threats into the ears of the stubborn. They know that public pronouncements usually do more harm than good. Publicly-stated stands bind you to a rigid position in which you find little room to maneuver. Game types prefer to be non-committal in public. No good copy here for a journalist.

Game types fail to provide good copy in another way. They avoid castigating others in public, since they know that one's enemy on issue X today could be one's ally on issue Y tomorrow. That cannot happen, though, if you have called that potential ally a liar or an idiot on national television. With their focus on fence-mending and coalition-building, game types avoid the hasty generalization and the harsh word that may prevent some future alliance. For that reason, they provide but modest fodder for the modern mass media.

It is an entirely different story with obligation types. They make just as good copy as status types, often better. With their purist perspectives and rigid moral code, they view political events through a simplistic, black-white, true-false lens. Thus, they speak in the kind of dramatic sound-bite language that journalists, especially those in the electronic media, love. Obligation types rarely say, "That's a complicated matter," in answer to a journalist's question. They are more likely to say, "That's nonsense!" "That's utterly wrong!" or "That policy has been totally discredited!"

They are also likely to cast aspersions, in no uncertain terms, on the moral character of others. "He's a first-rate liar!" is likely to get media attention. That attention will not be forthcoming if you say it this way: "I'm sure that my learned colleague has honorable reasons for taking the position that he does, although I cannot entirely agree with him on this point." Yet that's how program, game, and conviviality types would put it. In other words, they would disagree without being disagreeable, thereby gaining no media interest whatsoever.

It is clear that the strong, colorful, and dramatic adulation and mission types would also get media attention, come to prominence, and exacerbate conflict in systems where they might be found in serious numbers. Since their percentage of the political elite in modern societies seems small, we shall for reasons of space give them no further attention in this text.

Conclusion

We can now evaluate the link between the media and the personality profile of those who rise in politics. Media professionals love conflict-producing styles of political behavior. Politicians with rhetorical skills who generate controversy are precisely what Woodward–Bernstein hopefuls seek. Modern journalists cover cranky individualists, not quiet, informed team players. They thereby help confer power on one set of politicians, and not on another.

Colorful, outspoken figures who denounce opponents attract media attention. Negative statements and intriguing actors get attention. Contentious leaders will thrive in our media age and encourage, through their divisiveness, the already-existing trend toward a decline in social cohesion and political civility. That trend enhances the tendency of citizens to tune out the political process, encouraging the belief that "all politicians are corrupt."

The current structure of American politics disadvantages personalities oriented toward conflict reduction. Program, game and conviviality participants cannot achieve what they want when tensions are high and trust levels low. They will be less attracted to politics, as well as less successful at it, when the media are powerful and conflict-focused.

On the other hand, status and obligation politicians benefit from the current media system. Their conflict-provoking behavior nets them attention. They make names for themselves in the media, and that bolsters their chance of rising to positions of power. Once in power, they exacerbate the natural levels of conflict that always exist in politics. In an age of weak political parties and strong electronic media, levels of political conflict are likely to remain high for some time to come.

Questions for discussion

1 How many politicians do you know well? Do they fit into the incentive categories presented in this chapter?

2 How would you categorize the personalities of the last five or six American presidents (or any five or six leading politicians)? Do they all seem to have similar personalities, or are they significantly different from each other? (For this purpose, ignore their different party backgrounds and policy aims.)

3 Considering current social trends, do you think we're likely to see more program types or more status and obligation types entering politics in the next decade?

4 Do these personality categories seem useful for understanding political

leaders in other countries and cultures? Can you think of leaders abroad who fit one or another of these descriptions?

5   Many have criticized the approach presented in this chapter because "all personalities are a mix of various drives, desires, and motives." Does that strike you as a valid criticism?

16

THE IMPACT OF GLOBALIZATION
Democracy, anarchy, or . . .?

What comes next? We all want to know the future, but figuring it out is tricky. For example:

> After the invention of the telephone, a group of British experts concluded that the invention had no practical value, at least in their country: "The telephone may be appropriate for our American cousins, but not here, because we have an adequate supply of messenger boys."[1]

In like vein, the famous physicist, Lord Kelvin, declared in 1895 that "heavier-than-air flying machines are impossible." Wilfrid Laurier, Prime Minister of Canada in 1900, declared that "the twentieth century will be the century of Canada." A history teacher once told my class that in the fall of 1941, when he himself had been a student, he'd written a paper on "The Impregnability of Pearl Harbor." And of course, thousands of people over the centuries have predicted that the world would end on, say, March 11, 1923.

Clearly, it is not easy to predict the next developments in humanity's ongoing saga. "Experts" failed to predict the startling 1994 Republican takeover of the US House of Representatives. They never foresaw the dramatic budget surpluses of the late 1990s. Almost no one foretold the collapse of communism, the break-up of Yugoslavia, the rise of the Internet, or the end of *apartheid* in South Africa. If specialists have trouble seeing the future in their own areas of expertise, why should the rest of us even try?[2]

The answer is simple. We *have* to make educated guesses at the future. All our current decisions depend on having some idea of what is likely to happen next. We *must* make predictions and act on them, or we could not go on living in a normal way.

Take just one example: our decision to attend college. That is a key life choice and an expensive one. It may seem an obvious path to take, but it rests, at least partly, on our prediction that society will value college degrees in the future. We base many of our actions on our (often unconscious) predictions about the future.

Besides, we are all curious. We want to know how our current world is likely to evolve.

Unfortunately, making specific predictions is pointless. Who will be president 10 years from now? Where will the Dow Jones average stand? What wars will be raging? It is impossible to say. We might have better luck, however, speculating about broad political and social developments. Sensibly hedging my bets, I shall suggest five general scenarios that could occur. Any one of these, or some combination, might become the dominant sociocultural pattern of the next two or three decades.

Scenario 1: Anarchy and civilizational collapse

This is the option we all fear most. Variations on the theme are many, but it centers on a dramatic increase in violence and a decline in the powers of any state or organization to curb it. Some analysts believe that **asymmetric violence** is a hallmark of our time.[3] With technological advances, modern nations cannot fight wars against each other because they could both be destroyed in a short space of time. However, splinter and disaffected elements on the international scene, terrorist groups of one kind or another, can cause a great deal of havoc through unconventional means. The events of September 11, 2001, hammer this point home. Other examples include recent wars in Iraq, Afghanistan, and Chechnya, where large, well-equipped forces found themselves severely hampered by ragtag guerilla fighters.

Many fear a continuing series of attacks like those of 9–11–01 in the USA, 3–11–04 on Madrid commuter trains, or 7–7–05 in the London subways. Others envision catastrophes of greater magnitude. A commonly-mentioned scenario involves the smuggling of smallpox spores or small-scale atomic weapons into some industrial state via suitcases, container ships, or the like. Another fear suggests long-term unconventional warfare all other the globe. Iraqi-style insurgents, bolstered by thousands of suicide bombers, could spring up in dozens of places, creating chaos followed by calls for authoritarian repression. Still another prediction imagines accidental nuclear war, as additional nations become atomic powers. India and Pakistan have already fought each other several times since the Second World War. Now that they both have atomic bombs, why wouldn't they fight another war, this time with these weapons?

In short, the world could degenerate into chaos and anarchy as fanatic groups or deranged leaders use the awesome weaponry now available.

It is true that someone with determination can wreak a good deal of havoc. It is also true that beyond human will, simple natural processes could cause grave damage to life on this planet. A new disease could come along with no obvious cure. There are dire predictions about global warming, asteroid strikes, and so on.

Life offers no guarantees, of course, and we have little ability to prepare for most non-political developments. We will now focus, then, on disasters that could occur through political action.

Anything is possible, but I have my doubts about the increasing-anarchy thesis. Modern societies are versatile, stable, and resource-rich. They have many ways both to avert disaster and to bounce back from disaster. Neither Hurricane Katrina (New Orleans, 2005) nor the events of 9–11–01 had any *long-term* impact on ordinary social life in the USA. Of course, many people lost their lives in these events, the lives of many others were shattered, and various state and national policies changed significantly. But American social patterns, cultural outlooks, and political processes changed little. No one, as a result of these events, is calling for an end to democracy or capitalism (the two major patterns of our age). American institutions and deep-seated American values differ little today from what they were in the year 2000.

In the same way, neither the terrible bomb explosions in Madrid and London nor city riots by alienated Muslim youths in Paris (2006) caused any real disruption of life, society, and politics in Spain, Great Britain, and France. These dramatic events personally affected many people, got everyone's attention, and had short-term political ramifications. Still, they did not come close to producing a society-wide breakdown of law and order.

Large, modern, complex societies are strong and flexible. It would take developments of enormous magnitude to undermine their essential stability. One could argue that the last time an industrialized state "broke down" was Germany in the early 1930s—and that occurred only after a terrible 4-year war (First World War), the world's worst inflation (1923–1924), and the world's worst depression (1929–1939). We cannot promise that civilizational breakdown will not happen, but the odds seem stacked against it.[4]

The breakdown hypothesis seems all the less likely as we are constantly informed of its dangerous possibilities, both in learned journals and in popular outlets. Fore-warned is fore-armed (not always, but frequently). Take the surest way to cause social disorder: a devastating war. Some random weapon set off by terrorists, even an atomic weapon, would not undermine most stable, wealthy societies. But lengthy conventional wars or unrestricted atomic wars between major powers could produce social chaos. Scholars argue over the likelihood of these events, but knowledge of modern warfare's devastation surely reduces its likelihood.

Several nations, after all, have had atomic weapons since 1945, including bitter enemies like the USA and Russia. Still, two nations equipped with atomic arsenals have never fought against each other. They both know it is senseless; each would be completely destroyed. In real life those with suicide-bomber personalities do not rise to the status of national leader of an atom-armed nation. The institutional complexity of a nation developed enough to have an entire atomic arsenal (not just a bomb or two) makes that nation stable enough so that a single unhinged individual would not be able to give the orders that would destroy the entire society and possibly the world.

These statements, unfortunately, must be seen as probabilities, not certainties. As more nations reach an advanced stage of technological development, the odds increase that some leader somewhere will be willing to build and *use* the proverbial "weapons of mass destruction." Life never provides guarantees. I am suggesting, however, that the likelihood of this development is small.

Scenario 2: Rise of a new world hegemon

This scenario is entirely plausible. Throughout history, nations and empires have risen and fallen. Change is the only constant. At one time or another, major world powers have been Babylonian, Egyptian, Chinese, Persian, Greek, Roman, Arab, Mongol, Spanish, French, British, Japanese, German, and American. Other powers will rise (or rise again) in the next few decades.

The current money rests on India and China as the fastest-rising civilizations and the world powers of the near future. Some analysts point to the growing power and unity of the European Union (the EU). Japan, of course, is still a major economic power and could, with a spurt of will, become an engine of military might once again. Even Russia could be poised for a comeback, following its ignominious decline after the collapse of communism. Some observers see Brazil as a possible twenty-first contender for big-power status.

What's certain is that the current world dominance of the USA, both militarily and economically, will not last forever. Its standing will constantly be challenged by these and other powers in the coming decades. The "American era" that began roughly with the conclusion of the First World War (1918), came into its own at the end of the Second World War (1945), and took center stage with the fall of the Soviet Union (1989) could well be over in another few decades. China is an atomic power, has a billion people *more* than the USA, and is growing at the rate of 8–10 percent a year (to the USA's 3 percent). India too is an atomic power, has a billion citizens in all, and is growing at a rate double that of the USA. In a few decades, the center of world power could easily shift to East and Southeast Asia.

In neither economic nor military matters, however, does one nation's rise require the downfall of another. The USA will remain a major player on the world stage for some time. Britain and France are still significant world powers, long after the end of their empires. A likely scenario for the next few decades is simply that the USA declines *relative* to other nations (like China, India, and the EU). It will remain one of the world's power-houses, but not *the* world superpower. In that case we could return to the pattern of world politics familiar to historians of the nineteenth century: a **balance-of-power** situation.

Scenario 3: New and changing balance-of-power alignments

Although there have been similar eras in the past, historians see the nineteenth-century as a classic balance-of-power age. Specifically, this period begins with the end of the Napoleonic Wars (1815) and ends with the start of the First World War (1914). In balance-of-power circumstances, no country dominates the others. Many nations have varying degrees of power. Among both major and minor states, alliances shift regularly to prevent any one nation (or alliance of nations) from establishing **hegemony**.

When balance-of-power systems work well, war is rare. The balance among nations (or alliances of nations) is fairly close to equal. In this state of near-equality, all actors remain uncertain about the outcome of any potential war. Hence, all will be circumspect about starting one. This outlook dominated the 100-year period leading up to the First World War. The major world powers of the time (Russia, Prussia, Austria, Turkey, France, and Britain) fought no full-scale wars against each other.

There were wars, of course. Several minor conflicts occurred between the major powers (e.g., the Crimean War of 1853–1856, the Austro-Prussian War of 1866, and the Franco-Prussian War of 1870–1871). In addition, all the major powers fought wars against other states (e.g., Britain versus South Africa, 1899–1902; Russia versus Japan, 1905[5]). And smaller states fought wars against each other (e.g., the Italo-Sicilian War, 1860–1861; the Serbo-Bulgarian War, 1885–1886).

Balance of power systems do not prevent violent confrontations, and they certainly do not prevent serious international tension. They do, however, minimize the number of confrontations between *major* world powers. They also damp down the scale of the violent clashes that do occur, because *all-out* war is perceived by everyone as too risky to pursue.

Along these lines, we could see the emergence of a twenty-first century balance-of-power system. It would center on those powers already mentioned: the USA, China, Japan, India, the EU, and Russia. In such a system, each nation would be strong, but none dominant. None of these nations would want a full-scale war against any of the others for fear of the havoc that could ensue for itself.

China might think it could win a war against India, and the USA might be certain to win a war against Russia, but the ultimate cost would be so overwhelming that these nations would find a way to pull back from full-scale armed conflict. Furthermore, any country perceiving itself under threat might hastily align itself with another world power to deter attack. That's how balance-of-power systems work. Japan illustrates the value of this tactic. It has not been militarily significant since 1945, but its close ties to the USA keep China from starting a war of conquest against it.

Balance of power systems have a certain instability. Like most aspects of life, they require a precarious balancing act. Nations can misjudge a situation. Just because country A *says* it has an alliance with country B and *will* come to its defense if B is attacked by country C, that does not mean it actually will. It certainly does not mean that C *believes* it will.

The nineteenth-century system broke down for just this reason: a lack of belief that stated alliances would hold. Austria and Germany failed to believe that Russia, France, and Britain *would* come to Serbia's aid if they attacked it—even though these countries were committed to do just that. Austria did attack Serbia, and Russia did come to its aid. Germany then came to Austria's aid, France and Britain joined with Russia, and the rest is history (First World War history).

Of course, all world situations have been unstable since the dawn of time. No balance-of-power situation lasts forever. Neither does the hegemony of any world power. The "pax romana," the long period of relative calm in the western world under the Roman Empire (BC27–180AD), eventually broke down as the Empire declined and "barbarians" surged. The long periods of stability in China under various dynasties always began to decline with the increasing decadence of each ruling class. Eventually, each dynasty was toppled, followed by an unsettled period of violent chaos until the establishment of a new leader and dynasty.

Some observers have developed an optimistic outlook, proclaiming that eras of conflict and chaos may be coming to an end as the world enters a phase of relative peace, stability, and wealth.[6] These theories usually begin with an indication that humanity is now living in a unique era for which past patterns no longer apply. Globalizing trends, they say, have changed the human landscape in wholly new and unrecognizable ways. Since these theories have been highly influential in our time, even affecting the main lines of American foreign policy, they deserve serious scrutiny.[7]

Scenario 4: Global democratization

When I was growing up, Spain was a fascist dictatorship. In fact, it became a dictatorship the year I was born. In 1939, General Francisco Franco saw the final victory of his forces in the brutal Spanish Civil War that began in 1936. Having overthrown the Spanish Republic, a fragile democracy, Franco established an authoritarian regime with himself at the helm.

I evolved, I grew, I got through high school, I entered college, and all the while Spain remained a fascist dictatorship. Nothing seemed more certain, after death and taxes, than the Franco regime. During all my years in the Army and in graduate school—yes, you guessed it: Spain stayed under dictatorial control. Like Soviet Communism, Spanish Fascism was simply a given of my time: a solid, central fact that I and everyone else just took for granted.

Finally, in my mid-30s, well into my teaching career, I picked up the paper one day and learned that Spain's fascist dictator had died. Two likely scenarios came quickly to mind. Surely, some other general, some long-time henchman of Franco's, would move into the top slot and maintain authoritarian control of this long-dormant country, or Spain would degenerate once again into the general political chaos that had characterized its public life before Franco.

Neither development occurred. Instead, with a suddenness that dumbfounded expert and casual observer alike, Spain moved quickly into the democratic world. Since Franco's death in 1974, Spain has held a regular series of free, competitive elections. Candidates from across the political spectrum have campaigned for office, dozens of parties have been organized and become active, and the rules of the democratic game have, with a few isolated exceptions, been widely respected. Contrary to all expectations, Spain quickly became a stable, robust democracy.

A similar development has occurred in a few other countries. South Korea and Taiwan both evolved rapidly from authoritarian regimes in the 1960s to competitive political systems in the 1980s. In both, democratic ideals now seem deeply entrenched. South Africa may be moving along this path as well. It has evolved from an oligarchy as late as the early 1990s (with perhaps 5 percent of its citizens enfranchised) to something like a competitive system by 2008. Whether it continues to evolve into a strong polyarchy is too soon to tell. But these and other examples suggest that a bleak attitude about the future of currently oppressive regimes may be unwarranted.

In fact, a wave of **democratization** has been sweeping the world since the latter years of the twentieth century.[8] Dozens of nations like Spain that not long ago sported authoritarian rulers now live under systems that include free elections, competing parties, a free (even raucous) press, and all the other paraphernalia of modern democracy. How can we explain this development that seems so much at odds with ideas outlined in earlier chapters about the longevity of cultural patterns?

I have three responses to this question. My first response is a warning. Yes, many nations have moved along the road toward democracy, but we must be cautious. We can hardly place Liberia, say, or even Argentina and Hungary in the same category of stable democracy that is occupied by older, more secure democratic states like Sweden and Australia. We must be conservative in labeling nations democratic. A few years of relatively non-violent conflict and reasonably open competition does not make a nation's political *culture* polyarchal.

Without the requisite underlying culture, surface democracies will always be fragile. Competitive but unstable systems have frequently fallen to dictators or succumbed to civil wars. Mature democracies can weather the short-term political crises that destroy systems with little history of democratic rule. It takes time to develop the depth of support in both mass and elite populations that allows democracy to survive hard times.

When can one call a nation a stable polyarchy? I believe one must see *at least* three decades of free, open, competitive politics.[9] I'd feel even more confident after five decades of that pattern. During this time the full array of democratic activities should occur. Differing parties and groups must struggle freely and non-violently for power. Control of government must alternate among various parties. The free expression of every viewpoint must flourish in diverse media outlets. All adult citizens must be allowed to vote. They must also be able (without fear of violent suppression) to join political groups, organize political protests, and seek political office. After 30, 40 or 50 years of these activities, *then* one can say that a nation is a deeply-rooted, full-fledged polyarchy.

This system takes time to construct. Like learning the violin, it takes practice; mastery does not come overnight. Many countries have had trial periods with democracy that ended badly. A German republic in the 1920s gave way to Hitler's totalitarianism. Several French experiments with democracy ended abruptly, as the nation fell back into older, authoritarian traditions. Peru has long alternated between periods of relatively free political competition and periods of repressive despotism. So too have Pakistan, Lebanon, Nigeria, and Malaysia.

The path toward democracy is hardly straight or easy. Many of the nations currently experimenting with it will fail. Some will return to traditional, autocratic, or violent ways of resolving disputes. Despite the worldwide trend toward democratization, we must remain realistic, even wary. Many nations simply have not achieved the fundamental social, economic, and cultural conditions necessary to underpin the democratic process.[10]

After that note of caution, however, let me suggest two reasons why democracy may nevertheless represent the wave of the future—the long-term future. The first reason is the more ephemeral of the two. It's based on a well-known sociological concept known as the "demonstration effect." It is also called **social learning**, or simply the "monkey see, monkey do" phenomenon. To simplify one aspect of this theory, *people learn by imitating the successful behavior of others*. Children everywhere copy the "moves" of famous athletes. Writers have long tried to duplicate the popular prose style of Ernest Hemingway. Many of us work at reproducing the stylish outfits and behavior of popular entertainers.

People model their actions on the successful examples they see around them. This point applies too in politics. On a global scale, democracies represent successful behavior. Democratic systems are the wealthiest in the world. Their people are militarily strong, live in peace, and are generally happy with their lot. Citizens of nations that have not traditionally been democratic look enviously at the people who do live in democratic systems. Many are concluding (rightly or wrongly) that there may be a correlation between democracy and the good life.

By the same token, autocratic regimes have produced a string of abysmal failures. As I write these words in 2007, people are starving in North Korea, they are isolated from the world in Cuba and Burma, they are suffering sickness and poverty in dictatorial African countries, and they have to put up with chaos and violence in places like Haiti, Colombia, Somalia, and Sri Lanka. Yet citizens in Norway, Italy, New Zealand, and Costa Rica are living comfortably, pleased with their lives. It is not hard to draw lessons here.

People jump on the bandwagon of winners. Today democracy represents political success. It is globally dominant, it produces a comfortable lifestyle, and it is morally justifiable. Thus, elites and activists everywhere are at least paying lip service to democratic ideals. In many places, these public statements of support for democracy have actually moved countries toward action. Elites have begun to allow democratic institutions like competitive elections and a free press. Or in some cases, it would be more accurate to say that elites *haven't been able to prevent* the formation of those institutions.

Of course, the calculations that lie behind these imitations of democracy seem shallow. In some places, the democratic façade will crumble at the first hint of serious political disagreement or at the first evidence that "people who don't share our values" could win the next election. In places like Belarus, Uzbekistan, or Burma, the demonstration effect has had little impact. Local conditions and non-democratic traditions are too strong to overcome. A deeper set of socioeconomic changes must occur if we are to have any hope for the long-term success of the democratic enterprise.

It is precisely those long-term, sweeping cultural changes, however, that one *does* expect to occur. The world movement toward wealthy, tolerant societies—what Inglehart and others call "human development"—seems well entrenched.[11] Many people refer to this pattern as **globalization**.[12]

At any given moment, the world seems static, but we can see huge changes if we take a two-centuries-long perspective. It seems plausible to imagine that the less developed nations of the world will soon move along the path of the 200-year-long modernization process that allowed democratic conditions to flourish in the richest nations. Literate, affluent, self-confident people do not like living under either dictatorship or chaos. As more nations move into modernity and find themselves populated with educated, competent citizens, leaders will find it harder to govern those citizens without providing them the democratic rights that they are going to insist on anyway. Democracy, in this scenario, becomes inevitable. It won't occur easily or peacefully, but it is hard to see how it could be avoided.

The history of polyarchy

To see the likelihood of this scenario, let's extrapolate from what we know of human history. We start by noting that a change of enormous magnitude occurred, starting roughly in the middle of the eighteenth century. It produced transformations beyond anything previously seen in the several-thousand-year history of humankind. That well-worn phrase,

318

"the Industrial Revolution," encapsulates these developments. Essentially, the world learned to create wealth for the many, wealth that surpassed the imaginings of the most powerful rulers from earlier eras.

These dramatic economic advances went hand in hand with startling political change. In 1800, no real democracy existed on the planet. One could, by squinting, discern the beginnings of democracy in a few places. "Elite competition" (not full-fledged democracy) is a term that could possibly be applied to the politics of that time in the USA, Switzerland, Iceland, and possibly Britain.

By 1900, each of these nations had moved some distance down the road toward democracy. Civil rights for many were secure, a large percentage of citizens had the right to vote, a free press flourished. In addition, other countries had started down this same path: France, Holland, the Scandinavian nations, Canada, and more. The electorate had been expanded in many lands. Peaceful competition for power had in many places become a long-standing practice and a deeply-held norm.

Still, even in 1900, nowhere could even a majority of citizens exercise political power.[13] The vote was still denied to women and to many other groups, such as African-Americans in the USA. And in many places those who expressed unpopular views were denied political rights, even beaten and jailed.

By 2000, several dozen nations boasted stable, well-entrenched democratic institutions, and over a hundred more were experimenting, to one degree or another, with democratic structures. In a typical finding, Gene Schackman and colleagues estimate that the number of people living in democracies grew from 31 percent of the world's population in 1950 to 58 percent in 2000.[14] Data gathered by Freedom House reinforces this conclusion. Their researchers conclude that in 2005, 46 percent of the world's population lived in "free" countries, while only 36 percent lived in places that were clearly "not free."[15]

As we learned in Chapter 5, Freedom House has for decades been tracking civil and political rights. Each year it labels each country as either "free," "partly free," or "not free." Let's concentrate on the "free" countries, which we can safely assume are strong polyarchies, and on those that are clearly not polyarchies (the "not free" places). Table 16.1 plainly shows an increasing number of polyarchies, along with a corresponding decline in countries that are clearly not polyarchal.[16]

Despite the (inevitable) short-term setbacks, the long-term trend toward democratization is clear. As more people become modern—as they leave the land and become part of industrial or post-industrial society, as they gain an education, as they move beyond hand-to-mouth subsistence living—more and more societies achieve the conditions that make democratic governance possible.

It would appear that **modernity**, the experience of living in wealthy,

Table 16.1 Number of polyarchies between 1975 and 2005

Year	"Free" countries		"Not free" countries	
	n	*(%)*	*n*	*(%)*
1975	40	25	65	41
1985	56	34	55	33
1995	76	40	53	28
2005	89	46	45	24

educated, industrial society, brings with it a set of beliefs about equality, freedom, individual autonomy, and self-reliance that make it impossible to sustain any ideological justification for tyrannical rule. To the degree that the trend of the world is toward modernity, democratization trends are likely to continue apace.

Unfortunately, the best prediction that social scientists can make about the *details* of democratic transition is that it will not be easy. Democratization has never been easy. Every democratic nation today was not democratic one or two centuries ago, so we have lots of evidence about how democratization proceeds. It almost always entails extremely high levels of tension, accompanied by violence.

Problems of democratization

Democratization is difficult because it involves power shifts. In any country at any moment, some people have more power than others. In a non-democratic society, just a few people have power. They rightly fear the loss of their privileged status that would ensue under democracy. Like any threatened group, they will resist. Frequently, the privileged few represent a group that is radically different from the population at large. Its members belong to a different class, caste, religion, or ethnic group. Fears and hatreds on both sides of the power divide are heightened by these obvious differences.

Now what happens as new political demands arise? Groups that previously did not have power start getting the idea that they *should* have power. This development usually coincides with their starting to obtain the resources (money, education, skills, self-confidence) that allow them to act in effective ways. They learn to channel their newfound voice and competence into demands for power.

Remember that in every political system at any moment a **status quo** exists.[17] Power always lies with a particular group of people. Naturally those people will look askance at other groups' demands for some (or all) of that power. To put it bluntly, *those with power don't willingly give it up.*

They are especially likely to resist giving power to new, previously unempowered elements of the population that differ from them in significant ways. *The greater the gap in social status between power-holders and the unempowered, the greater is the likelihood that the road toward empowerment will entail serious violence and ruthless suppression.* When illiterate peasants try to obtain power in a system run by sophisticated aristocrats, resistance by the elite will be extreme, oppression likely, and a violent reaction by the oppressed even likelier. The bloodiest revolutions occur under these conditions. One thinks immediately of the three most significant revolutions of the last millennium: those in France (1789–1793), Russia (1917–1921), and China (1945–1950). In the first, thousands went to the guillotine. In the latter two, literally millions of people lost their lives.

At the other end of the spectrum, we note that almost no violence or repression accompanied the movement in the early nineteenth century in the USA to give political rights (primarily, the right to vote) to white men who did not own property. At the time, social status differences were minimal between the enfranchised and those seeking to be enfranchised. Both groups consisted of white males over the age of 20, and the vast majority on both sides of this power gap had modest levels of wealth. Those who could vote were for the most part small landholders. Those who could not were tenants or renters. In these circumstances, the white males who owned modest amounts of property did not feel particularly threatened at the idea of giving the vote to other white males who were just like them in every way but one.[18]

Thus, societies moving toward democracy will experience less conflict if the social gap is narrow between the groups demanding more power and the groups already holding power.

The ratio of powerful to powerless

A second axiom helps us understand when the transition to democracy is likely to be more violent: The smaller the number of people with power compared with those without power, the greater is the likelihood that democratizing efforts will produce violence. The few with power will retreat into defensiveness and fear. They will lash out to protect themselves from what they (correctly) see as a tidal wave of enemies. The many, as they become aware of their low status and high numbers, will become increasingly vocal in their demands. That will frighten the elite still further, leading it to take oppressive measures "to keep the masses in line." Those measures will only enrage the powerless and make revolutionary action more likely.

A prime illustration of this phenomenon can be seen in the **decolonization** period after the Second World War. Nations that had been ruled by a tiny foreign elite, supplemented by a small, foreign-trained native elite (India, Pakistan, most of Africa and South Asia) revolted *en masse* against their former rulers. These revolts were often quite violent, producing in turn violent counter-measures and much bloodshed, before national independence was finally obtained.

In the decolonization example, the ratio of empowered to non-empowered people was often in the range of 1:99, or at best 5:95. That is, for each person with power, there were dozens of people without power.

When the ratio is quite different from this (say, 80:20, or 90:10), one would expect relatively little trouble when those not empowered seek to gain political rights. That is, when most people hold full legal rights and just a few additional people wish to attain the same status, their empowerment will cause little defensiveness or worry to those already empowered. Their inclusion should be relatively peaceful, all the more so if they represent no distinctive social group.

An extreme example of peaceful empowerment occurred in 1971 when Americans lowered the voting age from 21 to 18. Here was a case in which the ratio of people with power to those without power was on the order of perhaps 95:5. Those with power could hardly feel threatened by those without. The small number of young people in the 18–20-year-old bracket could scarcely constitute a credible threat to the vast majority of the population.

Extending the vote to America's young people occurred exactly as our theory suggests. It took just a few months to amend the US Constitution for this purpose.

The swiftness of the process was unusual, given the usual difficulty of achieving constitutional change. Most proposed amendments in the USA are never ratified. Just 15 were added to the Constitution in the 200 years from 1804 to 2004. The voting rights extension of 1971 was a rare event in American political life, yet this grant of power by the many to a few took place through peaceful civil and legal procedures that caused scarcely a ripple on the political waters. It illustrates the point that the fewer the number of people to be empowered in relation to those with power, the more peaceful the extension of power will be.

In this episode, it surely helped that another factor we have already discussed came into play. Hardly any social gap separated those entering the electorate from those already in it. Eighteen-year-olds were not different from other Americans in terms of race, religion, or ethnic group. They differed only in age, representing simply the grown children of a cross-section of the American people. One additional fact insured passage of this amendment. American men aged 18–20 had for years been fighting and dying in Vietnam. A widespread sentiment at the time held that "if you're old enough to fight, you're old enough to vote."

Another example of American citizens extending political rights occurred with much more tension and violence. Determined resistance flared in reaction to the twentieth-century's Civil Rights Movement, which sought to win political rights for African Americans. Unlike young Americans, minority Americans experienced great difficulty in advancing their cause. Our earlier propositions explain why.

First, the ratio of those seeking power to those *with* power was quite different in these two cases. Black-Americans constituted around 15 percent of the population, at least triple the number of young people between 18 and 20. More important, in the specific areas where they were disenfranchised (10 or 12 Southern states), they comprised 20–50 percent of the population. In some Southern towns disenfranchised blacks constituted a majority of residents. Thus, the prospect of their empowerment stood as a strong threat to status quo interests. Furthermore, the dramatic difference in class and race between those with power (wealthy whites) and those without (poor blacks) greatly exacerbated tensions.

In short, during the era of the American Civil Rights Movement (1950s to 1970s), the group demanding power was *large*, and it was *different* from the group already holding power. What needs explaining is not why violence occurred, but why African Americans succeeded in gaining political rights with relatively *little* violence. To understand how this happened, we must consider one additional phenomenon.

The effect of history on democratization

The variable of a people's political history—or better, *the expectations that people derive from interpreting their history*—may represent the most important factor determining whether democratization will occur smoothly. If extensions of political rights have occurred in the past, especially if they have occurred smoothly and with some regularity, then a pattern of expectation arises. The demand for inclusion by new groups will not seem threatening to existing elites. Experience has taught them that similar demands in the past could be accommodated, and the world did not come to an end.

Similarly, the new groups asking for rights have reason to believe that their demands will be heard and accepted. They will not feel it necessary to resort to violence. They may instead modify their tactics. By moderating their demands and acting in a peaceful fashion, previously disenfranchised citizens may persuade authorities to avoid repression and give them some of what they want. *The more often a society peacefully empowers formerly powerless citizens, the more likely it is that new groups can also gain power peacefully.* A tradition arises of dealing with new equality claims via civil procedures, legal actions, and nonviolent political decisions rather than through force, counter-force, violence, and suppression.

The UK and the USA provide familiar examples of this pattern. Both nations operated under systems that some have called "competitive oligarchies" in the late eighteenth century. Both had evolved to a state of mature democracy by the late twentieth century. Still, it is hard to name the exact date at which they "achieved democracy," because of the gradual nature of the development.

In the USA, perhaps 10 percent of the population (white males with property) had political power before 1800. This percentage slowly expanded from Jefferson's day to Jackson's (early 1800s to early 1830s), as state after state allowed all white males to vote, regardless of property status. Thus, by 1840, 35–40 percent of the American population could be said to hold political power.

That number increased, at least nominally, to roughly 50 percent after the Civil War with the formal inclusion into citizenship of African-American males. In actuality, most American-Blacks did not achieve true political rights until after the civil rights gains of the 1960s, 100 years later. A huge and real increase in the number of power-holders did occur with the passage of the Nineteenth Amendment in 1920 allowing women the right to vote. At a stroke the number of people with political power doubled. The Civil Rights Acts and the Voting Rights Act of the 1960s, along with the Twenty-Sixth Amendment (1971) that gave 18-year-olds the right to vote, essentially completed the process of empowering American citizens.

A similar series of events occurred in the UK. As the result of various reform measures over the decades that gradually enfranchised more and more citizens, the UK found itself in the 1970s in the same circumstance as Americans. Essentially, all citizens over 18 held full political rights.

Many are the counter-examples to the British and American cases of gradual movement toward widespread empowerment. Often in the last two centuries, the majority of a nation's population has *suddenly* been given full political rights. Nearly as often, the use of those rights produced unstable, non-democratic government. The textbook example is France. After the "Revolution of 1848" (actually, just a modest uprising), nearly all French males, previously with no voting rights, were suddenly allowed to choose their national leader. What did these newly enfranchised citizens do? They proceeded to elect themselves a dictator!

To be specific, in the first competitive election after the Revolution (Dec. 10, 1848), French voters freely chose Louis Napoléon as their president. This gentleman, a nephew of the brilliant but tyrannical Napoléon Bonaparte, soon abolished democratic institutions and proceeded to rule along the authoritarian lines of his famous uncle. He cancelled future elections, jailed members of the opposition, silenced critical journalists, and set up a dictatorship based on the police and the military. In grandiose fashion, he called himself Emperor Napoléon III, but his critics (like Victor Hugo) dubbed this run-of-the-mill tyrant, "Napoléon the Little."

In the end, Napoléon III tried to emulate his uncle's military exploits and was soundly defeated by Bismarck in the Franco-Prussian War (1870–1871). He was forced from power, and France entered a long period of democratic instability that became known as the Third Republic (1870–1940). It was an era punctuated by a series of unconstitutional attempts by one group or another to seize power from the legitimate authorities. It ended ignominiously after Hitler's conquest of France. Parliamentarians fled to Bordeaux, where they met one last time and voted the republic out of existence. These democratically-elected representatives granted dictatorial powers to a popular French general, Marshal Pétain.

After three more decades of rocky political lurching (fascist government in the Second World War, unstable Fourth Republic, 1946–1958, martial powers to Charles de Gaulle to resolve the Algerian War crisis, semi-authoritarian Gaullist rule into the 1970s), France slowly emerged into the camp of stable polyarchies. That moment was perhaps best symbolized by the presidential victory of François Mitterrand in 1981. When Mitterrand entered the presidential palace, it marked a peaceful transition of power from right to left. It also suggested complete acceptance of the existing democratic system (the Fifth Republic) by all major political forces in France. That was unusual in France, where huge political blocs have often been on record as wanting to overthrow the existing system. It was especially significant in Mitterrand's case, as he had once been an outspoken opponent of Fifth Republic institutions.

Lessons from the history of democratization

The case of France is instructive. *Gradual and peaceful progress toward democracy is the exception.* Much more common has been the French pattern of staggering toward democracy. This pattern usually involves a dramatic fall "backward" from time to time, as fledgling democratic institutions are ditched for dictatorship or anarchy. It is especially likely to occur in the early days after citizens have gained a right to vote.

A recent example is the former Soviet puppet state of Belarus. In 1994 voters there, at last free to make real choices at the polls, chose a hard-line, quasi-communist dictator, Aleksandr Lukashenko. He moved immediately to wipe out democratic gains and reinstall a repressive dictatorship.

That type of action is common when people with little experience of democracy are suddenly given the vote. In the past century, countries as diverse as Germany, Italy, Pakistan, Argentina, and Ghana have democratically voted dictatorial rulers into power. Each choice occurred no more than a few years after a rapid expansion of political rights.

This pattern is far from absolute. Indian voters, suddenly enfranchised after independence in 1947, have by and large avoided the dictatorial temptation. Even in India, however, one must note the exception of Indira Gandhi.

Mrs Gandhi became Prime Minister democratically in the 1960s, and remained in power for several years under democratic conditions (elections, free press, multiple parties). But when a scandal threatened her tenure in

1975, she assumed dictatorial powers, cancelled elections, suspended civil liberties, arrested opponents, and generally behaved like a standard-issue dictator. No mass movement or legal action drove her from power. Oddly, she stepped down after a democratic election. Mrs Gandhi became so certain of her own popularity that she actually re-introduced free elections. In those elections the voters of India promptly disavowed her, and she obeyed their strong message to leave office.

The incident is striking. Here we have one of the few times in history when a dictator allowed free elections and one of the fewer times when the dictator accepted the result of those elections. This episode solidified India's position as the modern world's most interesting exception to the standard pattern of democratization. For all its diversity and domestic turmoil, and despite the rapid enfranchisement of its masses, post-Second-World-War India has remained relatively free and democratic.

On the surface, the case of India is a puzzle. When it became independent in 1947, domestic conditions hardly seemed promising for democracy. Most Indians were poor and illiterate; rampant caste, class, and ethnic divisions prevailed. Yet India has maintained a moderately positive record of freedom and democracy since its independence. For political scientists, it is clearly an anomaly.

We can start to explain India's solid democratic record using an insight of the brilliant political scientist, Robert Dahl. Dahl argued that *mass democracy is most likely to develop in places with historical traditions of peaceful competition among elites for the right to rule*. An example of this proposition would be the competition between Whigs and Tories that occurred for over 100 years in the British Parliament. Both groups represented elements of the British upper class, yet much was gained by their open, non-violent conflict in a non-democratic age.

During the long but peaceful competition between Whigs and Tories, Britain absorbed a series of norms central to democratic governance. Chief among these were (a) the notion that loyal opposition to an existing government is possible, (b) the idea that political winners do not kill (imprison, impoverish) their opponents, and (c) the understanding that political differences can be resolved by debates and votes within an assembly, rather than by military force on a battlefield. Once these ideas take hold in a people's consciousness, new entrants to the political scene absorb them, act on them, and thereby avoid the violence and repression typical of other political systems. Over the long period of British rule on the sub-continent, it would appear that Indian elites absorbed these and eventually, they passed these norms down to lower-ranking but politically-involved members of Indian society.

On the other hand, Dahl says, in places where peaceful competition has rarely occurred, new entrants to the political process, suddenly empowered, will hold an older perspective on politics. That traditional view says winners get to exterminate losers and impose their will on the population. Naturally, potential losers, faced with this attitude, do not go gently into that good night. Instead, they take up arms to defend themselves. When a formerly powerless citizenry is suddenly enfranchised, the result is often bloody civil war, followed by the brutal, authoritarian rule of whichever side stumbles though to victory.

The sad history of Rwanda and Burundi in the 1990s, among many other cases, illustrates this pattern. A sudden enfranchisement of the bulk of the population allowed the formerly-dominated Hutus—now a majority in both states—to vote their own leaders into government. Those new leaders promptly called on all Hutus simply to massacre all Tutsis, the former ruling group. The resultant bloodshed (by the especially gruesome means of machetes) cost at least half a million deaths in these small countries in just 3 years. Civil wars ensued, and in the end the Tutsis triumphed, going on to re-establish their non-democratic hold on power.[19] The conclusion is clear. *Sudden democratization, in lands with no tradition of peaceful political competition, often results in anarchy and eventual dictatorship.*

What future for democracy?

What do these examples and propositions tell us about the likely future for democracy? Its short-term prospects are mixed. The outlook is surely dark in many places, but the long-term outlook is strong. Certainly over the next few decades a number of nations are going to have enormous difficulty building stable, open, non-violent, non–oppressive political systems. The citizens of those nations will be poor, unskilled, and poorly educated. The culture will have few traditions of peaceful inter-elite competition. The societies will be fragmented into disparate groups representing radically different races, ethnicities, religions, class outlooks, and sectional loyalties. Tolerance toward opponents, a key democratic norm, will be sorely lacking.

Countries exhibiting these traits today include Haiti and Guatemala, Burma and Sri Lanka, Congo and Burkina Faso, Afghanistan and Iraq. Certainly in these nations and in thirty or forty others with similar characteristics, the outlook is bleak. While the long, slow process of modernization develops in these places, citizens there can expect to live either under oppressive governments or in varying states of chaos and anarchy.

The short-term prospect for dozens of other countries is much more hopeful. Many of the former puppet states of the Soviet Union are moving toward democratic governance. Places like Hungary, the Czech Republic, and Poland have several things going for them. They are relatively unified lands where ferocious sub-group animosities are less likely to disrupt political discourse. They are advanced societies in both an economic and a cultural sense. Finally, they have had, at some time in their past, periods in which nonviolent inter-elite competition occurred. Thus, a tradition of sorts does exist for the democratic management of social conflict.

A number of Latin American cultures also satisfy some of the key criteria for democracy. Brazil, Argentina, Chile, Uruguay, Mexico, and others: these nations stand midway on the path from poverty to affluence. Many of their citizens have the education, skills, and wealth needed to act effectively within a democratic system. Furthermore, all these nations have had lengthy periods of history during which reasonably peaceful competition occurred among various claimants to power.

On the negative side, these lands have all experienced eras of brutal and autocratic rule. Furthermore, their societies are not homogeneous. They experience strong ethnic, sectional, and class rivalries. Thus, we cannot claim that they have entered an era of stable, peaceful democracy. Some of them could fall back into fragmentation or authoritarian rule. Still, the prospects seem moderately strong that many of these states could develop into stable polyarchies over the next few decades.

In Asia, several nations may be moving toward democracy via another route. In Taiwan, Japan, Singapore, South Korea, to a lesser degree Malaysia, Indonesia, Thailand, and ultimately China, economies have been strong and growing rapidly. Many citizens have become affluent and educated. Few crushing ethnic or religious differences exist that could tear these societies apart if citizens are freely allowed to express their political desires.

The major drawback toward effective democracy in these places is a centuries-old practice of authoritarianism. Cultural expectations support the tradition of autocratic rulers and submissive citizens. Still, a few decades of wealth and education can do a lot to develop an assertive populace. The long-term prospects for democratization in Asia look good.

Scenario 5: The "democratic peace"

Many scholars see deep significance in the world trend toward democratization. Democracy, they argue, does more than provide the freedoms found in no other system, important as that is. They also believe that increasing democratization could produce a more peaceful world.

This argument is usually labeled **democratic peace theory**.[20] Its central tenet can be easily summarized: *Democracies don't go to war with each other.* Or at least, goes the theory, they are much less likely to fight wars against each other than they are to fight wars with non-democracies. And non-democracies are especially prone to fight wars with each other. In a world of democracies, say proponents of this idea, war will become much less common. Thus, democratization is a dramatic and positive development in human history. All current democracies, say supporters of this theory, should encourage this process in other nations, if for nothing other than their own security needs.

It is a powerful argument—and an influential one. President George W. Bush has used it to justify an American foreign policy that encourages democratization everywhere. For Bush, a democratic world is a safer world. Democratization, in this view, clearly advances US interests and should be high on the agenda of American foreign policy. We will now examine this influential theory in detail, including some major critiques that have been lodged against it.[21]

Democracies are not likely to fight each other, says the theory, because they have developed habits of nonviolence in settling disputes. Domestically, citizens and leaders alike become socialized to believe that political disagreements should be dealt with in open debate and settled in a peaceful manner. In systems of polyarchy, habits of tolerance and acceptance of the humanity of opponents develop. Democratic leaders become skilled in, and used to, negotiation as a prime tactic for achieving their goals. In mature democracies few (and certainly no one who is credible) suggest killing those in another party. Few again suggest that a given dispute should be resolved by force. Politics everywhere can be harsh, but few political leaders in the USA, Italy, Norway, or New Zealand argue that jailing opponents would be the best way to handle some current quarrel.

In short, democracy instills habits of rational argument, compromise, conciliation, and respect for law. These habits make a resort to violent solutions unlikely. As long as democratic citizens believe they are dealing with "people like ourselves," they will fall back on these habits. When democratic nations find themselves in disagreement, it is natural to confront the dispute in ways they have always used in domestic affairs. That is, people from each side will talk with each other, put forth their best arguments, listen to the arguments of the other side, try to persuade the other side of the error of its ways, and, failing that, reach the best compromise agreement possible. In some cases, both sides will agree to submit to a mediating third party or to an international legal authority. Again, this pattern reflects domestic life in democracies where many disputes are resolved through the court system.

What is *least* likely to happen when democracies disagree is armed conflict. Force is anathema to the democratic idea. Humans are the central value in a democratic culture. Each individual is believed to have basic rights, and the right to be treated with respect is high on that list. Democracies extend that right particularly to those who value it. People who agree with and abide by the key democratic principles are deemed worthy of being treated the way members of one's own society are treated. Thus, when democratic citizens deal with other democratic citizens, disagreements may wax hot and heavy, shouting and table-pounding may take place, but guns will rarely be used.

This avoidance of force to resolve political disputes practically defines democratic life. When some actors use violent means to achieve political ends, it is major news and widely condemned in all democracies. Americans are shocked and repulsed by people like Timothy McVeigh and abortion-doctor murderers on the Right and by anti-globalization activists on the Left. The French are horrified at the street violence of young Muslim activists, the Spanish are outraged at the brutality of Basque separatists, and the Japanese are shocked at the poison-gas attacks of a fringe group in the Tokyo subway. Force and brutality are far outside the norm in democratic society.[22]

The first inclination of democratic citizens, then, is to find non-violent ways to handle disagreement. When both sides to a dispute come from democratic systems, both will think in this manner, making it likely that they find ways to resolve an argument peacefully, just as they do for domestic disputes. It would be deemed outrageous for Republicans to send troops against Democrats to settle a budget issue. So too does it seem outrageous for Americans to send troops against Canadians to settle a trade dispute.

So goes the democratic-peace argument. It continues, turning its focus on non-democracies. These regimes, it argues, have few scruples in dealing with other countries. In non-democracies, issues are often resolved by force. Violence is both threatened and used—often. In authoritarian systems, leaders give orders, and those who disagree find themselves confronting not irate media talk-show hosts, but irate soldiers or secret police. Leaders in non-democracies develop the habit of getting what they want by force. Armed aggression against opponents is their natural way of operating. Why should it differ in the international arena? When disputes arise beyond their boundaries, they will be less hesitant than democratic leaders to deploy troops to get what they want.

That includes disputes with democracies as well as non-democracies. The violence-prone nature of non-democratic regimes makes them blind to the character of the system they are dealing with. They will take what they can. Their calculation is not the regime type, but the *power* of the regime they are confronting. The leaders of non-democracies are (usually) rational. They are not crazed maniacs, as often portrayed in popular books and movies. They do not start wars they think they would lose. Thus, Saddam Hussein of Iraq attacked Iran and Kuwait. He never declared war on the USA, Russia, or India.

We see why democracies are perfectly likely to go to war with non-democracies. Those regimes *expect* to use violence to get their way. They do so within their borders, and they will do so beyond their borders, if it serves their interest and they think they can get away with it. Democratic leaders know these facts. When democracies find themselves threatened by a non-democracy, they will not necessarily imagine that argument and discussion will produce an acceptable result. The evidence of centuries shows that force or the threat of force is the final weapon in disputes of this type.

Furthermore, the goodwill that democratic leaders may feel toward democratically-elected leaders of other countries does not apply to the leaders of non-democracies. Those people have gained and hold power through brutal tactics. Thus, the USA has fought numerous autocratic regimes, like Germany, Japan, and Iraq. Despite many disagreements over the years, it has never fought democratic regimes like Canada, Britain, or France. (And since Germany and Japan have become polyarchal, it hasn't fought them, either.) When in the War of 1812, the USA did fight Britain and "Canada" (not yet a real country), none of these entities was close to being democratic or polyarchal.

Criticism of the "democratic peace"

We will look now at the critics of democratic peace theory. Often called realists or neo-realists, they charge their opponents with naïveté. Given human nature, they say, leaders of any group (whatever its internal characteristics) must stand up for the interests of that group. Group interest will always prevail. It will always overwhelm abstract ideals. When the interests of two groups collide, whether those groups are democratic or not, tensions can skyrocket. If the interests are sufficiently central to the members of both groups, and if they involve matters difficult to compromise over, antagonisms can arise that will ultimately lead to violence.

In short, nations will always be at odds with each other on a host of matters, and some of these inevitable conflicts could become violent. The nature of the contending regimes is irrelevant. For realists in international affairs, *interest* determines all, and when interests collide, violence always becomes possible.

In rebuttal, democratic–peace theorists point to a powerful fact. *No mature democracy has ever gone to war against another mature democracy.* The key word here is "mature" (other synonyms include "stable," "full-fledged," and "developed"). The mature democracies are usually taken to be those described throughout this book as polyarchies. They are countries in which all citizens have had full democratic rights for decades, where numerous free, competitive elections have taken place, and where peaceful alternation in power of opposing elites is common. Under that definition, the claim holds up that wars don't occur between democracies.[23]

The problem, say critics in reply, is that "mature democracies" of this sort have existed for a just short time in world history. When democracy is defined in this highly restricted manner, we simply do not have enough data for a true test of the hypothesis.

France, for instance, did not allow women to vote until 1945. In addition, it acted like an unstable democracy (think Spain in the 1930s) until well into the 1970s. Spain, we already know, can just barely be thought of as a mature democracy, after perhaps three decades of democratic history. South Korea, South Africa, and Poland have used democratic forms for less time than that. The list goes on.

Only a handful of countries have a long enough history of full-fledged democracy to make a legitimate test of the democratic-peace proposition. True, the USA and Canada have not fought each other since 1812, Britain and France have not fought each other since 1815, and Australia and New Zealand have never fought each other. The few mature, long-term democracies have indeed not fought wars with each other. Still, we just do not have enough evidence to make a judgment call on democratic-peace theory.

In addition, say the critics, at least *partially*-democratic countries *have* fought each other. The American Civil War was fought between regions of a democratizing nation. Britain and France never fought each other in the democratic age, true, but during the latter part of the nineteenth century (when both were well on the way toward democracy) they had some intense disagreements that came very close to producing violent confrontation.

But this is nit-picking, say democratic-peace theorists. The fact remains that no stable, developed democracy has ever fought a war against a similar state. One scholar even put it this strongly: "The absence of war between democracies comes as close as anything we have to an empirical law in international relations."[24]

The future of democratic-peace theory

We must leave the dispute to be settled by time. In weighing the arguments, however, I do see real power in democratic-peace theory. Democracies do seem to develop norms and behavior patterns that help them resolve conflict in non-violent ways. There is also supporting evidence for the theory. Since the Second World War, it *is* hard to find a case of democracies at war with each other. Furthermore, the number of democracies has grown significantly, while the number of international conflicts has declined.

That may be a spurious correlation. It may not be democracy alone, but democracy combined with **economic modernization** that makes war less likely. Add this variable of socioeconomic development to the equation, and it strengthens the probability that the use of force in international affairs will decline. It seems fair to postulate that people in wealthy countries (whether democratic or not) have so much to lose from war that they will prefer to avoid military action, if possible.

One might develop this variant of democratic-peace theory: *rich (or developed) countries don't fight wars against each other*. Thomas Friedman once argued this point by suggesting that no nation with a McDonald's restaurant has ever fought a war against another nation with a McDonald's restaurant.[25] Erich Weede goes further and labels peaceful relations among modern democracies as a "capitalist peace" rather than a democratic peace.[26]

It is hard to sort all this out, since national wealth, as we have seen, correlates strongly with democracy.[27] Still, to the extent that wealth produces satisfaction with one's earthly condition and a desire not to lose what one has, it is likely to make those with riches unwilling to risk the military devastation that can come from starting a war they might lose. And starting a war against another wealthy country could cause just that result.

Modest evidence suggesting the utility of this hypothesis can be seen in the types of people who enter the military in modern, wealthy nations. Everywhere, those who enlist in their country's armed forces represent the lower socioeconomic echelons.[28] It was well known, during the Iraq War, that practically no children of the Washington elite were serving in the Middle East. Wealthy people just do not seem militarily inclined. As more and more people gain wealth, we may well see a decline in people's readiness to resort to violence as a means of resolving conflict.

Given the available evidence, it seems safe to conclude that wealthy, democratic countries are extremely unlikely to go to war with each other. Since the past two centuries have seen a dramatic increase in the number of people living both under affluence and democracy, the chances for an increasingly peaceful world seem strong.[29]

Conclusion

Of the various scenarios, I have spent longest on the possibility of a world of peaceful and wealthy democracies. Nothing is fore-ordained, as we know. Any number of events could prevent the seemingly inexorable global trend toward economic development, polyarchal culture, and democratic govern-ance. If you had to lay odds, bet on democracy becoming the world's dominant mode of decision-making by the middle of the twenty-first cen-tury—and bet also on that development leading to a more peaceful world.

If it doesn't turn out this way, however, don't sue me. One of the other scenarios may prove the correct one—or an entirely different trend will develop, as yet wholly unsuspected. No one in 1750 predicted the coming industrial revolution that transformed history. No one in 1200 predicted the Renaissance. Human invention has achieved many things, but a crystal ball into the future has yet to be perfected. The fun lies in watching what hap-pens. It's this uncertainty about important events that makes the study of human affairs both exciting and rewarding.

Questions for discussion

1   What will be the three most significant political developments of the next 5 years? Will a new political party arise? What nation will invade what other nation? Will terrorism increase or decrease? Write your predictions down and discuss them with friends and colleagues. How much agree-ment did you find? Now put those predictions away for 5 years, take them out, and see how well you did. Is predicting the future easy?

2 Do you agree with the author that the events of 9–11–01 and Hurricane Katrina had little "*long-term* impact on ordinary social life in the USA?"

3 If the rest of the world really believed in balance-of-power theory, what should be the foreign policy alignments of mid-level powers like France, Brazil, and South Africa?

4 Given the author's reasoning in this chapter, how easy will it be for women and minority groups to gain the right to vote in traditionally-autocratic and patriarchal societies?

5 From your own knowledge of history and politics, can you think of any instance of two democratic nations fighting each other in a war?

6 What countries (not mentioned in the text) would seem to be poorly positioned for democratic development in the next few decades? What countries *are* well positioned to become democracies? For all your examples, explain why or why not.

NOTES

1   Alert readers will wonder how Truman could legally have *run* for president in 1952. The Twenty-Second Amendment to the US Constitution limits presidents to two terms. However, that amendment was not ratified until 1951 and was specifically written so as not to apply to the president in office at the time of its passage through Congress. That person turned out to be Truman, making him the last American president not affected by the constitutionally-mandated two-term limit.

2   Kansas Republican Robert Dole, another unsuccessful presidential candidate, re-tells this story (with a slight variation) in Bob Dole, *Great Political Wit: Laughing (Almost) All the Way to the White House* (New York: Doubleday, 1998, p. 22).

3   Oliver H. Woshinsky, *Culture and Politics: An Introduction to Mass and Elite Political Behavior* (Englewood Cliffs, NJ: Prentice Hall, 1995), pp. xiii–xv.

INTRODUCTION

1   For an introduction to the election of 2000, see two good collections of essays: Michael Nelson, ed. *The Elections of 2000* (Washington, DC: CQ Press, 2001), and Gerald M. Pomper, ed. *The Election of 2000: Reports and Interpretations* (New York: Chatham House, 2001). In an excellent article on American presidential elections focused especially on 2004, James E. Campbell argues that three factors—presidential popularity, perceptions of the economy, and length of time in office by the ruling party—are crucial for determining electoral outcomes; see Campbell, "Why Bush won the Presidential Election of 2004: incumbency, ideology, terrorism, and turnout," *Political Science Quarterly* 120:2 (2005), pp. 219–241.

2   See pp. 185–195.

3   We're talking, of course, about men with personalities *like* those of Cuomo and Powell. Neither Cuomo nor Powell *themselves* could have become president in nineteenth-century America because of another environmental/situational constraint: the country was hardly ready in those years to elect either a Catholic or an African-American to high office. Even today (early 2008), no African-American has been elected president, and so far only one Catholic: John F. Kennedy in 1960.

4   This equation and its utility for political analysis is given extended treatment by James Chowning Davies, "Where from and where to?" in Jeanne N. Knutson, ed. *Handbook of Political Psychology* (San Francisco: Jossey-Bass Publishers, 1973, pp. 1–27).

5   Within Wisconsin alone, one finds tremendous variation among politicians. The ultra-conservative McCarthy became Senator by replacing the much more liberal Robert M. Lafollette, Jr, and was himself followed by the strong liberal, William Proxmire.

CHAPTER 1

1   For an engaging account of the social significance of body language in different cultures, see Roger E. Axtell, *Gestures: The Do's and Taboos of Body Language around the World* (New York: John Wiley & Sons, 1991).
2   P.J. O'Rourke, *Holidays in Hell* (London: Pan Books, 1989, p. 36).
3   An American analogy might be our mythical multi-millionaire who conspicuously lights his cigar with a hundred-dollar bill. This may never happen outside of comic books, but the idea illustrates the same aim as in Kwakiutl culture. It betokens a desire to awe others by displaying one's own unimaginable level of wealth. ("A hundred-dollar bill means no more to me than a match.")
4   See the classic description of Kwakiutl culture in Ruth Benedict, *Patterns of Culture* (New York: New American Library, 1934, pp. 156–195).
5   A vast literature exists on the connections between politics, culture, and society. For an excellent review of this material, as well as an extended bibliography, see David E. Apter, "Comparative Politics, Old and New," in Robert E. Goodin and Hans-Dieter Klingemann, eds. *A New Handbook of Political Science* (Oxford: Oxford University Press, 1996, pp. 372–397).
6   The advantages of education became more and more apparent in the scientific-industrial era. Concurrently, the demand for an educated populace rose, while the growing wealth of industrialized nations made it possible to implement that demand. Slowly and in piecemeal fashion over the course of the twentieth century, American states (and all modern nations) came to provide and then expand educational opportunities. Today, all states require children to be schooled to the age of 16; half the states make that requirement 17 or 18. The same phenomenon can be seen in all other wealthy countries.
7   See poll results online, available at: http://people-press.org/reports/display.php3?ReportID=312 (accessed May 16, 2007).
8   See the website run by Louis D. Johnston and Samuel H. Williamson, "The Annual Real and Nominal GDP for the United States, 1790-Present." *Economic History Services*, April 1, 2006. Online. Available: http://eh.net/hmit/gdp (accessed May 16, 2007).
9   The beliefs of socialists, libertarians, and other political activists are discussed in Chs 8 and 9.

CHAPTER 2

1   Or think they know well. In this era of rapid communication, most of us receive daily images from around the world, leading us to *think* we know about groups of other people, even though we may know nothing about them but a few non-typical facts. The power of this information may lead us to develop positive or negative stereotypes about people on the basis of little personal experience. In a sense, the era of worldwide communication has globalized the possibilities for both conflict and cooperation.
2   In this and following chapters, we shall be examining the factors that lead to these extremes of both conflict and cooperation.
3   Theorists like Plato and Marx (and many others, including Kant and Nietzsche)

looked forward to some ideal time when conflict in human affairs would be eliminated (or hugely reduced). On the other hand, well-known thinkers who stressed the inevitability of conflict include Aristotle, Machiavelli, and James Madison. Supporting the latter perspective, my colleague, Ronald J. Schmidt, Jr., writes (in a private communication): "Too many theorists . . . want to avoid conflict, which leads them to try to construct entire political theories premised on the eradication of politics." For a thorough discussion of these issues, see Bonnie Honig, *Political Theory and the Displacement of Politics* (Ithaca, NY: Cornell University Press, 1993). See also Thomas J. Bernard, *The Consensus-Conflict Debate: Form and Content in Social Theories* (New York: Columbia University Press, 1983). For classic refutations of the idea that conflict in human affairs can be eliminated, see Karl Popper, *The Open Society and Its Enemies* (Princeton: Princeton University Press, 1963), and Isaiah Berlin, *Four Essays on Liberty* (Oxford: Oxford University Press, 1969, esp. pp. 167–172).

4 See Ch. 3, for a thorough discussion of cooperation in human affairs.

5 Jean Baker Miller, *Toward A New Psychology of Women* (Boston: Beacon Press, 1976, p. 13).

6 *Ibid.*

7 *Ibid.*, p. 125.

8 Peter Berkowitz, describing the perspective of political theorist, Judith Shklar; see his review of Shklar's last two books in Berkowitz, "Fear and Loathing," *The New Republic* (July 13, 1998, pp. 34–39; quote on p. 34).

9 Madison today would no doubt state his point in gender-free language. These well-known words occur in *Federalist Paper* Number 51. For this specific quote, see Alexander Hamilton, James Madison, and John Jay, *The Federalist Papers*, with an introduction and commentary by Gary Wills (Toronto: Bantam Books, 1982, p. 262).

10 Madison, *Federalist Paper* Number 10, *ibid.*, p. 30.

11 This is an old theme in human history. Artists have long found tragedy, as well as humor, in the insatiability of human desires. The famous writer, Isaac Bashevis Singer, had one of his characters say, "Everyone tries in his own way with all his means to grab as many honors and as much love and prestige as he can." Singer, "The cafeteria," in *The Collected Stories of Isaac Bashevis Singer* (New York: Farrar, Straus, Giroux, 1991, pp. 287–288).

12 One sociologist interviewed dozens of big lottery winners and found that most had numerous miseries, gripes, and grievances to air, based on their experiences with new-found wealth. See H. Roy Kaplan, *Lottery Winners: How They Won and How Winning Changed Their Lives* (New York: Harper & Row, 1978).

13 As Princeton University's Daniel Kahneman points out, the standard of living in advanced nations "has increased dramatically and happiness has increased not at all" since the 1950s. In fact, he goes on, "there is a lot of evidence that being richer . . . isn't making us happier." See April 30, 2006, BBC news report on happiness studies. Online. Available at: http://newsvote.bbc.co.uk/2/hi/programmes/happiness_formula/4783836.stm (accessed January 19, 2007).

14 Madison lays out his celebrated argument in *Federalist Paper* Number 51. For the specific quote, see Madison, Hamilton, and Jay, *The Federalist Papers, op. cit.*, p. 262.

15 The classic expression of this perspective can be found in the well-known (and controversial) study by Donella H. Meadows *et al.*, *The Limits to Growth: A Report for the Club of Rome's Project on the Predicament of Mankind* (New York: Universe Books, 1972). The study was updated 30 years later with the same message. See Meadows *et al.*, *The Limits to Growth: The 30-Year Update* (White River Junction, VT: Chelsea Green Publishers, 2004).

16 "Homo sum: humani nil a me alienum puto," from Terrence, *Heauton Timoru-menos (The Self-Tormentor),* Act I, Scene 1.

17 Those skilled at human interactions are not only richer and higher in status than loners and social isolates; they even lead healthier lives and live longer. See the extensive data provided in the classic book on social cohesion, Robert D. Putnam, *Bowling Alone: The Collapse and Revival of American Community* (New York: Simon and Schuster, 2000).

18 Adolph Hitler, *Mein Kampf* (Boston: Houghton Mifflin Company, 1939 [original copyright, 1925], p. 84 (italics in the original text).

19 In the same vein, Republicans were struck by the enormity of the perjury charge against Bill Clinton, while downplaying as small potatoes the perjury charges several years later against a top White House aide, Lewis Libby (who just happened to be a Republican). Democrats, of course, took the opposite view on both charges—Clinton's perjury was minor, Libby's earth-shattering. On it goes.

20 As it turns out, term-limit supporters lost this vote by a 227–204 margin. It had been a key plank in the much-ballyhooed Republican "Contract for America" that helped Republicans take over the House in 1994 after 40 years as the minority party there. The party's inability to push this proposal through the House, while doing so with nearly all the other ideas in the Contract, none of which touched directly on the lives and well-being of the legislators themselves, strongly illustrates our point about the power of self-interest.

21 For a range of arguments, see the collection of articles in Edward B. Crane and Roger Pilon, eds. *The Politics and Law of Term Limits* (Washington, DC: The Cato Institute, 1994). I confess to lacking neutrality on this issue, having once argued that term limits is an "elitist proposal." See Oliver H. Woshinsky, "Term Limits: Political Boon or Monstrosity?" *Christian Science Monitor,* November 27, 1992, p. 9.

22 For an excellent introduction to this phenomenon, see Ralph K. White, "Misperception and the Vietnam War," *Journal of Social Issues* 22:3 (1966), pp. 1–167.

23 This story has been told many times. For one solid account, see Jonathan Sumption, *The Albigensian Crusade* (London: Faber & Faber, 1978, esp. pp. 88–103). See also Malcolm Lambert, *The Cathars* (Oxford: Blackwell Publishers, 1998, esp. pp. 102–107).

CHAPTER 3

1 One of the first systematic studies of members of Congress found this pattern clearly. One Senator told researcher Donald R. Matthews, "During the past year and a half . . ., I have done favors for about 3,000 persons. When you consider the word-of-mouth spread, this amounts to a substantial number of voters." And a Senator's aide noted that "when you get somebody $25.00 from the Social Security Administration, he talks to his friends and neighbors about it. After a while the story grows until you've single-handedly obtained $2,500 for a constituent who was on the brink of starvation." See Matthews, *U.S. Senators and Their World* (Chapel Hill, NC: University of North Carolina Press, 1960, p. 226).

2 Social theorists have wrestled with the question of what induces individuals to join groups and take leadership roles. Mancur Olson, an economist, provided an influential contribution to this discussion in *The Logic of Collective Action: Public Goods and the Theory of Groups* (Cambridge, MA: Harvard University Press, 1965). He argued that "rational" people often *don't* join groups, because the modest benefits that they might achieve through group activity are outweighed by the costs of their group involvement. Robert Putnam and Francis Fukuyama suggest that group activity is the natural consequence of learned social and cultural

norms that encourage cooperative involvement with others. Fukuyama calls this set of attitudes "trust" and Putnam uses the term "social capital." See Fukuyama, *Trust: Social Virtues and the Creation of Prosperity* (New York: Free Press, 1995), and Putnam, *Bowling Alone, op. cit.* My discussion about the psychology of political involvement (see Ch. 15) argues that at leadership level, people become active in social and political groups not for "rational" reasons (as economists define rationality), but to satisfy deep-seated personality needs and drives.

3 In Minneapolis, the mayor vetoed it, so the anti-pornography bill never got off the ground. It did become law in conservative Indianapolis, however, where the mayor was an enthusiastic supporter. Courts later struck down this legislation as an unconstitutional infringement on the First Amendment rights of free speech and freedom of the press.

4 See Putnam, *Bowling Alone*, and Fukuyama, *Trust*, both cited in Note 2.

5 Alan Moorehead, *The White Nile* (New York: Harper & Brothers, 1960, p. 49).

6 *Ibid.*

7 See Moorehead's account of Mutesa and his court in *ibid.*, pp. 47–50 and 52–55.

8 In a previous book (*Culture and Politics*, Prentice Hall, 1995, *op. cit.*, especially pp. 36–67), I describe these three methods for dealing with conflict and the political systems associated with these processes. I also described a fourth style of politics based on empire. Since this fourth style of politics has radically declined in the modern age, I have omitted detailed discussion of it from this volume.

9 In Chapter 16, I suggest that democratization may be the wave of the future.

10 "Lebanese Civil War," see Wikipedia: http://en.wikipedia.org/wiki/Lebanese_Civil_War (accessed May 18, 2007).

11 See the discussion of this point in Ch. 16.

12 Illustrative of this point is a well-known political science study that called congressional seats "unsafe at any margin." It argued that even though most members of Congress hold supposedly safe seats, no elected representative can take anything for granted in the shifting, complex world of democratic electoral politics. See Thomas E. Mann, *Unsafe at Any Margin: Interpreting Congressional Elections* (Washington, DC: American Enterprise Press, 1987).

13 The cynic H.L. Mencken once wrote: "Democracy is the theory that the common people know what they want and deserve to get it good and hard."

14 This argument has been made in many places by many astute observers of political and social life. For a well-known exposition of these ideas, see R.J. Rummel, *Power Kills: Democracy as a Method of Nonviolence* (New Brunswick, NJ: Transaction Publishers, 1997, esp. pp. 129–202).

CHAPTER 4

1 Note that "sociocultural change" can in some instances be instigated by political decisions. For instance, Mustafa Kemal Atatürk, leader of Turkey in the 1920s and 1930s, made political decisions that forced a partial modernization of Turkish society and hence produced a modest change in cultural attitudes. Many other examples can be found of strong leaders making decisions that forced some degree of cultural change that would not have occurred without their insistence. Still, the political decisions they made would not have remained significant unless the underlying sociocultural changes were deeply-rooted and well-established. One can find many examples of failed attempts to change the long-term political system, because superficial changes at the top never touched the underlying culture. The USA invaded Cuba in 1906, forcing a free election to occur, but Cuba was still not democratic 100 years later. Imposing a democratic structure

from on top without creating a democratic culture at the bottom produces a strong likelihood of failure. For an extended discussion of these ideas, see the writings of Harry Eckstein, particularly his *Division and Cohesion in Democracy: A Study of Norway* (Princeton, NJ: Princeton University Press, 1966) and (with Ted Robert Gurr) *Patterns of Authority: A Structural Basis for Political Inquiry* (New York: Wiley, 1975).

2 In 1995, I wrote that "Iraq will not tomorrow become a peaceful democracy." (Woshinsky, *Culture and Politics, op. cit.*, p. 41.) It still isn't, as I write these words (12 years later). However, I have substituted another non-democratic regime for Iraq to avoid getting into contemporary partisan debate about the democratic outlook for this country. But given that Iraq went through 57 changes in government in the period from 1921 to 1958 and later sustained a repressive authoritarian regime under Saddam Hussein for over three decades until the American invasion of 2003, one would hardly expect a stable democracy to emerge here soon. For historical perspective on Iraq (and other Middle Eastern non-democratic cultures), see Elie Kedourie, *Democracy and Arab Political Culture* (London: Frank Cass & Co., Ltd., 1994, esp. pp. 25–35 and 83–105).

3 There's a fourth style of politics, parochial, that is less common in our age. It is discussed later, pp. 55–59.

4 On American–Canadian differences, for example, see Seymour Martin Lipset, *Continental Divide: The Values and Institutions of the United States and Canada* (New York: Routledge, 1990). On Swedish–Norwegian differences, see David Klingman, *Social Change, Political Change, and Public Policy: Norway and Sweden, 1875–1965* (London: Sage Publications, 1976).

5 These terms are explained in detail later, pp. 48–60.

6 See, for example, the portrayal of the USA in Robert A. Dahl, *A Preface to Democratic Theory* (Chicago: University of Chicago Press, 1956, pp. 124–151), and the description of the USA and Great Britain in Gabriel A. Almond and Sidney Verba, *The Civic Culture: Political Attitudes and Democracy in Five Nations* (Princeton, NJ: Princeton University Press, 1963, pp. 360–367).

7 Berelson *et al.*, for example, seem to be arguing that continuously high levels of citizen activism are destabilizing. See Bernard R. Berelson, Paul F. Lazarsfeld, and William N. McPhee, *Voting: A Study of Opinion Formation in a Presidential Campaign* (Chicago: University of Chicago Press, 1954, esp. the last chapter, "Democratic Practice and Democratic Theory," pp. 305–323). For a similar line of reasoning, see also Almond and Verba, *op. cit.*, pp. 356–360.

8 See the discussion on this point in G. Bingham Powell, Jr., *Contemporary Democracies: Participation, Stability, and Violence* (Cambridge, MA: Harvard University Press, 1982, pp. 175–200).

9 James L. Payne first called my attention to the phenomenon of violence as an integral part of the political process in some countries. He used the provocative term "democracy by violence" to express this idea. See his discussion in *Labor and Politics in Peru* (New Haven, CT: Yale University Press, 1965, pp. 268–272). See also Samuel P. Huntington, *Political Order in Changing Societies* (New Haven: Yale University Press, 1968).

10 France at that time appears to have been a society moving from a heterogeneous-active to a homogeneous-active one. Its history during the several decades of the Fifth Republic (1958 to our time) shows growing agreement by a majority of French citizens on key social values and institutions. In the 1950s, at least 40 percent of the population (represented primarily by Gaullists and Communists) wanted political institutions *different* from those provided at the time by the Fourth Republic. Today, almost no one disputes the desirability of Fifth Republic arrangements.

11 For more information on this type of culture, see my discussion of it, and the citations presented, in Woshinsky, *Culture and Politics, op. cit.*, pp. 57–60 and 63–64.

12 He deals most extensively with this idea in Robert A. Dahl, *Polyarchy: Participation and Opposition* (New Haven, CT: Yale University Press, 1971). See also his *Preface to Democratic Theory, op. cit.*, and *Democracy and Its Critics* (New Haven, CT: Yale University Press, 1989). For a recent summary of Dahl's views, see his "What political institutions does large-scale democracy require?" *Political Science Quarterly* (Summer, 2005, pp. 187–197). The term "polyarchy" is also associated with Dahl's early close collaborator, Charles E. Lindblom, but over the years, Dahl has been more persistent in writing about the forms, causes, and consequences of polyarchal political systems.

13 I do not advocate throwing out the term altogether. The word democracy has its uses, especially in suggesting some ideal state toward which political systems should strive. But that, of course, is another matter.

14 See, e.g., Samuel P. Huntington and Joan Nelson, *No Easy Choice: Political Participation in Developing Countries* (Cambridge: Harvard University Press, 1976); Arend Lijphart, ed., *Conflict and Coexistence in Belgium: The Dynamics of a Culturally Divided Society* (Berkeley, CA: Institute of International Studies, 1981); Arend Lijphart, *Democracy in Plural Societies* (New Haven, CT: Yale University Press, 1977); Gabriel A. Almond and James S. Coleman, eds., *Politics of the Developing Areas* (Princeton, NJ: Princeton University Press, 1960); and Kenneth D. McRae, *Consociational Democracy: Political Accommodation in Segmented Societies* (Toronto: McClelland and Stewart, 1974).

15 Using good social science jargon, we say the typology is "heuristic."

CHAPTER 5

1 On the difficulty of creating polyarchies by design, see Dahl, *Polyarchy, op. cit.*, pp. 208–227, and Robert Putnam, with Robert Leonardi and Raffaella Nanetti, *Making Democracy Work: Civic Traditions in Modern Italy* (Princeton, NJ: Princeton University Press, 1993, pp. 121–185).

2 See his classic account of the pre-Revolutionary tax-collection system in Alexis de Tocqueville, *The Old Régime and the French Revolution* (Garden City, NY: Doubleday, 1955, pp. 125–128).

3 Only males were involved here. It was a long time ago.

4 I draw heavily here on Dahl's discussion of the conditions necessary for polyarchy in *Polyarchy, op. cit.*, esp. pp. 202–207 and the table on his p. 203.

5 Two leading political scientists put it this way: "The tendency for democracy to go with high levels of socioeconomic development has become one of the most extensively validated statistical linkages in the social sciences." Ronald Inglehart and Christian Welzel, *Modernization, Cultural Change, and Democracy: The Human Development Sequence* (Cambridge: Cambridge University Press, 2005, p. 160). The influential social scientist, Seymour Martin Lipset, was one of the first researchers to explore the wealth-democracy connection. See his early report, "Some social requisites of democracy: economic development and political legitimacy," *American Political Science Review* 53:1 (1959), pp. 69–105.

6 For Freedom House's methodology and results, see their website. Online. Available at: http://www.freedomhouse.org/template.cfm?page=1

7 Many different measures have been devised to compare nations by wealth. We are using here a common one, GDP *per capita* (for 2005) in international dollars, taking account of purchasing price parity (PPP). This data has been gathered by

various organizations, including the International Monetary Fund (IMF), the University of Pennsylvania, the World Bank, and the US Central Intelligence Agency. The information can be found at: http://www.answers.com/topic/list-of-countries-by-gdp-ppp-per-capita, or at the website containing the CIA's *Factbook* on nations of the world: https://www.cia.gov/cia/publications/factbook/index.html

8 Dahl, *Polyarchy*, p. 64.

9 Studies on the wealth-happiness correlation often produce contradictory, ambiguous, or inconclusive results, but there does seem to be general agreement that more money leads to greater happiness at the lower to middle levels of income—and this finding is significant since that's where the vast majority of people in the world find themselves. That is, an additional US$30,000 may not add a lot of happiness to the lives of people already making US$200,000, but an additional US$10,000 to someone making US$20,000 definitely does. Since wealth levels for most people throughout the world range from US$1,000 a year (or less) to US$30,000 or US$40,000 (and more for a small percentage of the world's citizens), we can assume that people in any nation with an average wealth level of US$25,000 are quite a bit "happier" than those in nations with wealth levels at US$5,000 to US$10,000. See the extensive work on this topic by Andrew Oswalt and associates (for example, Rafael di Tella, Robert J. MacCulloch, and Andrew J. Oswalt, "The macroeconomics of happiness," *Review of Economics and Statistics* 85 (2003), pp. 809–827, and recent summaries of happiness studies in Daniel Todd Gilbert, *Stumbling on Happiness* (New York: A.A. Knopf, 2006) and Ed Diener and Robert Biswas-Diener, "Will money increase subjective well-being? A literature review and guide to needed research," *Social Indicators Research* 57 (2002), pp. 119–169.

10 "Political activists" are here loosely defined as those who devote large blocs of their time to politics, as distinct from "average citizens" who devote relatively little time to politics beyond voting. For a lengthy discussion of activists and their influence, see Chs 7, 8, 9, and 15.

11 Robert Putnam explores the effect of elite values on political culture in *The Beliefs of Politicians: Ideology, Conflict, and Democracy in Britain and Italy* (New Haven, CT: Yale University Press, 1973). See also two classic studies on this topic: Samuel Stouffer, *Communism, Conformity, and Civil Liberties: A Cross-Section of the Nation Speaks Its Mind* (Garden City, NY: Doubleday, 1955) and Herbert McCloskey and Alida Brill, *Dimensions of Tolerance: What Americans Believe about Civil Liberties* (New York: Russell Sage Foundation, 1983).

12 Thanks to my colleague and friend, William Coogan, for calling my attention to this point.

13 The current political science phrase for this phenomenon is "path-dependence." It encapsulates the idea that the past cannot be re-written. Once something happens, other things happen as a result of that event, and a chain of further events follows, none of which would have happened in that exact way had the initial event not occurred. The popular version of this insight can be found in the famous poem of Robert Frost, "The Road Not Taken." In it, Frost meditates on the consequences of taking an action that thereby precludes a series of other actions that were equally probable *before* the decision, but impossible afterward. "I kept the first [path]," he writes, "for another day!/Yet knowing how way leads on to way,/I doubted if I should ever come back.") And of course, we all know that in the end his choice of one almost identical path over another "made all the difference."

14 I leave it to the reader to evaluate American efforts to democratize Iraq after its invasion of that country in 2003.

15 Dahl, *Polyarchy, op. cit.*, p. 203 [emphasis added]. See also the extended argument in this same vein by Edward D. Mansfield and Jack Snyder, *Electing to Fight: Why Emerging Democracies Go to War* (Cambridge, MA: MIT Press, 2005). Mansfield and Snyder argue that nations that allow mass citizen involvement before the establishment of rule-of-law norms and strong political institutions will be fragile domestically and especially willing to undertake wars on their neighbors as a way of shoring up popular support for current leaders.

16 It was only in the 1990s that the majority of India's citizens finally achieved literacy.

17 *Note:* I reproduced the older quote with just one minor change (to avoid identifying its era). The word [Cabinet] (in brackets in the second quote) replaces the actual words "Giolitti Ministry." Otherwise, the passage reads just as it was written in the late nineteenth century.

18 Alexis de Tocqueville, *Democracy in America*, edited by J. P. Mayer and Max Lerner (New York: Harper & Row, 1966), originally published in 1835.

19 *Ibid.*, p. 262.

20 *Ibid.*, pp. 262–263.

21 *Ibid.*, p. 261.

22 *Ibid.*, pp. 223–224.

23 *Ibid.*, p. 169.

24 *Ibid.*, p. 170.

25 *Ibid.*, p. 283.

26 Comparative survey research always shows Americans more publicly devoted to religion than the citizens of other countries. For a summary of evidence on the importance of religion to Americans, see Kenneth D. Wald and Allison Calhoun-Brown, *Religion and Politics in the United States*, 5th edn. (Lanham: Rowman and Littlefield, 2007).

27 Lucian W. Pye, *China: An Introduction* (Boston: Little Brown and Company, 1972, p. 344).

28 Putnam, *Making Democracy Work, op. cit.*, pp. 121–162.

29 James L. Payne, *Patterns of Conflict in Colombia* (New Haven: Yale University Press, 1968, p. 3).

30 *Ibid.*, pp. 4–5.

31 So were many other works making the same point. See, among others, John D. Martz, *Colombia: A Contemporary Political Survey* (Chapel Hill, NC: University of North Carolina Press, 1962) and Robert H. Dix, *Colombia: The Political Dimensions of Change* (New Haven, CT: Yale University Press, 1967).

32 Suzanne Massie, *Land of the Firebird: The Beauty of Old Russia* (New York: Simon and Schuster, 1980, p. 37).

33 *Ibid.*, p. 38.

CHAPTER 6

1 This discussion draws on material from the following works: Angus Campbell, Philip E. Converse, Warren E. Miller, and Donald G. Stokes, *The American Voter* (New York: Wiley, 1960); Sidney Verba and Norman H. Nie, *Participation in America: Political Democracy and Social Equality* (New York: Harper & Row, 1972); Norman H. Nie, Sidney Verba, and John R. Petrocik, *The Changing American Voter* (Cambridge, MA: Harvard University Press, 1976); David Butler and Donald Stokes, *Political Change in Britain* (New York: St. Martin's Press, 1974); M. Margaret Conway, *Political Participation in the United States*, 3rd edn. (Washington, DC: CQ Press, 2000); William Crotty, ed., *Political Participation and American Democracy*

(New York: Greenwood Press, 1991); Mark Franklin, Tom Mackie, Tom Valen *et al.*, *Electoral Change: Responses to Evolving Social and Attitudinal Structures in Western Countries* (Cambridge: Cambridge University Press, 1992); Mark N. Franklin, *Voter Turnout and the Dynamics of Electoral Competition in Established Democracies since 1945* (Cambridge: Cambridge University Press, 2004); Steven J. Rosenstone and John Mark Hansen, *Mobilization, Participation, and Democracy in America* (New York: Macmillan, 1993); Raymond E. Wolfinger and Steven J. Rosenstone, *Who Votes?* (New Haven: CT: Yale University Press, 1980); and Sidney Verba, Kay Lehman Schlozman, and Henry E. Brady, *Voice and Equality: Civic Voluntarism in American Politics* (Cambridge, MA: Harvard University Press, 1995). For a recent summary of these and other studies of participation, see Russell J. Dalton, *Citizen Politics: Public Opinion and Political Parties in Advanced Industrial Democracies*, 4th edn. (Washington, DC: CQ Press, 2006, pp. 35–61).

2 See John P. Robinson, Philip E. Converse, and Alexander Szalai, "Everyday life in twelve countries," in Alexander Szalai, ed. *The Use of Time: Daily Activities of Urban and Suburban Populations in Twelve Countries* (The Hague: Mouton, 1972, pp. 113–144).

3 See the evidence presented in Ronald Inglehart and Pippa Norris, *Rising Tide: Gender Equality and Cultural Change Around the World* (Cambridge, UK: Cambridge University Press, 2003, esp. pp. 101–146).

4 Inglehart and Norris, *ibid.*, pp. 149–164, consider the likelihood of this development and come down cautiously on the side of expecting it to occur.

5 Obviously, women and the issues they care about will fare less well in policy outcomes if they're a small minority in power positions than if they're a large majority. For more on issues of gender and politics, see later in this chapter, pp. 95–8, and also the discussion in Chapter 7, pp. 111 and 117–20.

6 See the evidence presented in Mikael Pelz, "The Political Effects of Evangelical Religiosity: A Comparative Approach" (Paper presented at the annual meeting of the Midwest Political Science Association, Chicago, April 15, 2004). Online. Available at: http://www.allacademic.com/meta/p82595_index.html. See also an early presentation of research on this topic, Fredrick C. Harris, "Something within: religion as a mobilizer of African-American political activism," *Journal of Politics* 56:1 (1994), pp. 42–68.

7 For evidence on age and turnout, see the data in Table 405, in "Voting-age population, percent reporting registered and voting: 1992 to 2004," from the *Statistical Abstract of the United States: 2006.* Online. Available at: http://72.14.209.104/search?q=cache:trEdSURxL4AJ:www.census.gov/prod/2005pubs/06statab/election.pdf+percent22Table+405.+Voting+Age+Population percent22&hl=en&gl=us&ct=clnk&cd=2 (accessed November 2, 2006).

8 Dahl makes this point in his classic study of power and participation; see Robert A. Dahl, *Who Governs? Democracy and Power in an American City* (New Haven: Yale University Press, 1961, p. 227).

9 See earlier, pp. 5–6.

10 Daniel J. Elazar developed the notion that three different cultures have shaped American society: the moralistic, the traditionalistic, and the individualistic. Of these, Maine (and New England, in general) has been most strongly influenced by the moralistic traditions of the early Pilgrims and Puritans. See Elazar, *American Federalism: A View from the States*, 2nd edn. (New York: Thomas Y. Crowell and Company, 1972, esp. pp. 84–126).

11 See Elazar, *ibid.*

12 Woshinsky, *Culture and Politics, op. cit.*, p. 119.

CHAPTER 7

1 Arizona's Hayden served in the US House of Representatives from 1912 until 1926, when he was elected to the US Senate, where he remained until 1968. He gained his first public office in 1902 as Town Councilor of Tempe, thus winning his first office before the age of the automobile and holding his last office well into the age of nuclear weapons and space exploration.

2 See, in particular, the discussion of Influentials' beliefs (Chs 8 and 9), and an analysis of Influentials' personality patterns (Ch. 15). In addition, much of the discussion of institutions in Chapters 10–14 implicitly centers on the behavior of Influentials in political structures.

3 The ideas presented in the paragraphs that follow and summarized in Figure 7.1 rely heavily on evidence presented in W. Russell Neuman, *The Parade of Mass Politics: Knowledge and Opinion in the American Electorate* (Cambridge: Harvard University Press, 1986, esp. Ch. 2); Sidney Verba, Norman H. Nie, and Jae-on Kim, *Participation and Political Equality: A Seven-Nation Study* (New York: Cambridge University Press, 1978); and Alan Marsh, *Political Action in Europe and the U.S.A.* (London: Macmillan, 1990). See in particular the data presented in Marsh, p. 14 (Table 1.1). See also the mass of evidence presented in the works cited in Note 1 of Chapter 6.

4 These two variables always reinforce each other. I personally have no interest in the game of bridge; consequently, I have shown weak skills at it during the few times that I've played the game. On the other hand, had I shown some skill at bridge when I was introduced to it, I might well have developed an interest in it.

5 For the variables that make people more or less likely to engage in political activity and therefore to fall into one or another of these categories, see Chapter 6.

6 See the argument in Lester W. Milbrath and Madan L. Goel, *Political Participation: How and Why do People Get Involved in Politics?* (Chicago: Rand McNally, 1977, pp. 98–102).

7 There *are* research specialists who devote themselves to examining this group, its characteristics, and ways in which it might be induced into greater levels of political activity. See, e.g., the extensive writings of Frances Fox Piven and Richard Cloward, including *Poor People's Movements: Why They Succeed, How They Fail* (New York: Vintage, 1978), and *Regulating the Poor: The Functions of Public Welfare*, 2nd edn. (New York: Vintage, 1993). See also Frances Fox Piven, *Challenging Authority: How Ordinary People Change America* (New York: Rowman and Littlefield, 2006).

8 For Lenin's tirades against "right-wing Marxism" (especially Economists and Mensheviks), see V. I. Lenin, *What Is To Be Done?* (Oxford: Clarendon Press, 1970 [1902]) and *One Step Forward, Two Steps Back: The Crisis in Our Party* (Moscow: Progress Publishers, 1969 [1904]). For his jeremiad against left-leaning communists, see *"Left-Wing" Communism: An Infantile Disorder* (Peking: Foreign Language Press, 1975 [1920]).

9 For one way to make sense of an election outside the Left–Right framework, see Donald E. Stokes and John J. DiIulio, Jr, "The setting: valence politics in modern elections," in Michael Nelson, ed. *The Elections of 1992* (Washington, DC: CQ Press, 1993, pp. 1–20).

10 One important reason derives from the Civil War and the intense identification it caused Southerners to feel for the Democratic Party and Northerners for the Republican Party. These strong emotional ties left little room for other parties to capture the allegiance of American voters. See the discussion later, pp. 125–128. Another reason has to do with the effects of our particular electoral system,

which favors a two-party system and disadvantages third parties. See the discussion of that point later, pp. 194–195.

11 The classic attempt to explain why two parties are natural, even inevitable, in a consensual, middle-of-the-road culture is Anthony Downs, *An Economic Theory of Democracy* (New York: Harper & Row, 1957, esp. pp. 114–122). For a recent elaboration of this approach, often called the "median voter theory," see Roger Congleton, "The Median Voter Model," in Charles Kershaw Rowley and Friedrich Schneider, eds. *The Encyclopedia of Public Choice* (Boston: Kluwer Academic Publishers, 2004, Vol. 2, pp. 382–387).

12 See data in the *New York Times*, November 5, 1992, p. B-9.

13 See the data supplied by Laura R. Olson and John C. Green, "Introduction: 'Gapology' and the Presidential Vote," *PS: Political Science and Politics* 39:3 (2006), p. 444, esp. Table 1.

14 Nolan McCarty, Keith T. Poole, and Howard Rosenthal, *Polarized America: The Dance of Ideology and Unequal Riches* (Cambridge: MIT Press, 2006, pp. 106–107).

15 Morris P. Fiorina, with Samuel J. Abrams and Jeremy C. Pope, *Culture War? The Myth of a Polarized America* (New York: Pearson Longman, 2005, p. 103).

16 On working-class voting patterns in Western nations, see Russell J. Dalton, *Citizen Politics: Public Opinion and Political Parties in Advanced Industrial Democracies* (Washington, DC: CQ Press, 2006, esp. pp. 148–157). Note, in particular, Table 8.1, p. 152.

17 Scholars have long tried to explain this phenomenon. Most explanations stress American individualism, egalitarianism, and zeal for upward social mobility— deeply-rooted values that leave the bulk of citizens committed to a laissez-faire capitalism. As early as 1906, for instance, the German sociologist Werner Sombart, asked *Why Is There No Socialism in the U.S.?* See a recent translation of this book by Patricia M. Hocking and C. T. Husbands (White Plains: International Arts and Sciences Press, 1976). Hundreds of writers since have tried to explain why the American electorate is not more to the Left (or the Right). Most attempts at explanation stress differences between the USA and all other countries, fitting into a tradition of historical analysis usually given the name "American exceptionalism." Tocqueville first brought the world's attention to this idea in his famous *Democracy in America* (1835), but the concept has been around since the beginning of the nation. John Winthrop enunciated it in 1630 when he said that America would be a moral beacon to the world, unlike the corrupt and decadent Europeans. When it comes to politics, hundreds of scholars, political analysts, and casual observers have noted the centrist, consensual aspects of American political life. Two strong statements of this pattern, and attempts to explain it, can be found in Louis Hartz, *The Liberal Tradition in America: An Interpretation of American Political Thought since the Revolution* (New York: Harcourt, Brace, 1955), and Seymour Martin Lipset, *American Exceptionalism: A Double-Edged Sword* (New York: W.W. Norton, 1996). Recently, many have come to question whether the USA can be seen as an exception to general historical and sociopolitical forces. For examples of this view, see Sean Wilentz, "Against Exceptionalism: class consciousness and the American labor movement, 1790–1920," *International Labor and Working Class History* 26 (1984), pp. 1–24, and Ian Tyrrell, "American Exceptionalism in an age of international history," *American Historical Review* 96:4 (1991), pp. 1031–1055.

18 I first encountered this idea in an essay of Seymour Martin Lipset. See his "American intellectuals: Their politics and status," in Lipset, *Political Man: The Social Bases of Politics* (Garden City, NY: Doubleday & Company, Inc., 1960, pp. 332–371). When I was a college student in the late 1950s, a campus wag

coined a term for those middle-class students who wore scruffy clothes and spouted Marxist diatribes against the middle-class. He called them *"les nouveaux pauvres."*

19 For supporting data from one recent typical American election (2000), see Table 6.2 in Gerald M. Pomper, "The Presidential Election," in Pomper *et al., The Election of 2000: Reports and Interpretations* (New York: Chatham House, 2001, p. 138).

20 See the evidence presented in Inglehart and Norris, *Rising Tide, op. cit.*, pp. 75–100. They conclude (p. 86) that "the gender gap in political ideology is consistently linked with the process of modernization." On the gender gap in the USA, see Janet M. Box-Steffensmeier, Suzanna De Boef, and Tse-min Lin, "The dynamics of the partisan gender gap," *American Political Science Review* 98:3 (2004), pp. 515–528, and Karen M. Kaufman, "The Gender Gap," *PS: Political Science and Politics* 39:3 (2006), pp. 447–453.

21 See the discussion of religiosity in Chapter 6, pp. 91–92.

22 As Fiorina, *Culture War? op. cit.*, p. 98, puts it concerning the USA, "the more religious an individual, the more likely he or she is to vote for and identify as a Republican."

23 Summarizing the American evidence, two scholars note that "those who attend church at least once a week have become stalwarts of the Republican Party; those who attend church infrequently or not at all are now disproportionately Democratic." (Marc J. Hetherington and William J. Keefe, *Parties, Politics and Public Policy in America*, 10th edn. (Washington, DC: CQ Press, 2007, p. 194). See also the evidence presented in Laura R. Olson and John C. Green, "The religion gap," *PS: Political Science & Politics* 39:3 (2006), pp. 455–459. Norris and Inglehart state that "religion was by far the strongest predictor of who voted for Bush and who voted for Gore [in 2000]—dwarfing the explanatory power of social class, occupation, or region." (Pippa Norris and Ronald Inglehart, *Sacred and Secular: Religion and Politics Worldwide* (Cambridge, UK: Cambridge University Press, 2004, p. 197.) Norris and Inglehart go on to argue (p. 211) that generally "in postindustrial nations, religious values continue to predict a sense of affiliation with the political right." See also the evidence presented in Dalton, *Citizen Politics, op. cit.*, pp. 158–166.

24 In many cases, they weren't even seen as "white." See the fascinating study by Noel Ignatiev, *How the Irish Became White* (New York: Routledge, 1995).

25 See Ch. 6, pp. 98–100.

26 See the classic study of the suburbanization phenomenon, Herbert J. Gans, *The Levittowners: Ways of Life and Politics in a New Suburban Community* (New York: Pantheon Books, 1967).

27 See his description in Joel Gaveau, *Edge City: Life on the New Frontier* (New York: Doubleday, 1991).

28 Oddly, on social (as opposed to economic) issues, suburbanites tend to be *more* liberal than urban voters—largely because they are better-educated. Education, as it turns out, makes one more liberal on social policies, though less liberal on economic ones. See Ch. 9 for a discussion of the differences between social and economic conservatism.

29 The classic expression of this statement can be found in Hartz, *The Liberal Tradition in America, op. cit.* See also Samuel P. Huntington, *American Politics: The Promise of Disharmony* (Cambridge: Harvard University Press, 1981).

30 Cash's is a good book to begin understanding the American South. W.J. Cash, *The Mind of the South* (New York: A. Knopf, 1941).

31 For another influential view on differences between the South and the rest of the

USA, see David Hackett Fischer, *Albion's Seed: Four British Folkways in America* (New York: Oxford University Press, 1991).

32 See the discussion of Elazar and political sub-cultures, pp. 99–100 and 126.

33 See, e.g., Edward G. Carmines and James A. Stimson, *Issue Evolution: Race and the Transformation of American Politics* (Princeton: Princeton University Press, 1989).

34 For a detailed look at this process, see three important books by Earl and Merle Black, *Politics and Society in the South* (Cambridge, MA: Harvard University Press, 1987); *The Vital South: How Presidents Are Elected* (Cambridge, MA: Harvard University Press, 1992); and *The Rise of Southern Republicans* (Cambridge, MA: Harvard University Press, 2002).

35 This finding has been reinforced in study after study for decades. For a recent summary of the evidence, see Donald Green, Bradley Palmquist, and Eric Schickler, *Partisan Hearts and Minds: Political Parties and the Social Identities of Voters* (New Haven, CT: Yale University Press, 2002).

CHAPTER 8

1 For a short introduction to this topic, see M. Margaret Conway, *Political Participation in the United States*, 3rd edn. (Washington, DC: CQ Press, 2000); especially the chapter on "The psychology of political participation," pp. 48–75. See also Russell J. Dalton, *Citizen Politics: Public Opinion and Political Parties in Advanced Industrial Democracies*, 4th edn. (Washington, DC: CQ Press, 2006, especially the chapter on "Political participation," pp. 35–61). For an extended discussion of the motives of political leaders (the "Influentials"), see Ch. 15, this volume.

2 This finding has been exhaustively documented. Philip E. Converse was one of the first modern political scientists to call attention to the phenomenon in his seminal article, "The Nature of Belief Systems in Mass Publics," in David E. Apter, ed., *Ideology and Discontent* (New York: Free Press, 1964, pp. 206–261). For two recent perspectives, see Dalton, *Citizen Politics, op. cit.*, pp. 15–34, and Nolan McCarty, Keith T. Poole, and Howard Rosenthal, *Polarized America: The Dance of Ideology and Unequal Riches* (Cambridge, MA: MIT Press, 2006, pp. 14–70).

3 The well-known social psychologist, Robert B. Cialdini, devotes an entire chapter of his popular introductory text to the topic of consistency. See Cialdini, *Influence: How and Why People Agree to Things* (New York: William Morrow, 1984, pp. 55–114).

4 See the classic study of this subject (known as cognitive dissonance) by Leon Festinger, Henry W. Riecken, and Stanley Schachter, *When Prophecy Fails* (Minneapolis, MN: University of Minnesota Press, 1956). See also Leon Festinger, *A Theory of Cognitive Dissonance* (Stanford, CA: Stanford University Press, 1957).

5 One leading scholar says it's "only natural" that "people who take the time and effort to participate in politics . . . have strong feelings about issues." Morris P. Fiorina, with Samuel J. Abrams and Jeremy C. Pope, *Culture War? The Myth of a Polarized America* (New York: Pearson Longman, 2005, p. 78).

6 As Russell J. Dalton, summarizing a large body of research, puts it: "party choices have meaningful policy consequences." See Dalton, *Citizen Politics, op. cit.*, p. 239.

7 I expand on this point later, in my discussion of the media in Chapter 14.

8 For several excellent discussions of this issue, see the essays in Adam Przeworski, Susan C. Stokes, and Bernard Manin, eds., *Democracy, Accountability, and Representation* (New York: Cambridge University Press, 1999).

9 The most thorough study of this matter has been that of Jeff Fishel, *Presidents and Promises* (Washington, DC: Congressional Quarterly Press, 1985), who showed that half to two-thirds of the campaign pledges of Presidents Kennedy, Johnson,

Nixon, Carter, and Reagan were entirely or partially fulfilled. His work supported earlier findings in the same vein by Gerald Pomper, who studied what became of the winning party's platform pledges from 1944 to 1976. See Pomper, *Elections in America* (New York: Longman, 1980, pp. 128–178). Later research finds that Bill Clinton too fulfilled the great majority of his campaign promises; see Carolyn Shaw, "Has President Clinton Fulfilled His 1992 Campaign Promises?" paper delivered at the 1996 convention of the American Political Science Association, San Francisco, August, 1996.

10 Naurin, "The Pledge Paradox: Why Do People Think Parties Break Their Promises?" paper delivered at a workshop of the European Consortium of Political Research, Turin, March, 2002.

11 See the extended discussion of this point in Michael Gallagher, Michael Laver, and Peter Mair, *Representative Government in Modern Europe*, 4th edn. (New York: McGraw-Hill, 2006, pp .422–440).

12 The term "CFA rating" refers to a number produced by the interest group, Consumer Federation of America. This number represents the percentage of times that a Senator voted for bills judged crucial to consumer interests by the CFA during the year indicated. To illustrate, 100 would mean perfect support for CFA issues, while 0 would indicate no support at all. Information on voting scores was gleaned from the standard reference source, *The Almanac of American Politics*, for the years 1978 and 1998.

13 Poole, "Changing Minds? Not in Congress!" unpublished paper, University of Houston, January 13, 2003. Summarizing a good deal of research on Congress, Jeffery A. Jenkins notes that "members' voting records remain essentially the same, regardless of whether they plan to retire . . ., plan to run for a higher office . . ., serve in a higher office . . ., or have their districts redrawn . . .", see Jenkins, "Examining the robustness of ideological voting: evidence from the Confederate House of Representatives," *American Journal of Political Science* 44:4 (2000), p. 811. See also the conclusion of two other scholars summarizing a good deal of research on this topic: "Congressmen's voting records are quite stable over time." Bruce Bender and John R. Lott, Jr, "Legislator voting and shirking: a critical review of the literature," *Public Choice* 87:1–2 (1996), p. 89.

14 Many will recognize this phrase as a take-off on Harold Lasswell's famous definition of politics: "Who gets what, when, how?", see Harold D. Lasswell, *Politics: Who Gets What, When, How?* (New York: Whittlesey House/McGraw-Hill, 1936). This was a good definition for the detached observer, the "objective" social scientist. Actual political participants, however, are concerned not just with understanding the current distribution of resources, but with the rightness or wrongness of this distribution and what, if anything, should be done about it. Hence, my formulation of the question produces a normative twist appropriate to the mind-set of Activists and Influentials.

15 We must note, of course, that the *degree* of inequality from one society to another varies greatly. The upper and lower strata of society are much closer to each other in Finland than they are in the contemporary USA or in Peru. Furthermore, in many modern societies all but the very lowest groups live relatively well—especially compared with world averages over the ages. So socioeconomic inequality does not necessarily mean that the mass of people in society is oppressed and miserable. That is certainly not the case in dozens of relatively wealthy, modern societies today.

16 With the possible exception of pre-agricultural, hunter/gatherer societies which, according to all accounts, operated with an extremely high level of equality among adult members of the group. Still, the conditions that produced that level

of equality were so special that we must not imagine they will occur again soon (nor would most readers of this book *want* to live in a hunter-gatherer culture, no matter how devoted they may be to the ideal of social equality). For an overview of academic thinking on hunter-gatherer cultures, see Richard B. Lee and Richard Daley, eds. *The Cambridge Encyclopedia of Hunters and Gatherers* (Cambridge: Cambridge University Press, 2004).

17 For complex historical reasons that seem paradoxical—indeed, incomprehensible—to Americans, those labeled "liberal" in Europe tend to be pro-business centrists. (European liberalism even encompasses moderately Right-of-Center free-enterprise advocates.) In this book, I use the term "liberal" in its American sense, as describing someone who is moderately Left-of-Center.

18 For the classic liberal perspective, one could do worse than consult the works of the prolific American economist, John Kenneth Galbraith. See especially, *The Affluent Society* (Boston: Houghton Mifflin, 1958) and *The New Industrial State* (Boston: Houghton Mifflin, 1971). Forerunners of modern liberalism include the philosophers John Locke, Voltaire, John Stuart Mill, and John Dewey; many of the leading figures of the early American Republic: Benjamin Franklin, Thomas Jefferson, Alexander Hamilton, James Madison; and economists Thorstein Veblen and John Maynard Keynes. For more recent liberal perspectives, see Arthur M. Schlesinger, Jr, *The Age of Roosevelt* (Boston: Houghton Mifflin, 1957); Amartya Sen, *Development as Freedom* (New York: Anchor Books, 1999); Isaiah Berlin, *Four Essays on Liberty* (New York: Oxford University Press, 1970); and John Rawls, *A Theory of Justice*, rev. edn. (Cambridge, MA: Belknap Press of Harvard University Press, 1999).

19 For a good introduction to this subject, see Warren Lerner, *A History of Socialism and Communism in Modern Times Theorists, Activists, and Humanists*, 2nd edn. (Englewood Cliffs, NJ: Prentice Hall, 1994).

20 The phrase in quotes is a common catch-phrase of the radical Left. When you hear it, you know you are speaking with someone to the Left of liberalism.

21 See this volume, p. 142.

22 Whether these idealistic claims of the radical Left work in practice is open to much debate. This is not the place to discuss the validity of any of the positions along the Left–Right spectrum. The aim here is to present, not critique, the key ideas adopted by the major ideological groups.

23 Marxists laugh with scorn when presented with cases of government turnover after a democratic election. All that happened, they say, is that Tweedledum replaced Tweedledee. Both the ingoing and the outgoing party (or coalition of parties) represent indistinguishable factions from within "the ruling class." These changeovers resemble nothing more than the superficial shifting of chairs at a bridge party. They are not the wholesale redistribution of socioeconomic power that Marxists say is needed.

24 All who accept communist rule, that is, and excluding all those who have been killed, imprisoned, or banished during the revolutionary upheavals.

25 Classic conservatives from the past include the philosophers Plato, Augustine, and Hegel; the political activists and writers, Edmund Burke and John Calhoun; and the twentieth century writers Friedrich von Hayek, Ludwig von Mises, Michael Oakeshott, Leo Strauss, and William F. Buckley, Jr. For two readable introductions to conservatism, see Russell Kirk, *The Conservative Mind: From Burke to Eliot*, 7th rev. edn. (Chicago: Regnery Books, 1986), and Milton and Rose Friedman, *Free to Choose: A Personal Statement* (San Diego: Harcourt Brace Jovanovich, 1990). See also Bruce Frohnen, Jeremy Beer, and Jeffrey O. Nelson, eds. *American Conservatism: An Encyclopedia* (Wilmington, DE: Intercollegiate Studies Institute, 2006).

26 The classic works on totalitarianism are Carl J. Friedrich and Zbigniew K. Brzezinski, *Totalitarian Dictatorship and Autocracy* (Cambridge, MA: Harvard University Press, 1956), and Hannah Arendt, *The Origins of Totalitarianism* (New York: Harcourt Brace, 1951). See also Eric Hoffer, *The True Believer: Thoughts on the Nature of Mass Movements* (New York: Harper and Row, 1951).

27 Many novels have captured the nightmarish quality of life under totalitarian régimes. Two of the most famous and influential are by George Orwell: *Animal Farm* (New York: Harcourt Brace, 1946) and *1984* (New York: Harcourt Brace, 1949). For an introduction to the way specific totalitarian regimes worked, see (for Russia under communism) Merle Fainsod, *How Russia is Ruled*, rev. edn. (Cambridge, MA: Harvard University Press, 1963); (for Nazi Germany) Michael Burleigh, *The Third Reich: A New History* (New York: Hill and Wang, 2000); and (for communist China) Maurice Meisner, *Mao's China and After: A History of the People's Republic*, 3rd edn. (New York: Free Press, 1999). Of course, the literature on this subject is immense and could consume the rest of your lifetime.

28 There is no magic number, of course. It will depend on the culture and history of a place, and even on chance events. Italy in the 1950s limped along with a fragile polyarchal system even though 30–40 percent of all activists were either communists or fascists. On the other hand, a determined leader like Lenin could engineer the downfall of a democratically-elected government in Russia in 1917, even though his group of communists had just modest support in the public at large.

CHAPTER 9

1 Of course, "other factors" always impinge on behavior. A host of variables influence the actual policies that governments undertake. These include domestic economic conditions; the presence or absence of aggressors on the border; the size of the government's majority; the skill of both government and opposition leaders; and much more. Still, the ideology of government officials must be counted as one of the key variables in understanding just what current policies a government is likely to undertake.

2 Inglehart's original statement can be found in *The Silent Revolution: Changing Values and Political Styles* (Princeton, NJ: Princeton University Press, 1977). For more recent thinking on politics and post-industrial values, see Inglehart, *Modernization and Postmodernization: Cultural, Economic, and Political Change in 43 Societies* (Princeton, NJ: Princeton University Press, 1997), and Inglehart and Christian Welzel, *Modernization, Cultural Change, and Democracy: The Human Development Sequence* (Cambridge, UK: Cambridge University Press, 2005).

3 For additional discussion of likely future trends, see Ch. 16.

4 This argument derives from the influential book of Daniel Bell, *The Coming of Post-Industrial Society: A Venture in Social Forecasting* (New York: Basic Books, 1973).

5 In one of the first books to call attention to this phenomenon, Richard M. Scammon and Ben J. Wattenberg differentiated between "the Economic Issue" (the traditional Left–Right division) and "the Social Issue" (the emerging set of divisions over social and cultural values). See Scammon and Wattenberg, *The Real Majority* (New York: Coward-McCann, 1970).

6 I first heard this line from a barber while I was a college student in the 1950s. Since that time, the country's industrial output has probably quintupled, and the standard of living has surged. *Somebody* must have been working hard all those years!

7 This is a key argument in Morris P. Fiorina, with Samuel J. Abrams and Jeremy C. Pope, *Culture War? The Myth of a Polarized America* (New York: Pearson Longman, 2005). For a similar argument and supporting data, see Jacob S. Hacker and Paul Pierson, *Off Center: The Republican Revolution and the Erosion of American Democracy* (New Haven: Yale University Press, 2005).

8 See his essay, "Working-class authoritarianism," in Lipset, *Political Man: The Social Bases of Politics* (Garden City, NY: Doubleday & Co., Inc., 1960, pp. 97–130).

9 For a similar take on the four types presented here, see Gary Miller and Norman Schofield, "Activists and partisan realignment in the United States," *American Political Science Review* 97:2 (2003), pp. 245–260. Miller and Schofield use the term, "populists," to describe this fourth group. The *Issues2000* website, at: http://www.issues2000.org/default.htm also calls people in this category "populists." See also the Political Compass website, at: http://www.digitalronin.f2s.com/politicalcompass/index.php, which calls people in this group "left authoritarians." David Nolan created a popular version of this schema, specifically to develop support for the libertarian position. See Advocates for Self-Government, *The Nolan Chart Reader* (Atlanta, GA: Advocates for Self-Government, 1995). Nolan calls people in this quadrant "authoritarians." Russell J. Dalton proposes a similar four-fold categorization of political ideologies in *Citizen Politics: Public Opinion and Political Parties in Advanced Industrial Democracies* (Washington, DC: CQ Press, 2006, pp. 136–140). He does not label people in each quadrant, but suggests the axes represent "Old Politics" splits and "New Politics" splits. Fiorina, *Culture War? op cit.*, pp. 118–131, also presents a quadrant of political positions based on the traditional economic dimension and a second "moral" dimension. He does not label people on this second dimension, but talks about activists aligning from the "orthodox" to the "progressive" position along this axis.

10 For a good discussion of this development, see Dalton, *Citizen Politics, op. cit.*, pp. 188–200.

11 Reasons for low voter turnout in the USA are many. One cause is the electoral system, which puts most voters in non-competitive districts where there is little incentive to vote because the result is a foregone conclusion. Another factor derives from election laws that require citizens to make some effort to get on the polling lists. (Governments perform this task in most democratic nations.) Another factor is the sheer number of American elections; "voter fatigue" may set in for many after four or five different elections in the same year. Most countries average less than one election a year. There is also the weakness of party organizations that fail to get voters to the polls, as well as the weakness of other politically-oriented groups such as unions. In most other countries, these groups are stronger than in the USA and wield more influence in turning out voters on election days. Finally, the separation-of-powers system in the USA creates a complex system that makes it hard for less-interested citizens (a large bloc, we know) to figure out who's to blame (or praise) for current conditions and leads many of them not to bother to vote at all. These are just some of the variables that have been suggested to explain America's low voting pattern. The classic study of this issue is Raymond E. Wolfinger and Steven J. Rosenstone, *Who Votes?* (New Haven: CT: Yale University Press, 1980). For a recent overview, see Mark N. Franklin, *Voter Turnout and the Dynamics of Electoral Competition in Established Democracies Since 1945* (Cambridge, UK: Cambridge University Press, 2004).

12 The Libertarian Party itself has averaged just one-half of 1 percent (0.5%) of the national vote in seven presidential elections from 1980 through 2004. Undoubtedly, there are many additional Americans whose philosophy tends toward libertarianism, but who vote for one of the two major parties to avoid "wasting" their

vote. The actual number of libertarians is a matter of some debate. In a typical poll done for the Annenberg Public Policy Center in May, 2005, for instance, only *2 percent* of respondents called themselves "libertarian." On the other hand, the Cato Institute (usually identified as "a libertarian think tank") claims that when asked a series of policy questions, about *13 percent* of Americans polled give answers that place them in the libertarian camp. (David Boaz and David Kirby, "The Libertarian vote," *Policy Analysis* (2006), pp. 1–28). Most politicians continue to act as if the lower number were the more accurate: few major campaigns have been based on appeals to the libertarian outlook.

13 The American presidential election of 2004 failed to conform to this pattern. Both parties decided to focus on "rallying the base" rather than on "converting the undecideds." It is debatable whether this election represents a change in the general pattern of American politics. The contest of 2004 may represent some fairly specialized circumstances: highly polarized parties, an evenly-divided elect-orate, few undecideds. These conditions have rarely existed in the past and seem unlikely to prove a long-term pattern.

14 "Perceived" is the key word here. In actuality, Democrats were hardly an "out" party in 1992, having controlled the US House of Representatives for 38 straight years and the Senate for the previous 6 years as well as for 32 of the previous 38 years. But since American voters identify "government" with "the president," they tend to blame the current president (and his party) when things go wrong. To a lesser extent, they reward him and his party when things go right. They pay little attention to party control of Congress (and often have no idea what party does control Congress).

15 Of course, I am leaving aside another problem: in Jesse Jackson's heyday, the country was surely not ready for an African-American president.

16 For years, it was taken for granted by activists and analysts alike that social security was the "third rail" of American politics. That is, like the third rail on some subway systems, if you touch it, you die. As if to test that hypothesis, George W. Bush did touch the rail. He didn't die, exactly, but his proposal did. He suggested privatizing parts of the social security system, but the idea went nowhere, and his standing with the American public began to decline almost immediately. It is a perfect illustration of my point: proposing an idea to the public at large that's popular with your base often makes you *un*popular with that broader public.

CHAPTER 10

1 This is often called a "first-past-the-post" system. Technically, specialists usually call it a "single-member-district plurality" system. For detailed analysis of this system, see the discussion on pp. 196–203.

2 In the official tally of Florida votes, Bush beat Gore by 537 votes out of 5,962,657, a margin of less than one one-hundredth of 1 percent (<0.01 percent). In the Electoral College, Bush beat Gore by five of the 537 votes cast, thus winning the presidency with 50.5 percent of voting Electors. Arguments about the "actual" outcome of this election (as opposed to the official count) will go on forever, with many analysts (and most Democratic partisans) believing that Republicans "stole" the election. Literally hundreds of books and articles have been written on the subject. For two opposing views, see Richard A. Posner, *Breaking the Deadlock: The 2000 Election, the Constitution, and the Courts* (Prince-ton, NJ: Princeton University Press, 2001), and Lance deHaven Smith, *The Battle for Florida: An Annotated Compendium of Materials from the 2000 Presidential Election* (Gainesville, FL: University Press of Florida, 2005).

3 Given the politics of that day, Clay might have faltered (he had his enemies). Still, one historian put it this way: "There was not the slightest doubt in anyone's mind, especially Clay's, that if the election did go to the House and Clay was one of the three, then he would be the next President." Robert V. Remini, *Henry Clay: Statesman for the Union* (New York: W. W. Norton & Company, 1991), p. 237; see pp. 234–272 for an overview of the election of 1824. See also Norman J. Ornstein, "Three Disputed Elections: 1800, 1824, 1876," in John C. Fortier, ed., *After the People Vote: A Guide to the Electoral College*, 3rd edn. (Washington, DC: The AEI Press, 2004, esp. pp. 31–34).

4 In a cruel twist of fate, Clay was deprived of four New York electors who ended up voting for Crawford after a complex series of Byzantine political maneuvers in Albany. If this bizarre set of events had turned in his favor, Clay would almost certainly have won the presidential election of 1824. On this incident, see George Dangerfield, *The Era of Good Feeling* (New York: Harcourt, Brace & World, 1952, pp. 331–345). See also Ornstein, "Three Disputed Elections," in *op. cit.*, p. 32), who points out that "questions were raised about the legitimacy of several" of the electoral votes received by "the ill and paralytic Crawford."

5 If you are truly ornery, you will ask what happens if the Senate splits 50–50 in its attempt to choose the next vice-president. Luckily, the Constitution provides a way to deal with Senate ties. The Senate would be meeting in December after the election to make its decision. The current Vice-President's term extends to January 20, allowing him to perform his constitutional functions of presiding over the Senate and breaking ties. In the extraordinary case that we are discussing, the Vice-President could single-handedly determine the next leader of the country. It is quite possible that the person he ended up choosing could be . . . himself! That could happen if the Vice-President had been running for a second term, and his ticket had come in either first or second in the Electoral College (but without a majority of electors).

6 Of course, many analysts worry that the odds are not small enough and from time to time have proposed various ways to change or abolish the Electoral College system to make the choice of president less quirky. All proposals have failed for many different reasons, but chief among them is the institution of the US Constitution itself, which makes changing the Constitution almost impossible. According to Article V of the Constitution, amendments to change that document can be approved only with two-thirds of both houses of Congress and three-quarters of the states—and that's a very tall order indeed! Since 1791, only 17 amendments have been approved via this process. Once something's in the Constitution, it is seemingly there for eternity because it is almost impossible to get that much agreement on a change in the basic rules of the game.

7 In 1828, Jackson won 56 percent of the popular vote and 68 percent of the Electoral College vote.

8 Just to keep life interesting, there will always be people who, for one reason or another, cannot work within the two-party system. Usually on the grounds of ideological principle or thwarted personal ambition, they start (or join) one of the many tiny "third parties" that always dot the American political landscape. Given the American institutions of the Electoral College and the SMDP voting system, the odds that any member of any third party will gain real power in the USA are vanishingly small.

9 These examples, which may sound arcane, will become clear by the end of this section.

10 For an in-depth explanation of electoral systems, see Pippa Norris, *Electoral*

Engineering: Voting Rules and Political Behavior (Cambridge, UK: Cambridge University Press, 2004).

11 This plurality rule does not apply to every election in the USA. We have already seen above, that the presidency has unique election rules. Additionally, some places (e.g., Louisiana) have run-off elections a week to a month after a first round of voting, in case no one wins a majority. In the run-off, only the top two candidates can compete, insuring a majority vote for someone. Furthermore, elections *within* American parties (during primaries, caucuses, and conventions) often provide for some form of proportional representation. And some American cities (Cambridge, Massachusetts, is the best-known example) use a proportional system for choosing councilors. Outside the USA, presidents in a number of countries are elected through a run-off system. France provides the standard illustration of this system; it is the nation with the longest continuous history of using this method for choosing its national leader (since the election of 1965).

12 Many scholars prefer the simpler label of SMP.

13 As Pippa Norris puts it, SMDP systems "systematically exaggerat[e] the seat lead for the . . . party with the largest share of votes." Norris, *Electoral Engineering, op. cit.*, p. 72.

14 See James E. Campbell, *Cheap Seats: The Democratic Party's Advantage in U. S. House Elections* (Columbus, OH: Ohio State University Press, 1996, pp. 34–43, esp. the table on p. 35). (This table gives Democratic vote and seat percentages for House elections from 1954 to 1992. I converted the percentages to numbers of House seats and came up with the figure of 25 "extra" Democratic seats.)

15 These numbers reflect the famous (to political scientists) "cube law," which states that in SMDP systems, the ratio of seats (party A to party B) will be the cube of the ratio of votes (party A to party B). Thus, if Party A and B divide votes by a ratio of 55–45, parliamentary seats will be divided by the ratio of 55 cubed to 45 cubed—or 64.6 to 35.4. Try this math on your own with other ratios. It is easy to do and eye-opening about the effects of SMDP.

16 This government under Harold Wilson, limped along for a few months, was forced to call new elections in October, 1974, and was then returned with a three-seat *majority* of seats after winning just 39.2 percent of the votes.

17 Vernon Bogdanor, *The People and the Party System: The Referendum and Electoral Reform in British Politics* (Cambridge, UK: Cambridge University Press, 1981), p. 148.

18 People in this situation are said to exemplify the "free-rider problem." That is, they get the result they want with no expenditure of resources. The problem in a free-rider situation is that if everyone thinks this way, then no one shows up to do the necessary job, it does not happen, and everyone loses. In practice, most people *don't* think this way, and the ones with this attitude probably divide about equally between majority and minority parties. Thus, it does not affect who wins—but it probably does cause a modest downturn in participation and voting rates. Political scientists have long known that competitive elections modestly increase turnout rates, as well as other measures of interest and involvement.

19 Some studies show a modest correlation between levels of turnout and levels of competition, but the connection is complex. For a review of recent findings, see David Hill, *American Voter Turnout: An Institutional Perspective* (Boulder, CO: Westview Press, 2006), pp. 71–114. In any case, PR systems do increase the likely turnout at any given election. As Pippa Norris concludes after her exhaustive study of election systems: "institutional rules do indeed matter: voting participation is maximized in elections using PR." Norris, *Electoral Engineering, op. cit.*, p. 257.

20 There is a way around this seeming need for multi-member districts, however; see below, pp. 205–208.
21 This was the radical Zionist, Meir Kahane. In 1990, Kahane was assassinated in New York by El Sayyid Nosair, an Arab terrorist, who was later involved in the 1993 effort to blow up the World Trade Center. Nosair was eventually sentenced to life in prison.
22 See the discussion of this point above, p. 197.
23 For a thorough overview of this type of electoral system, see Federico Ferrara, Erik S. Herron, and Misa Nishakawa, *Mixed Electoral Systems: Contamination and Its Consequences* (New York: Palgrave Macmillan, 2005).
24 Since two of the parties that have met this test (the Christian Democratic Union and the Christian Social Union) are always close allies, they are usually seen, for all intents and purposes, as the same party. Thus, since 1953 the only parties to gain representation in the West German Bundestag and (after 1989) the German Bundestag under this electoral system are the CDU/CSU, the Social Democrats (the SPD), the Free Democrats (the FDP), the Greens, and the former Communist Party of East Germany (the PDS).
25 Ferrara, Herron, and Nishikawa, *Mixed Electoral Systems, op. cit.*, p. 146.

CHAPTER 11

1 For a good summary of this perspective, see Fred W. Riggs, "Presidentialism vs. Parliamentarism: Implications for Representativeness and Legitimacy," *International Political Science Review* 18:3 (1997), pp. 253–278.
2 For a recent presentation of this argument, see José Antonio Cheibub, *Presidentialism, Parliamentarism, and Democracy* (Cambridge: Cambridge University Press, 2007).
3 See discussion of this point on pp. 215–220.
4 Variations exist. The norm in most parliamentary systems is a legislature with two houses (one popularly-elected and dominant, one weak—or at least weaker—and chosen in some way *other* than through direct popular election). But this norm is not universal. Sweden has abolished its second house and now has just one, while Italy has two nearly-equal houses that are both popularly-elected.
5 This situation is changing rapidly, as courts in many countries have recently gained (and are using) powers to slap down legislative actions. See the discussion of courts in Ch. 12.
6 As usual, there are exceptions to this general description of the typical parliamentary system. In Germany, the second house (the Bundesrat) must give its consent to any legislation that concerns *länder* (provincial) matters; it can therefore block the dominant house (the Bundestag) on provincial issues, if it chooses to do so. France (and some of the newer, less-stable polyarchies like Poland and the Czech Republic) have "mixed" parliamentary-presidential systems, where directly-elected presidents and the dominant house of parliament often clash with each other (and can check each other in various ways). Italy is perhaps the clearest exception to the one-house-dominant rule in parliamentary systems. It has two legislative bodies, a Chamber of Deputies and a Senate, that are essentially co-equal (as in the American system). Both are directly elected by the mass electorate, and governments (Prime Ministers) must have majorities in both houses to continue in office.
7 Most countries have this second, weaker, non-popularly-elected house. In Canada, members of the Senate are appointed by the Prime Minister. In Britain, members of the House of Lords are either appointed by the Prime Minister or inherit a

family seat that was bestowed on an ancestor earlier in history. In France, every 3 years, one-third of the members of the Senate are chosen for 9-year terms by groups of local and regional officials in a complex election process. These second, weaker houses of parliament have varying powers, depending on the country, but most can eventually be over-ridden by the stronger house, if push comes to shove. As mentioned earlier, some countries (like Sweden) have dispensed with a weak second house altogether.

8 Different countries have different names for the top executive official (Chancellor in Germany, Taoiseach in Ireland, etc.), but "Prime Minister" is most common and will be used throughout this text.

9 Other possibilities exist. Occasionally, a minority government is formed, but it tends to be short-lived. Occasionally, too (for various reasons), it is not the leader of the largest party who's named Prime Minister. We concentrate here on the most common outcomes after elections in parliamentary systems. For detail on all the possibilities, see Gallagher, Laver, and Mair, *Representative Government in Modern Europe*, 4th edn. (New York: McGraw Hill, 2005, pp. 381–421).

10 Union pour la Démocratie Française. The UDF split during the presidential and parliamentary elections of May and June, 2007, and its future is currently uncertain.

11 Of course, Prime Ministers do resign for reasons of health or other personal matters, and some have died in office, but those are chance events that can happen in all systems. We are dealing here with *political* reasons for a government changeover.

12 Parliaments can express their loss of confidence in the government in two ways: (1) through a formal vote of no-confidence and (2) through a negative vote on a major policy of the government. As an example of the second possibility, if the government's overall budget is defeated, or if it loses a vote on one of its central initiatives, it has effectively been told that parliament has lost confidence in it. It must then resign—unless it decides to call for new elections. See below, pp. 215–220, for a discussion of which option a given government is likely to choose.

13 Chamberlain's downfall was inevitable after the collapse of his appeasement policy toward Hitler. When war came, despite his futile efforts to avoid it, he had little choice but to resign. Luckily for his Conservative Party, they held a strong majority in the House of Commons and could easily replace him with Churchill, thus avoiding the need to dissolve parliament and face new elections.

14 Sweden used to elect parliaments every 3 years, but changed to 4-year terms in 1994.

CHAPTER 12

1 Karl Marx, *The Eighteenth Brumaire of Louis Napoléon* (New York: International Publishers, 1963 [original text, 1852], p. 15).

2 Of course, the sovereignty of national governments depends on an additional factor, an extra-legal one: their ability to defend themselves from outside aggressors or to enter into alliances that insure their defense from outside aggressors. Most countries most of the time are able to meet this requirement.

3 Oddly, there is one exotic exception to this rule in the constitutional amendment process of the USA. One way to amend the American constitution is for two-thirds of the states to call for a special convention to write one or more amendments, and those amendments could then be ratified by three-fourths of the states (either by state legislatures or by special state conventions chosen for this purpose). If the amendments in questions radically re-defined the powers of the

federal government, it might be possible to say that the American national government's sovereignty had been seriously breached by other entities (voters in the states, special state bodies). This event has never occurred in the 220 years of the American Republic, and it seems so unlikely that it's worth pointing out only in this obscure Note!

4 US Constitution, Article IV, Section 3.

5 That's in theory. In practice, it is highly complicated, and constitutional experts endlessly debate whether the federal government has "implied powers" beyond the "enumerated powers" given to it in the Constitution—and if so, what those implied powers consist of.

6 Six of these came about in 1964, when the growing Paris region was sub-divided into several smaller units. Later, the single unit of Corsica was split into two *départements*, and still later the status of several overseas territories was changed to make them *départements*. Of course, the entire *département* system, in the first place, was created out of thin air in 1790 by the French Constituent Assembly in Paris.

7 Fourteen, if one counts the territories of Yukon, Nunavut, and the Northwest Territories.

8 I am grateful to my University of Southern Maine colleague, Richard Maiman, for his perceptive comments on this section of the text.

9 An excellent series of essays on the role of courts in the American political system can be found in Kermit L. Hall and Kevin T. McGuire, eds. *The Judicial Branch* (Oxford: Oxford University Press, 2005).

10 James Eisenstein, *Politics and the Legal Process* (New York: Harper and Row, 1973, p. 4).

11 The political power of courts has grown in most countries since the 1960s, but in the mid-twentieth century, nearly all courts outside the USA had little political clout. See the discussion in this chapter.

12 Abraham Lincoln, "First Inaugural Address," cited in Keith E. Whittington, "Judicial Review and Interpretation: Have the Courts Become Sovereign When Interpreting the Constitution?" in Hall and McGuire, *The Judicial Branch, op. cit.*, p. 119.

13 See the extended discussion of Tocqueville's views on American culture, pp. 77–80.

14 Tocqueville, *Democracy in America, op. cit.*, p. 248.

15 For a good introduction to issues and cases in American constitutional law, see Lee Epstein and Thomas G. Walker, *Constitutional Law for a Changing America: Institutional Powers and Constraints*, 6th edn. (Washington, DC: CQ Press, 2007).

16 See the discussion of American exceptionalism (and accompanying references) in Note 19 of Ch. 7.

17 Numerous scholars have produced useful comparative perspectives on the role of law and courts in various countries. For some recent works, see: Tim Koopmans, *Courts and Political Institutions: A Comparative View* (Cambridge: Cambridge University Press, 2003); Alec Stone-Sweet, *Governing with Judges: Constitutional Politics in Europe* (Oxford: Oxford University Press, 2000); Charles Epp, *The Rights Revolution: Lawyers, Activists, and Supreme Courts in Comparative Perspective* (Chicago: University of Chicago Press, 1998); Herbert Jacob, Erhard Blankenburg, Herbert M. Kritzer, and Doris Marie Provine, *Courts, Law, and Politics in Comparative Perspective* (New Haven: Yale University Press, 1996); and C. Neal Tate and Torbjorn Vallinder, eds., *The Global Expansion of Judicial Power* (New York: New York University Press, 1995).

18 For a provocative attempt to link American judicial processes to American culture, see Oscar G. Chase, *Law, Culture, and Ritual: Disputing Systems in Cross-Cultural Context* (New York: New York University Press, 2005).

19 We need not focus on whether this mythology is accurate. We need simply remember that if people believe something to be true, they will act as if it were true. Americans, at least a critical mass of them, did believe in these "truths" and acted on them.

20 For evidence, see Tom R. Tyler, *Why People Obey the Law*, rev. ed. (Princeton, NJ: Princeton University Press, 2006). Tyler argues that Americans obey laws from a deep-seated belief in the legitimacy of the legal process, rather than from simple fear of punishment if they disobeyed the law.

21 Marbury v. Madison, 5 U.S. 137 (1803).

22 Jefferson did voice disagreement with the Marbury decision, but not too loudly, and ultimately did nothing about it.

23 See, for instance, the strongly-worded critique of the court for this very development by John T. Noonan, Jr., *Narrowing the Nation's Power: The Supreme Court Sides with the States* (Berkeley, CA: University of California Press, 2003).

24 For a good introduction to policy issues that courts have handled over the years, see Epstein and Walker, *Constitutional Law for a Changing America, op. cit.*, and David O. Friedrichs, *Law in our Lives: An Introduction*, 2nd edn. (Los Angeles: Roxbury Publishing Company, 2006).

25 Finley Peter Dunne, *Mr. Dooley's Opinions* (New York: R. H. Russell, 1901), p. 26. Dunne had his fictional hero, Mr Dooley (a Chicago bar-tender), speaking in an Irish dialect, so he actually said, "th' supreme coort follows th' iliction returns."

26 Cass R. Sunstein, "Judges and democracy: the changing role of the United States Supreme Court," in Hall and McGuire, *The Judicial Branch, op. cit.*, p. 33.

27 Richard A. Brisbin, Jr., "The Judiciary and the Separation of Powers," in *ibid.*, p. 98.

28 Robert A. Dahl, "Decision-making in a democracy: The Supreme Court as a National policy-maker," *Journal of Public Law* 6:2 (1957), p. 285.

29 See Keith E. Whittington, *Political Foundations of Judicial Supremacy: The Presidency, The Supreme Court, and Constitutional Leadership in U. S. History* (Princeton, NJ: Princeton University Press, 2007).

30 A 2004 poll conducted by the American Bar Association found that 62 percent of Americans had been called for jury duty at some time in their lives, and 29 percent had actually served on a jury. See the report on this research. Online. Available at: http://72.14.209.104/search?q=cache:znS4Xum-mGQJ. www.abanews.org/releases/juryreport.pdf+How+many+Americans+have+served+on+a+jury&hl=en&ct=clnk&cd=1&gl=us (accessed May, 2007).

31 See Charles R. Epp, *The Rights Revolution, op. cit.*, and Epp, "Courts and the rights revolution," in Hall and McGuire, *The Judicial Branch, op. cit.*, pp. 343–374.

32 For a good overview of this development, see Kermit L. Hall, "Judicial Independence and the Majoritarian Difficulty," in Hall and McGuire, *The Judicial Branch, op. cit.*, pp. 60–85.

33 Donald P. Kommers, "American Courts and Democracy: A Comparative Perspective," in Hall and McGuire, *The Judicial Branch, op. cit.*, pp. 200–230.

34 For a fascinating popular account that suggests the gains and the limits of this development, see Jianying Zha, "Letter from Beijing: Enemy of the State," *The New Yorker*, April 23, 2007, pp. 46–57.

35 Kermit L. Hall, "Judicial Independence and the Majoritarian Difficulty," *op. cit.*, p. 69.

36 T. B. Friedman, "The politicization of the judiciary," *Judicature* 82: 1 (1998), pp. 6–7.

37 Ran Hirschl, *Towards Juristocracy: The Origins and Consequences of the New Constitutionalism* (Cambridge, MA: Harvard University Press, 2004).

38 Eisenstein, *op. cit.*, p. 340. On the courts as status-quo enforcers, see pp. 307

39 This support occurs in several ways: high tariffs on imported sugar; quotas on sugar imports; and subsidies to sugar producers, sugar-beet farmers, and sugar-cane growers. For information on the American Sugar Alliance's lobbying efforts and expenditures. Online. Available at: OpenSecrets.org: http:// www.opensecrets.org/lobbyists/clientsum.asp?year=2006&txtname=American +Sugar+Alliance (accessed May, 2007). On the total monetary value of assistance to the sugar industry from the federal government, see Bruce Ingersoll, "Sugar producers get $1.6 billion of Federal help," *Wall Street Journal* (May 15, 2000), p. B-4.

40 Tocqueville, *op. cit.*, p. 485.

41 Theodore J. Lowi, Benjamin Ginsberg, and Kenneth A, Shepsle, *American Government: Freedom and Power*, brief 2006 edition (New York: W. W. Norton & Company, 2006, p. 302). [Italics added].

42 Few subjects have been more studied than American interest groups. The first contribution to "group theory" was Arthur F. Bentley, *The Process of Government* (Chicago: University of Chicago Press, 1908). Three early and influential studies of interest group politics were Pendleton Herring, *Group Representation before Congress* (Washington, DC: Brookings, 1929); E. E. Schattschneider, *Politics, Pressures, and the Tariff* (New York: Prentice Hall, 1935); and Earl Latham, *The Group Basis of Politics: A Study in Basing-Point Legislation* (Ithaca, NY: Cornell University Press, 1952). The classic book on interest group politics is David B. Truman, *The Governmental Process* (New York: Knopf, 1951). More recent studies of group politics include Robert H. Salisbury, "An exchange theory of interest groups," *Midwest Journal of Political Science* 13:1 (1969), pp. 1–32; Jack L. Walker, Jr, *Mobilizing Interest Groups in America: Patrons, Professions, and Social Movements* (Ann Arbor, MI: University of Michigan Press, 1991); John P. Heinz, Edward Q. Laumann, Robert L. Nelson, and Robert H. Salisbury, *The Hollow Core: Private Interests in National Policy Making* (Cambridge, MA: Harvard University Press, 1993); Frank R. Baumgartner and Beth L. Leech, *The Importance of Groups in Politics and Political Science* (Princeton, NJ: Princeton University Press, 1998); David Lowery and Holly Brasher, *Organized Interests and American Government* (New York: McGraw Hill, 2004); Allan J. Cigler and Burdett A. Loomis, eds., *Interest Group Politics*, 7th edn. (Washington, DC: CQ Press, 2007); and Jeffrey M. Berry and Clyde Wilcox, *The Interest Group Society*, 4th edn. (New York: Longman, 2007).

43 Philip M. Stern, *The Best Congress Money Can Buy* (New York: Pantheon, 1988).

44 John B. Judis, *The Paradox of American Democracy: Elites, Special Interests, and the Betrayal of the Public Trust* (New York: Routledge, 2001).

45 This negative view of interest groups can be seen in the writings of one of the early students of the subject, E.E. Schattschneider. See his *Politics, Pressures, and the Tariff, op. cit.* It also predominates in the work of another leading scholar of interest groups, Theodore J. Lowi; see *The End of Liberalism: The Second Republic of the United States*, 2nd edn. (New York: W.W. Norton, 1979). See also Mancur Olson, Jr, *The Logic of Collective Action* (Cambridge, MA: Harvard University Press, 1965).

46 The well-known phrase, "the mobilization of bias," is centrally connected to the work of E.E. Schattschneider. He develops the idea at length in *The Semi-Sovereign People: A Realist's View of Democracy in America* (New York: Holt, Rinehart and Winston, 1960). See also Lowi, Ginsberg, and Shepsle, *American Government, op. cit.*, p. 302: "Politics in which interest groups predominate is politics with a distinctly upper-class bias." For others who see an upper-status bias to interest group activity, see Kay Lehman Schlozman and John T. Tierney, *Organized Interests and American Democracy* (New York: Harper and Row, 1986), and Theda

Skocpol, "Voice and Inequality: The Transformation of American Civic Democracy," *Perspectives on Politics* 2:1 (2004), pp. 1–18.

47 This is a central point in the influential argument of Mancur Olson, *The Logic of Collective Action, op. cit.*

48 Michael Parenti, *Democracy for the Few*, 8th edn. (New York: Thomson Publishing Company, 2008).

49 See Lowi, *The End of Liberalism, op. cit.*

50 Many of the works cited in Note 42 above take this approach. See in particular Berry and Wilcox, *The Interest Group Society*, and Walker, *Mobilizing Political Interests.*

51 Robert A. Dahl, *A Preface to Democratic Theory*, expanded edition (Chicago: University of Chicago Press, 2006 [originally published, 1956], p. 145). Dahl wrote those words in 1956. Decades later, he took a less optimistic view of the political system's responsiveness to group claims, especially to claims coming from the socioeconomically disadvantaged. See Dahl, *Democracy and Its Critics* (New Haven, CT: Yale University Press, 1989).

52 See the argument in Heinz, *et al., The Hollow Core, op. cit.*

53 These ideas are widespread in the discipline of political science, but especially connected with the work of Robert Putnam, especially his *Bowling Alone, op. cit.*

54 For an explanation of these terms and a good overview of the history of interest group analysis, see Andrew S. McFarland, *Neopluralism: The Evolution of Political Process Theory* (Lawrence, KS: University of Kansas Press, 2004). He develops the traditional pluralist perspective into a more sophisticated perspective that he labels "cooperative pluralism."

CHAPTER 13

1 For a typical discussion of this topic, see the explanation of "why two major parties have dominated the political landscape in the United States for almost two centuries", in Barbara A. Bardes, Mark C. Shelley, II, and Steffen W. Schmidt, *American Government and Politics Today: The Essentials* (Belmont: CA: Thomson Wadsworth, 2007, pp. 268–270).

2 See discussion on pp. 194–195 and also 255–256.

3 Exceptions include the small number of tiny parties organized along authoritarian and quasi-military lines. They can be found in any democracy. These parties wish to impose dictatorial rule on the country, so they attract followers who feel comfortable in closed, hierarchical organizations. In stable polyarchies, parties of this sort rarely appeal to more than a small percentage of voters, although exceptions exist. The *Front National* in France, a proto-fascist party, stands out as the largest and longest-lived deviant case among parties in stable polyarchies. It has had support levels ranging from 10 to 17 percent in French elections for two decades and more, starting in the mid-1980s.

4 This is not a precise number, the way 32° Fahrenheit signals the freezing temperature of water. It is just a rough rule of thumb. Like all such rules, it could evolve or be modified as times change and conditions develop. It matters how big the legislature is, for instance. Five seats in Israel (120-member Knesset) is much more significant than five seats in France (577-member National Assembly).

5 See the earlier discussion of this point in Ch. 10.

6 During the extraordinary circumstances of the Second World War, the major parties in the UK joined together to form a National Government, under Winston Churchill. A national government was also formed during the First World War, under Lloyd George.

7 In West Germany a "Grand Coalition" of the two large parties governed from 1966 to 1969. In a unified Germany, this same coalition formed in late 2005 and continues in power as of this writing (2007).

8 This might not happen if the largest party were an extremist group with whom no one else is willing to align, or if two or more parties campaigned together and, combined, have more seats than the largest party.

9 Parties are sensitive to vote swings from one election to the next, since voters do know where parties stand and cast their votes at least partly based on those stands. As a result, parties modify their positions, at least partially, to take account of changing public preferences. (Or if they do not adapt to new voter desires, they decline at the polls.) For information on the correlation between voters and parties, see G. Bingham Powell, Jr, "Political Representation in Comparative Politics," *Annual Review of Political Science* 7 (2004), pp. 273–296. See also Mikko Mattila and Tapio Raunio, ""Opinion Congruence between Voters and Parties on the EU Dimension," Paper presented at the European Election Study Conference, Budapest, May 20–23, 2005.

10 See discussion on pp. 218–220.

11 For two excellent books that provide in-depth perspective on how unstable, multi-party systems work, see Joseph LaPalombara, *Democracy, Italian Style* (New Haven, CT: Yale University Press, 1987), and (on France) Philip M. Williams, *Crisis and Compromise: Politics in the Fourth Republic* (Hamden, CT: Archon Books, 1963).

12 See Ronald Inglehart and Christian Welzel, *Modernization, Cultural Change, and Democracy: The Human Development Sequence* (Cambridge: Cambridge University Press, 2005, p. 254).

13 See evidence presented in Russell J. Dalton, *Citizen Politics: Public Opinion and Political Parties in Advanced Industrial Democracies*, 4th edn. (Washington, DC: CQ Press, 2006. p. 40 and pp. 258–259).

14 See his discussion in LaPalombara, *Democracy, Italian Style, op. cit.*, pp. 258–286.

15 *Ibid.*, p. 285.

16 Bryan must have been an extraordinary speaker to win the nomination at 36. The youngest president in American history up to that time had been national hero, Ulysses S. Grant, middle-aged at 46. Even today, the youngest person ever to *win* the presidency was the 43-year-old John F. Kennedy. Teddy Roosevelt, the youngest president ever, was just shy of 43 when he took office after McKinley's assassination.

17 Donald Green, Bradley Palmquist, and Eric Schickler, *Partisan Hearts and Minds: Political Parties and the Social Identities of Voters* (New Haven, CT: Yale University Press, 2002, p. 3). They go on to say that "for many new voters, the parties are not terribly different from clandestine organizations that one learns about through rumor" (p. 228).

18 Hanna is reputed to have said, "There are two things that are important in politics. The first is money, and I can't remember what the second one is."

19 Republicans and Democrats together win well over 99 percent of all *partisan* races. Although independent candidates and candidates of "third parties" occasionally win elections, it is a rare event. Nearly all *serious* political actors run for office knowing that they can win only with the word "Republican" or "Democrat" next to their name on the ballot paper.

20 These people were all men, of course. Only men could vote in those days, so party leaders put little effort into pleasing women. In fact, most party figures vehemently opposed women's suffrage, believing (correctly) that prohibition stood a greater chance of passage if women could vote.

CHAPTER 14

1 For a thorough and positive account of Wilkie, see the biography by Charles Peters, *Five Days in Philadelphia: The Amazing "We Want Wilkie!" Convention of 1940 and How It Freed FDR to Save the Western World* (New York: Public Affairs, 2005). See also Steve Neal, *Dark Horse: A Biography of Wendell Wilkie* (Garden City, NY: Doubleday, 1984).

2 See the extended argument to this effect in Robert J. Klotz, *The Politics of Internet Communication* (Lanham, MD: Rowman and Littlefield, 2004).

3 For more on democratization trends, see the extended discussion in Ch. 16.

4 The thesis I am expounding here has been eloquently argued in dozens of contemporary analyses of the modern mass media. One of the most cogent is Thomas E. Patterson, *Out of Order* (New York: Knopf, 1993). See also James M. Fallows, *Breaking the News: How the Media Undermine American Democracy* (New York: Pantheon Books, 1996), and Neil Postman, *Amusing Ourselves to Death: Public Discourse in the Age of Show Business*, 20th anniversary edn. (New York: Penguin, 2006 [originally published 1986]). An early and brilliant perspective making many of the same points can be found in Walter Lippmann, *Public Opinion* (New York: The Free Press, 1949 [originally written in 1922]); see especially his four chapters on "Newspapers," pp. 201–230.

5 Thomas E. Patterson, "Bad News, Period," *PS: Political Science and Politics* 29:1 (1996), p. 17.

6 For a typical discussion of this point in a standard text on the media, see Doris A. Graber, *Mass Media and American Politics*, 7th edn. (Washington, DC: CQ Press, 2005), pp. 98–102. See also the works cited in footnote 4 above, among many others.

7 This fallacy goes by a number of formal terms, but I think this phrase most clearly summarizes its meaning. Other ways to express it are "the fallacy of hasty generalization," "the fallacy of the biased sample," "the fallacy of the insufficient sample," "the fallacy of misleading vividness," and "the statistics of small numbers fallacy."

8 Stephen Hess, *Live from Capitol Hill! Studies of Congress and the Media* (Washington, DC: Brookings Institution, 1991), p. 106.

9 Power elite theory ultimately traces back to Marx, but it was given its most popular expression in the writings of the mid-twentieth-century American sociologist, C. Wright Mills. See especially, *The Power Elite* (New York: Oxford University Press, 1956). Another prominent purveyor of this perspective has been G. William Domhoff. Typical of his many writings are *Who Rules America?* (Englewood Cliffs, NJ: Prentice Hall, 1967); *The Power Elite and the State: How Policy Is Made in America* (New York: A. de Gruyter, 1990); and *Who Rules America: Power and Politics* (Boston: McGraw Hill, 2002).

10 I present this argument in pared-down form. For a detailed elucidation, see any of Michael Parenti's numerous writings on the media—in particular, *Inventing Reality: The Politics of News Media*, 2nd edn. (New York, NY: St. Martin's Press, 1993).

11 For a classic presentation of the pluralist perspective, see Nelson W. Polsby, *Community Power and Political Theory* (New Haven, CT: Yale University Press, 1962). See also Robert A. Dahl, *Who Governs? Democracy and Power in an American City* (New Haven: Yale University Press, 1961).

12 Eight other presidencies came to an end through death: four men died of natural causes, four by assassination.

13 Woodward himself (admittedly, a biased source) argues this point in one of his later books. See Robert Woodward, *Shadow: Five Presidents and the Legacy of Watergate* (New York: Simon and Schuster, 1999).

14 Carl Bernstein and Bob Woodward, *All the President's Men* (New York: Simon and Schuster, 1974).

15 For a good introduction to media scandal-mongering, see Larry Sabato, *Feeding Frenzy: How Attack Journalism has Transformed American Politics* (New York: Free Press, 1991). See also Larry J. Sabato, Mark Stencel, and S. Robert Lichter, *Peepshow: Media and Politics in an Age of Scandal* (Lanham, MD: Rowman & Littlefield, 2000).

16 Robert Putnam, among many others, has been strenuously making this argument for years. For a full presentation of the thesis, see *Bowling Alone: The Collapse and Revival of American Community* (New York: Simon and Schuster, 2000).

17 The best summary of this research can be found in Thomas E. Patterson, *Out of Order, op cit.* See also Doris Graber, *Mass Media and American Politics, op. cit.*, esp. pp. 98–102. Other good reviews of the way the modern mass media cover politics include Stephen Ansolabehere, Roy Behr, and Shanto Iyengar, *The Media Game: American Politics in the Media Age* (New York: Macmillan, 1993), and Timothy E. Cook, *Governing with the News: The News Media as a Political Institution*, 2nd edn. (Chicago: University of Chicago Press, 2005). For a good journalistic take on the media by a top-notch reporter, see James Fallows, *Breaking the News, op. cit.*

18 Politics not being a precise science, the word "major" here will vary in interpretation, according to year and circumstance. A committee that carried great weight in the 1950s may be insignificant in the 1980s (and vice-versa). The head of the House un-American Activities Committee got lots of attention in 1947, but practically none in 1967. The chair of the Senate Foreign Relations Committee was always in the news in the 1960s but rarely in the 1990s. Changing circumstances, changing personalities, and changing media trends will determine which power positions get attention. For more on this subject, see the argument in Stephen Hess, *News and Newsmaking* (Washington, DC: Brookings Institution, 1996), pp. 46–60. See also Hess, *Live from Capitol Hill, op. cit.*

19 See discussion of this point in Ch. 13.

20 This famous term was given wide publicity in the fascinating work of Eric Hoffer, *The True Believer* (Canada: HarperCollins, 2002).

21 See Ch. 9, for the ideological outlook of these types.

CHAPTER 15

1 See the discussion in Ch. 7, pp. 102–106.

2 In this chapter, all quotes attributed to Maine political activists derive, unless otherwise indicated, from my interviews during the summer and fall of 1984. The names I have used are pseudonyms, and I have taken additional precautions to disguise their true identity.

3 Harold D. Lasswell, *Psychopathology and Politics* (Chicago: University of Chicago Press, 1930). See also Lasswell's later work, *Power and Personality* (New York: W.W. Norton, 1948).

4 Barber conducted research on dozens of Connecticut legislators for his Yale doctoral dissertation, which later became *The Lawmakers: Recruitment and Adaptation to Legislative Life* (New Haven: Yale University Press, 1965). In *The Lawmakers*, Barber worked out a typology of political personality types. He later used the same schema for his influential study of American executives, *The Presidential Character: Predicting Performance in the White House* (Englewood Cliffs, NJ: Prentice-Hall, 1972).

5 I discuss a number of studies of personality types in Woshinsky, *The French Deputy: Incentives and Behavior in the National Assembly* (Lexington, MA: Heath

and Company, Lexington Books, 1973), pp. 2–12. Michael Maccoby in 1976 completed a study of businessmen that reached conclusions similar to those reported here concerning politicians. See Maccoby, *The Gamesman: The New Corporate Leaders* (New York: Simon and Schuster, 1976). Maccoby discovered, among businessmen, personality types resembling those described in this chapter. As the title makes clear, he paid special attention to the gamesman type, a business leader whose motivation and behavior pattern corresponds well to the "game type" described in this chapter.

6 This research and its major findings are summarized in Ch. 11 of my book, *Culture and Politics* (Prentice Hall, 1995, pp. 159–184). The presentation that follows here draws on that source and on the research cited there. For an overview and summary of this work, see James L. Payne, Oliver H. Woshinsky, Eric P. Veblen, William H. Coogan, and Gene E. Bigler, *The Motivation of Politicians* (Chicago: Nelson-Hall, 1984).

7 Obviously, the presentation of types in Table 15.1 is seriously abbreviated. For a detailed description of each type, along with the theory and research underpinning the findings, see the references in Notes 3 through 6 of this chapter.

8 Morris Fiorina seems to be referring to this type when he calls attention to the rising number of conflict-provoking "purists" in American politics. He claims that purists are deeply-committed ideologues who have helped create an unhealthy system of elite polarization in American politics. See Morris P. Fiorina, with Samuel J. Abrams and Jeremy C. Pope, *Culture War? The Myth of a Polarized America* (New York: Pearson Longman, 2005, pp. 138–142.)

9 Payne *et al. The Motivation of Politicians, op. cit.*, p. 163.

10 Eric Hoffer, *The True Believer* (Canada: HarperCollins, 2002).

11 Payne *et al., The Motivation of Politicians, op. cit.*, p. 165.

12 *Ibid.*

CHAPTER 16

1 W.A. Sherden, *The Fortune Sellers: The Big Business of Buying and Selling Predictions* (New York: John Wiley and Sons, 1998) quoted in Gerd Gigerenzer, "I Think, There I Err," *Social Research* 72:1 (2005), p. 195.

2 Sherden, *ibid., passim*, examined the predictions of experts in seven different fields: meteorology, economics, investments, technology assessment, demography, futurology, and organizational planning. Those predictions hit the mark at a rate little better than chance. In other words, if you or I flipped a coin, our predictions would come out about as well as those of major authorities in highly developed fields of specialization.

3 See Ivan Arreguin-Toft, *How the Weak Win Wars: A Theory of Asymmetric Conflict* (New York: Cambridge University Press, 2005), and Jonathan B. Tucker, "Asymmetric warfare: like the young David with his sling-shot, hostile nations armed with cheap but effective weapons pose an increasing threat to the Goliath of US Military Might," *Forum for Applied Research and Public Policy* 14:2 (1999), pp. 32–38.

4 One might argue that the break-up of Yugoslavia in the 1990s was an exception to the rule enunciated here ("no civilizational breakdown of modern industrialized states"). One could also argue, however, that Yugoslavia was hardly a "modern industrialized state" in 1990. In any case, one arguable exception in 70 years hardly undermines a general rule.

5 Japan's victory in this conflict propelled *it* into the ranks of major world powers.

6 The most famous exposition of this theory can be found in Francis Fukuyama,

The End of History and the Last Man (New York: Free Press, 1992). For a vehement opposing perspective, see John J. Mearsheimer, *The Tragedy of Great Power Politics* (New York: W.W. Norton & Company, 2001).

7 As the "weapons of mass destruction" argument for the Iraq War fizzled, the George W. Bush administration began instead to emphasize the "democratic peace" argument. This theory holds that supporting democratization in non-democratic countries (e.g., Iraq) helps to enhance the security of the USA.

8 See the influential discussion of this topic by Samuel P. Huntington, *The Third Wave: Democratization in the Late Twentieth Century* (Norman, OK: University of Oklahoma Press, 1991). See also John Markoff, *Waves of Democracy: Social Movements and Political Change* (Thousand Oaks, CA: Pine Forge Press, 1996), and Renske Doorenspleet, *Democratic Transitions: Exploring the Structural Sources of the Fourth Wave* (Boulder, CO: Lynne Rienner, 2005).

9 That was the essence of my criteria for characterizing nations as "strong polyarchies" in Ch. 6. See pp. 72–73.

10 All current stable polyarchies took decades to evolve and suffered setbacks along the way. Many other countries have adopted democratic institutions at one time or another, only to fall back after a time into patterns of authoritarianism or anarchy. Nevertheless, the long-term, 200-year pattern shows a general movement toward an ever-increasing number of democracies (or what we have been calling polyarchies).

11 See, in particular, Ronald Inglehart and Christian Welzel, *Modernization, Cultural Change, and Democracy: The Human Development Sequence* (Cambridge: Cambridge University Press, 2005).

12 For a readable introduction to this complex phenomenon, see Alex MacGillivray, *A Brief History of Globalization: The Untold Story of Our Incredible Shrinking Planet* (London: Robinson, 2006). Globalization means many things to many people. MacGillivray points out (p. 1) that by December, 2004, over 5,000 books on the subject had been published. Among the more influential of these are Benjamin R. Barber, *Jihad vs. McWorld: How Globalism and Tribalism Are Reshaping the World* (New York: Ballantine, 1996), and two by Thomas L. Friedman, *The Lexus and the Olive Tree: Understanding Globalization* (New York: Farrar, Strauss and Giroux, 2000), and *The World Is Flat: A Brief History of the Twentieth-First Century* (New York: Farrar, Strauss and Giroux, 2005).

13 Some argue that New Zealand might have passed the "full-fledged democracy" test when it allowed women to vote in 1893, but New Zealand was not even a country yet, just an appendage of the British Empire. Besides, it provided no rights at all to its substantial minority population, the Maori.

14 See Gene Shackman, Ya-Lin Liu and Xun Wang, "Brief review of world political trends," 2004. Online. Available at: http://gsociology.icaap.org/report/polsum.html (accessed June, 2007).

15 See Freedom House, *Freedom in the World, 2006* (New York: Freedom House, 2006, p. 2). Report. Online. Available at: http://www.freedomhouse.org/template.cfm?page=1 (accessed June, 2007).

16 Data taken from *Ibid.*, p. 3.

17 See the discussion of this term on pp. 140–141.

18 Even today, there is little social differentiation in the USA between property-owners and tenants. Americans talk about, and the media focus much energy on, the gender gap, racial differences, sectional, ethnic, religious, and sometimes class conflicts, but never do people get up in arms about the "landlord-tenant schism" in American society.

19 This terrible story has been told in many places. See in particular Philip

Gourevitch, *We Wish to Inform You That Tomorrow We Will Be Killed with Our Families: Stories from Rwanda* (New York: Farrar Straus and Giroux, 1998), and Romeo Dallaire, *Shake Hands with the Devil: The Failure of Humanity in Rwanda* (Toronto: Random House, 2003). See also the well-received MGM movie, *Hotel Rwanda* (2004).

20 The literature on this subject has been rapidly expanding. The idea was first put forth by the philosopher, Immanuel Kant, in *Perpetual Peace* (New York: Columbia University Press, 1939 [originally written in German in 1795]). It was given its first modern expression in an obscure 1964 paper by sociologist Dean V. Babst, "Elective governments: a force for peace," *The Wisconsin Sociologist* 3:1 (1964), pp. 9–14. Two leading scholars associated with the idea are Rudolph J. Rummel and Bruce M. Russett; both have published extensively on the peaceful nature of democracies. See in particular, Rummel's *Power Kills: Democracy as a Method of Nonviolence* (New Brunswick, NJ: Transaction Publishers, 1997), and Russett's *Grasping the Democratic Peace: Principles for a Post-Cold-War World* (Princeton, NJ: Princeton University Press, 1993). For another leading proponent of this theory, see Spencer R. Weart, *Never at War: Why Democracies Will Not Fight One Another* (New Haven, CT: Yale University Press, 1998). For a recent perspective, see Human Security Report, 2005 "Why the Dramatic Decline in Armed Conflict?" Online. Available at: http://www.humansecurityreport.info/ HSR2005_HTML/Part5/index.htm (accessed November 1, 2006). A good short introduction to democratic peace theory can be found on the Wikipedia website. Online. Available at: http://en.wikipedia.org/wiki/Democratic_ peace_theory (accessed November 1, 2006).

21 Among major critics of democratic peace theory, see Mearsheimer, *The Tragedy of Great Power Politics, op. cit.*; Joanne Gowa, *Ballots and Bullets: The Elusive Democratic Peace* (Princeton, NJ: Princeton University Press, 2000); Edward D. Mansfield and Jack Snyder, *Electing to Fight: Why Emerging Democracies Go to War* (Cambridge, MA: MIT Press, 2005); and Eric Gartzke, "Economic freedom and peace," in James Gwartney *et al.*, *Economic Freedom of the World: 2005 Annual Report* (Vancouver: The Fraser Institute, 2005).

22 The leading democratic peace theorist, R.J. Rummel, puts it this way: "Democracy is a method of nonviolence because democratic freedoms create a spontaneous society whose culture promotes negotiation and compromise; and whose social, economic, political, and cultural diversity and cross-cutting bonds inhibit violence" (in *Power Kills, op. cit.*, pp. 8–9). Rummel goes on to argue (p. 114) "that of the nearly 170 million people that governments have murdered in our century, nearly 99 percent were killed by nondemocracies."

23 To take the extreme case, look at the list of "strong polyarchies" in Table 5.4 in this volume. *None* of those countries has fought a war against *any* of the other countries for decades, and certainly never during the time when they were both polyarchal.

24 Jack S. Levy, "Domestic politics and war," in Robert I. Rotberg and Theodore K. Rabb, eds. *The Origin and Prevention of Major Wars* (Cambridge: Cambridge University Press, 1988, p. 88).

25 He laid down that proposition in 1999. See Thomas A. Friedman, *The Lexus and the Olive Tree* (New York: Farrar, Strauss, Giroux, 1999, pp. 195–198).

26 Erich Weede, "The diffusion of prosperity and peace by globalization," *The Independent Review* 9:2 (2004), pp. 165–186.

27 See earlier, pp. 62–65.

28 As one study put it, "young people with the fewest alternatives, which tends to mean those from less advantaged backgrounds or who [(as minorities] face

discrimination in civilian labor markets, are most likely to seek service in the military." Congressional Budget Office, *Social Representation in the U.S. Military* (Washington, DC: CBO, US Congress, 1989, p. xv). One scholar points out that in the USA, "peacetime regulars in the 19th century consisted mostly of drifters and immigrants" (Richard H. Kohn, "The American Soldier: Myths in Need of History" in Garry D. Ryan and Timothy K. Nenninger, eds. *Soldiers and Civilians: the U.S. Army and the American People* (Washington, DC: National Archives and Records Administration, 1987, p. 54).

29 James L. Payne reaches these same conclusions for somewhat different reasons in his extensive study of violence over the centuries. See his *A History of Force: Exploring the Worldwide Movement Against Habits of Coercion, Bloodshed, and Mayhem* (Sandpoint, ID: Lytton Publishing, 2004).

GLOSSARY

Activation   Process whereby a group or political party rouses its members from passivity to work on its behalf (usually to vote, in the case of a party).

Activists, political (or **Participants, political**)   The 20 percent or so of any population with a strong interest in political life, willing to engage in a variety of political activities from discussing politics to working on campaigns.

Administrator   One of several political types conceived by Harold Lasswell; one who avoids the dramatic and conflictual side of politics, stresses the details of policy work, and focuses on creating rules and routines in any positions held.

Adulation type   One of several political types observed by James Payne *et al.*; one who seeks the admiration of throngs of adoring followers.

Advertiser   One of several political types observed by James David Barber; one who seeks high office for the status it confers, but who is bored with (and avoids) detailed work on laws and policies. (See also **status type**.)

Age   One of the key variables that determine political **behavior**; older people are more politically active and more set in their political tendencies than younger people.

Agitator   One of several political types conceived by Harold Lasswell; a self-dramatizing personality who seeks to rally the public behind grand reform proposals.

Alienation, political   A feeling that the political system and its representatives have no concern for you as a person or for your material interests; a cynical, negative view of all things political.

American exceptionalism   A belief, held by many Americans, that the USA is not an "ordinary" country; it stands out as morally superior to other nations and does not obey the same historical laws that they are bound by.

Anarchic   Adjective derived from "anarchy;" in politics; applies to societies in which governments are weak and levels of political violence high.

Anarchism A political theory associated with the nineteenth-century Russian philosopher-activist, Mikhail Bakunin, arguing that all governments are repressive and that the best form of society involves mutual, peaceful cooperation among free and equal citizens.

Anarchy Technically, a society with no government; usually used to describe a country in which social chaos reigns, with a weak government trying ineffectually to restrain violence among warring political factions.

Anocracy A nation in a state of anarchy.

Apathetics (or **Disaffecteds**) That large group of any population (one-fifth to two-fifths) with almost no interest in, or involvement with, the political process.

Ascriptive Adjective describing traits or statuses that people have no control over, such as age, sex, race, or ethnic group, as opposed to "achievement" traits like one's profession or income.

Asymmetric violence Describes a state of confrontation between two groups in which the weaker one uses unconventional means of violence to undermine the will of the stronger; e.g., guerilla warfare by Afghans against Soviet forces in the 1980s, and suicide bombings by Iraqi insurgents against American troops in the 2000s.

Attitudes, political Opinions of a positive or negative nature about issues, policies, or leaders of the day.

Authoritarian *People*: Those whose personality inclines them toward abject obedience to those above them and contempt for those below them.

    Political system: Characterized by strong, unchecked rulers and passive, obedient subjects.

Autocracy (see **Dictatorship**)

Autocratic Dictatorial; brooking no opposition, imperious.

B = f [OE] theorem A formula to underline the theory that all behavior results from the interaction of an organism with its **environment**; in other words, we must understand both external (social) forces and internal (psychological) forces to know why people behave as they do.

Bad-news-bias The tendency of most media outlets to focus on the negative (confrontational, violent, and sensational) aspects of the news, as opposed to positive or constructive developments.

Balance-of-power politics A theory in international relations holding that states always work to promote their own interests and do so in part by making or breaking alliances with other states in ways that they hope will insure their own security while undermining the power bases of close competitors.

Behavior Action taken by people or groups that can be systematically described and measured.

Cabinet The highest-ranking executive officials in a nation; each member is usually the head of a major government department. In a **parliamentary system**, members of the Cabinet are also the most powerful members of the dominant party or coalition. In non-parliamentary systems, like the USA, cabinet members may be specialized technocrats or mid-level political figures.

Centrists   Moderates who place themselves at the center of the traditional **Left–Right spectrum** of political ideas; they generally support the **status quo**, but are willing to work with both **liberals** and **conservatives** to make modest adjustments to it.

Checks and balances   A system of **government** based on a fear of concentrated power; set up so that various units (or "branches") of government can block actions of the others, necessitating bargaining and coalitions, while decreasing the likelihood of unrestrained action by any one unit or person

Citizens   Broadly, members of a nation who hold full legal rights, including the right to vote and take part in political activities. As used in this text, it refers to that large bloc of people in most countries who do little more, in terms of political action, than vote.

Civic duty   A widely-held norm in stable **polyarchies** suggesting that people owe their society an obligation to get involved in social and political life for the betterment of their fellow citizens.

Class   A social science concept aimed at categorizing people by their objective social status: "working-class," "middle-class," etc.

Class system   A favorite concept of **Left** theorists (esp. **socialists** and **communists**), it refers to the distribution of classes within a society, which ones are dominant, etc.

Coalition government   In **parliamentary systems**, a **government** formed by the alliance of two or more political parties, usually after an agreement among them on the main lines of policy to be pursued and on the distribution of **Cabinet** posts. Coalitions usually occur because no single party has a majority in parliament.

Collectivism   A type of culture that stresses social unity, obedience to national leaders, and harsh punishment for dissenters.

Competence   (see **Social competence**)

Conflict   The inevitable clash of interests and values that occur everywhere between individuals, groups, and nations. Conflict can take either violent or non-violent form.

Conservatism   A set of political beliefs stressing support for order, tradition, and just rewards for the most productive members of society.

Conservatives   Those who adhere to the philosophy of **conservatism**. In some places, conservatives are specifically members of the country's Conservative Party (e.g., UK). (See also **traditional conservatives**.)

Constituency   (see **District**)

Conviviality type   One of several political types observed by James Payne *et al.*; one who seeks friendship and warm support from others, particularly those with power and position.

Cooperation   One of the strongest defining human characteristics, the ability to work with others for common goals.

Cross-cutting cleavages   Social ties that move people in opposite directions, often leading to behavioral stalemate (e.g., wealthy members of a minority group may be unable to decide whether to vote **Left** or **Right**, so end up abstaining). It can also lead to political moderation—they vote **Centrist** (if that is an option).

Cultural dimension of politics   A term used to describe a range of political attitudes that do not fit into the traditional **Left–Right continuum** focused on economic questions. Issues with a cultural dimension reflect concerns raised by **feminists**, environmentalists, conservative religious followers, and proponents of "lifestyle" freedom.

Culture   The set of **norms**, values, beliefs, and **behaviors** that distinguish the world view of one group of people and differentiates them from all others.

Decolonization   The process, frequently violent, whereby a conquered and occupied people overthrow the nation that rules them and gain independence. The term often refers to the period from roughly 1945–1960, when many developing countries successfully ejected the Western imperial powers that had long dominated them.

Democracy   Term for a complex political system based loosely on the idea that free people can govern themselves or, at the least, are wise enough to choose effective **leaders** from among themselves.

Democratic peace theory   A theory stressing the peaceful nature of democratic states; it holds that democracies are less prone than other political systems to use violence in domestic governance and also less likely to use violence in their relations with each other.

Democratic values   A set of beliefs—including support for individualism, freedom, tolerance, and equality—that are congruent with democratic systems and make democratic behavior more likely to occur.

Democratization   The long, slow process whereby a formerly non-democratic political system develops democratic institutions and the **democratic values** that support those institutions.

Demographic variables   Objective, easily-designated, and easily-obtained characteristics of any given human population (e.g., **gender, age, race**, language, marital status, birth order).

Demonstration effect   The impact on our **behavior** that comes from witnessing the behavior of others. (Successful behavior is imitated; unsuccessful behavior is avoided.)

Dictatorship   A system of government built around the **authoritarian** rule of an **elite**, usually one headed by a specific, tyrannical **leader**.

Disaffecteds   (see **Apathetics**)

District   A geographic area drawn for the political purpose of allowing residents thereof to choose one or more of their number to represent them in some political body (legislature, council, board). Districts can be **single-member** or **multi-member**.

Early election   In **parliamentary systems**, an election called well before the legally-mandated time for a new election.

Edge city   A term popularized by journalist Joel Garreau, to describe the nearly-self contained, densely-populated settlements that spring up on the outskirts of major urban areas.

Education (level of)   One of the key variables influencing individual political **behavior**; education correlates with political participation, with **conservative** economic views, and with **liberal** social attitudes.

Effective party   A party with some chance of gaining representation on a regular basis in the national legislature or in provincial assemblies.

Egalitarian   Adjective derived from the concept of **egalitarianism**, stressing the importance of treating every human being equally.

Egalitarianism   An outlook associated with **Left**-oriented activists, stressing the importance of equal social, economic, political, and legal treatment for all citizens. The more Left one goes, the more one stresses equality of results, as well as equality of opportunity.

Electoral College   The system by which American executives are chosen. Each State has a number of **Electors** corresponding broadly to its population size; citizens vote for president by State; and the plurality winner in each state wins all that State's Electors (with two minor exceptions). Electors then vote for president, and the person who wins a majority of Electors becomes president. Devised in the late eighteenth century, to prevent the popular election of presidents and to empower the States, the College appears dated today, but cannot easily be changed because it is embedded in a Constitution that is difficult to modify.

Electoral system   The term to describe the method that a particular political entity uses to choose its elected officials; electoral systems can vary almost infinitely, but the main types include some form of (a) **proportional representation**, (b) the **single-member-district-plurality system**, or (c) a combination of these two.

Electors   Members of the American **Electoral College**, currently totaling 538 (one for every member of Congress, plus 3 for the District of Columbia). Winning a majority of Electors (270) is necessary to become President; otherwise, the president is chosen by the US House of Representatives.

Elite   Usually refers to a small group of people with high social status who are presumed to "run things." More generally, indicates the small percent of the population who get deeply involved in politics and gain power therein.

Elitism   As an *attitude*, it is a belief that **government** *should* be run by the "better" elements of society, those people with high social status from the "right" families or background. As a *theory*, it is a belief that government *is* run by a small, unrepresentative group of upper-class power-holders (and should not be).

Enlightened self-interest   A concept associated with eighteenth-century Enlightenment thinkers, it suggests that people who act in single-minded fashion for their own short-term gain may lose in the long run through the consequences of the ill-will that they generate, while people who consider the point of view of competitors and give away more than strictly necessary in transactions today may gain in the long run through the good will and cooperation of these people in the future.

Environment   The external circumstances that impinge on and influence individual **behavior**.

Equal distribution of resources   A concept beloved by **political activists** on the **Left**; the more Left one is, the stronger one's wish to promote this aim.

Ethnic group   A set of people who share a common background, similar traits, a mutual history, or simply the belief that they are "a unique people," distinct from others.

Ethnicity   The sense of belonging to a particular **ethnic group**; it is one of many sociological variables with political significance, because members of the same ethnic group behave similarly in politics, but unlike members of other groups, especially during elections.

Ethnocentrism   The belief that one's own group is (or should be) the world's favored group, thus allowing group members to justify actions, even of the harshest sort, to promote their group's interests and position, while hurting any group believed to be standing in their way.

Exceptionalism   (see **American exceptionalism**)

Failed state   Refers to a country with a weak **government** that is unable to quell widespread outbreaks of **violence** among warring factions of society.

Fallacy of the dramatic example   The mistake of imagining that a colorful but unusual event is typical of a social pattern rather than an exception or a deviant case.

Fascists   Followers of a point of view at the far **Right** of the political spectrum; they believe that only a small part of humanity deserves to rule and reap the rewards society has to offer, while all other people should follow and serve this dominant group—or be wiped out by it.

Fatalism   The belief, often associated with **parochial** cultures, that humans are not masters of their fates and can do little to change or improve their situations.

Federal system   A method of dividing power between a central **government** and regional governments, so that political institutions at both levels have certain policy areas in which they are recognized as preeminent. In practice, the struggle for dominance between levels is never-ending, and units at both levels have ways of interfering with or checking units in the other.

Feminism A theory (or set of theories) centered on the belief that women are equal to men and should be treated as equals—socially, economically, politically, and legally. Most versions stress the need for corrective action to overcome the centuries of women's mistreatment at the hands of men.

Feminist movement The movement aimed at implementing the ideals of **feminism**. Its modern origins are usually traced to the Seneca Falls (New York) Convention of 1848, and the most recent revival of feminism in the USA began in the 1960s, with the publication of Betty Friedan's *The Feminine Mystique* (1963).

Feminists People who believe in the ideals of **feminism** (not limited to women).

First-past-the-post system (or **FPTP**) An electoral system also known as the **single-member-district-plurality system** (or **SMDP**).

Fixed-term system A method of electing government officials to a specific number of years in office, with an unvarying date for the next election. Differs from most parliamentary systems, where elections can be called at any time before the legally-mandated date for the next election.

FPTP (see **First-past-the-post system**)

Fragmented culture A society characterized by low levels of trust and high levels of **violence** among social groups.

Free elections Institutions that stand at the core of the democratic process, they are characterized by balloting in which any individual or group can compete, no restrictions are placed on attempts to contact and persuade voters, citizens vote in secret with no pressure or coercion, the counting of ballots is done fairly by impartial officials, and the declared winners take office peacefully.

Free-rider problem The difficulty of getting all who benefit from a broad, publicly-provided good to pay their fair share or make an equal contribution.

Game type One of several political types observed by James Payne *et al.*; one who enters politics through a love of competition and a joy in political manipulation.

Gatekeeping In **media** parlance, the act of weeding out, from the almost infinite number of breaking developments, those items that will be presented to the public as "the news of the day."

Gender One of the most significant of the **demographic variables**; men and women behave differently and hold different attitudes on many dimensions of life, including politics.

Gender gap Refers to the tendency of women in most **polyarchies** these days to vote and to hold **attitudes** somewhat to the **Left** of men.

Genocide   The systematic attempt to massacre an entire set of people based on one of their **demographic** characteristics (**race, religion, ethnicity**).

Geography   One of several factors that help explain political behavior; place of residence (urban or rural? East or West? etc.) influences voting decisions and other political choices.

Globalization   A complex concept stressing, at its core, that modern technology has made all borders porous, so that all people everywhere are now interconnected, economically, socially, and politically.

Globalization of judicial review   Refers to increasing support worldwide of the American practice of court oversight of legislative and executive actions.

Government   The ruling **institutions** of society that are especially focused on ways to deal with social **conflict**. Often refers to the particular administration or set of rulers holding power in a country at any given moment—as in, "The government announced today . . ." or "The government fell today after a vote . . ."

Hegemon   The dominant nation of a region, or even of the world.

Hegemony   The establishment of dominance within a geographical region, or even throughout the world.

Heterogeneous–active culture   A society in which citizens disagree about basic values but act positively to promote their own interests, a pattern that often provokes high levels of societal violence. (See **fragmented culture**.)

Heterogeneous–passive culture   A society in which citizens disagree about basic values but passively accept the rule of **authoritarian** leaders. (See **parochial culture**.)

Homogeneous–active culture   A society in which citizens agree on basic values while acting positively to promote their own interests, thus encouraging a democratic (or **polyarchal**) political pattern. (See **polyarchy**.)

Homogeneous–passive culture   A society where citizens agree on basic values, but do not act to promote their own interests, accepting instead the decisions of the **elite** that runs things. (See **collectivism**.)

Identification   A psychological sense of connection with a set of people, an institution, or an outlook (as in "I'm middle-class"; "I'm American"; "I'm a Democrat").

Ideology   (see **Political ideology**)

Image   A shallow stereotype we carry around in our minds to serve as a short cut for understanding some complex phenomenon.

Incentive types   Refers to a system (developed by James Payne *et al.*) of categorizing **Influentials** by their dominant motive for political activity; seven different drives or needs (**incentives**) have been identified and described.

Incentives   In **political psychology**, the needs, motives, or drives that lead people to engage in full-time, long-term political activism.

Influentials   The tiny number of people in any society (3 percent at most, 1 percent more likely), who devote most of their lives to full-time political activity.

In-group   The set of people that any individual most closely identifies with ("*my* group").

Instant-runoff voting system   A variant of the **single-member-district-plurality** voting system that insures a majority winner; voters rank all candidates on the ballot; if no one has 50 percent of the first-place votes, then second and third place votes are distributed and so on, until someone achieves a majority.

Institutions   Social structures characterized by stable habits of behavior, customary practices, and widely-accepted norms. Strong, deeply-entrenched institutions (churches, governments, parties) can have enormous impact on the way groups and individuals behave.

Intellectuals   A social group distinguished by its connection to the world of ideas; intellectuals are writers, teachers, journalists, researchers, or people who identify with these professions.

Interest group   A set of people united by a common perspective or goal, who join to influence **government** or society to take action that would benefit them materially or satisfy them ideologically.

Internal warfare   Term to describe intra-state group **conflict** that degenerates into major forms of long-term violence: guerilla warfare, civil war, mass insurrections, and the like.

Iron triangle   Phrase to suggest the supposedly cozy connection between an **interest group**, a legislative committee, and the executive department that administers programs affecting the interest group.

Judicial review   Theory holding that courts have (a) the right to review laws for constitutionality and (b) the power to overturn laws that they deem "unconstitutional."

Law of unintended consequences   A proposition calling attention to the unforeseeability of the future; it suggests that any attempt to change current social patterns, even if successful, will always produce other, unexpected, and usually undesired results.

Lawmaker   One of several political types observed by James David Barber; one who enters politics out of a desire to influence policy decisions. (See also **program type**.)

Leaders   People in that tiny segment of the population who make politics their life's work and who succeed at gaining power and influence in their chosen field. (See also "**Elite**," "**Influentials**.")

Left   Refers to a broad set of political positions that share one thing in common: the desire to use **government** powers to promote **egalitarian** policies.

Left–Right spectrum A common way of imagining the relationship between various **political ideologies**. It is a continuum of beliefs ranging from support for extreme **elitism** (far **Right**) to support for extreme **egalitarianism** (far **Left**).

Liberals **Activists** in the USA who hold a position somewhat to the **Left** of center; known in Europe as **Social Democrats**, they urge state intervention to achieve a modest **redistribution of values** with the aim of producing an **egalitarian** society.

Libertarians **Political activists** who place their highest priority on the values of individual liberty and freedom, preferring the weakest **government** possible and the widest possible range for citizen choice.

Litigiousness A social combativeness that is often expressed in an easy readiness to undertake legal action to promote or defend one's interests, a trait often associated with the aggressive individualism of American **culture**.

Love of the game Describes an **attitude** held by many political activists and stands as one reason why they enter and remain in politics. (See also the **game type**.)

Loyal opposition The idea, central to **democratic values**, that people can oppose their current **government** and its policies without being traitors.

Majority voting A form of balloting that insures a majority of votes to the eventual election winner; this can be achieved in several ways, primarily through an **instant run-off** system or a second round of voting on another day with just the two strongest candidates left in the race.

Marbury v. Madison The first major decision handed down by the American Supreme Court (1803), its significance stemming from the power of **judicial review** that the court gave itself after reviewing this case.

Media (or "the media") Always plural, **the media** comprise all communications outlets within a culture. In modern societies, the primary media forms are newspapers, magazines, radio, television, film, and the Internet.

Merit system A method of choosing people for employment (especially **government** employment) on the basis of talent, ability, and achievement, rather than connections. Devised in the late nineteenth century and now widespread in modern cultures, it aims at undermining the power of **patronage** parties and the corruption associated with them.

Middle-class professionals A term to describe the large bloc of people in modern cultures who earn their living in careers that require high levels of education and little physical labor (for example, lawyers, accountants, managers, real-estate brokers, pharmacists, doctors, journalists, and teachers).

Ministers (usually "government ministers") Term for high-ranking members of the governing party in **parliamentary systems** who have been given executive branch duties: head of a department, second in command of a department; head of an agency; and so forth. The highest-ranking ministers form the **Cabinet**; others are known as "junior ministers."

Minority group   A set of people with a common **identity** who have been treated in the past or are currently being treated in unequal fashion by the dominant members of society. Political ramifications include the likelihood that they will vote together as a bloc, usually to the **Left**.

Mirror–image misperception   Describes the likelihood that two groups in **conflict** will view each other with similar negative stereotypes, enhancing the difficulty of achieving peaceful resolution of disagreements.

Mission type   One of several political types observed by James Payne *et al.*; one who enters politics to promote the ideals of some all-encompassing doctrine.

Mixed economy   Term to describe modern economic systems, which are governed by the basic principles of free-market capitalism but regulated and restrained by large governments that account for 25–50 percent of the economy.

Mixed electoral system   A voting system that combines elements of the **single-member-district-plurality** system (**SMDP**) and **proportional representation** (**PR**).

Mobilization of bias   A term to describe the supposed slant or leaning of modern political systems in favor of the better-organized and wealthier interests of society.

Moderates   (see **Centrists**)

Modernity   An attitude towards life that arose and spread in the late nineteenth century, stressing the values of progress, efficiency, achievement, secularism, rationality, and the scientific method. It describes the outlook of many people around the world today, especially those in advanced industrial nations and in the modern sectors of other societies.

Modernization   The long, slow process, whereby traditional agrarian societies move into the scientifically-advanced, industrialized world.

Multi–member districts   Large districts in **PR** systems with numerous members of **parliament** (from a few to several dozen). Winners are decided by the proportion of a party's vote; a party with 10 percent of the vote in a 10-member district wins one seat.

Multi–party system   Society in which a number of parties regularly compete for and win a significant share of the available offices.

Multiple elites   A term reflecting the view that while no single **power elite** exists in modern states, public policy is often made in specialized sub-fields, in each of which an interested **elite** dominates on the issues most significant to it.

Nazis **Activists** at the far **Right** of the political spectrum; specifically those in (or sympathetic to) the party of Adolf Hitler, who claimed that Germans were the "master race" and were obliged to wipe out "inferior peoples," especially Jews.

Nazism The far **Right** doctrine advocated by Hitler (see **Nazis**).

Neopluralism A complex and sophisticated extension of the theory of **pluralism**, developed in the work of political scientist, Andrew McFarland.

News hole Term for the amount of news that a given **media** outlet needs to provide; it is a certain number of pages per day in the case of print journalism, and a certain number of hours per day in the case of electronic journalism.

No-confidence vote A vote taken in the dominant legislative body of a **parliamentary system** which, if successful, forces the resignation of the **Prime Minister** and the downfall of the **government**. At that point, either a new government will be formed or an election called, depending on circumstance.

Norm A deep-seated belief within a **culture** or **subculture** about how people should behave; sanctions are usually visited upon those who violate the norm.

Obligation type One of several political types observed by James Payne *et al.*; one who enters politics out of a sense of duty, eager to bring his moral perspectives and ethical standards into the "shady" world of politics.

Oligarchy Term for a political system governed by a small group of people who rule in an **authoritarian** manner for the benefit of themselves and their supporters.

One-party system A non-democratic political system with all power concentrated in a single **institution** (the ruling party). The system could be either **authoritarian** or **totalitarian**, depending on the **ideology** and aims of its leaders.

Out-group Term for people not part of one's **in-group**. They are usually presumed to share a host of negative characteristics.

Parliamentarism Term for the kind of politics that occur under a **parliamentary system**.

Parliamentary system A form of governing based on electing a legislative body and then asking the leading members of the winning party or parties to take over the top executive positions in government and run the country for as long as they retain a legislative majority or until the date of the next mandated election. Among democracies, its primary competitor is the **presidential system**.

Parochial Someone with a narrow perspective, non-political, focused mainly on the survival of self and family under harsh circumstances.

Parochial culture A society in which most people take the **fatalistic**

view of the illiterate peasant that they can do nothing to change their lives for the better and must simply go along with things, including their **autocratic leaders**, just to survive.

Participants, political (see **Activists, political**)

Party identification A deep-seated feeling of loyalty to, and psychological connection with, a particular political party; leads to high support levels for the party when it counts, especially at election time.

Party list Used in **PR** systems to choose members of **parliament**. If a party wins 30 percent of the vote in a 10-member **district**, then three of the 10 names on that party's list (usually the top three) are named winners and take parliamentary seats.

Party primary Almost exclusively an American phenomenon, it is an election in which almost anyone can participate for the purpose of selecting party nominees for office.

Patronage The act of granting favors to political followers, usually by placing them in governmental offices that one controls. (See **patronage party**.)

Patronage party A political party based on favor-doing and job-providing; usually associated with the corrupt urban politics of 50–150 years ago.

Personality A broad term referring to an individual's general outlook on life, ways of dealing with others, values and **attitudes**, and style of **behavior**. All of these elements that make up a person's character can have political ramifications, and they all form the subject of numerous research projects.

Pluralism One of the major theories in political science, most closely associated with David Truman and Robert Dahl. It argues that no one power point or group exists in American politics; rather, a large number of groups with varying degrees of influence compete, allowing wide (though hardly equal) public input into the political process.

Pluralistic Adjective derived from pluralism, suggesting a situation with multiple, competing political players and multiple access points for the attainment of power.

Plurality voting Method of voting that makes a winner of the person with the most votes; differs from **majority voting** and voting by **proportional representation**.

Policy networks Term derived from interest-group studies; it suggests that instead of the cozy **iron triangle** pattern, policy is made in specialized sub-fields where multiple conflicting interests clash and compete for dominance.

Political activists (see **Activists, political**)
Political alienation (see **Alienation, political**)
Political attitudes (see **Attitudes, political**)

Political efficacy   The subjective feeling that one's political actions can be effective in swaying public officials. This "I *can* fight City Hall" **attitude** is strongly correlated with likelihood of political involvement.

Political ideology   Term for a doctrine or set of beliefs about how politics should work; most **political activists** adhere to one of the small number of ideologies dominant in the world today, seeking to order public policy along the lines of their beliefs.

Political leaders   (see **Leaders**)

Political participants   (see **Activists, political**)

Political psychology   A social science sub-field that attempts to explain political behavior from the point of view of **personality, attitudes**, and beliefs (as opposed to explanations based on **institutional** factors).

Political recruitment   The largely-unorganized and uncoordinated process whereby a society encourages some of its members to enter the political arena and move up within it.

Politics   The complex interplay of competing, conflicting, cooperating groups and people struggling to gain their ends. It is the way societies deal with the inevitable conflicts that result from human struggles for advantage.

Polyarchy   Term promoted in the writings of Robert Dahl to describe the way politics works in free, modern societies. It means, literally, "many rule."

Post-industrial values   Ideals that focus on non-tangible, public goods, such as concern for a clean environment, a just distribution of society's resources, and fair treatment for **minority-group** members. (See **post-industrialists**.)

Post-industrialists   Term popularized by Ronald Inglehart and associates; it describes those citizens everywhere (most common in stable **polyarchies**) who have adopted values like environmentalism, **feminism**, and support for minority rights, that go beyond people's traditional focus on narrow material advantage.

Power elite   The small, unified group of high-status citizens who control politics and dominate the upper echelons of society, according to **power elite theory**.

Power elite theory   The argument that a small, unified group of upper-status people "run things:" i.e., dictate most government policies and keep society structured in ways that benefit them and their supporters.

PR   (see **Proportional representation**)

Presidential system (or **Presidentialism**)   A system of government associated primarily with the USA, in which the core of political power rests with a nationally-elected executive, independent of the legislature.

Primary   (see **Party primary**)

Prime Minister   Head of the **government** in **parliamentary systems**.

Program type   One of several political types observed by James Payne *et al.*; one who enters politics out of an interest in solving issue or policy problems. (See also **Lawmaker.**)

Proletariat   Technically, "the working-class," but the word is loaded with ideological overtones. For Marxists, it is the group most oppressed by the current system, whose "historical mission" is to rise up and overthrow capitalism.

Proportional representation (PR)   A set of voting systems which all have the effect of producing a legislative body where party representation is nearly identical to the distribution of party votes in the last election.

Psychological self-identification   (see **Identification**)

Public interest   A vague, indefinable term that people use to justify the political course they wish to pursue.

Race   One of the most powerful of the **demographic variables** for explaining behavior, including political action. In particular, members of a clear racial minority will vote together as a bloc and most often in a **Left** direction.

Radicals   As a generic term, it describes people at the edges of the political spectrum—either to the **Right** or (most often) the **Left**. In historical terms, Radicals were members of the anti-clerical Radical Party that played a prominent role in several European countries (especially France) from the late-nineteenth to the mid-twentieth century.

Rationalization of interests   The general human tendency to explain the pursuit of one's own interests as tending somehow to support a supposed **public interest** or the good of all.

Reactionaries   People toward the far **Right** of the political spectrum who believe in rank and hierarchy and wish to return society to the way it was structured before the democratic reforms of the last hundred years.

Recruitment   (see **Political recruitment**)

Redistribution of values   A phrase dear to **Leftists**, especially those on the far **Left**; it signifies a wish to move wealth and status from the haves to the have-nots.

Region   One of the key variables influencing political action; the dominant **attitudes** associated with a particular region will influence the political choices of region members.

Reinforcement   The psychological process whereby groups send messages to followers to remind them of their dormant attachments and reinvigorate them to contribute to group welfare with their time, money, and votes. It is one of the key activities of political parties during the latter stages of any campaign.

Religion   One of the key variables that determine political **behavior**; your particular religion and the depth of your commitment to it strongly influence your likelihood of political involvement and the direction of that involvement. (See also **religiosity.**)

Religiosity Deep commitment to one's religious faith, as evidenced by regular attendance at services and attempts to live by the faith's teachings; correlates strongly with political **conservatism**.

Reluctant One of several political types observed by James David Barber; one who enters politics out of a sense of duty, does not particularly enjoy it, takes few strong actions, and leaves voluntarily in short order.

Resources The assets one can use in trying to wield political influence; these can vary from obvious factors like money and connections to more intangible matters like rhetorical skills or simply the spare time needed to devote to public affairs.

Right Refers to a broad set of political positions that share one thing in common: the desire to structure society so that rewards go to those who most deserve them (and not to all indiscriminately).

Rights revolution The growing demand throughout the world, especially in developing **polyarchies** and democratizing societies, for legal protection of individual freedoms and liberties, with the claims of this sort most frequently pushed in the arena of the courts.

Rule of law A system in which government policies are based on an objective set of rules known to all and applied equally to all; differentiated from systems where rules are ambiguous, favor the strong and the well-connected, and can be twisted to help those willing to use bribery or threats.

Ruling class A term so hackneyed that it now has with little meaning, beyond signifying the user of the term's dislike for the supposed power of some despised out-group. The term is often associated with a simplistic Marxism, suggesting as it does the political dominance of the unified upper segment of capitalist society.

Safety net The set of policies designed by **governments** in modern **welfare states** to keep people from falling below a certain socioeconomic level (the precise level varying by country).

Self-esteem A psychological variable strongly correlated with likelihood of political involvement; the higher one's level of self-confidence (or ego strength), the more likely one is to become politically active, and vice versa.

Sense of civic duty (see **Civic duty**)

Separation of powers A political system designed to disperse governmental authority among various institutions, so as to prevent any one unit from dominating the others; a theory enunciated by Montesquieu and associated most clearly with the USA, whose Constitution was specifically written with the separation-of-powers concept firmly in mind.

SES Abbreviation for **Socioeconomic status**

Single-member-district-plurality system (or **SMDP**) One of the most common voting systems. Each district chooses just one person for any office, and the candidate with the most votes wins, whether or not the votes add up to a **majority**. (See **single-member-district system**.)

Single-member-district system A method of electing members to a political body by dividing the relevant geographical space into districts that each elect a single person. That person can then be chosen via **plurality** or **majority** voting methods.

SMDP (see **Single-member-district-plurality system**)

Social capital A term popularized by Robert Putnam in his book, *Bowling Alone*; it refers to the social connections that bind people to each other through attitudes of **trust** and respect.

Social competence The feelings of ease and confidence within human relationships that allow one to join groups and develop connections to others; strongly correlated with likelihood of political involvement.

Social connectedness A feeling of affiliation with others in your **culture** or society, usually derived from active experiences of cooperation and work with others

Social Darwinism Based on a crude understanding of evolutionary theory, this outlook applies a "survival of the fittest" notion to human beings and accepts the idea that those who do well in society deserve their rewards and those who fail deserve their fate. It is an outlook that has been popular on the **Right** and far-Right of the political spectrum.

Social Democrats Term for those **political activists** outside the USA (mostly in Europe) who hold essentially the same political views as do American **liberals**.

Social divisions Refers to the inevitable distinctions and conflicts between groups that characterize any society. Social divisions always produce political competition, but the resulting confrontations are not necessarily violent.

Social identification, Social identity (see **Identification**)

Social learning A theory stressing the acquisition of knowledge through observation of the **behavior** of others; one then acts to imitate the desired behavior (or to avoid the undesired behavior).

Social trust A concept in social psychology stressing the level of confidence people have in the good will of others and their willingness to expect the best in their fellow humans. Social trust strongly correlates with support for the democratic process and with one's likelihood of involvement in politics.

Socialization The process by which new members of society (children, immigrants) learn the basic **norms** and **behavior** patterns of their **culture** in order to integrate into the system.

Socioeconomic status A concept devised by social scientists to rank people by their standing in society; it takes account of numerous indicators of rank, including income, property holdings, profession or job, education level, and the like.

Sound bite   A short, pithy, often sensational phrase or statement, sure to catch people's attention, that the modern **media** play up in order to entertain and expand their audience.

Sovereignty   A word applied to a political entity that has full legal authority (the "final say") on decision-making within its geographic space.

Spectator   One of several political types observed by James David Barber; a genial but passive person who sees politics as a lively show put on for one's benefit rather than an activity to engage in oneself. (See the similar **conviviality type**.)

Spin   The interpretation of current political events to favor the point of view of the speaker and the speaker's party or group.

Spin master (colloquial: "**Spin meister**")   Someone skilled at **spin**; spin masters are often invited onto television shows to enliven political debate, and the most adept of them become well-known **media** personalities

Spoils system   A term explaining how politics works in countries lacking a civil service based on the **merit system**; under the spoils system, most or all government positions are based on favoritism, going to those who best promoted the fortunes of the eventual election winners

Stable multi-party system   A political system in which three to six parties regularly win seats in **parliament**, and in which the two largest parties alternate in power after forming stable, long-term alliances with one (occasionally two) of the other parties.

States' rights theory   An approach to **government** developed in the USA by the nineteenth-century politician, John C. Calhoun, suggesting that ultimate **sovereignty** in the American system rests with the states and that therefore states can, in the final analysis, determine what policies they will and will not uphold, including even the "policy" of remaining part of the country.

Status quo   An important concept in political science; all discussions of what to do next must start from this reference point: where we are now (i.e., the status quo). Also an important concept in international relations, where one finds status quo powers (content with current world power arrangements) and aggressor powers (pushing to change the current power distribution in their favor).

Status type   One of several political types described by James Payne *et al.*; one who enters politics out of a need to attain glory and prestige; focuses on the attainment of high office and the trappings of office rather than on the policies to be undertaken once office is attained.

Subculture   The beliefs, **norms**, and values of a set of people who stand out in some clear way from the broader society of which they are a part. Subcultures have political significance because people within them tend to behave differently in politics from other citizens.

Suburbia   Term used in juxtaposition to both **urban** and **rural**; it describes a third geographical option, the open space where the city ends and the country begins where middle-class people have moved to avoid the grittiness of the city and the poverty of the countryside.

Theorist   One of several political types conceived by Harold Lasswell; one who focuses on ideas and doctrines rather than on the interplay of political relationships or the workaday examination of policy details.

Third party   Term to describe *any* party in a **two-party-dominant system** that is not one of the two dominant parties.

Totalitarian   Aimed at controlling all aspects of a person's or a group's life; (see **totalitarianism**).

Totalitarianism   A term widely used by social scientists to describe systems of government that try to control all aspects of life, not just political institutions as in **authoritarian** systems; the most commonly-cited examples are Soviet Russia (especially 1928–53), Nazi Germany (1933–45), and Mao's China (especially 1949–69).

Traditional conservatives   **Political activists** who are **conservative** on both economic and cultural matters. In the USA, they represent the mainstream position within the Republican Party.

Traditional liberals   **Political activists** who are **liberal** on both economic and cultural matters. In the USA, they represent the mainstream position within the Democratic Party.

Traditionalists   Term for people on the "conservative" side of the **cultural dimension of politics**. They tend to be deeply religious, horrified by drug use, abortion, and pornography, opposed to "lax" immigration laws, and enraged by the "declining standards of moral life" in modern society.

Two-party system   (see **two-party-dominant system**)

Two-party-dominant system   A form of **polyarchal** politics in which just two parties win control of most political offices, alternate forming the **government**, and between them win 80 percent or more of parliamentary seats after most elections. The purest form of this is the **two-party system** in the USA, where just two parties win essentially every election and hold every position of political power.

Typology   An intellectual construct used to categorize parts of a whole (kinds of political system, methods of political action, systems of voting, etc.).

Unitary system   A political system that places **sovereignty** ("the final say on things") in the hands of the national **government**, making regional governments weak and dependent on the central authority for their powers and even for their very existence.

Unstable multi-party system   A **parliamentary system** in which a large number of parties regularly compete for and win legislative seats, necessitating a continuing set of shifting coalitions to produce shaky **governments** that rarely last more than a year or two.

Urban–rural split   A term suggesting the difference in outlook between city-dwellers and people from the country; politically, the former are likely to lean **Left** and the latter likely to lean **Right**.

Violence   The physical aggression that occurs when **conflict** becomes too intense to be resolved through negotiation, bargaining, discussion, and voting. It can take many forms, from a simple fistfight to full-fledged warfare. (See also, **Asymmetric violence**.)

Ward heeler   Slang term to describe a party official in a **patronage system** whose job is to "walk the district" and cultivate good will for the party, largely by distributing favors.

Welfare state   Term to describe **governments** in most modern societies; it stresses the role of government as an agent of assistance and support, the provider of health, education, and medical benefits to the mass of citizens.

Welfare–state traditionalists   People in modern societies (the USA, in particular) who accept government's liberal role as a provider of economic benefits, but who oppose liberal cultural policies involving abortion, church-state separation, and immigration.

Working–class authoritarian   A term coined by the influential social scientist, Seymour Martin Lipset, to characterize people who are economic **liberals** but cultural **conservatives**.

Written constitution   A "super-document" stating the principles that all ordinary laws must adhere to. Starting with the USA in 1787, nearly all countries now have written constitutions (with the notable exception of the UK). This institution makes the case for **judicial review** plausible, as some political entity is needed to decide whether laws do or do not adhere to the Constitution, and courts seem best suited for that task.

Zombie Dietmen   Members of the Japanese **parliament** (the Diet) defeated in their attempts to win seats in **constituency** races, but later appointed to the assembly anyway via the **party-list** system; they represent an anomaly of the **mixed electoral system**: "representatives of the people" who were actually rejected by the people in an election.

INDEX

abolition (of slavery, USA) 68
abortion 43, 48, 159, 162, 163, 164, 165,
167, 238, 242, 330
Abramoff, Jack 276
Abu Ghraib 282
accidents of history 61, 62, 67–8, 109,
209
activation 175, 369
active-negative (personality type) 298
active-positive (personality type) 298
activism, political 49–53, 55, 57, 120,
249; absence in homogeneous-passive
culture 53–4; factors that induce
88–98, 101; levels of 102–06; *see also*
participation
activists, political 87, 103–6, 108, 139,
150, 157, 160, 208, 231–2, 237, 254,
261; and democratization 272, 318;
beliefs of 65–6, 133*ff*; characteristics of
89–98; defined 102–3, 369; party
activists 176–80, 263–6, 269;
personality of 291–308; relations with
the media 287–9; *see also* elites; leaders;
participants; politicians
Adams, John 185, 186
Adams, John Quincy 186–8, 190–1, 193,
194
administrator (as political type) 298,
369
adulation incentive 300, 304, 307–8, 369
advertiser (as political type) 298, 369
Afghanistan 20, 40, 53, 73, 74, 75, 311,
327
Africa 67, 318, 321–2
African Americans 48, 80, 90–1, 122–3,
128, 130, 175, 241–2, 319; and
Civil Rights Movement 322–4; *see
also* Blacks (USA)

Age: and election turnout 94; as key
demographic variable 108, 369; effect
on political participation 94–5, 98;
impact on voting decisions 128–30
agitator (as political type) 298, 369
Alaska 138, 174
Alberta 235
Alexander the Great 23, 39
Algerian War 325
alienation 58, 67, 97–8, 99–101, 369;
produced by media's bad-news bias
283, 284, 289
All the President's Men 281
Allen, George 276
Alliance for Marriage 246, 247
Alsace-Lorraine 116
amendments *see* Constitution (USA)
America 88, 124, 82, 154–5, 173, 175,
259, 268, 313, 315; values 239, 266,
311; *see also* Americans; USA
American exceptionalism 238–9, 253,
369
American Medical Association 35
American Sugar Alliance 245–6, 247,
248
Americans 35, 44, 46, 47, 48, 80, 94, 105,
107, 114, 121–2, 174, 176, 189, 195,
209, 211, 250, 301, 330; and jury
service 244; and the parliamentary
system 226–7; dedication to
materialism 78–80; described by
Tocqueville 77–80; electoral system
185–95; frequently resort to the law
238–9; joiner mentality 246;
litigiousness 244; religious
commitment 79–80; shocked at use of
violence 329–30; skeptical of leaders
239; sub-cultures of 125; two-party

weak in heterogeneous–active culture 53; *see also* coalition government; majority government; minority government
Governors (USA) 188–9
Graham, Katherine 281–2
Grant, Ulysses S. 173, 292
Great Britain 71, 80–1, 109, 125–6, 211, 214, 292, 314, 331, 332; and colonial rule 67; and start of First World War 315; and tradition of peaceful politics 323–4, 326; beginnings of democracy 319; education policy 230; effect of 7–7–05 312; election of February, 1974 198–9, 220; empire 313; recent leaders 292; two elections in 1974 220; two-party-dominant system 256; voting patterns in 115, 125; war against South Africa 314
Great Depression *see* Depression
Great Society 171
Greece 73, 74, 313
Green Party (Germany) 213
Greens 112, 213, 255
groups: demand for power 320–1; differences among 88; some divisions hard to fit on Left–Right spectrum 112; hostility between, causes of 25–32; hostility, and mirror-image misperception 30; hostility, exacerbated by power differences 320–1; interests 331–3; political tendencies 88; stimulus to political participation 92–4, 98; voting patterns 122–3
Guatemala 14, 327
guerillas 190, 311

Haiti 318, 327
Hamlet 208
Hanna, Mark 264
happiness 23, 24, 78, 170–1
Harding, Warren 292
Hart, Gary 2, 3, 4–5
haves and have-nots 110, 149, 163
Hayden, Carl 103
healthcare 27, 35, 159, 175, 180
hegemon 313, 376
hegemony 314, 315, 376
Helms, Senator Jesse 138, 139
Henry VIII 1–2, 16

Hesse 207
heterogeneous–active cultures 51–3, 55, 376
heterogeneous–passive cultures 55, 376
Hindus 11, 24, 30
Hispanics 120, 121, 246
history: accidents of 67–8; as shaper of the present 228; effect on culture 66–71; effect on democratization 323–7; of polyarchy 318–20
Hitler, Adolf 23, 24, 26, 36, 47, 156, 217, 317, 325
Hobbes, Thomas 40
Hoffer, Eric 304
Holland 209, 216, 217, 230, 319
Holmes, Oliver Wendell 148
home ownership 94–5, 98
homogeneity, cultural 55, 75–6
homogeneous–active cultures 49–51, 55, 376
homogeneous–passive cultures 53–4, 55, 376
homophobes 135, 162
horserace, media focus on 285–6
House of Commons (English-speaking countries) 211
House of Commons (UK) 199
House of Representatives (Maine) 293, 296
House of Representatives (USA) 29, 186, 191–3, 196, 197, 200–1, 205, 206, 211, 221, 269, 276, 283, 310
Hugo, Victor 324
human development 318
human nature 20, 22–5, 62, 331
human rights 241–2
Hungary 316, 327
Hurricane Katrina 215, 312
Hussein, Saddam 24, 57, 330
Hutus 45, 327

Iceland 319
Idaho 88, 174, 251, 266
identification: class 131, 173; defined 376; group 122–3, 127–8; party 131; psychological 131–2, 269; social 91–2
identity, social 48, 53, 91
ideology 112, 180–1, 304; and post-industrial issues 161–7, 180–1; chart of 158–9; defined 382; introduction to 133–41; leftist 142–9,

of news 280; the modern mass media
272–5
media professionals *see* journalists
Mensheviks 110
merit system 265, 268, 378
Mexico 328
Michigan 2
middle class 144, 173, 268
Middle East 41, 122, 333
middle-class professionals 89, 96, 116,
130, 173, 245, 378
Midwest (USA) 173
militarism 17, 59, 67, 156, 274
military 153, 155, 159; enlistees 333
Miller, Jean Baker 22
Milosevic, Slobodan 37, 38
minimum wage 14, 134–5, 143, 178–9.
242–3,
ministers *see* government ministers
Minnesota 61, 99, 123, 188–9
minorities 1, 48, 56, 111, 122–3, 124,
143, 172, 177, 231, 241–2, 247, 250
minority government 256
minority group 80, 90–2, 106–7, 122–3,
126, 128, 165, 242, 247, 379
minority, political 173, 226
Miranda v. Arizona *see* Supreme Court
(USA)
mirror-image misperception 30, 379
mission incentive 300, 303–4, 307–8,
379
Mitterrand, François 325
mixed economy 144, 379
mixed electoral system 206–7, 379
mobilization of bias 247, 379
Moderate Left 112, 142–4, 148
moderates 109, 112, 141, 158–9, 161,
166, 289; *see also* centrism; centrists
modernity 90, 318, 319–20, 379
modernization 318, 327, 332, 379
monetary system 152
money: key role in modern campaigns
266
Mongol empire 66–7, 313
Monica Lewinsky scandal *see* Lewinsky,
Monica
Monroe, James 185, 186
Montana 189
Moore, Joan (pseudonym, Maine state
legislator) 293, 294, 295, 297, 301
Moorhead, Alan 37
Moscow 82

motivation for politics *see* incentives
motives *see* incentives
muckraking *see* media negativity
multi-member districts 200–01, 204–7,
379
multi-party system 203, 212, 219, 224,
253, 256; defined 379; stable 257–8;
unstable 259–61
multiple elites 379
Muslims 30, 31, 36, 37, 235, 312, 330
Mutesa I 37, 38

NAACP *see* National Association for the
Advancement of Colored People
Nader, Ralph 3, 35, 115
Napoléon I 67, 324
Napoléon III (Louis Napoléon) 324
Napoleonic Wars 314
National Assembly, France 201–2, 203,
211, 255; *see also* France, National
Assembly
National Assembly, Québec 211;
see also Canada
National Association for the
Advancement of Colored People
(NAACP) 250
National Council of La Raza 246, 247,
248
National Front (France) 203, 255
nationalists 153; Scottish 199
nationalization (of industry) 145, 158–9
Native Americans 13, 186
NATO *see* North Atlantic Treaty
Organization
Nazis 41, 71, 112, 157, 158–9, 380;
see also Germany; Nazism
Nazism 156, 380
NDP *see* New Democrats (Canada)
needs *see* drives; incentives
negativity (of the media) *see* media
negativity
negotiation (as political style) 45, 48,
158, 221, 302, 329
neopluralism 250, 380
neo-realists 331
New Deal 107, 171, 238, 242
New Democrats (Canada) 198
New England 20, 173, 205
New Hampshire 174, 205, 251
New Orleans: Battle of 186; Hurricane
Katrina 284, 312
New York City 68, 149, 233

sovereignty 229–30, 232–4; defined 386
Soviet Union 36, 47, 313, 327; *see also* Russia
Spain 67, 71, 228, 312, 313, 315–6, 330, 331
special interests 247
spectator (personality type) 298, 386
spin 266, 286; defined 386
spin master, spin meister 286, 386
spoils system 265, 386
Sri Lanka 45, 47, 53, 318, 327
stability (of political system) 77, 105, 131, 170, 189, 192, 206, 312, 315
stable multi-party system 256–7, 386
Stalin, Josif 35, 82, 292
state legislators *see* legislators
states (political subdivision) 228, 230, 233–4
states' rights theory 231, 232, 386
status incentive 300, 302–3, 386
status quo 110, 111, 122–3, 126, 140, 144, 145, 158; courts as enforcers of 245; defined 386; exists in every political system 320
status type *see* status incentive
status, social or socio-economic *see* class
Stevenson, Adlai Ewing xii-xiii, 6
strategy *see* campaign strategy
strikes 15, 52
students 50, 73–6, 230, 273
subcultures 66, 99, 120, 125; defined 386
Subjectivity (in self-identification) 132; concerning class 115–17; concerning gender 117–20
subsidies 153, 159, 246, 277, 306
suburbia 123–5, 386–7
Sudan 40, 46
sugar 245–6, 247, 248
suicide, assisted 162
suicide bombers 311, 312–3
Supreme Court (Colombia) 44–5
Supreme Court (Florida) 232
Supreme Court (USA) 44, 190, 211, 221, 229, 238, 239; and public opinion 243–4; as model for other countries 244–5; Brandenburg v. Ohio 242; Brown v. Board of Education of Topeka, Kansas 242, 245; Bush v. Gore 232; Dred Scott v. Sandford 238, 241; Marbury v. Madison 239–41, 378; McCulloch v. Maryland 241; Miranda v. Arizona 242; New York Times

Company v. Sullivan 242; New York Times Company v. United States 242; Plessy v. Ferguson 231, 241; Roe v. Wade 242, 245; rulings affecting business and industry 242–3
survival of the fittest 16
Sweden 17, 50, 56, 73, 74, 94, 118, 187, 196, 257, 316
Switzerland 20, 61, 73, 74, 257, 319
Syria 73, 74, 75

Taiwan 72, 316, 328
talk radio 175
Tanzania 74
Tatar empire 66–7, 81–2
tax collection system (pre-Revolutionary France) 61–2
taxation 148, 153–4, 242
taxes 143, 148, 179, 229
teachers 27, 235
television: 88, 266, 272, 273, 297, 307; and the dissemination of news, 276, 283, 284; as entertainment 276–7, 289; *see also* media
term-limits 28–9, 289
terror 40, 45, 82,
terrorism 162, 311, 312
Texas 103
Thailand 14, 328
Thatcher, Margaret 214, 292
theorist (as political type) 298, 387
think tanks 175, 247, 248
Third Estate 109
third party 3, 189, 199, 387
Third Republic *see* France
Thirty Years War (Germany) 30
Tocqueville, Alexis de 61–2, 77–81, 238, 246
Togo, General 292
tolerance: 36, 58, 69, 289; affected by education level 75; impact on political participation rate 98; norm in polyarchal culture 66, 79, 160, 327, 329
Tories (UK) 326
totalitarian rule 38, 41, 54, 56, 244, 387
totalitarianism 157, 317, 387
traditional conservatives 166, 167–9, 174, 176, 177, 178, 289, 387
traditional liberals 166, 170–1, 174, 176, 177, 289, 387

U.S.S.R. *see* Soviet Union; Russia
Uzbekistan 318

values 49, 50–2, 70, 75–6, 77, 78, 79, 108,
110, 159, 172, 240, 245; American
240, 266, 268, 312; *see also* attitudes;
beliefs; democratic values;
post-industrial values; culture; norms
Ventura, Jesse 189
Vermont 2–, 128, 205, 299
veto 211, 221
vice-president (USA) 192–3
Viet Cong 123
Vietnam 2–3, 7, 35, 73, 74, 127, 250, 322
violence 38–9, 50, 158, 318; and
democratization 320–7; and judicial
policy disputes 44–5; as common way
to deal with conflict 20–2; as future
possibility for world 311; associated
with Far-Left positions 147–9;
associated with Far-Right positions
156–7; between non-democracies
330–1; declines in wealthy societies
332–3; defined 388; during American
Civil Rights Movement 322–3;
during decolonization 321–2; in
authoritarian systems 330; in
Colombia 44–5, 81; in fragmented
cultures 56; in heterogeneous-active
cultures 51–3; in homogeneous-active
cultures 50–1; in international affairs
331–2; in parochial cultures 66; in
Yugoslavia, 37–38; increases with the
number of extremists 157, 160; less
common in democracies 41–3; *see also*
asymmetric violence; conflict; war
virtual parties 268–9
Voltaire 70, 287
voters 42–3, 165, 174, 176, 225, 263; in
unstable multi-party systems 261; role
in patronage- party systems 264–5; *see
also* voting; citizens
voting 104, 107; and age 128–30; and
class 113–7; and ethnicity 122–3; and
gender 117–20; and group identity
122–3; and race 122–3; and region
123–8; and religion 120–2; and
subjective factors 115–7; and
urban-rural differences 123; in
suburbia 123–5; laws 229;
psychological factors 127–8;
restrictions on 159; rights 321, 324;

straight-line party-voting in
parliamentary systems 222–4; turnout
see turnout, voter; variables that
influence 113*ff*; *see also* election;
elections; voter turnout
Voting Rights Act (USA) 324
voting systems *see* electoral systems
vouchers, school 162

war 2–3, 48, 156, 250, 311, 312, 314, 332;
see also civil war; Cold War; conflict;
democratic peace theory; First World
War; Korean War; Second World War;
violence;
War of 1812 186, 331
war on drugs 168, 169
ward heeler 264, 388
Warren, Earl 237–8
Wars of Religion 125
Washington Post 280–2
Washington, George 77, 275, 280, 292
WASPs (white Anglo-Saxon
Protestants) 268
wasted vote 199–201
Watergate 280–2, 284
wealth: correlated with conservatism
113; correlated with peaceful dispute
resolution 332–3 correlated with
satisfaction 65; created by the
Industrial Revolution 319; effect on
political participation 95, 98; effect on
voting preferences 113–15; equality
of, as condition for polyarchy 65;
factor in sustaining polyarchy 62–5;
per capita, USA 16; rapid increase in,
after Second World War 163–4;
see also class
weapons of mass destruction 313
Weede, Erich 332
Weimar Germany *see* Germany
welfare programs 158–9, 171
welfare state 14–15, 16, 144, 159, 267,
268, 388
welfare-state traditionalists 166, 172,
176, 177, 178–80, 388
Welsh Nationalists see Plaid Cymru
Welzel, Christian 260
West (USA) 120
West Germany *see* Germany
West Virginia (USA) 103
Western Europe 67, 69
Whigs (UK) 326